crest rail, or bow

arm rail (steam-bent)

oval seat

THE

WINDSOR STYLE

in

AMERICA

Volumes I and II

The Definitive Pictorial Study of the History and Regional Characteristics of the Most Popular Furniture Form of Eighteenth-Century America

1730–1840

Featuring new discoveries, an expanded list of Windsor makers, and more than 500 photographs and illustrations

By Charles Santore

Edited by Thomas M. Voss
Photographs by Bill Holland

COURAGE BOOKS

AN IMPRINT OF RUNNING PRESS
PHILADELPHIA • LONDON

Library of Congress Cataloging-in-Publication Number
91-52789

ISBN 0-7624-0190-7

Dust jacket design by Toby Schmidt
Dust jacket photographs by Bill Holland

Volume I was designed by Dava Lurie Jennings and set in Goudy Oldstyle by Graphic Arts Composition, Philadelphia, Pennsylvania. The following photographs were provided for Volume I courtesy of: Sotheby Parke Bernet, Inc.—figures 22, 52, 75, 79, 114, 178, 248; Deno Papageorge—figures 50, 53, 112, 119, 134, 170, 183, 192, 226, 237, 251; Samuel Pennington—figures 155, 179; Robert Whitley—figures 159, 167; Courtauld Institute of Art—figure 6; Joseph Adams—figure 10; Moreton Marsh—figure 13; Thomas K. Woodard, Antiques—figures 78 and 133; and National Gallery of Art—figure 186.

Volume II was set in type by Deputy Crown, Camden, NJ, with display type by Composing Room, Philadelphia, Pennsylvania. Drawings on pages 17-24 © 1987, 1981 by Charles Santore. The following photographs were provided for Volume II courtesy of: Bill Holland—pages ii, 26–30, 34–39; figures 1–4, 6–8, 10–16A, 18, 19, 23–34, 36, 39, 42–44, 46, 47, 49–61, 63–68, 70–85, 87–90, 93–110, 112, 114–117, 119–122, 124, 126, 128–138, 141–144, 146, 147, 149, 150, 152–154, 156–164, 166–170, 172–175, 177, 179–184, 187, 189, 190, 194–197, 199–201, 203–205, 208, 210–213A, 216–224, 226, 228–231, 234, 235, 238–245, 247–265, 268, 270; pages 242, 243, (lower l. and r.), 244 (center and lower r.), 245 (upper l. and r.), 246 (upper l. and upper r.), 247 (r.), 248 (r.), 249 (l.), 250 (l.), 251 (r.), 252 (l. and lower r.), 253, 254 (upper l.), 255 (r.) 256, 257 (lower l. and r.), 258, 259 (l. and upper r.), 260 (l. and lower r.) 261 (center), 262 (upper r.), 263 (r.), 264 (lower l., upper and lower r.), 265, 266 (center and lower r.), 267 (lower l.), 268 (upper and center r.), 269. Photographs for figure 40 and for page 247 (center) copyright © 1987 by Luigi Pellettieri. Photograph for figure 271 is courtesy of Sotheby's, Inc., New York. Will Brown's photograph for figure 272 is courtesy of Dietrich Collection, Philadelphia. Photograph for figure 280 is courtesy of Skinner, Inc., Boston. George J. Fistrovich's photograph for page 257 (lower r.) is courtesy of Chester County Historical Society, West Chester, PA. Wayne Pratt's photographs are courtesy of John J. Courville. Photograph of Oliver Swan label, page 264, reprinted from *The Folk Tradition: Early Arts and Crafts of the Susquehanna Valley* compiled by Richard Barons, copyright © 1982 by The Roberson Center, Binghamton, NY

Printed in the United Kingdom by Butler & Tanner Limited

This book may be ordered by mail from the publisher.
But try your bookstore first!

Published by Courage Books, an imprint of
Running Press Book Publishers
125 South Twenty-second Street
Philadelphia, Pennsylvania 19103-4399

Contents

Introduction

There will probably always be one more unusual Windsor chair, settee, stool, or table to be added to any volume on this subject, one more previously unidentified chairmaker to be included in the ever-growing checklist of Windsor craftsmen. My first book on the subject, *The Windsor Style in America,* was published in 1981. Soon afterward, many more fine examples became known—enough new material to publish *The Windsor Style in America, Volume II,* in 1987.

Since the publication of *Volume II,* this phenomenon has occurred again, and several more important examples of Windsor chairmaking have surfaced. Previously unpublished, these superb Windsors are essential, in my opinion, to a further understanding of the high level of Windsor design and craftsmanship achieved by competing chairmakers in a flourishing Windsor market—at its zenith by the end of the eighteenth century in America.

As I discover new information and additional important examples of Windsor chairmaking, I am constantly amazed by the imagination and ingenuity of those great early chairmakers. I hope to continue to add to the Windsor story in America by adding to *The Windsor Style in America.*

The Windsor Style in America
1730–1830
Volume I

CONTENTS

Foreword

It was not until the twentieth century that Windsor furniture became the subject of serious academic study, as well as a desirable antique commodity among collectors. The latter preceded the former.

It seems highly probable that the collecting of Windsor furniture in America was fostered by the handcrafts movement of the late nineteenth century. Work of the hand was supposed to contribute to the building of one's moral character. Such philosophy found a zealous disciple in a minister named Wallace Nutting.

It is extraordinary that even before the collecting rage of the 1920s, Nutting published *A Windsor Handbook* (1917). He had obviously given serious study to the Windsor chair for some time before that date, through which he gained knowledge of regional types; and he sermonized the parvenue collector on the good, better, and best of them.

However precocious Nutting may have been in recognizing the aesthetic merits of fine Windsor furniture, it appears that but a handful of collectors followed suit, the most notable being the late J. Stodgell Stokes, whose exceptional collection was sold at public auction in 1948. A few articles about Windsors appeared in magazines and books during the 1920s and 1930s, but another monograph on the subject did not appear in print until 1962, when Thomas H. Ormsbee published *The Windsor Chair*. Ormsbee built upon the corpus of information Nutting had supplied by discussing the structural details of Windsor furniture and by appending a checklist of the makers then known to him.

Today the collecting and appreciation of Windsor furniture is growing apace, and new works on the subject are sorely needed. Following in the footsteps of Nutting, Stokes, and Ormsbee—and blazing some trails of his own—is Charles Santore, a collector and connoisseur of American Windsor furniture, a nationally prominent illustrator, and now the author of *The Windsor Style in America, 1730–1830*. Mr. Santore's comparative analyses of the great number of Windsor furniture forms he has personally examined, and his insight in translating the artistic vocabulary of line, form, color, and technique into historical narrative, open a spirited and welcome new chapter in the historiography of Windsor furniture.

JOHN C. MILLEY
Chief of Museum Operations
Independence National Historical Park

Preface

I spent my childhood in Philadelphia, growing up in the shadow of Independence Hall. Today, that historic building is filled with uniformed guards, visitors take guided tours through the rooms, and the Liberty Bell has been moved to its own oddly anachronistic steel-and-glass building, where tourists must queue up for a look.

But during my childhood, and perhaps as a testimony to the tenor of the times during the 1940s, my friends and I had the run of Independence Hall—and run we did through the Assembly Room, the Courtroom, and the venerable corridors. Guided tours were unheard of, and guards were few and far between. You had to be exceptionally mischievous to annoy a guard enough so that he would ask you to leave. And of course our "gang" was, I admit, occasionally ejected—once for using the Liberty Bell as a jungle gym!

If Independence Hall was a place to play, then what were its furnishings? In a strange sense, and through my familiarity with them, they became commonplace and acceptable, certainly not exotic echoes of a time long gone. The furnishings simply *belonged* to Independence Hall, and I never imagined that similar pieces could be, or were, bought and sold, or that anyone would ever want to own any of them.

Why, then, did I become a collector of American Windsor furniture? That is a question that I have been asked many times over the years, and my answer is that I was fortunate enough to have begun my career as an illustrator in a studio just two blocks from the auction house of Samuel T. Freeman and Company, in Philadelphia. I started visiting Freeman's with the hope of finding the things an artist needs—easels, filing cabinets, drawing tables, and the like. Sometimes I was lucky, and with the guidance of the legendary Bill Kissane of Freeman's, I eventually furnished my studio quite nicely. But more important, those visits to Freeman's were for me a second introduction to eighteenth-century American furniture and the fact that, if one had a mind to, one could bid on it, take it home, and live with it.

The task of furnishing our first apartment was no easy matter for my wife and me. But after being invited to innumerable dinner parties at the homes of our friends in the advertising business, we became certain of what we did *not* want to live with: contemporary furniture. (Those were the days of Paul McCobb, Herman Miller, and Charles Eames furniture.) So, we held our breath and bought our first piece of antique furniture, an English gate-leg table.

Of course, once you have a table, you need chairs to go around it. Once again, Bill Kissane came to the rescue. One morning at Freeman's he noticed my wife and I huddled around a small armchair with sticks for the back, a rather nicely shaped seat, and turned legs. "That's a good one," he said. "If you like it, you should buy it." "Fine," I said. "How much will it cost?" "Not too much," he replied.

The next morning I rushed to Freeman's and discovered that I was the proud owner of a sixty-dollar chair. I didn't know whether to feel elated or foolish. In any case, the following afternoon I presented my purchase to a furniture refinisher and said these immortal words: "Please remove this dirty, old, flaking green paint and give me a chair with a walnut stain." (The thought of my saying that still gives me the chills.) The refinisher scrutinized the chair and said, "How much did it cost you?" And when I told him, he said, "You paid too much."

Next day the refinisher telephoned to say that he could not get the chair apart to properly refinish it. With its dowels and pins and wedges, the chair was "too well made," and so it was "probably an antique."

I decided I had to know more about the chair, and so I headed for the library, where I discovered Wallace Nutting's book, *Furniture Treasury*. Mr. Nutting informed me that my chair was a Philadelphia comb-back Windsor, 1750-1760. Anxious for more information, I took my chair to the curator of American furniture at our local museum, but the curator could not elaborate on Nutting.

I began haunting Freeman's, visiting antique shops, and reading everything I could about Windsors, which I soon discovered was not very much. I became desperate for information and preoccupied with Windsors. After all, I needed five more comb-backs to go around my gate-leg table. . . .

So, that's how my romance with Windsors began. But why write a book about Windsors? For several reasons. First, although Windsors have become one of the most highly sought-after forms of American furniture, there is still not a comprehensive book on the subject. Second, although much solid research is done in the area of American Windsors, which is usually published in article form, there is one great flaw in most of the researchers' writings: the lack of interest in, or inability to, read the stylistic "language" of Windsors. Certainly the researchers have been compiling valuable facts from documents and brands and woods, but they have consistently ignored an obvious fact—that pieces of Windsor furniture are themselves the primary "documents."

Part of the problem is that most researchers have simply not asked the right questions about Windsors. If one merely *looks* at a Windsor in a general sort of way, all one will see is a bunch of spindles, ears, turnings, and what have you. But if one *sees* the style of Windsors, one begins to ask questions. Why were certain woods used? Why did the Philadelphia blunt-arrow foot evolve into the Philadelphia and then the New England tapered leg? Why were bamboo turnings used? Why did the D-shape become an oval seat? And hundreds of other similar questions.

Simply by asking such questions, one will have made some progress. Then if one begins to be able to answer those questions, a whole new world will begin to open up, and one will actually begin to understand American Windsor furniture.

But in order to even think of asking those questions in the first place, one must be able to see American Windsor furniture as part of an organic, evolving process that began and ended and also had a very interesting middle. That is what I have tried to do in *The Windsor Style in America:* to show what I see when I am presented with a piece of Windsor furniture. And I've tried to do it by **asking** and answering many questions, such as:

If American Windsors were influenced by English Windsors, why do they look so different? I've tried to show the connection of American Windsors to English Windsors and provide a concise view of the development of the American Windsor chair. The opinion is often expressed that American Windsor design was influenced by English design, but that the influence stopped. That, however, is not the case. American Windsor design was constantly influenced by that of England, both positively and negatively. That is, some of the reaction was *against* English design and, indeed, against England herself.

How did the American Windsor style develop in time and by region? I've tried to answer that question with a detailed, readable text, by providing photographs of Windsors of the best possible quality (most of them commissioned especially for this book), and by arranging those photographs in such a way that the evolution of American Windsor design will be clarified.

What makes one Windsor better than another? That question is answered by a careful juxtaposition of photographs and with a text that points up qualitative differences and also merchandising pressures that in many cases were detrimental to design excellence.

How important are the painted surfaces of Windsors? I've answered that question both in the text and with a section of full-color photographs that focuses on those painted surfaces.

How can I really show you the diversity of Windsors? That question is answered by a portfolio of drawings I've done from life, which show the design and construction details of Windsors. For no matter how good they may be, photographs tend to slightly distort the details and perspective of objects. But life drawings have the advantage of a three-dimensional perspective—not merely a frozen moment but a million perspectives synthesized in the way the human eye actually sees. The portfolio of drawings is an accurate summation of reality that is as close to actual visual experience as one can get on the printed page.

I have also included several Appendixes covering the construction of Windsors, questions collectors often ask me about Windsors, how I helped to recreate Thomas Jefferson's swivel Windsor, and a checklist of Windsor makers.

CHARLES SANTORE

NOTE: The captions in this book give the dimensions of furniture in inches and use the following abbreviations: SW (seat width), SD (seat depth), SH (seat height), OH (overall height).

Acknowledgments

I could not have written this book without the effort, concern, knowledge, and most of all genuine interest of many others—some of them scholars, collectors, and dealers I have known for many years and some whom I have met in the course of writing this book. Now I would like to offer them my sincere appreciation and thanks.

First, I would like to thank Tom Voss not only for encouraging me but also for insisting that it was nothing less than my absolute duty to write this book! Without his editing, writing, research, insights, and badgering this book would never have been possible. Furthermore, he has become a good friend.

Speaking of friends, Bill Holland has brought this book to life with his superb photographs. His sensitivity and good taste illuminate not only the Windsors in this book but also everything else he turns his attention to. *Quality* is the word for Bill Holland, both the man and his work.

Roy and Carol Allen, whose knowledge of Windsors is second to none, could not have been more helpful. We have discussed Windsors for many hours over many years. They generously put their Windsor collection at my disposal, and for that I am deeply grateful.

John C. Milley, Chief of Museum Operations, Independence National Historical Park, has been an invaluable friend and advisor. He made available to me the Park's research library, source materials, and wonderful collection of Philadelphia Windsors. For their help, I would also like to thank Assistant Curator Charles G. Dorman, Jane Coulter, Robert Ganini, Fred Hansen, Lynne Leopold Sharp, and the entire staff of Independence National Historical Park.

My great thanks go to Colonial Williamsburg and Chief Curator Wallace Gussler, who so graciously shared the resources of their superlative collection, and to Barbara Luck of the Abby Aldridge Rockefeller Folk Art Center for her hospitality and assistance. On several occasions Willman Spawn, of the American Philosophical Society, pointed me to important material, much of it uncovered through his own research and years of experience. I am also indebted to the State-in-Schuylkill and especially to Chairman of the Board L. Rodman Page for his cooperation and interest.

For their invaluable assistance I thank William K. du Pont, Dean Failey, Catherine and Howard Feldman, Burton and Helaine Fendelman, Janie and Dr. Peter Gross, Isobel and Harvey Kahn, Steven and Helen Kellogg, Steven Kesselman, William Oliver, Lita Solis-Cohen, Lawrence Teacher, and Judy and Allen Wexler. My special thanks go to Virginia Aceti, Mark and Marjorie Allen, Marna Anderson, Mrs. George D. Batcheler, Philip Bradley, The Bohns, Skip and Lee Ellen Chalfont, Michael Dunbar, James and Nancy Glazer, Phyllis and Louis Gross, Don and Trish Herr, George Ireland, Israel Sack, Inc., Earl Jamison, Ross Levett, Moreton Marsh, Alan Miller, Mrs. John A. Miller, Deno Papageorge, Samuel Pennington, Barbara and Eugene Pettinelli, David Pottinger, Wayne Pratt, C. L. Prickett, Patricia Ann Reed, Jacqueline Schneider, David Schorsch, Mr. and Mrs. Richard Flanders-Smith, Robert Stallfort, Leon Stark, William Stahl, Robert Stuart, Howard Szmolko, Mary Walton, Robert Whitley, and Thomas K. Woodard.

I am grateful for the assistance provided by The Art Institute of Chicago; The Carpenters' Company of Philadelphia; The Chester County Historical Society; The Corcoran Gallery of Art; The Courtauld Institute of Art, London; The Design Council, London; Greenfield Village and The Henry Ford Museum; The Henry Francis du Pont Winterthur Museum, Director, James Morton Smith; The Lancaster Heritage Society, Dr. George W. Scott, Lancaster Masonic Lodge No. 43; The Mercer Museum, Director, Lynn Poirier; The Metropolitan Museum of Art, Curator of American Decorative Arts, Morrison Heckscher; The Museum of Fine Arts, Boston; The Museum of the Rhode Island School of Design; National Gallery of Art; New Haven Colony Historical Society; The Northampton Historical Society; The Pennsylvania Historical Society; The Philadelphia Museum of Art; The Redwood Library, Newport, Rhode Island; The Society for the Preservation of Long Island Antiquities; Stenton Mansion, Philadelphia; The Victoria and Albert Museum, London; The Wadsworth Atheneum; The Whaling Museum, Massachusetts; The Yale University Art Gallery.

I appreciate the assistance of Jay Badger, Noreen Cooke Bello, Sam Bruccoleri, Dale J. Butterworth, Frank P. Dingley, Jo Anne Fuerst, Joan M. Goldburgh, George R. Hamell, Jane Herrick, Buol Hinman, Jacqueline Homan, Doris E. Hoot, Paul Koda, Jane McClafferty, Forbes MacGregor, James D. Meltzer, Ann Rahn, Barbara Soltis, and John F. Stanley.

I would also like to acknowledge my debt to three pioneers in the collecting of American furniture: William Macpherson Hornor, Wallace Nutting, and J. Stodgell Stokes, who had a romance with Windsors long before my time.

I would like to thank my wife, Olenka, most of all, for sharing this mad passion.

This book is dedicated to my brother, Bobby Hart, 1936–1978

A PORTFOLIO OF DRAWINGS

Philadelphia Windsor armchair, 1750–1770.

Drawing 1. Evolution of the Windsor leg. Left to right: *Philadelphia cylinder-and-ball-foot leg, 1740–1765; Philadelphia baluster-and-ring tapered leg, 1765–1790; Connecticut baluster-and-ring tapered leg, 1770–1800.*

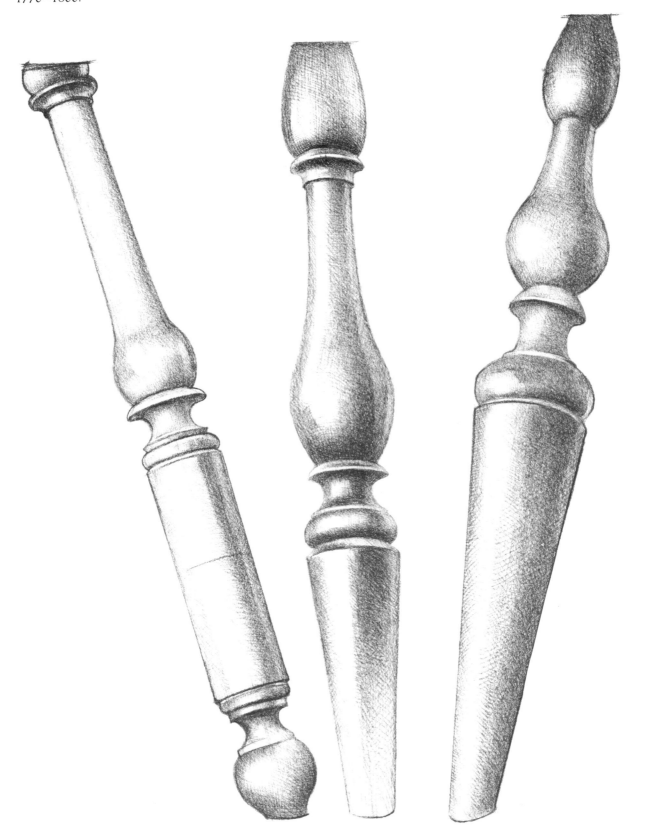

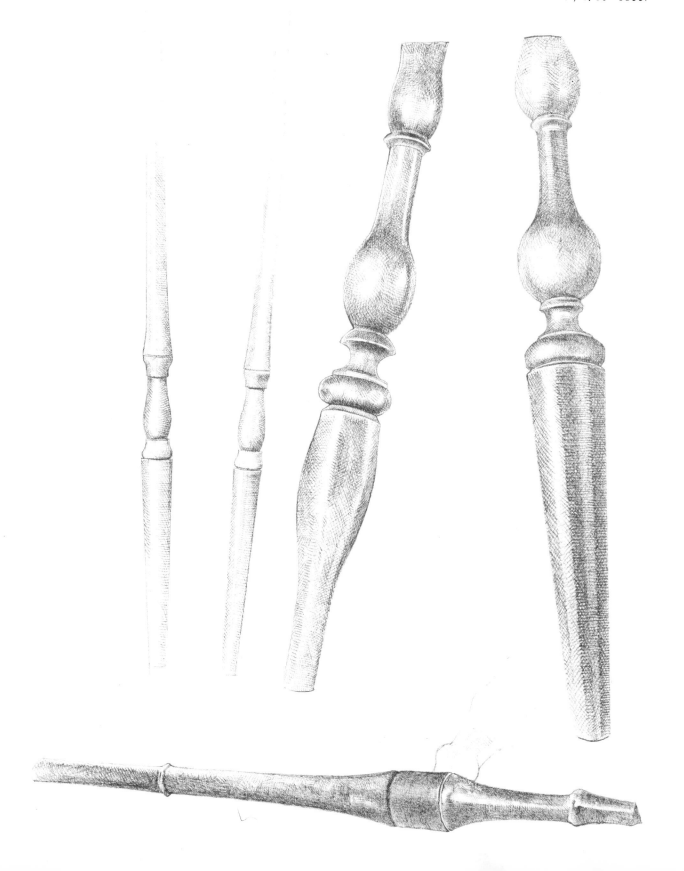

Drawing 2. Rhode Island and New York turning patterns. Left to right: Rhode Island bow-back or continuous-arm chair back spindles, 1780–1800; Rhode Island leg, 1780–1800; New York leg, 1770–1800. Bottom: Rhode Island sack-back side stretcher, 1780–1800.

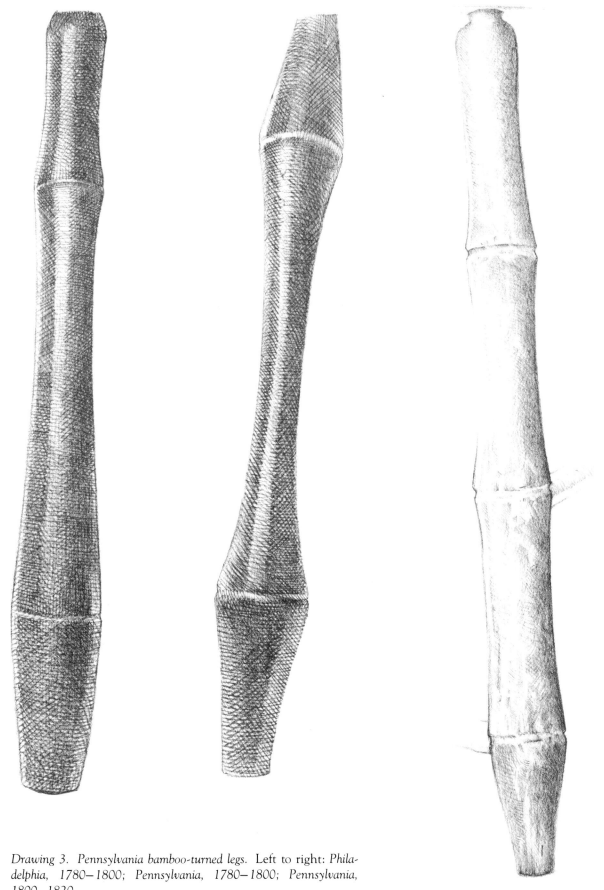

Drawing 3. Pennsylvania bamboo-turned legs. Left to right: Phila-delphia, 1780–1800; Pennsylvania, 1780–1800; Pennsylvania, 1800–1820.

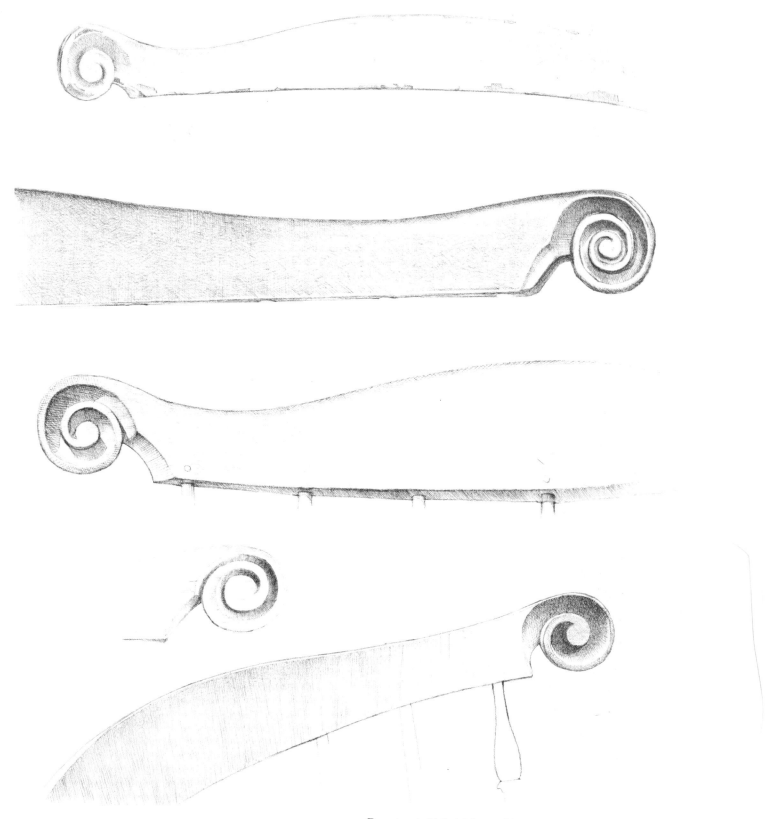

Drawing 4. Philadelphia and New England comb-pieces with carved ears. Top to bottom: *Philadelphia side chair, 1765–1790; Philadelphia armchair, 1740–1770; Connecticut armchair, 1760–1780; Massachusetts armchair, 1765–1790; Rhode Island side chair, 1765–1790.*

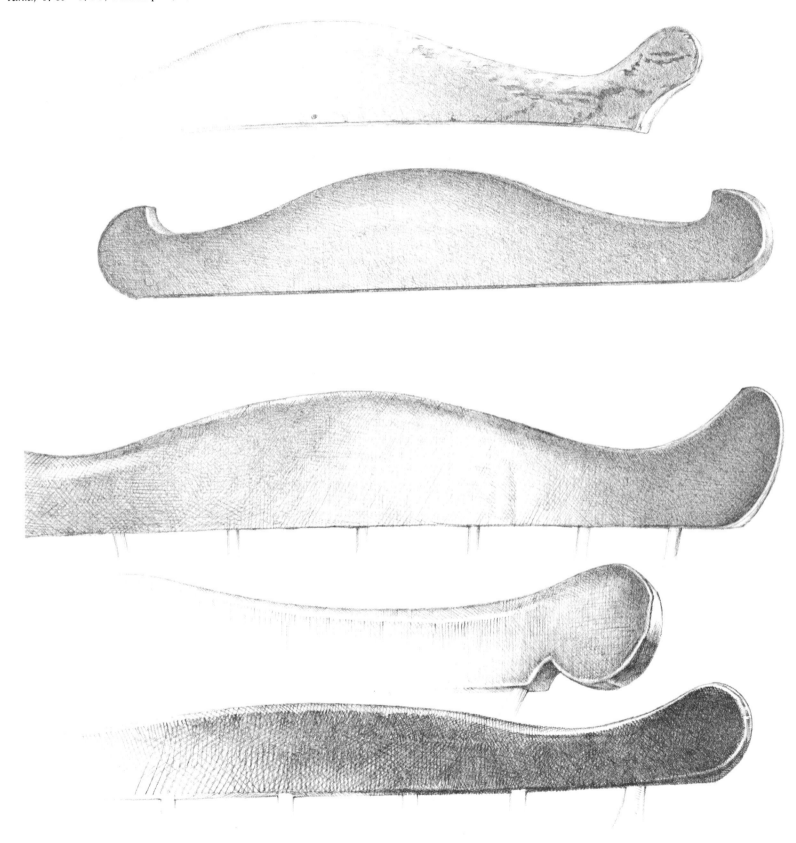

Drawing 5. *New England and Pennsylvania comb pieces with uncarved ears. Top to bottom: Connecticut, 1765–1790; Connecticut, 1765–1790; Connecticut, 1765–1790; Lancaster County, Pennsylvania, 1765–1790; Philadelphia, 1765–1780.*

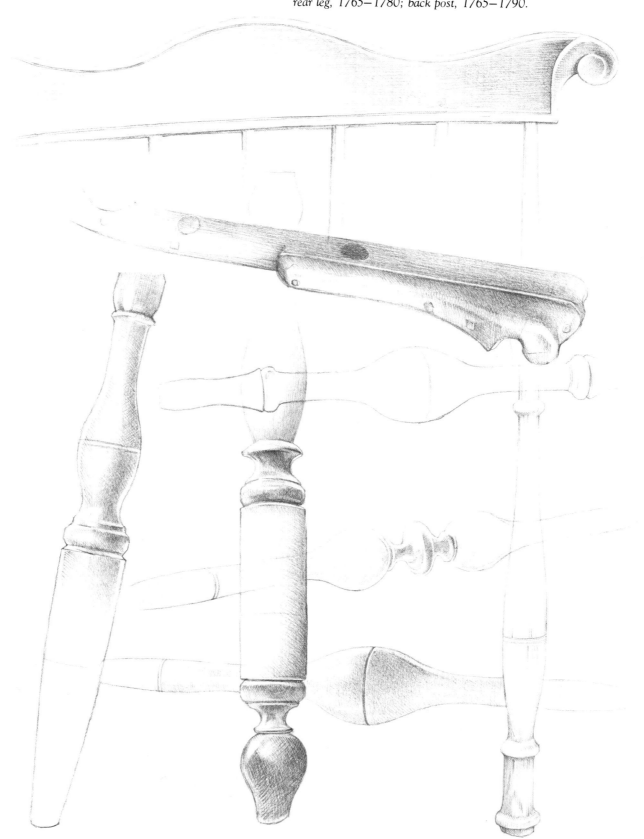

Drawing 6. Lancaster County, Pennsylvania, details. Top to bottom: *comb piece, 1765–1790; knuckle handhold, 1765–1790; medial stretcher, 1765–1790; medial stretcher, 1765–1780; side stretcher, 1765–1790.* Left to right: *rear leg, 1765–1790; front or rear leg, 1765–1780; back post, 1765–1790.*

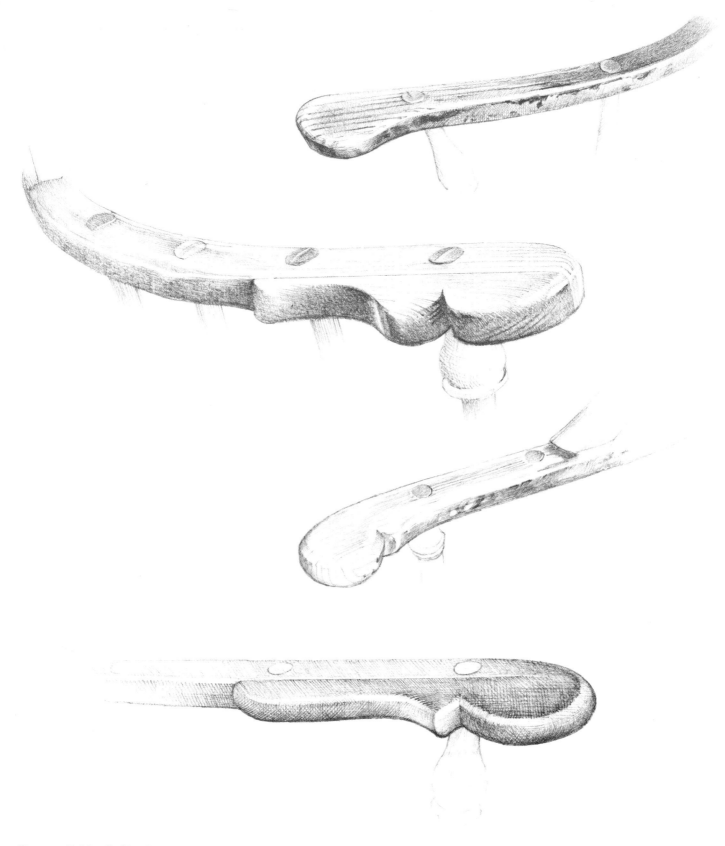

Drawing 7. Handholds of steam-bent arms, New England and Phila-delphia. Top to bottom: Connecticut, 1760–1800; Philadelphia, 1740–1765; Rhode Island, 1780–1800; Connecticut, 1760–1790.

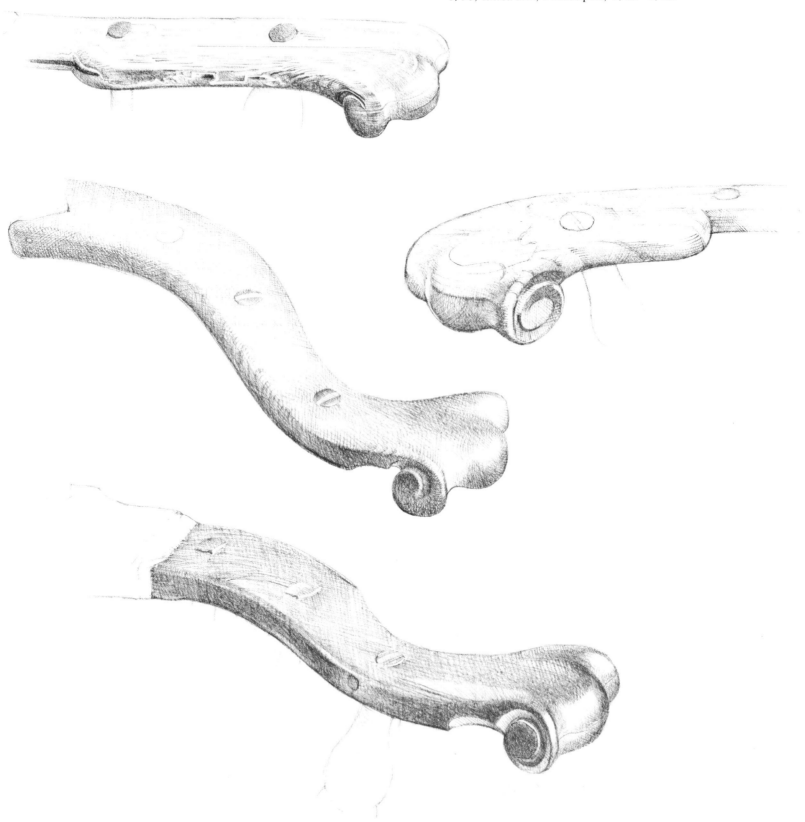

Drawing 8. Knuckle handholds, Philadelphia and New England. Top to bottom: *steam-bent arm, Philadelphia, 1765–1790; steam-bent arm, Connecticut, 1765–1790; sawed arm, Massachusetts, 1765–1790; sawed arm, Philadelphia, 1765–1785.*

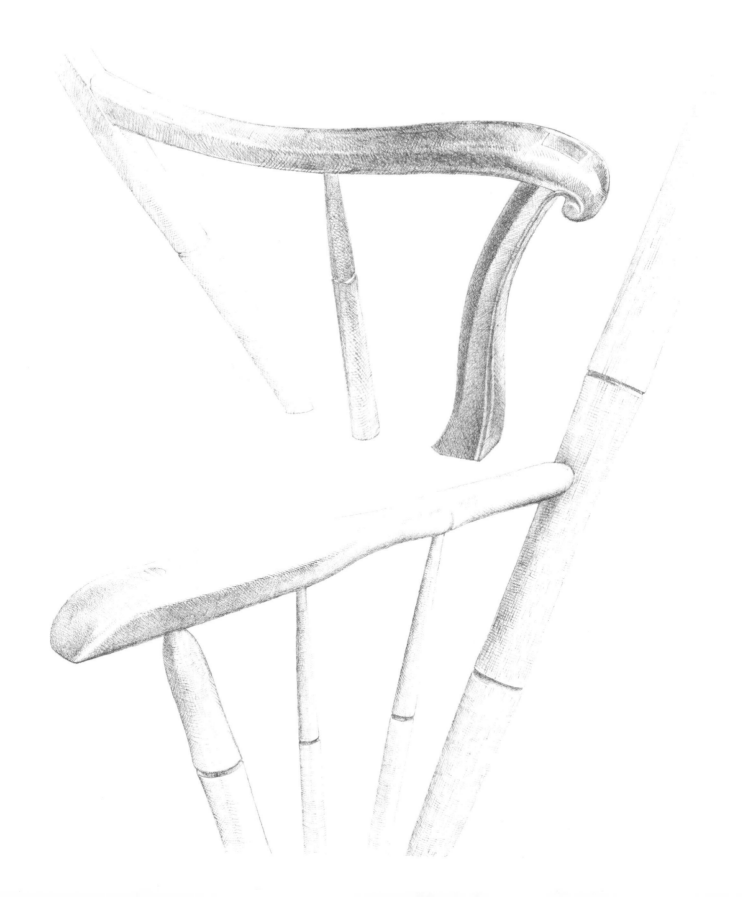

Drawing 9. *Pennsylvania tenoned arms.* Top to bottom: *Philadel-phia, 1780–1800; Pennsylvania, 1800–1820.*

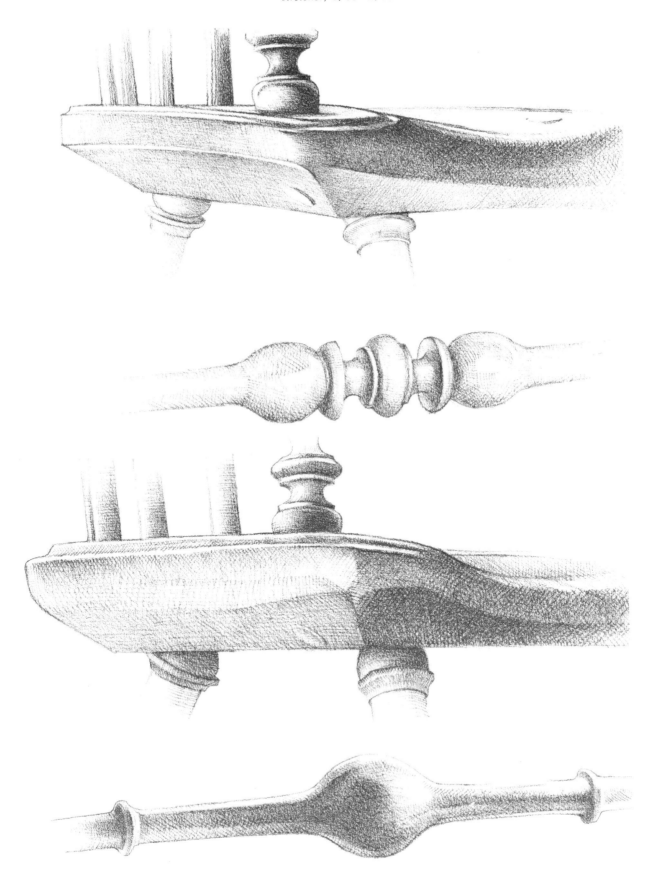

Drawing 10. Details of two Philadelphia comb-back chairs. Top to bottom: *seat and medial stretcher, 1740–1765; seat and medial stretcher, 1760–1780.*

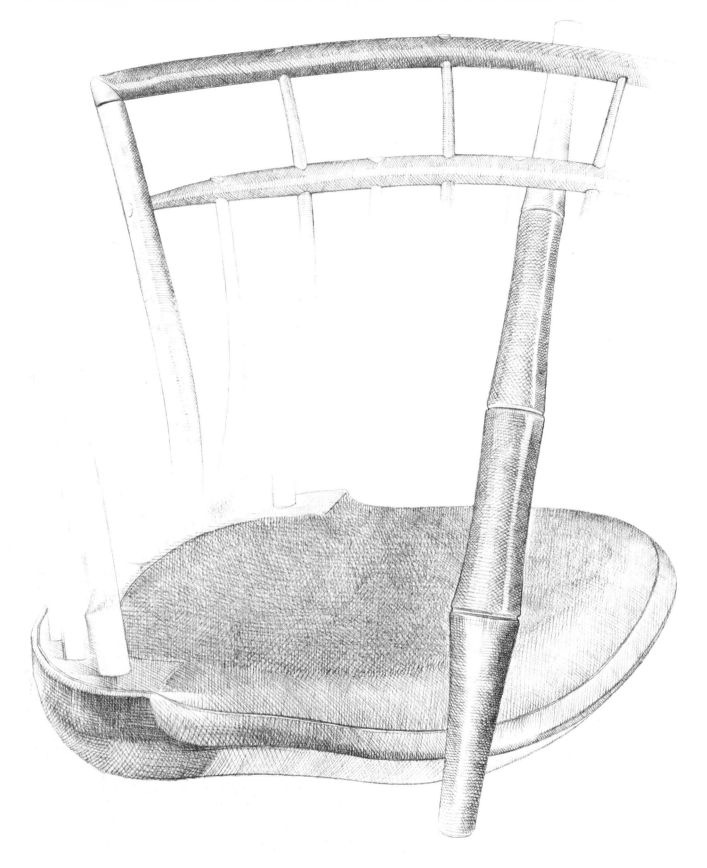

Drawing 11. Details of a New England rod-back side chair, 1800–1820.

Introduction:
A History of the Windsor Style

WHEN ROGER SHERMAN—a Connecticut cobbler, a statesman, and the only man of his time to sign the Declaration of Independence, the Articles of Association, the Articles of Confederation, and the Constitution of the United States—sat for his portrait by Ralph Earl, he chose a Philadelphia low-back Windsor chair in which to be seated (figure 1).

When the First Continental Congress met at Carpenters' Hall in Philadelphia on September 5, 1774, Windsor armchairs furnished the room for that historic occasion (see, for example, figure 39).

In Robert Edge Pine's well-known painting, *The Congress Voting Independence, July 4, 1776*, Benjamin Franklin, Charles Carroll, and others can be seen seated in sack-back Windsor chairs (figure 2).[1]

In 1796 George Washington purchased from Philadelphia Windsor-chair makers Robert and Gilbert Gaw twenty-seven bow-back Windsor side chairs for use on the portico of his Mount Vernon home. John Adams had a favorite Windsor chair. And Thomas Jefferson is said to have composed the first draft of the Declaration of Independence while sitting in an unusual swivel Windsor chair, a Philadelphia type of the 1770s (figure 3).[2]

Windsor furniture is, I believe, the most characteristically American and the most historically significant furniture style to emerge from eighteenth-century America. It is a democratic style, one which appealed to and was used by all levels of American society. Windsor furniture was practical indoors or out, in public buildings or in private residences, in the country or in the city. It accommodated children or adults. Furthermore, the Windsor style was adapted to a wider variety of furniture forms. Chairs, settees, tables, stands, stools, cradles—all lent themselves to adaptations in the Windsor style.

Indeed, the changing status and attitudes of the Colonial craftsman vis-à-vis England in the mid-eighteenth century are so

1. Portrait of Roger Sherman (1721-1793) by Ralph Earl (1721-1801). (Yale University Art Gallery; gift of Roger Sherman White)

eloquently revealed in American Windsor furniture—particularly the chairs—that by the time the Revolution had begun, the American Windsor chair had become established as the single most popular form of furniture in the Colonies and perhaps the most popular form of furniture ever to be made in America.

DESIGN PSYCHOLOGY

The term *Windsor* refers to a specific form of furniture, which has also been called *stick furniture* because of the method of its construction. A solid plank wooden seat, about two inches thick, is the keystone of the Windsor chair. Spindles are socketed into this seat to form the back of the chair. Similarly, to form the undercarriage of the chair, the legs are socketed into the bottom of the seat. Thus, unlike those of most other forms of chair, the

2. (below) The Congress Voting Independence, July 4, 1776, *by Robert Edge Pine. (Historical Society of Pennsylvania)*

3. (right) *Swivel armchair. Philadelphia, c. 1770. The writing arm and undercarriage are nineteenth-century replacements. (American Philosophical Society)*

rear legs of Windsors are not extensions of the back posts; neither are the front legs extensions of the arm supports, if the latter are present. It is in these elements, extending up and down from, and socketed into, a central hub (the seat), held in place with a steam-bent hoop, arm rail, or crest rail, that one can sense a psychology of construction more closely associated with wheelwrights than with joiners, the makers of more traditional furniture constructed with mortise-and-tenon joints. In addition, the use of steam-bending itself to form furniture seems to have been a new idea.

William Macpherson Hornor, Jr., has said that,

in tracing chairmakers, it is obvious that the cabinet makers drifted into the construction of the finer chairs through their similarity to tables and other standing pieces of furniture which they were fabricating at the time. On the other hand, rushbottom chairs, together with Windsors, were primarily the work of turners. [3]

Now, in a sense Hornor is quite correct. We know, for example, that Windsor-chair makers (like many cabinetmakers) depended on the services of turners, and many were themselves trained as turners. But in the eighteenth century the product of the turner was part of a very long tradition of furniture making, whereas the product of the Windsor-chair maker was anything but. Turners, for example, made joined tables, banister-back chairs, joined stools, and more,—all of which in one way or another required precisely the same knowledge of joinery as that needed in the "finer" cabriole-leg Queen Anne tables and chairs. However, Windsor chairs are based on a different—I am tempted to say *radically* different—construction method and design psychology. And so, although Windsor chairs may have been made by turners, the development of the Windsor form itself in no way depends on the construction methods that turners traditionally used.

ROYAL ORIGINS

How and where did the Windsor chair originate? Anyone who has ever had more than a passing interest in American furniture in general, and in Windsor furniture in particular, might ask that question. And perhaps it can best be answered by asking another question: why are these chairs called *Windsor* chairs in the first place?

That question is often answered with a story, parroted time and again in one variation or another in books, magazine and encyclopaedia articles, lectures, and conversation among collectors and dealers. The story is that George II of England—or George I or George III—was on a fox hunt or on a picnic when it began to rain or it became chilly. In any case, for some reason the monarch sought shelter in the simple home of one of his simple subjects, where, near the blazing hearth, he came upon a simple chair.

This chair had a seat made from a single plank of wood; the legs were attached to the seat through holes drilled into it. The back of the chair consisted of spokelike sticks that, like the legs, were stuck into holes in the seat, too. So enthralled was the king with this humble but comfortable piece of furniture that, on his return to Windsor Castle, he ordered several made after the same pattern. Hence, of course, the legendary derivation of both the chair and the name of the chair.

Today, although the story is still repeated, it is often dismissed as only legend. [4] But might there not be some truth to the legend? Indeed, it seems there is.

Figure 4 is a painting titled *The Tobacco Parliament (Das Tabakskollegium)*, executed in 1739. It depicts Frederick William I of Prussia (1688-1740), father of Frederick the Great, and his ministers, puffing away on long-stem pipes and sitting in English, or at least English-style, comb-back Windsor chairs. But how can that be? Why should a group of Prussian aristocrats be sitting in Windsor chairs?

One very good reason is that the wife of Frederick William I, Sophia Dorothea, was the daughter of George I of England (1660-1727), who ascended the throne after Queen Anne died and who ruled from 1714 to 1727. Indeed, George I was himself a German prince who could not speak English, had two German mistresses, and had Frederick William I as a son-in-law. It is entirely possible that George I favored Windsor chairs, used them at Windsor Castle, and passed on his taste for Windsors to Frederick William I, who commissioned a painting of himself and his ministers sitting in the chairs. If so, the legend of George I discovering a Windsor in a humble setting becomes more plausible.

Another interesting, however tentative connection between George I and the Windsor chair can be found in America. Patrick Gordon was governor of Pennsylvania from 1726 until his death in 1736. The inventory of his opulent Philadelphia mansion, compiled at his death, reveals, among the walnut, leather, mohair, cane, and easy chairs—five Windsor chairs. [5] Furthermore, Gordon, a wealthy Loyalist, had two portraits of George I on his walls. Perhaps Gordon's taste in chairs was influenced by that of his king.

In any case, we know that in England of the 1720s and 1730s "Windsor chairs were extremely fashionable indoors and out, particularly in Palladian settings." [6] That, I think, should not be surprising, since whatever caught King George I's fancy was, by definition, *the* fashion among the English aristocracy and the hangers-on at court. Furthermore, if the George I connection stands up under scrutiny, it strongly suggests that Windsor chairs were in use in England before 1720.

In England it is quite common for the regional names of shires or towns to be used as descriptive appellations for the objects produced in those shires or towns and environs. Thus Yorkshire chairs, Buttersfield chairs, Lancashire chairs, Cotswold chairs, Mendelsham chairs, Buckinghamshire chairs, and High Wycombe chairs are but a few of the names given to Windsors. The chairs I have just mentioned seem always to have been produced in their particular area by local craftsmen for local use. However, Windsor chairs were produced in the southern counties of England to a far greater degree than they were in the north. And if it could be said that there is such a thing as a typical English Windsor chair, it would be the type that was produced in the southern counties to supply the taverns and tea gardens of the London suburbs.

It may have been at this point in stepped-up production and

4. The Tobacco Parliament
(Das Tabakskollegium) *by
Dismar Degen (?), 1739.
(Staatliche Schlösser und Gär-
ten, Potsdam-Sans Souci)*

distribution that the generic term *Windsor* came into use. As the appearance of the stick chairs in London increased, they simply became known as the chairs one could buy at Windsor. It is interesting to note that there are not only Windsor chairs but Windsor curtains, beans, loam, soap, bricks, and tubs, all named after the town where they were first introduced or could be purchased.

As far as I know, the first document that actually mentions a Windsor chair is a description by the first earl of Egmont (1683-1748), who stated in 1724 that on a visit to the garden of Hall Barn, near Beaconsfield, Buckinghamshire, his "wife was carry'd in a Windsor chair like those at Versailles."[7] To be "carry'd in a Windsor chair" may at first seem odd, but figure 5 helps explain it. This detail of a print of the 1730s depicts a scene at Stowe Gardens, Buckinghamshire. An aristocratic man and woman are seated in Windsor chairs, which were placed upon wheeled platforms that could be pushed from behind and were steerable with a tiller. This wheeled Windsor chair is probably an early version of the Bath chair, a hooded wheelchair used by invalids at the fashionable English spa. Furthermore, the wheeled Windsor is

5. Detail of a print of Stowe Gardens, Buckinghamshire, by J. Rigaud, c. 1733, published 1739. (The Metropolitan Museum of Art; Harris Brisbane Dick Fund, 1942)

conceptually like the upholstered wheeled armchairs used in the Versailles gardens and mentioned by the Earl of Egmont. It is significant that the town of Windsor itself is only thirty-five miles from the town of Stowe, the scene of the print, and only eight miles from Hall Barn, where the Countess of Egmont was "carry'd."

Although this early wheeled Windsor was probably a fairly uncommon contraption, "immobile" Windsors flourished in England as garden furniture. Indeed, Windsors seem to have been the furniture of choice in early eighteenth-century English gardens. The see-through construction of the back of the Windsor would permit a quantity of these chairs to furnish a garden or veranda without obstructing the view or, if the chair were occupied, the flow of air in pleasant weather. Furthermore, because of this see-through construction Windsor chairs do not blow over in heavy winds—at least they did not in my own experiments with them. These outdoor Windsors were usually painted green, which both allowed them to blend with the landscaped gardens and protected them from the weather.

It was not long before most proper English gardens were furnished with Windsors. Thus, we read about garden Windsors in such early English advertisements as one from 1730 for a "John Brown in St. Paul's Churchyard, all sorts of Windsor Garden Chairs of all sizes painted green or in the wood." In 1738 Earl Fitzwalter paid two pounds to the pumpmaker in Moulsham, Essex, "for 2 Windsor chairs for the garden" of his house there.

33

Paintings by Arthur Devis from the 1750s depict such Windsor garden chairs, which appear to be relatively simple, straightforward pieces of furniture (figure 6). And although it was painted 140 years later, *The Tea Party* by Edwin Austin Abbey gives us a clear idea of how the English upper classes used their Windsor furniture out of doors (figure 7). (Abbey spent the better part of his painting career in England, steeped in English subject matter.)

Windsor furniture created for indoor use was quite elaborate, and early English references to these pieces are rather impressive. In 1725 there were "seaven Japan'd Windsor chairs" in the library of the duke of Chandos at Canons in Stanmore, Middlesex. Between 1729 and 1733 Henry Williams, a joiner in London, supplied a "very neat mahogany Windsor side chair" to the Prince of Wales Library in St. James Place and "2 mahogany Windsor chairs richly carved" for the Blue Room there. The contents of the luxurious house of Sir William Stanhope, sold in 1733, included a "Windsor chair covered in quilted crimson damask." In 1738 the Red Gallery at Newstead Abbey, Nottinghamshire, counted "Four Double Windsor Chairs [that is, four settees] one Treble ditto," the Great Gallery "Four Treble Wind-

6. (above) Horace Walpole Presenting Kitty Clive with a Piece of Honeysuckle *by Arthur Devis, c. 1750 (Lady Douglas)*

7. (right) The Tea Party *by Edwin Austin Abbey (1852– 1911). Watercolor. Abbey was an American painter; however, the watercolor was executed in England. (Yale University Art Gallery; The Edwin Austin Abbey Collection)*

sor Chairs Six Single ditto," the Little Gallery "Two Windsor Chairs," and the Blue Gallery "One Treble Windsor Chairs Eight Single ditto."

Interestingly, two Windsor-chair makers who were actually working near Windsor between 1755 and 1780—John Pitt and Richard Hewett—were not only chairmakers but also wheelwrights. In London, however—where Windsor-chair making demanded such decorative niceties as the carving and joining of cabriole legs to seats in the manner of high-style furniture—the work was no doubt performed by such joiners as the aforementioned Henry Williams, rather than by turners or wheelwrights. Indeed, the production of urban English Windsors required the workmanship of not only joiners, but of carvers, painters, gilders, and upholsterers.

LONDON'S INFLUENCE ON THE COLONIES

Judging from early inventories, the first Windsors were shipped to the Colonies—specifically, to Philadelphia—in the 1720s and 1730s. A more interesting question is why they were shipped at all.

It is unlikely that members of the working classes constituted much of a market for imported Windsors, and the same can be said for tavern and public building owners. Either potential customer would have made his own furniture or would have purchased local products. Indeed, the only justification for the added expense of buying imported common seating furniture—which in Philadelphia and in the Colonies in general was hardly in short supply—was fashion.

Those who could afford it looked to London for all the latest fashions—from clothing to wallpaper to eating utensils to furniture. Because Windsors used as outdoor furniture were almost a fad in London in the mid-1700s and because no proper Philadelphian could have a proper garden without the proper furniture, imported Windsors of the green-painted variety were almost certainly first used in America in the gardens of the wealthy. Indeed, before 1765, advertisements by American Windsor makers frequently describe their products exclusively as "fit for Piazza or Gardens."

Now, whereas the interior furnishings of a town house are personal and private, hidden from public view, the exterior furnishings, even when on private property, become part of the daily, common experience of the street. I do not mean to over-psychologize here, but it seems to me that the common man in eighteenth-century Philadelphia may have subconsciously associated the Windsor form with a democratic sort of availability, and one that he was quick to adapt to his own use. In a strange turnabout of events the Windsor chair became the most popular form of eighteenth-century American furniture not because of what it represented to the wealthy—fashionable exclusivity—but because of what it represented to the common man—democratic accessibility.

The Windsor chair was also accessible from the point of view of price. Whereas a typical high-style chair might cost upwards of two or three pounds, a typical Windsor could be supplied for anywhere from seven to fifteen shillings (twenty shillings to the pound). By contrast, three- or four-slat rush-bottom chairs cost between three and five shillings. Thus, although a Windsor might cost more than a slat-back chair, it cost considerably less than a framed, high-style chair.

AMERICAN PROTOTYPES

Based on the personal inventories of Philadelphians in the second quarter of the eighteenth century, I have, in the past, speculated that a few Philadelphia craftsmen were probably producing Windsor chairs during that period. But I felt that their chair production would have been limited to repairing or replacing Windsor chairs broken in shipment from London, or perhaps adding a chair or two to enlarge an imported set. Now, however, I believe that I have at least one piece of evidence that indicates Windsors made in a recognizably American style were produced in Philadelphia at a very early date.

Figure 8 shows what is, in my opinion, the earliest American Windsor chair yet discovered. This remarkable piece of furniture is the prototype for all subsequent Windsors in the American style. Many of the later chairs may surpass this one in elegance or stylishness, but none surpasses it in the boldness of its execution, the cohesiveness of its design, or the excellence of its construction. Interestingly, this chair was probably not made by a Windsor-chair maker at all, but rather, by an artisan who made primarily rush-bottom chairs and daybeds. Indeed, everything about this chair points to that conclusion, as well as to the fact that the chair is of very early vintage. How early? I believe it was made toward the end of the period of early Philadelphia banister-back chairs and daybeds—that is, around 1730—and I base this conclusion on stylistic evidence.

In addition to its overall appearance of age and the method of its construction, one dates a piece of antique furniture by its chronologically latest stylistic feature or features. That, of course, is only simple logic. A given piece of furniture may incorporate stylistic features from two, three, or even four different periods of furniture-making, but the latest feature will always reveal when it was made.

However, the comb-back Windsor chair shown in figure 8 has

8. Armchair. Philadelphia, 1730–1740.
Nineteenth-century red paint, over yellow,
over the original green. Crest rail, spindles,
and arm rail, hickory; seat, poplar; legs
and stretchers, maple. SW 24″, SD 16″,
SH 17″, OH 42½″. (Also see color plate
I.) (Olenka and Charles Santore)

8a. Armchair. Detail of crest rail.

8b. (below left) Armchair. Detail of arm supports.

8c. (below) Armchair. Detail of legs and stretchers.

no "latest" feature. Put another way, all of its stylistic features are earlier than, or as early as, those of any other known American Windsor chair. And the chair's latest feature, if it can be said to have one, is the very fact that it *is* a Windsor chair—that it has a steam-bent crest rail and arm rail, and that it is constructed in the Windsor manner. First, the turned parts of the chair are identical in pattern to the turnings found on early (1710 to 1740) Pennsylvania daybeds and banister-back chairs (figure 9). The ball foot and above it, the distinctive flaring collar or ring and, just above that, the definite inward curve of the cylindrical leg are all features of turned Philadelphia furniture in the classic William and Mary style. So, too, is the turning pattern of the stretchers of

9. *Leg detail of daybed. Pennsylvania, 1710–1740. Painted dark green. Maple. L 65". (David Pottinger)*

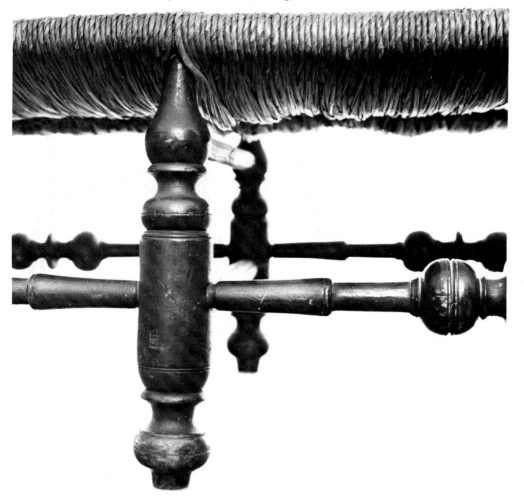

figure 8, which is often found on fine, early Philadelphia arch-head banister-back chairs.

Every other feature of this chair can also be dated early; the double scoring used as a decorative touch on the bulbous turnings; the double "rain gutter" (planing line) around the perimeter of the D-shaped seat; the arm rail and rolled-down, scrolled handholds (which are simply a steam-bent Windsor interpretation of the arm rail and handholds used on joined chairs from the last quarter of the seventeenth century and on rush-bottom chairs of the eighteenth century). The tapered arm rail is an extremely rare feature found only on a handful of early Pennsylvania Windsors. Also, consider the fact that the spindles have no taper and that the crest rail has paddlelike ends, heavily chamfered on the top edge (like the crest rail of an early Philadelphia banister-back chair) and with ears that do not turn upward. All of these are features of some of the great, early eighteenth-century Windsors as well as of figure 8, and infrequently found on American Windsors later than the 1750s. This great piece of American furniture, which has an almost experimental quality about it, was created by a master turner, and, given its early date it is little wonder that there are no other examples of this type of chair yet known. [8]

We now also have some fascinating evidence that English Windsors were being copied in America as late as 1750 to 1760, but, unfortunately, not at a date quite so early as the "Ur-Windsor" just discussed. Figure 10 shows such a chair, and figure 11, its English counterpart. Indeed, the chair in Figure 10 looks *so* English that at least one expert I know has dismissed it as such. But it is unquestionably American. First, the crest rail, arm crest, arms, arm supports, and rear legs of figure 10 are made of sugar maple, a distinctly American wood not found in English Windsors. Second, microanalysis of the wood of the seat shows it to be American butternut (*Juglans cinerea*). The chair itself is one of a pair that is now in the Floyd mansion, Brookhaven, in Mastic, Long Island, and is by tradition, said to have always been in the family. William Floyd was a signer of the Declaration of Independence.

Figure 11 is a typical English comb-back armchair of the mid-eighteenth century. It is no wonder that the Floyd chair in figure 10 seems to be English, given the striking similarities in their proportions and of the shapes of their crest rails, seats, arm supports, and leg turnings. However, although figure 10 is undoubtedly a purposeful imitation of an English Windsor, it has some distinctly un-English stylistic features. First, the spindles have a swelling or bulb in their centers; second, the baluster turning at the tops of the legs swells out slightly before entering the seat. Different also, are the arrow-shaped bulbs at the ends of

10. (left) Armchair. Probably Connecticut, 1750–1770. Blackish paint or varnish over the original green paint. Crest rail, arm crest, arm supports, and rear legs, sugar maple; spindles, front legs, and stretchers, hickory or ash; seat, American butternut (microanalysis by Gordon K. Saltar, Wilmington, Delaware, May 6, 1980). SW 17″, SD 16¼″, SH 17″, OH 37″. (National Park Service)

11. (above) Armchair. English, 1740–1760. Ash and elm. (Mary and Raymond Walton)

the three stretchers and the dishing of the seat, reminiscent of the seat in figure 76. These stylistic features of the Floyd Windsor, in addition to the scientific determination made about the seat wood, distinguish the chair as not only American but, I think the further assumption that it is a Connecticut piece can also be made. Later chapters examine and discuss many Connecticut Windsors with similar features.[9] For the moment, however, I shall add that the Connecticut provenance makes sense in another way. There was intense commerce in the eighteenth century between eastern Long Island and Connecticut, and, indeed, William Floyd lived in the Litchfield area of Connecticut for a number of years, as did members of his family, during the second half of the eighteenth century.[10]

The point here is that the Floyd chair is in fact American, demonstrating that American Windsor-chair makers were imitating English examples at least in the second half of the eighteenth century and, probably, in the first half as well. It remains to be seen how many other American chairs in the English style exist. But there must be others, some of which, like the Floyd chair, have been erroneously labeled as English and so have not yet come to light.

In any case, I think we can say with some confidence that, although Windsors must have been made in Philadelphia in the 1730s—both in the American and in the English style—there were no craftsmen who devoted their full energies to the manufacture of Windsors to the exclusion of other forms of turned furniture. The specialists were to come later.

PHILADELPHIA STYLE

By 1740 to 1750 Windsor furniture was being used in a wide variety of settings in Philadelphia. Private homes used Windsors indoors and out, as did public gathering places like taverns and meetinghouses. Furthermore, in Colonial America the popularity of Windsor furniture knew no social boundaries. Merchants, generals, shopkeepers, clergymen, craftsmen, bankers, and revolutionaries all used Windsors to furnish their seating requirements. Like the Colonist himself, the Windsor chair was flexible and quickly adapted to a variety of forms rarely associated with English Windsors.

Who were the craftsmen who were not only copying English Windsors but also making them in the new Philadelphia style? As I have indicated, from simple logic and from their advertisements we know that they were basically turners who were making, among other things, both rush-bottom *and* Windsor chairs. In creating an American style of Windsor, these craftsmen did what came naturally: they based the turning patterns and even the

12. A Windsor settee of the 1780s in the garden of the Stenton Mansion, Philadelphia. Now covered in brown paint, the piece was originally white with blue decoration. (For more details on this piece, see figure 193.)

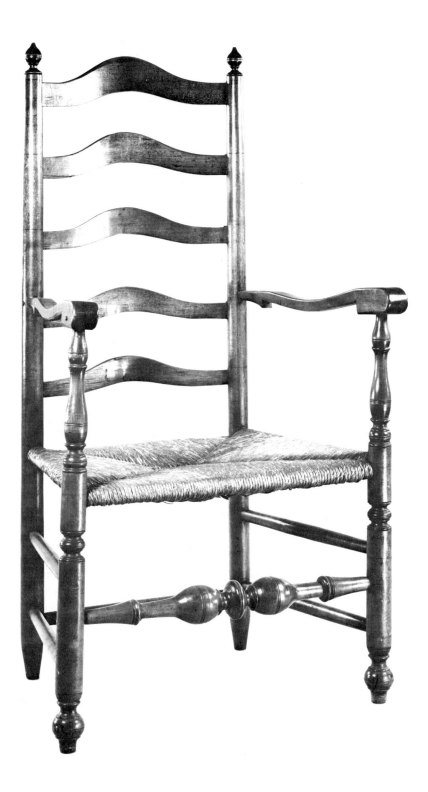

13. (below) Turner, *from Edward Hazen's* Panorama of Professions and Trades. *Philadelphia, 1839.*

14. (left) Armchair. *Philadelphia, 1735–1750. Primary wood, maple; seat, rush. (Independence National Historical Park)*

15. Armchair. English, 1720–1740. (Design Council)

16. Advertisement of Andrew Gautier, Windsor-chair maker, New York Journal, September 2, 1765. (Historical Society of Pennsylvania)

TO BE SOLD,
By ANDREW GAUTIER,

In Princes-Street, opposite Mr. Provooft's, near Broad-Street:

A Large and neat Affortment of Windsor Chairs, made in the beft and neateft Manner, & well painted, viz. High-back'd low-back'd and Sackback'd, Chairs and Settees, or double feated, fit for Piazza or Gardens.—Children's dining and low Chairs, &c.

N. B. As the above GAUTIER intends conftantly to keep a large Number of all Sorts of the above Chairs by him for Sale, all Perfons, wanting fuch, may depend on being fupplied with any Quantity Wholefale or Retail, at reafonable Rates.

42

overall design of their Windsor chairs on local turning patterns and on designs of rush-button chairs. Josiah Sherald advertised himself as a "rushbottom and Windsor Chair maker" in the *Pennsylvania Gazette* in 1762.

Consider the early Philadelphia slat-back armchair shown in figure 14, and compare it with figure 8 or with the early Philadelphia comb-back Windsors shown in figures 20 and 22. First, the legs of early Philadelphia Windsors are a direct descendant of the local turning styles of Delaware Valley rush-bottom chairs, both slat-back and banister-back: a cylindrical leg ending in a ball foot. Second, just as the rush-bottom chairs have a baluster-and-reel, or Queen Anne, front stretcher, so the early Philadelphia Windsors have Queen Anne medial stretchers. Finally, the turned arm supports of early Philadelphia Windsors are positioned at the front corners of the seat and echo both the positioning and the turning pattern of the front arm supports of Philadelphia rush-bottom chairs that are simply an extension of the front legs.

By contrast, the very popular and stylish Windsors from the south of England, especially London, have either swept-back or paddlelike arm supports, cabriole legs, and Queen Anne back splats (figure 15). The Philadelphia Windsor is much more stylistically influenced by the stick chairs of northern England, which have turned arm supports and no back splats. In part, this is due to the immigration of north country craftsmen to the Pennsylvania-New Jersey area in the second quarter of the eighteenth century. But even those craftsmen had the high-style English examples before them, and they must have made a conscious decision not only to ignore the most obviously London-ish features of most English Windsors—the back splat and the cabriole legs—but also to incorporate into their chairs distinctly local Delaware Valley turning patterns. Here, at last, was an American Windsor that could in no way be mistaken for an English one.

The earliest Philadelphia advertisement by a Windsor-chair maker that I am aware of appears in the *Pennsylvania Gazette* for August 18, 1748, and states that "David Chambers is removed from his house in Walnut Street, to his house in Plumb Street, on Society Hill, where he keeps shop, and makes Windsor chairs as formerly."[11] One could infer from this advertisement not only that Chambers had previously made Windsors at another location in Philadelphia but also, perhaps, that he made Windsors exclusively. If so, then he was certainly the first craftsman to specialize in this way. Unfortunately, no chair that is attributable to Chambers is known, but I think it is probable that he made chairs in the Philadelphia style.

In the 1750s advertisements and other references to Windsors became more frequent. In 1754 Jedediah Snowden, who was both a Windsor-chair maker and a cabinetmaker, billed Philadelphia merchant John Reynell three pounds for "2 Double Windsor Chairs with 6 legs."[12] This, by the way, is the earliest-known sale of a piece of Windsor furniture in America. As with Chambers, however, surviving pieces by Snowden are not known. On December 18, 1759, Francis Trumble, one of the earliest craftsmen to make Windsors in large numbers, received eight pounds eighteen shillings for twelve Windsor chairs and ten shillings for a child's Windsor from the merchant Garrett Meade.[13] Many of the chairs made by Trumble are known today. The June 8, 1758, inventory of one Abraham Lodge of New York City lists "4 high back Windsor chairs."[14] In the *New York Journal* for September 2, 1765, Andrew Gautier ran an advertisement showing a woodcut of a comb-back Windsor chair in the Philadelphia style (figure 16). The earliest branded (signed) Windsor chairs in the American style are comb-backs with cylindrical legs, ball feet, and Queen Anne medial stretchers by Philadelphia chairmaker Thomas Gilpin (1700-66; see, for example, figure 26), and similarly, low-backs by Francis Trumble (1716-1798). Such facts, along with our dating of the comb-back in figure 8, suggest that production of American Windsors began around 1735 and evolved into the fully developed Philadelphia form roughly between 1750 and 1765.

By the mid- to late 1760s Windsor chairs were so popular that it was economically feasible for a craftsman to specialize in their production, often to the exclusion of other forms of furniture. But although it was good for business, the chairs' tremendous popularity created a problem of supply and demand in the area of mass production. The early cylinder-and-ball-foot leg was relatively difficult to produce, requiring the time and skill of a master turner (drawing 1). In addition, this leg had to be custom-made because the height of the chair could not be lowered after purchase without cutting off the ball foot; thus ruining the design of the leg. A production shortcut had to be found, and it was the Philadelphia tapered leg.

To the Windsor-chair maker, the tapered leg had a number of distinct advantages over the cylinder-and-ball-foot leg. First, the tapered leg could be turned quickly by a less-skilled craftsman. And unlike the cylindrical leg, the tapered leg could be reproduced thousands of times in an identical pattern. The tapered leg could be made slightly long, the assembled chairs could be stockpiled, and the individual buyer could cut down the chair, or have it cut down, to the desired height without destroying the basic design of the leg, much as store-bought trousers can be shortened. Changing the Queen Anne medial stretcher to a simpler bobbin turning also permitted stepped-up production. In addition, the side stretchers of Philadelphia Windsors were altered. On the

early chairs these stretchers had been turned in an asymmetrical pattern; that is, the bobbin turning of the side stretchers was positioned off-center, and when the chair was assembled, the bobbin was closer to the rear of the chair than to the front. However, as production increased, the bobbin was turned in the very center of the side stretchers, a simpler procedure.

It was at about this time, in the mid- to late 1760s, that the name *Philadelphia chair* became a synonym in Colonial America for *Windsor chair*—exactly what had happened thirty years earlier with the town of Windsor in England. The Philadelphia Windsor-chair makers and the merchants who purchased their chairs in quantity exported thousands of tapered-leg Windsors up and down the eastern seaboard and to Europe. The southern states and the West Indies as far south as Grenada received regular shipments. In 1766 the *South Carolina Gazette* carried an advertisement of the firm of Sheed and White offering Philadelphia-made Windsor chairs that had been imported on the brig *Philadelphia Packet*. These chairs were described as "well painted, high back'd, low back'd, sack back'd, and settees or double seated, fit for piazzas or gardens." Twenty years later—from March 26, 1784, to August 24, 1786—the port of Philadelphia exported 1,760 Windsor chairs to Charleston, South Carolina; 1,734 chairs to Virginia; 538 to Georgia; 474 to North Carolina; and 1,180 to various ports in the West Indies.[15] The heavy demand for Windsor chairs and benches in the South and in the Caribbean stemmed from the same reasons it did in the North, perhaps even more so: Windsors made perfect garden furniture, especially in tropical climates.

At this time many Philadelphia Windsor-chair makers began stamping their names into the bottoms of the seats of their tapered-leg Windsors with red-hot branding irons (see figure 17), just as Thomas Gilpin and Francis Trumble had done on their stylistically earlier chairs with cylindrical legs and ball feet. This was done not only to show pride in workmanship but also as a form of advertising. Today, to those who understand the history of these chairs, the brand means something more: it is literally a brand name, the hallmark of the early assembly line, indicating that the chairs were, more often than not, made in large numbers for anonymous buyers. And with only a few exceptions—including the Gilpin and Trumble chairs mentioned above—all Philadelphia branded chairs known today have tapered legs or the even later bamboo-turned legs (drawing 3).

With the rapid spread in popularity of the "Philadelphia chair," the chairmakers of New York and New England were faced with the problem of how to get a piece of the action. Their solution, in the best New England tradition, was straightforward and simple: build a better Windsor and the customers would beat

17. Branding iron of A. CHAPMAN, American, early nineteenth century. Branding irons like this one were used by Windsor makers to stamp their names on their products, usually on the seat bottoms; Chapman himself may have been a Windsor maker. L 17¼" × W 2¾". (Howard Szmolko)

strong, beautifully painted, after the Philadelphia mode, warrented of good seasoned materials, so firmly put together as not to deceive the purchasers by an untimely coming to pieces." Even southern chairmaker Andrew Redmond advertised in South Carolina in 1784 that he made and sold "Philadelphia Windsor chairs, either armed or unarmed, as neat as any imported, and much better stuff."[16]

In fact, the New England and New York chairs of the 1770 to 1790 period *were* in many ways better than those being produced in Philadelphia. Without realizing it, Philadelphia Windsor makers had been seduced by the siren song of the assembly line into producing a standardized, uninspired tapered leg on their chairs. New England and New York chairmakers, however, were taking the tapered leg to a new height of design, with bold changes between the thicks and thins of the turnings, long and graceful tapering, dramatic leg splay, and high stretchers (drawings 1 and 2). They were also creating the innovative continuous-arm Windsor and the marvelous Rhode Island turnings of the 1770s.

This is not to say that some New England Windsors did not suffer from assembly-line methods. For example, Windsors made in large quantities in Boston also became standardized and relatively sterile because they were being sold to a generalized group of anonymous buyers. But like the imposing custom-made Philadelphia chairs, the large majority of the best New England and New York Windsors as well as those from Lancaster County, Pennsylvania, were *not* branded. These unbranded chairs were conscientiously tailored to individual buyers, or they were produced by local craftsmen for a relatively small community. They incorporate regional style idiosyncracies that, at their best, result in great American furniture design—at their worst quaintness, but never sterility.

As I have previously noted, the really important change that distinguishes American Windsors at a glance from most English prototypes is the absence of a splat and cabriole legs. This change came at a time when a growing spirit of independence and dissatisfaction with the mother country was felt. Discarding those two ornamental features was, I feel, an act of stylistic defiance toward England expressed by American craftsmen, a gesture that preceded the political defiance of American statesmen by two decades. By the 1760s more and more advertisements appeared in Colonial newspapers assuring the public of the quality of American-made goods and urging them to "buy American." Nor were the wealthy immune from such patriotic pressures. In 1765 the prominent Philadelphian Samuel Morris advised his nephew, who was on a sojourn in London, to refrain from purchasing furnishings abroad for his newly-planned Philadelphia mansion because "a man is in danger of becoming invidiously distin-

a path to their doors. To judge from early advertisements, competition between New England and Philadelphia for the domestic market was fierce and chauvinistic. New England chairmakers claimed that their products were every bit as good—even better—than anything being shipped north from the City of Brotherly Love.

For example, in 1786 Ebenezer Stone advertised in Boston that "Warrented Green Windsor chairs" could be had at his shop, "where is made, and for sale at a low price, round top chairs, fanback garden chairs, sofas, stuff-seat chairs, and a neat assortment of dining chairs, painted equally as well as those made in Philadelphia." Daniel Lawrence advertised in Providence, Rhode Island, in 1787 that he made and sold "all kinds of Windsor chairs . . . in the newest and best fashion, neat elegant and guished who buys anything in England which our tradesmen can furnish."[17]

Although some may disagree, I do not feel that it is an exaggeration to assert that the elimination of the two most obviously English features from American Windsors was prophetic. The Windsor, free of the splat, becomes open and democratic. Free of the cabriole leg, the turned legs are no longer confined to the front corners of the seat and can be socketed farther in, resulting in great, dramatic leg splay. Whereas the English chair is usually rigid and rather passive in design, the impact of the American chair is of flexibility and assertiveness.

Furthermore, most joined, turned, or framed chairs, including English Windsors, are designed to be viewed from the front, for it is from that vantage point only that both ornamentation and design coalesce sensibly—a design psychology based, no doubt, on the throne, a chair of ceremony or pretension. Such chairs exist unto themselves and, to anthropomorphize, they ignore their environment.

Not so the American Windsor. The form immediately becomes a part of its surroundings. One looks *at* a Windsor and *through* it at the same time. Its form is felt rather than seen. It can be aesthetically pleasing when viewed from any position: front, side, or back (figure 18). In a design sense an American Windsor never "turns its back on you."

By the mid-1770s the American Windsor had reached its full development: the design was totally American, the stance was aggressive, the craftsmanship superb. It is not through ornamentation or decorative detail that we recognize the American Windsor but, rather, through the total spirit of its design. And I think that if that spirit could be summed up in a single word, that word would be *independence*.

DEVELOPMENT OF
THE CRAFTSMAN-MERCHANT

To this point I have been discussing what might be called the classic, early Windsors—those with baluster-and-ring turnings made in the Middle Atlantic and New England areas from around 1735 through 1790. This was a period of transition not only for political America but for industrial America as well, if *industrial* is not an anachronism in this context. And for better or worse, the popularity of the Windsor chair played a significant role in the changing America.

To celebrate the ratification of the Constitution of the United States on June 21, 1788, a Grand Federal Procession was held in Philadelphia on July 4 of that year. About 5,000 citizens had been invited to join the line of march. Among them were 88

18. A Rhode Island continuous-arm Windsor chair, 1775–1800, rear view. (See figure 123 for details.)

different groups of marchers, 44 of which represented various trades and professions. Indeed, those 44 groups could themselves be further subdivided into 65 different trades and professions.

In the forty-third group marched the "Instrument-Makers, Turners, Windsor Chair and Spinning-wheel Makers." The group was

> conducted by Captain John Cornish, Mr. John Stow bearing the standard,—the turner's arms, with the addition of a spinning-wheel on one side and a Windsor chair on the other. Motto, "By faith we obtain."
>
> Messrs. George Stow and Michael Fox carrying columns representing the several branches of turning; Messrs. Anthony and Mason, with a group of musical instruments, followed by sixty persons dressed in green aprons.[18]

I mention this event not only for its purely historical interest but to emphasize the fact that specialization in the trades and professions had become the rule of the day in late eighteenth century America, a trend that, of course, today continues in full force. A whole class of craftsmen arose up and down the eastern seaboard who specialized in one product: the making of Windsor chairs. Windsor chairs were the first item to be mass-produced in America. This is not to say that Windsor-chair makers did not make other products. But it was the rare furniture craftsman who could conduct a business that produced a wide variety of products, and those that did had usually been well-established before the Revolution.

Along those same lines the manufacturing of Windsors was at the center of another area that still concerns us today: the division of labor and management. During most of the eighteenth century a would-be craftsman would apprentice himself to a master craftsman. After serving his apprenticeship and then his journeymanship, he could look forward to the possibility of some day becoming a master himself and running his own shop.

However, in the late eighteenth century that situation began to change rather radically for several reasons. First, specialization was running rampant not only among the various trades but *within* them as well. As production was stepped up and the size of the shops increased, the making of Windsors became a produc-

tion-line operation. Rather than learning the entire operation, as he had in the past, an apprentice would now become skillful in only one specialized area. Whether he became a journeyman or not, he would never learn to make a whole Windsor chair, and thus would be destined to perform a single chairmaking operation for the rest of his working life—a specialist within an already specialized field.

Second, for the sake of respectability and prestige, the master craftsmen were attempting, often successfully, to "elevate" themselves from craftsmen to merchants. The master began to function as a businessman who managed the shop but did not participate in the day-to-day, hands-on operation of it. Furniture was now made in a "manufactory" rather than in a shop (figure 19), and production became concentrated in the hands of a few master-managers, as competition increased and the smaller shops fell by the wayside. The terms *wareroom* and *chair store* began to appear in advertisements, meaning, of course, a place where furniture was stockpiled for immediate sale in large quantities. Thus the journeyman had almost no chance of ever breaking into the managerial merchant class, and an uncrossable line was drawn between labor and management that persists today. Indeed, the journeyman class itself began to dwindle as the managers found more and better ways to cut costs and hire worker-apprentices at rates lower than those that journeymen demanded.

The manufacturing of Windsors was not only particularly well-suited to this sort of social change but may have been partly responsible for it. As the enormous market for the chairs was ready-made, the chairs easily lent themselves to production by nonmaster craftsmen. In addition, around 1785 the turning style of Windsors was even further simplified from the baluster-and-ring pattern to the bamboo pattern, which required even less-skilled craftsmen and coincided with a change in America from the Chippendale style in furniture to the Hepplewhite and Sheraton styles.

We have already touched on the fact that Windsors were produced in enormous numbers, and this is well-documented in advertisements, bills, and inventories and account books of the late eighteenth and early nineteenth centuries. As early as 1775 Francis Trumble advertised in the *Pennsylvania Gazette* of December 27 that he not only sold all kinds of furniture, walking sticks, rolling pins, lemon squeezers, and the like, but also that he had on hand 1,200 Windsor chairs, no doubt for export from Philadelphia. In the same issue, Trumble advertised that he desired to purchase "40,000 hickory sticks for Windsor chairs."[19] An entry in an account book of one Claudius Paul Raguet, dated May 20, 1790, indicates that Raguet had placed an order with Philadelphia Windsor maker Anthony Steel "for 140 Dozen Windsor

19. Bill of John K. Cowperthwaite. New York City, dated May 11, 1825, showing his "Fancy & Windsor Chair Manufactory." (The New York Historical Society)

Fancy & Windsor Chair Manufactory.

An extensive assortment of the above articles constantly on hand, and for sale, Wholesale and Retail at the lowest prices, warranted well finished, at the long established factory

No 1 Chatham-Square, extending through to No. 2 Catherine-street.

chairs." In New York City, Thomas Hayes announced in the *Daily Advertiser* for November 3, 1800, that "Masters of Vessels or Merchants, can be supplied with from 1 to 1000 [Windsor] chairs in one hour." But the Raguet order and the Trumble and Hayes advertisements are modest compared to the advertisement of James Hallett, Jr., who boasted in the *New York Gazette* for October 22, 1801, that he had "For Sale 5,000 windsor chairs of various patterns, prepared for a Foreign market of the very best materials and workmanship." Even chairmakers in comparatively rural areas could and did develop a volume business in Windsors. Although the famous Windsor maker Ebenezer Tracy (1744-1803) of Lisbon, Connecticut, may not be a perfectly representative example—Tracy being a rather extraordinary craftsman and entrepreneur—nonetheless at his death his inventory listed in his shop 6,400 Windsor chair rounds and legs and 277 chair seats, the former enough for about 900 complete chairs.

Although innovation in the design of Windsors continued, the high point had been reached with the introduction of the new Hepplewhite and later Sheraton taste, and the chairs on the whole became progressively more simplified and standardized in the nineteenth century, still there were compensating factors. For example, Windsor makers Thomas and William Ash advertised in the *New York Packet* of March 3, 1785, that they

> have now ready at the Ware-house, a great number of very neat chairs and settees, some of which is very elegant, being stuffed in the seat and brass nailed, a mode peculiar to themselves and never before executed in America.

Although upholstered Windsors are something of a rarity, the desire for them apparently caught on to a certain extent. In the *Maryland Journal* of July 12, 1797, the following advertisement appeared:

> James Zwisler & Co.—Having established, in the vicinity of Balti-more-town, a Manufactory for Dressing Leather as Practiced in Turkey, . . . have . . . for Sale, a Variety of Arm and other Wind-sor Chairs and settees, the seats neatly stuffed and covered with red, green, yellow, blue and black Morocco coloured leather.

A more significant development in Windsor making, at least with respect to the chairs' availability to the collector today, was the Sheraton-style "fancy chair." Perhaps best known in their elaborately paint-stenciled "Hitchcock" form of the 1820s and 1830s, they were made at the turn of the century in sometimes beautifully hand-decorated forms. To keep pace with the latest fashion trends, many Windsor makers became Windsor *and* fancy chairmakers, as evidenced in many advertisements.

Earlier Windsors had generally been painted in a single color, usually green, and the color itself, used primarily to unify the

design of the chair and protect it from the elements, was subordinate to the overall design of the chair.

With the mid- to late-Federal Windsor, however, color played a more important role than ever before, compensating for a lack of great design and undoubtedly indicative of the fact that most of the later Windsors were used mostly in the home.

White, yellow, copper, mahogany, black, red, green, tan, gray, and blue—those are a few of the colors, used alone or in combination on Federal Windsors. From 1795 to 1799 John DeWitt & Co. of New York City advertised "Windsor Chairs japann'd and neatly flowered."[20] John Lambert of Philadelphia made five "roundtop" white Windsor settees in 1793. An advertisement in the *American Citizen* (New York City) of August 11, 1804, stated that

> Fifty dollars reward, will be paid by the subscriber for the detection of the thief who, on the 2nd instant, stole from No. 7 Burling-slip, six Windsor Chairs, green backs and black seats, ornamented with yellow. The frequent depredations committed, in this way, has determined us to prosecute the first detected to the full extent of the law. Christian & Paxton, Auctioneers.

But, supposing one wished to be in fashion by owning chairs in the "new" colors but did not care to purchase new Windsor chairs, then one could apply to James Always of New York City, who advertised in the *Weekly Museum* for February 28, 1801, that he not only had for sale "Windsor chairs of every description, both plain and fancy colors," but also that "he has good accommodations for drying old chairs, when re-painted, and he will take them from any part of town, and return them in good order. He will paint them green or any fancy color, in the best manner, at a very low price." Or one could look up Herman Vosburgh, who announced in the *Weekly Museum* for March 29, 1800, that one could come to him to have one's "Old Chairs re-painted in Fancy Colors [and] in hard varnishes, which will make them both elegant and durable." Of course, such advertisements account perfectly for the frequent discoveries of eighteenth-century Windsors with attractive nineteenth-century painted decorations covering their original green paint.

Although Windsors were being advertised as late as the 1850s, the designs had become static fifteen or twenty years earlier. Indeed, these late chairs had become so standardized and plain that today it is virtually impossible to determine by style alone in what region of America they were made.

PAINTED WINDSORS

Most Windsor chairs and other Windsor furniture were painted, as I have mentioned, for several reasons: to unify the appearance of the diverse woods used in their construction; to add decorative flourishes; and, if the furniture was used out-of-doors, to protect it. And to the collector, the most desirable Windsor is the one that retains its original coat of paint.

In most chairs made up to around 1780, the original paint is green. I've seen literally hundreds and hundreds of chairs originally painted green. When a green Windsor from this period is examined, this original paint will be found to have become crystallized. When it was originally applied, the paint was a rich, leaf-green color, but chemical changes over time will have produced a green patina not unlike that found on Persian Bronze Age artifacts.

More often than not, the original paint will be found covered by one or more coats of later paint, applied at various times in the life of the Windsor. Over the years I have discovered a remarkable number of Windsor chairs from a variety of geographical regions that have the same "paint history," or sequence of paint colors. Indeed, I have found this same paint history on chairs from Delaware, Philadelphia, Lancaster County, Pennsylvania, New York, Connecticut, Massachusetts, and Rhode Island. The surface color is black, probably applied in the late nineteenth century, dulled with age and with an alligator skin-like appearance. The coat below the black is bright red (early to mid-nineteenth century), and beneath the red is the original green.

To my eye, the sort of paint history just described creates a very pleasing effect, especially when the black surface coating is flaking from some parts of the chair and the various layers of color are exposed. I suppose the word *character* is as good a word as any to describe the added dimension and interest the exposed paint history of the chair brings to the surface, notably in the bulbous baluster-and-ring turnings.

Of course, there are a great many chairs with a different paint history. For example, many early chairs have just two layers of paint. The surface coat is a buff color—usually striped or ringed with black or dark green around the "rain gutter" (seat groove) and used to accent the turnings. This buff color usually covers the original green. It is brittle, and age has given it a surface of hairline cracks like those found on porcelain. It flakes easily to expose more green beneath it. Again, a very pleasing effect.

Chair parts that are made of hickory—for example, the spindles, the arm rail, and the crest rail—tend to flake and lose their later coats of paint more readily than do other parts of Windsors. At the other extreme I have seen and owned Windsors with eight or nine coats of paint over the original green. It is my feeling that the beauty of the turnings is obscured by four or more coats of paint, and I usually attempt to remove the outer coats to get down to the original. I do this by carefully chipping away at the paint with a knife, not by using paint removers or solvents that may smear or destroy the crystallized paint.

As I have already mentioned, it is in the fourth quarter of the eighteenth century that chairmakers began to branch out and paint their chairs in colors other than green. The mahogany color is one of the more interesting. It was achieved by first painting the entire chair a pink or salmon color and then applying a mahogany stain or varnish. I have seen many chairs painted this way, and the original surface tends to hold up surprisingly well over two centuries. I have also seen chairs that were originally and completely painted a mahogany color—including their authentic mahogany arms! The only reason I can deduce for this seemingly strange practice is that, as the paint wore off the chair's most vulnerable part—the arms—the authentic mahogany below would be exposed, thus obviating to a certain extent the necessity of repainting the arms.

During the early days of collecting American furniture in this century, it became the fashion to remove the paint from Windsors and to refinish them. I suppose the thinking at the time was that it made the chairs look cleaner, slicker, and easier to live with. Besides, what would one's friends or neighbors say if one's furniture were covered with peeling paint? Furthermore, if a Windsor needed repair or a replaced part, it was easier to strip the entire chair than to try to match a timeworn paint surface. This practice has, of course, resulted in a great many refinished Windsors—so many, in fact, that it is far more common to find stripped Windsors for sale than those with their original paint. Thus painted Windsors, now recognized as being rarer and more authentic, are more sought after and expensive.

Nonetheless, a Windsor with wonderful turnings and excellent proportions should not be scorned because it has been refinished. It may still be an asset to any collection. Conversely, a basically mediocre chair may be greatly enhanced by its original paint. For that reason and because of the current resurgence in the popularity of Windsors, many chairs that were refinished in the 1920s are being repainted to look old. Some of these repainted chairs are very convincing and bring much higher prices than they would in their refinished state. The best, and perhaps the only way to guard against buying a Windsor with a new "original" finish is to examine as many authentically old surfaces on Windsors as possible—in museums, antique shops, and such historic restorations as the Winterthur Museum, Old Sturbridge Village, and, especially, Colonial Williamsburg, which has in its collection some of the finest early American Windsor furniture with its old paint surfaces intact.

A STUDY OF WINDSOR SURFACES

PLATE I. *This rare, early, Philadelphia comb-back is so important as an early stylistic document because its paint surfaces are still intact—nineteenth century dark red over earlier nineteenth century yellow, over the original eighteenth century green. When a Windsor chair has no known counterpart, I cannot stress how important the surface condition is in determining its authenticity or whether it has gone through any changes. The untouched paint surface is one of the key factors in making this chair one of the truly great American Windsors. (See figure 8.)*

PLATE II. *This portrait of a Rhode Island gentleman, probably done between 1790 and 1810, shows an interesting continuous-arm Windsor with an upholstered back. Windsors with upholstered backs are rare but occasionally turn up. See figure 115. (Isobel and Harvey Kahn)*

PLATE III. *Side chair, probably Pennsylvania, 1780-1800. Early nineteenth century red paint over the original grayish-green. Crest rail, oak; spindles and back posts, hickory; seat, pine; legs and stretchers, maple. SW 16¾", SD 17", SH 15½", OH 35¾". (Privately owned)*

Covering the original grayish-green paint, the early nineteenth century red paint striped with yellow is an attempt to bring an "old fashioned" chair up to date with paint decoration popular in the first half of the nineteenth century. The color combination is typical of Pennsylvania German decorated chairs of the 1830s and 1840s.

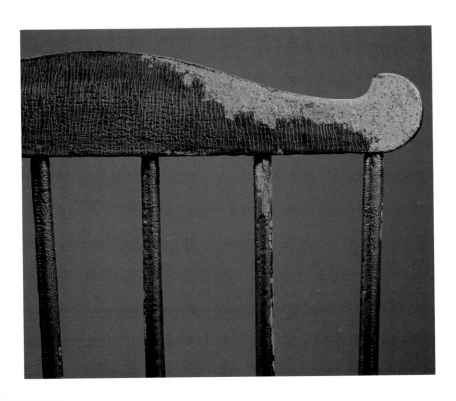

PLATE IV. *shows the slow results of the dry scraping process to remove a heavy coat of late nineteenth century black paint from figure 172, a Conn. writing-arm Windsor. The bright salmon red emerging is an early nineteenth century coat of paint over the original eighteenth century green. By not using a solvent to remove the outer coat, the red undercoat retains its crystallized patina. (See figure 172.)*

PLATE V. *Side chair. Farmington, Maine, c. 1820. Original color paint with red and green decoration. Crest rail, back posts, legs, and stretchers, probably maple; spindles, hickory or ash; seat, pine. SW 16¼″, SD 15¾″, SH 18″, OH 35¾″. (Burton and Helaine Fendelman)*

Made by Daniel Stewart, who worked in Farmington, Maine from 1812 to 1827, this chair is one of a set of six, which bears Stewart's label. Called a step-down Windsor because of the shape of its crest rail, this style was common in the nineteenth century. What sets this chair apart is its rare and exuberant red and green paint decoration (Stewart was a painter as well as a Windsor maker). The paint is used not simply to decorate, but to accent the architecture of the chair.

PLATE VI. *This lovely, early nineteenth century portrait shows a child's step-down Windsor painted and decorated. In a companion painting not shown here, the child's mother is seated on a chair of identical design, color and decoration. Sets of decorated Windsors often included highchairs as well. (See figure 157.)*

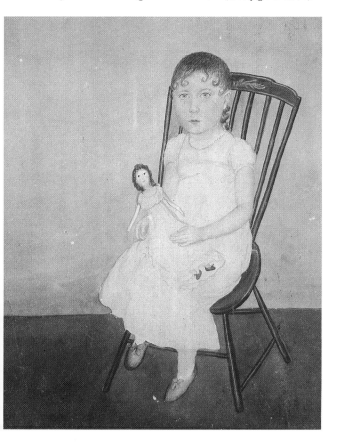

PLATE VII. Armchair. *Probably Bucks County, Pennsylvania, 1765–1780. Original olive green paint with black striping. Crest rail, oak; spindles and arm rail, hickory; arm supports, legs, and stretchers, maple; seat, poplar. SW 24⅜″, SD 16¼″, SH 17½″, OH 44⅜″. (James and Nancy Glazer)*

This is a large and graceful comb-back with greater leg splay and more attenuated turnings than similar chairs made in Philadelphia. It is rare to find such a chair in its original paint; eighteenth century Pennsylvania comb-back Windsors were eagerly sought at the beginning of the twentieth century, but many—perhaps the majority—were stripped clean. Furthermore, olive green is an unusual color for Pennsylvania comb-backs. The crest rail, arm rail, and ring turnings are nicely accented with black striping.

PLATE VIII. *Early nineteenth century portrait of gentleman seated on a chair with a back construction similar to* PLATE XI. *(Isobel and Harvey Kahn)*

PLATES IX and X. *The ornamentation of painted Windsors became popular at the beginning of the nineteenth century. The flat wooden medallions centered in the crest of many double rodback Windsors, and in various shapes (rectangular, oval, and square), were a perfect place for a small painting. The paintings were often symbolic, like the fine, golden rising sun in the oval crest medallion of PLATE X. I have also seen ornamentation detailing classical urns, portraits, landscapes, etc. (See figure 165.)*

PLATE XI. *Shows a motif of delicate, golden, climbing vines. The decoration, done in gold leaf, may have been inspired by the trellis-like construction of this chair's back. (See figure 160.)*

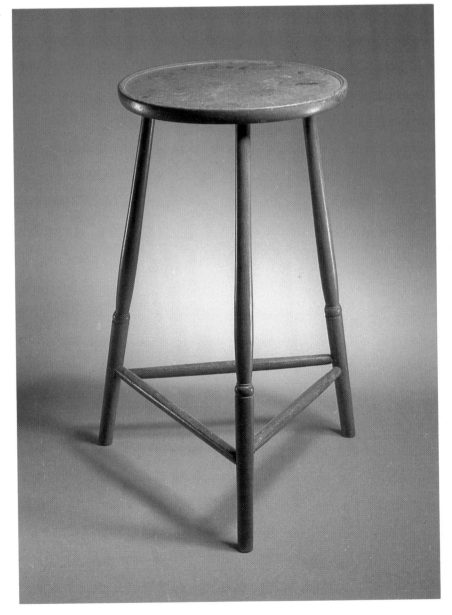

PLATE XII. *The charming little child's bow-back side chair in* PLATE XII *has a nineteenth century warm light grey color, striped and ringed with blue over the original dark green paint. To me, this is a delightful color for a child's Windsor, and I do not think removing it to expose the original green would, in this case, enhance the look of the chair. (See figure 208.)*

PLATE XIII. *Candlestand. Chester County, Pennsylvania, 1780-1800. Original blue paint. Made entirely in walnut. Top diameter 15″, H 29″. (Privately owned)*

This rare and delicate candlestand was covered with mid-nineteenth century, dark brown, grained paint. The effect was rather gloomy, and the turnings were sticklike. When the brown graining was removed by careful dry scraping, the original pale blue paint was revealed, and the importance of the original color to the total design became apparent. In pale blue, the slender turnings take on light and shadow, and the form is shown at its best.

PLATE XIV. The Windsor fan chair is another example of the importance the original paint and patina play in analyzing the authenticity of a chair. Had this fan chair been refinished, it would have been difficult to determine whether the fan apparatus was built when the chair was made or whether it was added later. Based on construction, the one obvious fact is that it was added, and is not an integral part of the original chair. What the original finish conveys is that the chair, fan and related parts are painted a straw color that was popular in the last years of the eighteenth century. In addition to color, the character of the paint, the crazing, and the crystallizing of it all indicate the time the chair was painted. Also there is no other color under the straw color on the fan equipment, while the chair does retain its familiar coat of crystallized green found on most eighteenth century Windsors. My conclusion is that the fan equipment, a Philadelphia invention, was adapted to a Long Island, New York Windsor in the 1790s and then the entire contraption was painted a straw color. This was done so the fan support that is attached to the chair back and indeed, the fan itself, when placed against a wall, would blend in to its surroundings and not loom over the sitter like a gallows. (See figure 235.)

PLATE XV. A form of paint ornamentation besides gilding and striping found on Windsors is the use of a name used to personalize the chair. The chair in PLATE XV is painted a bone white with gold leaf stripes edged in black and red on the arms, back crest, the front of the seat, and the front legs; the name Louie is painted in gold leaf on the arm crest. This chair was purchased by a dealer from the attic of a New Jersey home in absolutely untouched condition. The story that accompanied the chair was that it was ordered by the child's father when the boy was born. At 15 months old, the child, Louie, was drowned in a boating accident. Louie's parents could not bear to look at this chair, nor could they bear to have it repainted for use by other children—so the attic was the only alternative. (See figure 220.)

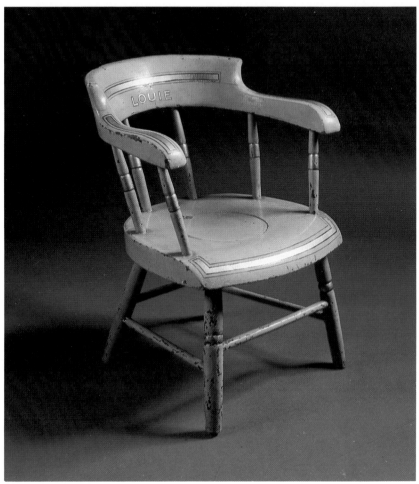

PLATE XVI. *Detail of the arm rail and support of the sack-back Windsor chair shown, right. Notice that the straw-colored paint over the original green has held firm to the hard close grained maple of the arm support, but has flaked badly from the hickory spindles. Hickory does not hold paint well. Practically every eighteenth century Windsor I have examined in original paint will show more evidence of flaking on hickory parts than parts made of other wood. The smooth wear of the paint from the arm is obviously from over two hundred years of use. (See figure 97.)*

PLATE XVII. *Sack-back Windsor chair. Philadelphia, 1765–1780. This chair is a fine example of that wonderful mellow surface patina that one finds on an absolutely untouched chair. An early nineteenth century straw-colored coat of paint covers the original eighteenth century green. The straw color is ornamental, with green striping on the turnings, seat and arm rail. The skin of this chair, as I like to refer to it, with all its imperfections—the wear, the flaking, and the crazing—only add the distinction of time to its grace and beauty. (See figure 97.)*

CHAPTER ONE
Comb-back Chairs

THE TERM *comb-back* refers to a type of Windsor which has a back that resembles a hair comb. Most comb-backs are armchairs, and the back is formed by a continuation of the spindles through the arm rail. The spindles are capped by a curved, steam-bent crest rail that usually has "ears," which project beyond the back spindles. The arm rail may be formed by a single, steam-bent piece of wood; or it may be formed from two pieces of wood sawed into a curve, which are capped in the rear of the chair with another sawed piece of wood: the arm crest.

Figures 20 through 23 represent a group of the earliest, rarest, and finest American comb-backs—the chair in figure 8 notwithstanding. These are classic examples of the Philadelphia chairs that began the Windsor revolution in America.

Note the tall, stately backs of figures 20, 21, and 22. The ears at the ends of the crest rail are carved with two to three volutes. These volutes and the general shape of the crest rail seem to be adaptations from the Philadelphia splat-back Queen Anne chairs of around 1740 and later, the center of whose crest rails have a similar curved shape and carved volutes (figure 24).[21] All of these large, early, classic Philadelphia comb-back armchairs have nine spindles in their backs with little or no taper. The steam-bent arm rails end in handholds with scrolled outer edges; the scrolls being applied, separate pieces of wood. Sometimes these chairs are found with knuckle-carved handholds.

Positioned at the front corners of the seats, the arm supports are very boldly and beautifully turned. Their turning pattern is intended to echo that of the Queen Anne medial stretcher. The first baluster turning of the arm supports, just beneath the handhold, has a compressed appearance, as does the final ball turning, which is sunk deeply into the seat. Actually, the latter is not a

20. Armchair. Philadelphia, 1740–1770. Nineteenth-century black paint over the original red. Crest rail, hickory or oak; arm rail and spindles, hickory; arm supports, legs, and stretchers, maple; seat, poplar. SW 24½", SD 17", SH 16", OH 44". (Independence National Historical Park)

ball turning at all, but a hemisphere with a dowel turned on the end, which is socketed into the seat.

As for the large seats, they are D-shaped and dished out with slight pommel at the front—a comfortable, body-conforming design. A single rain gutter surrounds all the vertical parts socketed into the seat. The underside of the seat is heavily chamfered, and its sides are squared off. The legs protrude through the seat and are secured with wedges, and the spindles are similarly attached to the arm rail.

At the tops of the legs the first baluster turning is socketed deeply into the seat, and there is a small ring turning just below the baluster. From that point down to the second baluster the leg is almost cylindrical, and the second baluster is rather abruptly turned. Next comes a ring, a reel, and a long cylinder, and the leg ends in a ball foot, or "blunt-arrow" design.

The side stretchers are somewhat square and are asymmetrical. That is, the bulbous turning is not in the center of the side stretcher but is positioned closer to the rear of the chair than to the front. As the decoratively turned Queen Anne medial stretcher is socketed into the side stretchers, it, too, is closer to the rear of the chair. As I mentioned in the Introduction, the turning pattern of this medial stretcher is an adaptation of the turned front stretchers of Philadelphia rush-bottom chairs.

These, then, are the principal design features of early Philadelphia comb-back Windsor chairs. One would be hard-pressed to choose among these imposing chairs, but the one in figure 22 is somewhat better in that its turnings are more refined and its crest rail, including the ears, has better proportions.

In figures 23 and 23A we see two views of one of a pair of the

22. Armchair. Philadelphia, 1740–1770.

most remarkable Windsor chairs recently to come to light. This chair is so rare that until now it had been thought not to exist. Why? Because it is the earliest comb-back side chair known, and there had been speculation that side chair companion pieces to the early comb-backs were not made. The turning patterns are virtually identical to those of figures 20 through 22. The side stretchers are asymmetrical, the seat D-shaped, and the legs end in blunt-arrow feet. Indeed, the chair resembles in some respects the one pictured in the Arthur Devis painting in figure 6. Especially interesting is the similarity in the shape of the tail piece that supports the bracing spindles. Noteworthy too, is the fact that the bracing spindles do not fan out but are vertical, a feature I have never seen on any other American brace-back Windsor.

Figures 25 through 27 are variants of early Philadelphia comb-backs, and figure 25 is probably unique. It is entirely original and has sustained very little damage over the years, except for the fact that about three-quarters of an inch of the center of the crest rail is missing and the feet have been worn down. As in figure 8, figure 25 has a double rain gutter (clearly visible in the detail photograph) and double scoring on the balusters, generally considered early features.

Most noteworthy, however, is the shell carving in the center of the crest rail and the carved volutes at the ends of the handholds and at the corners of the seat, extremely rare features on an

21. Armchair. Philadelphia, 1740–1770. Refinished; feet restored. Crest rail, oak; spindles, hickory; seat, poplar; arm supports, legs, and stretchers, maple. SW 23¾", SD 17", SH 16", OH 44½". (Privately owned)

23. (far left) *Side chair. Philadelphia, 1740–1770. Side view. Traces of green paint. Crest rail, oak; spindles, hickory; seat, poplar; legs and stretchers, maple. SW 17½″, SD 16½″, tail piece 4″ × 5½″, SH 17″, OH 37½″. (Olenka and Charles Santore)*

23A. *Side chair. Front view.*

American Windsor and ones that I have never seen before or since. Although rare on a Windsor, such shell carvings are standard motifs of high-style Philadelphia Queen Anne chairs from about mid-century, as shown in figure 24. Indeed, the shell carving on the crest rail of the Windsor chair is virtually identical to that on the crest rail of figure 24.

Chairs such as figure 24 have carved volutes at the ends of the handholds and in the corner brackets at the tops of the front legs. In figure 25, these Queen Anne motifs have been translated into the volutes at the tops of the handholds and at the corners of the seat, shown in the detail photographs. All those decorative flourishes—the shell and the volutes—were, it seems to me, adapted from the elegant Philadelphia Queen Anne furniture in order to lend an air of importance to a Windsor chair made for a wealthy Quaker family, combining a sense of "success" with Quaker simplicity. Which Quaker family? A brass plaque attached to the back of the comb-piece holds a clue: "This chair," reads the plaque, "belonged to William Penn and was presented by his son John Penn to the Colony in Schuylkill." (The Colony

in Schuylkill, now the State-in-Schuylkill, is a private club.)

Interesting as the legend on the plaque is, I have speculated that it is in error. The chair in figure 25 could not have been made before the second quarter of the eighteenth century. Its Queen Anne and Windsor features indicate that it was probably made about 1740. William Penn left the colony of Pennsylvania in 1701 and spent the rest of his life in England, where he died in 1718, so the chair could not have belonged to him.

Could the chair have belonged to William Penn's son John? Again, no. John was an infant when he returned to England with his father in 1701, and he never again returned to America. But there was another John Penn (1729-95), grandson of William Penn, son of Richard Penn, and lieutenant governor of Pennsylvania from 1763 to 1771 and from 1773 to 1776. It is possible that the chair had belonged to Richard Penn and was presented to the Colony in Schuylkill by *his* son John. Such speculations have been partially confirmed by the historian of the State-in-Schuylkill. The chair was presented to the fishing company of Fort St. David's, probably by John Penn. The club already pos-

sessed many Penn heirlooms, and the chair enhanced the collection. In 1780, Fort St. David's burned down, and the salvaged belongings were transported to State-in-Schuylkill when the two clubs merged. Even without such provenance the chair is exceptional—or *was* exceptional. Unfortunately, it was destroyed in a fire on December 22, 1980.

Figure 26 has the brand of Thomas Gilpin (1700-66) on its seat bottom, on the front chamfer of its seat, and on the back of its crest rail. As such, it is one of the earliest-known branded American Windsors. Like that of figure 25, the crest rail of figure 26 is nicely shaped but rather "tight" in that the ears do not project very much. The arm supports have an urn-shaped turning

at the top, and, as in figure 25, at their bottom is a cylinder rather than a compressed ball. Like figures 8 and 25, this chair has the early double rain gutter and double scoring on the balusters. Given the general stylistic similarities, it is quite possible that Gilpin made the chairs in figures 8 and 25 as well as the one in figure 26. On the whole, however, the turnings of figure 26 are not of the very highest, early quality.

Figure 27 is turned better than figure 26 and has better leg splay as well. It, too, has a double rain gutter, double scoring on the balusters, and, I think, a rather Gilpin-like quality. And there is something different about this chair: it has a simplified, earless crest rail, rail, paddlelike arm supports, and a tapered arm rail

25. Armchair. Philadelphia, 1740–1750. Original yellow paint over red filler; about ¾″ of center of crest rail missing. Crest rail and arm rail, ash; spindles, hickory; handhold scroll, maple; seat, poplar; legs and side stretchers, chestnut, medial stretcher, maple. SW 31½″, SD 17″, SH 17¼″, OH 47¾″. (State-in-Schuylkill) (Destroyed in fire, December 22, 1980.)

25A. Armchair. Detail of carved shell on crest rail.

25B. Armchair. Detail of scrolled seat and handhold.

61

26. Armchair. Philadelphia, 1740–1750. Branded under the seat and on back of comb piece "T. Gilpin." Painted black. Crest rail, spindles, and arms, hickory; arm supports, legs, and stretchers, maple (note: Gilpin also made chairs with oak legs); seat, poplar. SW 25", SH 17½", SD 16", OH 44¾". (David Stockwell, Inc.)

26A. Armchair. Detail of brand of Thomas Gilpin.

27. Armchair. Possibly Monmouth County, New Jersey, 1740–1770. Painted green. Crest rail and legs, oak; arm rail, spindles, and arm supports, hickory; seat, poplar. SW 24", SD 16¾", SH 17¾", OH 43". (Independence national Historical Park)

that shows no evidence of ever having had scrolled handholds. Those features are not unique to this chair, and over the years I have seen about a half-dozen similar chairs, most of which turned up in the Monmouth County area of New Jersey. But those features, combined with the flat front edge of the seat, give the chair an English quality, much like the chair in figure 15. A possible explanation for these features—and the overall fanciness of the base and plainness of the top—is that the maker was English, perhaps newly arrived in America. He may have purchased the turnings of the base from a local craftsman and attached them to the upper part of the chair, which he had made himself.

Figure 28 is also a variant of early Philadelphia comb-backs. It has two sawed arms with a heavy arm crest in the back. The two arms do not meet in the back but are cut off just beyond the sixth spindle on each side. The arm crest is then attached to the arms with a lap joint. Early Philadelphia comb-backs with this arm construction are quite rare and greatly sought after. On this particular chair the shape of the crest rail and the deep volutes in the ears are especially well-executed. The turnings are crisp and classic, and, all told, the chair conveys the strength and dignity of the best Quaker furniture.

The next period of Philadelphia Windsor production began around 1760. Although the blunt-arrow foot was slowly being phased out in favor of the tapered leg, many very fine blunt-arrow-foot chairs were still being made. Good examples of two

28. Armchair. Philadelphia, 1750–1760. Traces of the original green paint. Crest rail and arms, oak; arm crest and seat, poplar; spindles, hickory; arm supports, legs, and stretchers, maple. SW 24½", SD 17¼", SH 16", OH 43". (Mr. & Mrs. R. W. P. Allen)

Windsors produced during the same period and which I shall discuss in subsequent chapters. The spindles of the tapered-leg Philadelphia comb-backs acquire a taper of their own, as do the base of the arm supports where they enter the seat. The better chairs have knuckle handholds. Of course, I am making generalizations here, for on some chairs the early and late styles were intermingled.

Figures 31 and 32 represent the style changes that were taking place in Philadelphia Windsors of the 1760s. Figure 31 is a massive chair with eleven tapered back spindles and pleasing, if boxy, proportions. The carved ears and knuckle handholds add greatly to the success of the design. This is an impressive but conservative chair that should probably be looked on as a companion piece to the sack-back Windsors produced by such craftsmen as Joseph Henzey and Francis Trumble during the same period (see, for example, figure 96).

Figure 32 has the brand of Joseph Henzey under its seat. This chair is far more graceful than the one in figure 31. The proportions are better, and the comb fans out nicely. The fine turnings are in the distinctive Henzey pattern, with better thicks and thins than those of figure 31. The arm supports are positioned farther

such chairs are shown in figures 29 and 30. Compared with the earlier chairs, these have a quiet quality about them. The backs seem more airy. The arm supports are less dynamic, and the turning pattern is more elongated, which is especially noticeable in the shapes of both balusters. The balusters of the legs swell more gently than before. The medial stretcher is no longer turned in the Queen Anne pattern but has been reduced to a pleasing bulge, or bobbin, with a ring at either end. Although the seats are still large and D-shaped, something interesting has happened to them as well: the edges have become less sharp. This is especially obvious in comparing the left-hand edges of the seats of figures 20 and 30. In the latter, the edges have gradually begun to curl under the seat (drawing 10). All this bespeaks a kind of conservatism that had begun to overtake certain Philadelphia chairmakers.

The 1760s were something of a transitional period for Windsors. Not only was the blunt-arrow foot superseded by the tapered leg but the D-shaped seat was often replaced with one of an oval or shield shape—this in deference to the designs of other styles of

29. Armchair. Philadelphia, 1760–1775. Refinished. Crest rail and handhold scrolls, oak; spindles, hickory; arm rail, birch; arm supports, legs, and stretchers, maple; seat, poplar. SW 24½", SD 17", SH 17¾", OH 45½". (Privately owned)

30. (left) *Armchair. Philadelphia, 1760–1775. Nineteenth-century dark brown paint over the original green. Crest rail, oak; spindles and arm rail, hickory; arm supports, legs, and stretchers, maple; seat, poplar. SW 23", SD 17", SH 16", OH 43½". (Privately owned)*

31. (right) *Armchair. Philadelphia, 1760–1790. Nineteenth-century black paint over the original green. Crest rail, arm rail, and spindles, hickory; knuckles, oak; seat, poplar; arm supports, legs, and stretchers, maple. SW 23", SD 18½", SH 17", OH 41". (Independence National Historical Park)*

32. (below) *Armchair. Philadelphia, 1765–1785. Branded I. [Joseph] HENZEY. Covered with old varnish. Crest rail, arm supports, legs, and stretchers, maple; spindles and arm rail, hickory; seat, poplar. SW 21¾", SD 16¼", SH 17¼", OH 44". (Mr. and Mrs. R.W. P. Allen)*

back than those of figure 31, relieving the potential boxiness, and their bottom taper is buried deeply in the seat, the latter a Henzey characteristic. Originally this chair had full knuckles, but the bottom portion of them has been lost.

Figure 33 is a provincial chair that shows the heavy influence of the middle-period Philadelphia taste in comb-backs. It is a somewhat simplified chair. The ears are not carved, it has only seven spindles (a middle-period feature), the stretchers have no rings at their ends, and the turnings are toned-down versions of those in figure 32. Yet the chair has well-carved knuckles and an excellent patina.

Figure 34 shows the same type of middle-period comb-back as figure 32, but it is an even better chair. The turnings are bolder and the arm supports set farther back. In addition, the seat has better saddling. Note that although this chair has all the qualities of oval-seat comb-backs of the 1770s, it retains the cylinder-and-blunt-arrow legs of the 1750s. The explanation for this is that the chair was not made in Philadelphia but probably in Wilmington, Delaware, and probably as a custom order by craftsman Sampson Barnet. There is a virtually identical example with Barnet's label in the Historical Society of Delaware in Wilmington. Furniture that is made away from the centers of design is often far less standardized and thus more interesting than furniture made in them, and figure 34 is a good example of that theory.

That is doubly true of the comb-back in figure 35, made in Lancaster County, Pennsylvania. The crest rail of this chair is an especially beautiful feature, with its characteristic beading around the perimeter, flowing shape, and tall ears carved in a relief pattern. As the spindles curve outward, the crest rail seems to be a more logical extension of the spindles than something that merely sits astride them. Note also how the handholds project beyond the front edge of the seat and the relative simplicity of the knuckles, the center one of which also projects comparatively far forward. In typical Pennsylvania-German fashion, the knuckles of Lancaster County chairs are often secured to the arm rail with large, square wooden pins that pierce the arm rail completely from side to side. The seat is more of a kidney shape than an oval and heavily chamfered in the usual Lancaster County fashion. Double scoring is used as a decorative device, the medial stretch-

er is elaborately turned, and the legs end in a style of blunt-arrow foot that is locally called a "goat's foot." The baluster turnings of the arm supports and legs are more barrel shaped than those of the Philadelphia product, but the overall stance of the chair is tension-filled and dynamic. All told, this is a great, idiosyncratic Windsor.

Also from Lancaster County, the chair in figure 36 is almost certainly a product of the same shop that produced figure 101. Note the well-shaped comb-piece with its peaked center and uncarved ears, the unusual, bold arm supports with double reels at the bottom, and the spindles without a hint of taper. An interesting construction feature is the square wooden pin driven through the edge of the seat to secure the arm supports, visible on the right-hand edge of the seat in the photograph. Although more simplified than figure 35, this is a very good chair that demonstrates that excellence of design was not the sole province

33. Armchair. Pennsylvania, possibly Chester County, 1770–1800. Nineteenth-century black paint over the original green. Crest rail, arm rail, and knuckles, oak; spindles, hickory; arm supports, legs, and stretchers, maple; seat, poplar. SW 20″, SD 15⅜″, SH 16¼″, OH 42½″. (Privately owned)

34. Armchair. Probably Wilmington, Delaware, 1770–1790. Old varnish over early nineteenth-century orange paint. Crest rail, arm rail, and spindles, hickory; arm supports, legs, and stretchers, maple; seat, poplar. SW 21¼″, SD 16¼″, SH 17″, OH 40¾″. (Mr. and Mrs. R.W.P. Allen)

36. Armchair. Lancaster County, Pennsylvania, 1765–1790. Refinished. Crest rail, spindles, and arm rail, hickory; arm supports, legs, and stretchers, maple; seat, pine. SW 2 1", SD 16", SH 17¾", O 40". (Lawrence Teacher)

of the so-called design centers of the eastern seaboard.

Figures 37, 38, and 39 exhibit many of the fine features of middle-period Windsors as well as provide an opportunity for the sort of "detective work" many collectors like to do; for these chairs display so many similarities, they lead at least *this* collector to speculate that they are the products of the same shop.

These chairs show us the first definite influence of the Chippendale style on Windsors. Their carved-knuckle, sawed arms rake sharply outward, and their arm supports are set well back from the front corners of the seats. The arm crests at the rear of these chairs and others like them are a Philadelphia characteristic rarely found on chairs from other regions. Each chair is atypical in some way, and each was undoubtedly a custom order. Figure 37 is a chair of massive dimensions and was made for a large, if not obese, individual. Although of the earlier D-shape, the broad seat is quite rounded on its edges—an attempt, perhaps, to lighten the heaviness of the seat visually. The arms, arm supports, and short spindles are made of mahogany, a rare feature. The top surface of the arms are beaded about half an inch on either side. Note too, that not only the medial stretcher, but also the side stretchers are adorned with two rings as well as a central bobbin.

35. Armchair. Lancaster County, Pennsylvania, 1760–1780. Traces of green, red, and white paint. Crest rail, arm rail, and spindles, hickory; knuckles, curly maple; arm supports, legs, and stretchers, maple; seat, poplar. SW 21½", SD 16½", SH 16½", OH 43". (Olenka and Charles Santore)

The chair in figure 38 is quite remarkable. Most significantly, it has a Queen Anne splat in its back, a feature often thought to be an exclusive characteristic of English Windsors. The splat on this rare, beautifully proportioned chair is very well integrated into the crest rail, flowing smoothly into an arching design which is achieved by a slight under-cutting of the crest rail. Unlike the majority of English Windsors, the splat does not continue down to the seat but is mortised into the arm crest, a very effective conceit. As is the case with figure 37, the seat is D-shaped, the beaded arms and arm supports are mahogany, and the side stretchers have rings at both their ends.

37. (below) *Armchair. Philadelphia, 1760–1780. Crest rail, oak; long spindles, hickory; short spindles, arms, and arm supports, mahogany; arm crest, legs, and stretchers, maple; seat, poplar. SW 27", SD 20½", SH 16", OH 43¾". (Stenton Mansion)*

38. (below right) *Armchair. Philadelphia, 1760–1780. Dark red paint over the original green. Crest rail and splat, oak; spindles, hickory; arm crest and seat, poplar; arms, mahogany; legs and stretchers, maple. SW 34½", SD 25¼", OH 46¼". (The Henry Francis du Pont Winterthur Museum)*

Figure 39 shows a marvelously tall comb-back armchair, one of a pair in Carpenter's Hall, Philadelphia. Known as a *speaker's chair*, it has the oval seat typical of the mid-1760s and later. Once again, however, the arms are mahogany and the side stretchers have rings. The turning pattern of these chairs is very similar, and I feel that they were made to order by the same craftsman or shop.

A few more words about figure 39 are in order. This chair is of great interest because of its height, mahogany arms, and superb design. But it is also an important chair. Both it and its twin retain their original black paint; they were made along with ten sack-back, knuckle-arm chairs specifically for Carpenter's Hall, one of the most historically significant buildings in America. A discovery of an entry in the Carpenter's Company records, recently come to light, dated January 1773 notes, "to cash paid for chares [sic] for the Hall 20S [hillings] [each]." The concurring opinion is that this (figure 39) is, in all likelihood, one of those chairs. They were used by the First Continental Congress when it met at Carpenter's Hall on September 5, 1774; and, finally, they still stand in the very same room they were originally intended to occupy. That, in sum, is why I call this chair *important*—a word

39. Armchair. Philadelphia, 1773. Original black paint (two coats). Crest rail, probably oak; spindles, hickory; arm crest and seat, poplar; arms, mahogany; legs, stretchers, and arm supports, maple. SW 23″, SD 17½″, SH 25″, OH 53″. (Carpenter's Company of Philadelphia)

40. Armchair. Philadelphia, 1765–1780. Early nineteenth-century black paint over the original green. Crest rail and spindles, hickory; arms, arm crest, legs, and stretchers, maple; seat, poplar. SW 20½″, SH 16″, OH 40″. (C. L. Prickett)

41. (below) *Armchair. Philadelphia, 1765–1780. Black paint over the original green. Crest rail, oak or hickory; spindles, hickory; arm crest, arm supports, legs, and stretchers, maple; arms, mahogany; seat, poplar. SW 20¾″, SD 17¾″, SH 18″, OH 43¾″. (Privately owned)*

42. (right) *Armchair. Philadelphia, 1765–1780. Early nineteenth-century red grained paint over original green. Crest rail and arms, oak; spindles, hickory; arm crest and seat, poplar; arm supports, legs, and stretchers, maple. SW 21″, SD 17″, SH 17½″, OH 41¼″. (Privately owned)*

often loosely used to apply to *any* interesting piece of early furniture.

The chairs shown in figures 40, 41, and 42 represent a group that, at its best, is among the most graceful and successful of all Philadelphia comb-backs. These chairs usually have shield-shaped seats, rakish knuckle arms sometimes made of mahogany, and finely turned legs and arm supports. Because of the shape of the seat, the arm supports are set far back toward the rear of the chair. The chair in figure 40, while excellent on its own terms, has a seat and undercarriage that are a bit too broad for the width of its back and the height of its comb. Figure 41 is far more

successful: well-proportioned, tall, and with a well-saddled shield-shape seat. Nonetheless, when we compare it with figure 42, we see that it falls just short of being the best. True, at first glance the chairs seem almost identical (and may have been made in the same shop), but look at the leg turnings of each. The second baluster turnings of figure 41 are too thin and give the impression that the first baluster turning is swollen and out of proportion to the rest of the leg. On figure 42, however, the second baluster turnings are fully realized—just the right shape and thickness to make the first baluster turning and the leg taper "work."

Now look at the comb-pieces of the two chairs. That of figure 42 is a bit wider, more vertical, and hence better integrated into the design of the broad seat. Also, note the curved carving leading from the outer spindles to the volutes. On figure 42 this carving is full and deep; that of figure 41 is weaker and seems to be almost an afterthought. Such small details often make the difference between a chair that, while excellent and highly desirable, is nevertheless not quite the best of its type.

Figure 43 has good proportions and is undoubtedly a provincial interpretation of chairs like figures 41 and 42. The arm supports are idiosyncratic; the slim knuckles are made in one piece but are effective; the ears are well-scrolled. The arrowlike turnings at the ends of the medial stretcher are perhaps closer to 1780 than to 1770, but the ball feet, of course, hark back to the 1750s.

Another style of Pennsylvania shield-seat comb-back Windsor has the so-called "ram's-horn" arm supports, and two such chairs are shown in figures 44 and 45. Figure 44 is a graceful and stylish chair. The leg splay is very good, and the ears, turnings, crest and handholds are finely detailed. If the chair has a significant flaw, it is that the short spindle is positioned too close to the ram's-horn arm support. The latter feature, by the way, is derived from English Windsors.

44. *Armchair. Philadelphia, 1760–1780. Nineteenth-century black paint over the original green. Crest rail and arm supports, oak; spindles and arm rail, hickory; seat, poplar; legs and stretchers, maple. (James and Nancy Glazer)*

43. Armchair. Pennsylvania, 1770–1780. Painted black. Crest rail and arms, oak; spindles, hickory; arm crest, arm supports, legs, and stretchers, maple; seat, poplar. SW 20½", SD 16", SH 16¾", OH 40". (Mr. and Mrs. Howard Feldman)

Figure 44 is surpassed only by a chair like figure 45. The crest rail of this Windsor is beautifully shaped, with ears that are "perked up" almost as though they were listening. The wide sweep of the arms and the downward pull of the arm supports create a wonderful, tension-filled effect. The legs have great splay and are superbly turned in a far more compressed pattern than those of figure 44. Note, too, the slightly concave cylinder of the legs that flares out into the bold, blunt-arrow feet. The design of the medial stretcher, with its almost spherical turning in the center and "extra" baluster turning at the ends, is one I have seen on Lancaster County Windsors, and this magnificent chair may be from that area.

The chair pictured in figure 46 is one of a small group of early Philadelphia comb-backs exhibiting a strong English influence. Over the years I have seen about a dozen of these chairs, and they seem to have been the product of one or two shops. All but two have six long spindles in the back, and the remainder have seven. All have ram's-horn arm supports, and none has short spindles under the arm rail. Those features are derived from a particular type of mid-eighteenth-century English Windsor armchair not

45. Armchair. Philadelphia, 1760–1780. Early nineteenth-century brown paint with gilt, blue, and red decoration over the original green. Crest, oak; arm crest and seat, poplar; arm rail and spindles, hickory; arm supports, oak; legs and stretchers, maple. SW 19½", SD 16½", SH 17", OH 41¼". (Colonial Williamsburg)

carved ear. The comb is short, extending only about sixteen to seventeen inches above the arm rail. The seat is high, about eighteen inches above the floor. The legs are much more vigorously turned than the arm supports, although the success of the leg and stretcher turnings varies from chair to chair. The example in figure 47 is quite good. The seat is always shield-shaped and nicely saddled. Two other interesting features of these chairs are that they have only one short spindle between the arm supports and the back—most small comb-backs have two—and that they have arm supports that are positioned at the extreme rear of the seat. Indeed, in the chair pictured, the arm supports are actually socketed into the seat *behind* the point where the rear legs penetrate the seat—a very unusual feature.

The chair in figure 48 is, quite simply, one of the best New England comb-backs from the 1770 to 1790 period. The crest rail is about as fine as one could ask for—large, graceful, and with wonderfully tall scroll-carved ears. The back is open and light,

unlike the one shown in figure 11. The Philadelphia chairs differ from the English models in the turning pattern of the legs and stretchers and in the shape of the crest rail. Generally, the American chairs have the typical cylindrical leg and blunt-arrow foot. The ears are scroll-carved and they turn downward while the English ears turn upward. Furthermore, the American arm rail is steam-bent while the English chairs have sawed arm rails. This particular chair is a noteworthy variant. The maker has apparently chosen not to finish the leg with a ball foot, but rather, has allowed the cylinder to continue to the floor despite the fact that the leg is long enough to accommodate the blunt-arrow turning. In addition, the seat is carved with a sort of stepped platform in the back, into which the spindles and arm supports are socketed, an attractive feature.

In figure 47 we see not only our first New England interpretation of the comb-back but also a chair with many analogues. I have seen about twenty such chairs that had only slight variations in design. They are from Connecticut, and I believe they were produced by a single shop. The parts above the seat tend to be delicate. The back is narrow, the curve to the arm rail shallow. The crest rail always teminates in an elongated, upturned, un-

46. Armchair. Philadelphia, 1760–1780. Nineteenth-century black paint over the original green. SW 23¹³/₁₆", SD 23⅜", OH 42½". (The Henry Francis du Pont Winterthur Museum)

47. (left) Armchair. Connecticut, 1770–1790. Nineteenth-century red grained paint, over black, over the original green. Crest rail and spindles, hickory; arm rail, oak; one arm support, chestnut; other arm support, legs, and stretchers, maple; seat, pine. SW 17″, SD 16½″, SH 18¼″, OH 38¾″. (Janie and Dr. Peter Gross)

48. (below) Armchair. Connecticut, probably Westbrook area, 1770–1790. Traces of the original green paint. Crest rail, oak; arm rail and spindles, hickory; arm supports, legs, and stretchers, maple; seat, pine. SW 21″, SD 16″, SH 17¾″, OH 44″. (Mr. and Mrs. R. W. P. Allen)

49. (right) Armchair. Philadelphia, 1770–1790. (C. L. Prickett)

the spindles well-tapered with a slight swelling under the arm rail that adds just enough "weight" to fill the space and contrast nicely with the soaring quality of the spindles above the arm rail. The seat is very well shaped. The turnings of the arm supports and legs are in keeping with the best from Connecticut: bold and compressed with lots of thicks and thins. All of that is enhanced by the long leg taper, consequent high stretchers, and excellent leg splay. A truly fine Windsor.

Figure 49 shows a nice example of the simpler variety of combback, the type without carved ears or carved knuckles. This Philadelphia Windsor was probably more popular than the fancier chairs, and it is probably the sort that was mass-produced for immediate sale. It is a pleasing and well-proportioned chair but rather standardized. The Philadelphia craftsman William Cox made similar chairs; there is a virtually identical chair at Colonial Williamsburg branded *W. COX*.

Figure 50 also has plain ears and plain handholds, but there the comparison ends. The remarkable eleven-spindle back of this chair is very tall. The turnings, the seat, and the leg splay are excellent. The leg taper is long. It is no wonder that New York craftsmen could boast about the quality of their Windsors in comparison with those from Philadelphia. Even though figure 49 is a very good chair, figure 50 is simply better.

Although the comb-backs I have shown to this point have had their differences in design, they have also had much in common. But the large family of American Windsors has its quirky members as well as its upstanding citizens, and in figures 51 through 54 I show a few of the former. Windsors of idiosyncratic design should, I think, be viewed as highly personal expressions—almost as folk art. Design oddities may spring from the craftsman's desire to push his talent and imagination to the limit, and far from detracting from a piece, such oddities may simply add interest and should be respected.

Figure 51 is different for two reasons. First, it has a nearly round seat, a very unusual but not unattractive feature on a comb-back Windsor. Second, this chair has short arms that end in rather strange knuckles. Although they may not look it, the knuckles are in fact original to the chair and are not simply recarvings at the ends of arms that had broken off. Perhaps these crude knuckles look a bit silly, but the chair has fine lines and very nice turnings.

In figure 52 the back spindles bow the "wrong" way: inward instead of outward. Although this is unusual, other comb-back Windsors with this feature are known. In the past there had been speculation that perhaps the maker had made the crest rail too short and so, had to bend the spindles in to accommodate the length of the crest rail. But this chair is rather sophisticated, and its barrel-shaped back is just a stylistic flourish of the maker. The crest rail has Connecticut ears (see figure 47), and the distinct bulge of the spindles below the arm rail is also a Connecticut feature. The base of the chair has a weighty appearance with its thick balusters and stretchers. This is quite an interesting and pleasing comb-back.

Figure 53 is different in that it has two outer bamboo-turned back spindles that are mortised through the arm rail but do not continue to the seat. In addition, what would normally be a thick ring turning on the arm supports before it tapers into the seat has been "inflated" almost into a ball, giving the impression of three baluster turnings on the arm supports instead of the conventional two. The leg turnings are unusual as well, especially the proportion below the last turning, which moves from thin to thick and back to thin, echoing the bamboo shape of the outer back

50. Armchair. New York, 1770–1790.

51. Armchair. Connecticut, 1770–1790. Original dark gray-green paint. Crest rail, hickory; spindles, arms, arm supports, legs and stretchers, maple; seat, pine. SW 17¾", SD 16¾", SH 17", OH 39¾". (Mr. and Mrs. R. W. P. Allen)

73

spindles. The turning pattern, the concave feeling of the bottoms of the legs, and the small, disklike carving in the center of the ears makes me think the chair is from Rhode Island. The bamboo turnings are a late feature, and the chair probably dates from 1780 to 1800.

A wild and woolly turning pattern derived from English examples, can be found on figure 54. The base of the arm supports is a series of rings, reels, and balls, and the same pattern can be found on the medial stretcher and on the undulating legs. In addition, the crest rail of this chair has been put on backward! That is, the back side of the crest rail on comb-backs and fan-backs like this one is usually chamfered around the ears (see, for example, figure 36), but this chair has ears that are chamfered on the front side, leaving the impression that the crest rail has been steam-bent the wrong way. With its D-shaped seat and cylinder-and-ball-foot legs, the chair seems akin to Pennsylvania examples from the 1760s, but I think it is a later, probably provincial, tour-de-force interpretation of the earlier style. Late features include the very tapered back spindles; the forward thrust of the arm supports; the bamboo feeling of the first turning of the arm supports and legs; the general thinness of the side stretchers and of the legs; and the arrowlike turning at the ends of the medial stretcher. Although by no means a classic Pennsylvania comb-back, the chair is wonderfully exuberant. And I, for one, would certainly not pass up the opportunity to acquire such a chair.

53. (above) *Armchair. Probably Rhode Island, 1770–1790.*

54. (below) *Armchair. Probably Pennsylvania, 1780–1800. Nineteenth-century black and red paint. Crest rail, arm rail, and spindles, hickory; arm supports, legs, and stretchers, maple. SW 24", SD 17½", SH 16½", OH 44½". (Historical Society of Pennsylvania)*

52. *Armchair. Connecticut, 1770–1790.*

CHAPTER TWO
Low-back Chairs

LOW-BACK Windsors are always armchairs. Their backs are formed by short spindles, all more or less the same length, and by a flattened, sawed arm rail about three-fourths- to seven-eighths-inch thick that curves outward to form the handholds. At the rear of the chair is an arm crest. On most low-backs the arm crest is attached to the top of the arm rail with a lap joint, and the arm crest separates the inner ends of the arm rail; however, on Rhode Island low-backs the two inner ends of the arm rail meet at the rear of the chair, and the arm crest sits astride the arm rail but does not separate its two ends (figure 55). Furthermore, Rhode Island low-backs tend to have thicker arms than those of chairs from other regions, and the spindles do not penetrate the arms. It is not unusual to find a low-back with a quarter-inch diameter hole in the very center of the handhold, usually on the right-hand side; this hole was used for a swivel iron candle mounting. Most low-backs have D-shaped seats, and the arm supports are positioned at the front corners of the seat; there are, however, exceptions, as we shall see.

In the past, some furniture Darwinians have speculated that the low-back—derived from the Queen Anne corner chair—chronologically preceded the comb-back; that is, the comb-back

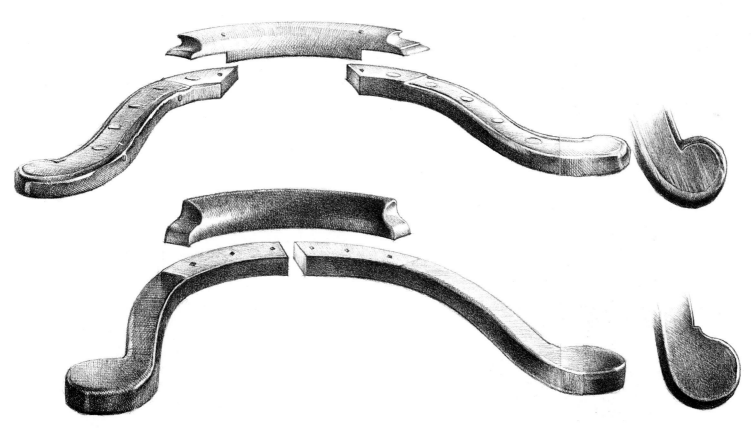

55. Arm and arm crest assembly of two low-back chairs. Top to bottom: *Philadelphia, 1750–1770. Rhode Island, 1750–1780. (Drawing by the author)*

75

56. *Armchair. Philadelphia, 1750–1760. Original green paint. Arms, red oak; seat, poplar; spindles, arm supports, legs, and stretchers, maple. SW 21⅞″, SH 17″. (Colonial Williamsburg)*

is nothing more than a low-back with a comb, and the comb-back evolved from the low-back when someone decided to put a comb on the latter. However, no evidence, direct or indirect, for this theory has ever been adduced, and I believe that the opposite may be true. First, I know of no American low-back Windsor with the very early features of the comb-back in figure 8; all low-backs appear to be later. Second, the English low-back Windsor with a splat, from which the splatless American version is derived, seems to have been made no earlier than around 1740—well after the English began to produce comb-back Windsors in the early eighteenth century. And I see no reason that the sequence of development should have been different in the American Colonies. In any case the low-back is a style of Windsor that never lost its popularity in America and it was revived in the mid-nineteenth century as the *captain's chair* or *firehouse Windsor*, still with a D-shaped seat.

In figure 56 we see a classic, early Philadelphia low-back, the best of its type with respect to turnings and medial stretcher proportions, and with the same features as the classic early Philadelphia comb-backs discussed in chapter one. Indeed, the only difference between this chair and the comb-backs is in the construction of their backs, and a chair such as, for example, the one in figure 28 is merely a comb-back version of figure 56.

Figure 57 shows a low-back that is probably from Bucks County, Pennsylvania, not Philadelphia. It still retains such early Philadelphia features as a heavily chamfered, squared-off seat edge, a Queen Anne medial stretcher, and asymmetrical side stretchers. But the rather large spaces between the turnings of the medial stretcher is a provincial interpretation of the Philadelphia style. Furthermore, the legs are not turned in the Philadelphia style and have a far more gradual second baluster turning. Those features, plus the fact that the first turning under the arm supports is elongated lead me to believe that the chair was made later than the 1750s. I should point out here that the blunt-arrow feet of this chair are replacements.

Figure 58 shows what I believe is a Connecticut or New York interpretation of the Philadelphia low-back. The arm supports are, if I may use the expression, voluptuously turned in a style more in keeping with the small tuckaway tables and joint stools made in the New York area from around 1700 through the 1760s. Note also the "extra" turning at either end of the side stretchers, a detail frequently found on Long Island and Connecticut Windsors. Finally, the seat is pine, a wood used often for the seats of New York and Connecticut Windsors but infrequently for those from Pennsylvania, where poplar was the wood of choice.

In figure 59 we see one of the finest early Rhode Island low-backs, constructed entirely in maple and curly maple. Strongly

57. (left) *Armchair. Probably Bucks County, Pennsylvania, 1750–1770. Refinished; traces of green paint; feet restored. Arm crest and seat, poplar; spindles, hickory; arms, oak; arm supports, legs, and stretchers, maple. SW 23¾″, SD 17¼″, SH 17½″, OH 30″. (William Oliver)*

58. (below) *Armchair. Connecticut or New York, 1750–1770. Mahogany-color paint over the original dark red. Arm crest, arms, arm supports, legs, and stretchers, maple; spindles, hickory; seat, pine. SW 24″, SD 15″, SH 16½″, OH 28″. (Independence National Historical Park)*

influenced by English designs, this chair, legend has it, was made by the Townsend family of craftsmen in Newport. The English influence can be seen in the decoratively turned spindles, the finely saddled seat with its flat front edge, outward turning front corners, and lack of a rain gutter, and in the turning pattern of the legs that, by the way, do not penetrate the seat. This is usually the case with these chairs. The chair, however, in no way appears English. The outer intersection of the arms and the handholds comes to a small, sharp point, echoing the shape of the front corners of the seat. The spindles are nicely turned in a pattern like that of the arm supports, and there is no back splat. The cross-stretcher device is derived from Rhode Island corner chairs of the period. Furthermore, the legs splay outward far more

than any analogous English chair—more, in fact, than many similar Rhode Island chairs.

Figures 60 through 63 show low-backs from the 1760 to 1790 period. Like figure 59, figure 60 is from Rhode Island, but it has become more "Americanized." The front edge of the seat is still flat where the arm supports are socketed, but beyond that point the edges become rounded. The seat is just as thick as that in

59. *Armchair. Rhode Island, 1750–1770. Made entirely in maple and curly maple. SW 22½", SD 15¾", SH 15½", OH 27¾". (Museum of Art, Rhode Island School of Design; gift of the estate of Mrs. Gustav Radeke)*

figure 59, but the illusion of thinness created by chamfering and rounding the front edge of the seat is very convincing here. The arm rail and the crest rail are virtually identical to those of figure 59, but the turnings of the arm supports and of the legs are quite different and more beautiful. In the turnings of the legs of this chair we see, I think, a forecast of the classic Rhode Island leg as seen, for example, in figure 123 (the sequence in time is figure 59, figure 60, figure 123). In figure 60 one can easily see the overlapping thick ring just above the bottom cylinder of the leg that would become, as it were, "standard equipment" on many Rhode Island Windsors but not on chairs from other regions. The

cylindrical turnings on the stretchers of figure 60 echo the shape of the legs, but a similar pattern can be found on English Windsors and, for that matter, other Rhode Island Windsors. Of course, this handsome chair could never be mistaken for an English one, but the English influence must be acknowledged.

The chair in figure 61 is from Philadelphia and shows a good view of the shape of the arm crest on these chairs. As was the case with Philadelphia comb-backs made during the same period, through its evolution this chair has lost the Queen Anne medial stretcher; the seat edge has become rounded; and the turnings have become somewhat elongated. This is a strong chair with a

pleasing surface patina of nineteenth-century black paint over the original green. While the leg turnings are not of the highest style, the arm supports are very good, and the overall original condition makes the piece desirable.

The chair in figure 62 is a fine low-back of the period as well as something of a mystery. The chair is branded *S. O. PAINE*, but no Paine appears in the Philadelphia directories or in any earlier record or in advertisements yet found in Philadelphia. On the other hand, a Stephen Paine did work in Charlestown, Massachusetts, from 1743 to 1752, whereupon he moved to Medford.[22] I cannot prove that S. O. and Stephen are the same Paine but can only suggest the possibility.

Figure 63 has several noteworthy features. First, the cylindrical portion of the leg is not, strictly speaking, a cylinder at all but has been turned with a slight concavity, an uncommon feature on blunt-arrow-foot chairs. More interesting is the baluster turning at the top of the leg, just beneath the seat. Although the photograph of that area is not particularly clear, you will have to trust me when I say that the turning strongly resembles those of figure 135 and, to a lesser degree, of figure 175. That is, the turning is a

79

63. (right) *Armchair. Possibly New York City, 1760–1780. Arm crest, arm supports, legs, and stretchers, maple; arms, oak; spindles, hickory; seat, poplar. SW 24½", SD 17", SH 17½", OH 29". (The Metropolitan Museum of Art; gift of Mrs. J. Insley Blair, 1947)*

64. (below) *Armchair. Philadelphia, 1765–1780. Nineteenth-century brown paint over the original grayish green. Arm crest and seat, poplar; arms, oak; spindles, hickory; arm supports, legs, and stretchers, maple. SW 22¾", SD 16¾", SH 17½", OH 29". (Privately owned)*

simple baluster with no ring directly beneath it. The piece in figure 135 is from New York State and the one in figure 175 is from Connecticut. I have never seen such a turning on a Pennsylvania chair, and that leads me to speculate that figure 63 is actually a New York version of the popular Philadelphia low-back. The similar flat seat front of figures 63, 135, and 66 (from Long Island) supports that conclusion.

With their tapered legs and oval seats, figures 64 and 65 are different from the low-backs we have examined thus far. They are from the 1765 to 1790 period and are extremely rare. Figure 64 is made in the same basic pattern as the comb-backs shown in figures 39 and 41. As you can see, the chair is a very beautiful one, and the concept works just as well in the low-back style as it does in the comb-back style. One subtle difference between the Philadelphia comb-backs and this low-back is in the spindles. On the comb-backs the spindles take a comparatively sharp taper before entering the arm crest; however, on figure 64 there is only a gentle taper, indicative of the fact that this chair was purposely made as a low-back and not simply as a comb-back with a missing comb. Figure 64 is, of course, all original and was undoubtedly made as a custom order. Figure 65, a New England version of figure 64, has very fine leg turnings and interesting arms with flaring, squared-off handholds. Although not as stylish as figure 64, it is nevertheless a very desirable low-back.

The chair in figure 66 is a good example of what happened to the low-back style near the turn of the century. It is one of a set of ten made for Captain William J. Rysam in 1794 by Nathaniel Dominy V of the well-known Dominy family of furniture makers on Long Island, a fact to which the inscription on the bottom of the seat attests (figure 66A). The arms are rounded on the top, an unusual but not unheard-of feature on low-backs. The arm supports are very simply turned, the legs and stretchers conservative. The side stretchers have that little extra turning at their ends, which, as I have previously stated, was found on Connecticut and Long Island furniture. This is a pleasing chair and important for its provenance, but only its seat is a classic feature. The chair's most remarkable feature is that it is made entirely in mahogany, apparently from Captain Rysam's own grove of Honduras mahogany.[23]

66. Armchair. East Hampton, New York, c. 1794. Inscribed on seat bottom, Nat Dominy [Nathaniel Dominy] / makg 10 / Novr 11, 1794 / W. R. Made entirely in mahogany. SW 21¾", SD 15¼", SH 17⅛", OH 28¼". (Society for the Preservation of Long Island Antiquities)

66A. Armchair. Detail of furniture maker Nathaniel Dominy's inscription.

65. (left) Armchair. Probably Connecticut, 1770–1790. Nineteenth-century dark green paint over the original green. Arm crest, spindles, arm supports, legs, and stretchers, maple; arms, maple and oak; seat, pine. SW 22", SD 16¼", SH 17¼", OH 28¾". (Mr. and Mrs. R. W. P. Allen)

CHAPTER THREE
Fan-back Chairs

THE PRIMARY difference between comb-back and fan-back Windsor chairs is that in the latter the spindles fan out from the seat and the back posts are decoratively turned. The spindles are still capped with a crest rail of some sort. The seats are oval, round, or shield-shaped. In addition fan-back armchairs are constructed quite differently from comb-back arm chairs. Instead of the arm rail of the comb-back, the fan-back's arms are mortised directly into the back posts, and there is no arm rail at all. Fan-back armchairs and side chairs may have bracing, V-like spindles running from a projecting tongue, or tailpiece, at the back of the seat up through the crest rail. On armchairs the effect is to strengthen the back that has lost the support of the arm rail, and the extra spindles also add movement and interest to the back of the chair. The American fan-back style is derived from English

68. Side chair. Philadelphia, 1765–1780. Crest rail, oak; spindles and back posts, hickory; seat, poplar; legs and stretchers, maple. SW 18″, SD 17″, SH 17¼″, OH 37″. (Privately owned)

fan-backs with round or shield-shaped seats, as shown in figure 67; this chair has the characteristic English back splat, flat back posts, and cabriole front legs.

Figures 68 and 69 are representative of the Philadelphia product—conservative expressions of Quaker chairmakers. The crest rails are pleasing enough but without much movement, and the arch between the ear and the back posts is short and rather shallow. The back posts seem exceedingly long, with a great space between the first and second balusters, almost as though the turnings had been pulled very slowly, like taffy. The taper of the back posts into the seat is rather short, more so on figure 69

67. Side chair. English, c. 1760. (Design Council)

69. *Side chair. Philadelphia, 1765–1780. Early nineteenth-century yellow paint over the original green. Crest rail, oak; spindles, hickory; back posts, chestnut; seat, poplar; legs and stretchers, maple. SW 16¼″, SD 17″, SH 18″, OH 37½″. (Privately owned)*

70. *Side chair. Wilmington, Delaware, 1780–1795. Dark reddish brown paint. Crest rail and spindles, hickory; seat, poplar; legs and stretchers, maple. SW 17″, SD 15″, SH 16½″, OH 35¾″. (Charles G. Dorman)*

70A. *Side chair. Detail showing brand of Sampson Barnet.*

71. *Side chair. Lancaster County, Pennsylvania, 1760–1780. Refinished. Crest rail, back posts, and spindles, hickory; legs and stretchers, maple; seat, poplar. SW 19″, SD 15″, SH 16½″, OH 36″. (Privately owned)*

than on figure 68. The seats are nicely shaped and are rounded off on all edges including the back edge, a feature often found on Philadelphia fan-backs. The legs are well turned with a fairly short leg taper to the floor. Make no mistake; these are very good chairs, but their design details add up to an overall impression of restraint. The chairs are not exciting and, in a sense, they seem to be "sagging" under their own weight.

The chair in figure 70 evokes a similar response. It is an example of how the Philadelphia fan-back was interpreted nearby in Wilmington, Delaware, by Windsor maker Sampson Barnet, whose brand appears on the underside of the seat (figure 70A). We can see slight variations in the more chamfered back edge of the seat and the slightly concave turning of the back posts where they enter the seat. This is a well-made piece and was originally probably less expensive since the ears are not carved.

Figures 71 and 72 graphically illustrate not only what was going on in nearby Lancaster County, Pennsylvania, but also offer a fascinating look at what can happen when two local styles become mixed. Figure 71 is pure Pennsylvania German. It has the typical Lancaster County crest rail: beaded, high-arching, and tall, relief-carved ears. The back is composed of only five spindles, rather than the usual seven or nine, that taper slightly both

84

at the top and the bottom, and the spindles appear almost vertical, not paralleling the angle of the back posts. The back posts do not rake outward, so the chair is an exception to our definition of *fan-back*. They are turned in a simple pattern of three rings, the bottom one of which rests directly on the seat, and they do not echo the turning pattern of the legs except for the double decorative score marks on the balusters. The undercarriage is also noticeably different from other fan-backs, for the front legs have blunt-arrow feet while the rear legs are tapered. Lancaster County chairs seem to be the only ones with this design, although all Lancaster County Windsors do not have it. The almost barrel-shaped second baluster with no flaring collar directly beneath it and the slight bulge at the ends of the side stretchers, decoratively scored, are also features associated with Pennsylvania German Windsors.

At first glance figure 72 repeats the pattern, but there are many differences between the two chairs. These are found chiefly in the more conventional, Philadelphia-turning style of the back posts and of the legs. A plausible explanation for these design differences may be found in the fact that figure 72 is branded *F.T.*

twice on the seat bottom. It was almost certainly made by one of the pioneering Philadelphia Windsor makers, Francis Trumble. Perhaps Trumble had seen the Lancaster County style and decided to try his hand at it, or perhaps he was filling a special order for a Lancaster resident. In any case Trumble's version of the Lancaster style is quite successful.

While the Pennsylvania Windsor makers were crafting very good fan-back side chairs, the New England makers were providing tough competition with often extraordinarily good ones. Figure 73 is from Connecticut. Its crest rail is well-shaped and the arch next to the ear is higher and longer than those of Pennsylvania fan-backs. The turnings of the back posts are more condensed, and the taper to the seat is longer. This results in an overall upward movement in the parts of the chair, enhanced by the wider fanning of the back posts and spindles and also, by the greater taper of the spindles from the seat to the crest rail. The legs have a somewhat longer taper than comparable Philadelphia chairs. If this fan-back has a significant flaw, it is in the seat. This has a narrower "waist" than the Philadelphia chairs, but it is not particularly well-saddled, and the front edges are not sharply

72. (far left) *Side chair. Philadelphia or Lancaster County, Pennsylvania, 1765–1780. Branded F.T. (probably Francis Trumble). Traces of green paint. Pine, oak, hickory, and maple. (Greenfield Village and the Henry Ford Museum, Dearborn, Michigan)*

73. *Side chair. Connecticut, 1770–1780. Painted green. Crest rail, oak; back posts, spindles, legs, and stretchers, maple; seat, pine. SW 16½", SD 16¼", SH 17½", OH 36½". (Mr. and Mrs. R. W. P. Allen)*

85

chamfered. Note, however, the almost squared-off rear edge of the seat, a recurring feature of Connecticut Windsors.

Figure 74 is a much better chair in every way. Although the ears are not carved, they are perked-up like those of many Connecticut Windsors (see, for example, figures 47 and 52). The back posts are beautifully turned with an interesting mirror-image baluster motif toward the top, a truncated version of which is also found on the back posts of certain Connecticut rush-bottom chairs. The seat has an excellent saddle with a thin front edge. The legs are bold, with a nice, narrow reel in the center and a very long taper; the splay of the legs is excellent. The two bracing spindles are joined to the tailpiece on either side with square wooden pins. This chair ranks among the best of the Connecticut fan-backs.

Figure 75 shows a fan-back of great individuality, not uncommon for all forms of Connecticut furniture. The focal point of this chair is its superbly stylized seat, with its pinched waist and crisp edges. This effect has been achieved in part because the seat is made from curly maple—a very hard wood that, although difficult to carve, lends itself to such crispness that it has retained it for over 200 years. The marvelously splayed back posts radiate from the seat. The entire movement of the back is upward and outward. The back posts not only splay but have an extremely long taper to the seat and point the way to the ears, which also point up and out. The effect is enhanced by the very rakish bracing spindles, which, unlike those of figure 74, are socketed into the extreme ends of the crest rail. Even the "cupid's bow" of the crest rail with its angled ends helps move the eye upward and then outward. The great splay of the finely turned legs and their long taper are in perfect keeping with the design of the upper portion of the chair. This is a dynamic and exciting piece of American Windsor furniture.

Although not as dynamic as figure 75, figure 76 is something of a masterpiece of design as well as of novelty. The crest rail is well-executed with one of the best sorts of uncarved Connecticut ear: large, flat, curving, and rising higher than the center of the crest rail. And one could not ask for better-defined turnings on a Windsor, or better spacing between them. The collar and ring turnings of the attenuated back posts are perfect miniaturized reflections of the bold leg turnings. The bulbous side stretchers are designed to echo the visual weight of the ears and of both baluster turnings of the legs. The seat is unusually well saddled with a distinctive, long pommel that meets a central, horseshoe-shaped depression (figure 76A). The sharply chamfered edges of the seat echo the crispness of the turnings. This is a beautifully developed, highly stylized chair.

Figure 77 is one of a handful of fan-backs known with identical

74. *Side chair. Connecticut, 1770–1790. Nineteenth-century black paint over the original green with gilt decoration. Crest rail, oak; back posts and spindles, hickory; seat, pine; legs and stretchers, maple. SW 16½", SD 15½", tail piece 3½", SH 17½", OH 38¼". (Mr. and Mrs. R. W. P. Allen)*

76. Side chair. Connecticut, 1760–1780. Brown paint over old red. SW 17¼″, SD 16″, SH 18″, OH 37¾″. (Mr. and Mrs. Howard Feldman)

76A. Side chair. Detail of seat.

75. Side chair. Connecticut, 1780–1800. Gilt-decorated old black paint over traces of red, green, and white. Crest rail, back posts, legs, and stretchers, maple; spindles, probably ash; seat, curly maple. SW 15¹/₁₆″, SD 18½″, SH 17⅝″, OH 34″.

features. It is a wonderful expression of Connecticut design and ornamentation. The great, scalloped crest rail reminds me of certain chests and highboys made by the Dunlap family of New Hampshire, and it has an almost zany feeling. The back posts are imaginatively turned with an urn shape in the center, and there are eighteenth-century precedents for such turnings in certain Connecticut tables. The elaborately turned medial stretcher echoes the leg turnings. Another chair shown in this book, figure 175, shows many similar features to figure 77, including the simple baluster at the tops of the legs. Both chairs may have been made in the same shop in the Westbrook–Old Lyme area of Connecticut.

Rhode Island Windsor makers also produced fine fan-back chairs. Figure 78 has a very lively design. The back posts splay and curve nicely, and the crest rail is handsome, with a characteristic disk in the center of each ear. The seat shape is quite good, and the leg turnings attractive. Nevertheless, this chair is not among the most sophisticated of Rhode Island fan-backs.

Figure 79, however, is. The tall, compact, finely-carved ears are much better. The turnings are superb with great thicks and

thins. The seat is sharply carved. Some Rhode Island fan-backs suffer from having backs that appear too short, but this chair has an appropriately tall back. As I have mentioned previously, the disks of the ears, the overlapping thick ring of the legs, and the concave taper are all Rhode Island characteristics, and all are extremely well done on this chair.

Figures 81 through 85 are fan-back armchairs that are all based, I feel, on the design of the English chair shown in figure 80. Of course, the English chair is a braced comb-back armchair, rather than a fan-back armchair, but that is unimportant. The fact is that English fan-back armchairs are rare, as are American braced comb-backs. What is important here are similarities, not differences.

The chair in figure 80 once belonged to the poet Oliver Goldsmith (1728-1774). A remarkably good English chair made

79. Side chair. Rhode Island, 1760–1790.

around 1750, it has a well-saddled, almost circular seat with a projecting tailpiece that supports the bracing spindles.

Derived from chairs like figure 80, figures 81 and 82 represent the finest examples of Philadelphia fan-back armchairs. In figure 81 we get a good view of the saddled circular seat with its tailpiece. Note in figure 81A that the grain of the wood of the seat runs on the diagonal. The reason for this has to do with a structural quality of wood: it is weakest *along* its grain, and, under stress, it tends to crack along the grain. Therefore wood is strongest *across* its grain. Consider, if the grain of the seat of figure 81 ran widthwise, and the tailpiece had been cut out of the end of the seat, the grain of the seat would be such that the tailpiece would have been constructed in the weakest possible way. Why, then, didn't the maker run the grain from front to back? Because he would have had to use an extremely wide board to do so. His solution is a compromise—he ran the grain on a slight diagonal, which allowed him to use a narrower board but retain most of the crossgrain strength of the seat wood. The crest rail of this chair is deeply carved. The back spindles are more or less parallel to each other; and the bracing spindles perfectly bisect the space between the back posts and the first back spin-

80. Armchair. English, 1740–1760. Black paint over dark green. Beech and ash. OH 37¾". (Victoria and Albert Museum)

89

81. (left) Armchair. Philadelphia, 1765–1780. Traces of green paint. Crest rail and arms, oak; spindles, hickory; back posts, arm supports, legs, and stretchers, maple; seat, poplar. SW 19″, SD 17″, tail piece 4″, SH 15″, OH 38¾″. (Privately owned)

81A. (above) Armchair. View of circular seat showing diagonal wood grain.

dles, thus keeping the spacing even between *all* the spindles. The finely carved knuckle arms, influenced by Chippendale designs, are mortised into a block on the back posts and pinned with a wooden peg. The turnings and proportions are excellent.

Figure 82 is a first cousin of figure 81 with just as many handsome features to commend it, especially the great, dynamic leg splay. But these two chairs, when viewed together, are somewhat problematical. The first, figure 81, is a type that consistently seems to have back posts whose turnings echo that of the arm supports and legs. But Philadelphia fan-back armchairs of the figure 82 variety usually have simple, ringed back posts and always paddlelike handholds and cylinder-and-blunt-arrow feet. I have puzzled for a while over the question of why a craftsman who was capable of creating the stylish figure 82 did not give it the more elegant knuckle arms of figure 81, and, conversely, why the maker of figure 81 did not give it the greater leg splay and blunt-arrow feet of figure 82. Unfortunately, I must admit that I have not yet solved the problem.

Figures 83, 84, and 85 are New England versions of the fan-back armchair, and are all, no doubt, from Massachusetts. Figures

83. *Armchair. Massachusetts, 1770–1790. Branded C. CHASE. Crest rail, spindles, and arms, ash, oak, or hickory; back posts, arm supports, legs, and stretchers, maple; seat, poplar. SW 22⅞", SD 21¼", SH 17", OH 47¾". (Colonial Williamsburg)*

82. (left) *Armchair. Philadelphia, 1765–1780. Dark brown paint, over green, over the original red. Crest rail and arms, oak; spindles, hickory; seat, poplar; arm supports, legs, and stretchers, maple. SW 19⅜", SD 17½", SH 15½", OH 40⅜". (The Art Institute of Chicago)*

83 and 84 are majestic chairs, wonderful examples of their type. The crest rails are of the best New England design. The knuckles are better on figure 84—stronger and more deeply carved. On both chairs the turnings are excellent and not overstated. Some of these chairs have decorative turnings on the back posts beneath the arms, but that is an extremely rare feature. Figure 83 is a brace-back, but it is constructed differently from figure 81. The seat is oval and very wide, and the wood grain runs across the width. Consequently, the maker had to mortise a *separate* tailpiece into the back of the seat of the chair, with the grain of the tailpiece running from front to back for strength. The middle back spindle runs through the seat and through the tailpiece, functioning as a locking pin. In addition two small square wooden pins run through the seat and into the tailpiece. Contrary to what one might think, this separate tailpiece construction is a common feature of braced New England fan-back armchairs.

84. (left) *Armchair. Massachusetts, 1770—1790. Nineteenth-century black paint over the original grayish green. Crest rail, oak; spindles, maple and hickory; back posts, hickory; arms, arm supports, legs, and stretchers, maple; seat, pine. SW 23⅝", SD 18½", SH 19¼", OH 47". (Mr. and Mrs. R. W. P. Allen)*

85. (above) *Armchair. Probably eastern Massachusetts, 1765—1780. Traces of green paint. Crest rail and arms, sycamore; spindles, hickory; back posts, arm supports, legs, and stretchers, birch; seat, pine. SW 21¾", SD 16½", tail piece 4", SH 13¼", OH 40½". (Privately owned)*

Furthermore, the arms, rather than being attached to the back posts with wooden pins as in figure 81, are held fast by rosehead nails driven through the back of the block on the back posts and into the backs of the arms. This, too, is a common New England construction method. Figure 84 has no bracing spindles. Consequently, both the spindles and the back posts of this chair are thicker than those of figure 83, providing extra strength to the back.

Figure 85 is also a rather elegant Massachusetts fan-back arm-

chair. At first it may seem to have been cut down, but in fact it was made just the way you see it, and the legs, though short, are perfectly proportioned. As in figure 83, the tailpiece of figure 85 is mortised in place, and the arms are attached with rosehead nails.

The chair in figure 86 is a rare Connecticut fan-back armchair. To tell the truth, the first time I saw one of these chairs from a distance, I thought it was a reproduction. But it is an authentic piece that simply was not made in great quantity. Its back has been made to be approximately the same height as that of a fan-back side chair, and, consequently, the turnings of the back posts are compressed rather than attenuated. The crest rail is a toned-down version of the one of figure 76, and the turning style is rather late in that it is simplified; for example, the final thick ring

86. Armchair. Connecticut, 1780-1800. Label under the seat reads, "This unusually made windsor chair I bought from Mr. Rodney Langdon in South- ington, Conn., September 26, 1877. I. W. Lyon." Traces of black and green paint. Crest rail, oak; spindles, hickory; back posts, arm supports, legs, and stretchers, maple; arms, black cherry; seat, poplar. SW 17¼", SD 18", SH 18", OH 39". (Yale University Art Gallery; Mabel Brady Garvan Collection)

turning, usually found just above the beginning of the tapered leg and the taper of the arm support, has been completely eliminat- ed. In its place is a slight bulging, or rounded shoulder, that can also be seen in the back posts. The seat has a characteristic Connecticut shape. All told, the chair presents a good solution to the problem of how to make a "down-sized" fan-back armchair, and, beyond that, the chair is noteworthy for its black cherry arms.

Figures 87 through 90 represent the fan-back chair at the turn

87. Side chair. Northampton, Massachusetts, 1795–1803. Label on underside of seat reads, "Ansel Goodrich, / Has on hand, and keeps / constantly for sale, a quan- /tity of war- ranted Chairs, / a few rods North of the / Court-House Northamp- / ton." Green and black paint over the original red. Basswood and maple. SW 16¼", SD 16⅜", OH 37¹⁵/₁₆". (Historic Deerfield, Inc.)

of the eighteenth century. Figure 87 was made by Northampton, Massachusetts, craftsman Ansel Goodrich sometime between 1795 and 1803. The crest rail is not particularly inspiring, and the back is quite straight. The turnings resemble those of other chairs from the area and are rather weak examples of the baluster- and-ring variety. The seat is quite interesting, however—thin on the edges and well chamfered. The chair is pleasing enough, but, except for the seat, it has a devitalized quality that makes it appear somewhat flimsy.

Figure 88 is from Connecticut. The high ring turnings of the legs and the long undulating taper are often seen on Connecticut chairs, but here they are quite simplified. The first baluster under the seat has been completely omitted (compare figure 86). How- ever, the back posts are fairly conventional. The angular crest rail with its molded, Chippendale ears and pronounced peak, al- though unusual on a Windsor, is a feature common to a group of chairs found in the lower Connecticut River Valley. Not only Windsors but rush-bottom "country Chippendale" chairs from this region often utilize Windsor spindles in the backs instead of the conventional pierced splat.

Figure 89 is also from Connecticut and displays the strong influence of the famous Windsor maker, Ebenezer Tracy, notably in the quite bulbous spindles; the chestnut seat with an almost circular depression and the lack of a rain gutter; deep, almost quarter-inch gouges that form the bamboo ringing of the legs; and the fact that the side stretchers are socketed into the legs below,

93

90. (right) *Side chair. New England, 1800–1815. Nineteenth-century yellow grained paint. Crest rail and spindles, hickory; seat, pine; legs and stretchers, maple. SW 16″, SD 15½″, SH 17″, OH 35¼″. (Mr. and Mrs. R. W. P. Allen)*

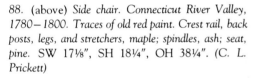

88. (above) *Side chair. Connecticut River Valley, 1780–1800. Traces of old red paint. Crest rail, back posts, legs, and stretchers, maple; spindles, ash; seat, pine. SW 17⅛″, SH 18¼″, OH 38¼″. (C. L. Prickett)*

89. (right) *Side chair. Connecticut, probably Norwich area, 1790–1800. Painted green over gray. Seat, chestnut. SW 16″, SD 16½″, SH 16½″, OH 35″. (Museum of Art, Rhode Island School of Design; gift of the estate of Mrs. Gustav Radeke.)*

rather than at, the second bamboo ring. As you have undoubtedly noticed, the chair combines early and late features. The crest rail has been reduced to a simple but effective flattened rod, probably in deference to the influential Sheraton style, and the ears at the ends of the crest rail have shrunk to nubbins. The back posts combine bamboo turnings with the more traditional Windsor style near the seat. Although at first the legs may seem well-turned but completely late, on second glance we notice that the maker, by attaching the side stretchers below the second bulge, has retained something of the flavor of earlier, baluster-and-ring-turned legs. I should point out here that, generally speaking, chairs with two bamboo rings on the legs are earlier than those with three, which became the hallmark of the late, Sheraton-influenced rod-back style of Windsor (discussed at length in chapter seven).

The side chair in figure 90 perfectly exemplifies the turn-of-the-century, bamboo-turned fan-back Windsor at its best. The bamboo turnings are quite good, deep and pronounced. The crest rail and the seat could easily be found on an earlier chair. Although there are three bamboo rings on the legs, as opposed to the earlier two, the maker has retained the H-stretcher arrangement instead of the later box stretcher of the rod-back Windsor. While succumbing to the pressures of a changing furniture style, the maker has managed to retain all of the best eighteenth-century qualities of the New England fan-back Windsor chair.

CHAPTER FOUR
Sack-back Chairs

THE SACK-BACK style of Windsor chair has a back formed by a bowlike, steam-bent crest rail that is mortised into an arm rail. It is, in effect, constructed very much like a comb-back Windsor but with a different sort of crest rail. The spindles of the sack-back extend from the seat, through the arm rail, and then into or through the crest rail. The arm rail is usually steam-bent, but some sack-backs have sawed arms and arm crests. Some sack-backs also have a comblike extension in the back formed by three to seven of the central spindles and topped by a crest rail of the sort found on comb-backs.

The large majority of sack-backs have oval seats, but there are some of the shield, or D-shaped variety. The last two styles, almost always of the custom-made sort, are more closely related to English sack-backs, one example of which is shown in figure 91. This is a good English Windsor, and if you compare it with the chair in figure 15, I think it will be apparent that, except for the bent bow, it is basically a comb-back in style.

Although most earlier chairs like comb-backs and low-backs were made to order, I believe that it is with the introduction of the sack-back in the 1760s that the American Windsor chair became truly utilitarian and available to the general public. Judging from the quantity of eighteenth-century sack-backs that have survived to the present, the style must have been far and away the most popular of the eighteenth-century until the introduction of bamboo-turned Windsors. And there is certainly no dearth of eighteenth- and nineteenth-century American paintings, both academic and folk, that depict such persons as wealthy dandies (figure 92), stolid merchants (figure 93), honorable statesmen (figure 2), and just plain folks sitting in sack-backs.

Furthermore, sack-backs are also the type of chair most often found branded with the names of the chairmaker. For example, Trumble, Henzey, Wire, Cox, Bowen, Burden, and Widdifield are a few of the names of Philadelphia craftsmen found on these chairs. Some of those chairmakers, like Trumble and Henzey, are known to have shipped large quantities of Windsors up and down the eastern seaboard. Since those shipments occurred in the 1770s and 1780s, when the sack-back was most fashionable, it is reasonable to assume that sack-backs made up a large portion of those shipments.

I have been told that the term *sack-back* is derived from the practice of pulling a sack, fashioned from a popular fabric of the time and trimmed with ribbons, over the back of the chair and securing it to the arm rail with the ribbons, the purpose being to shield the sitter from drafts in chilly rooms. As we shall see, there may be some truth to that notion. In any case I should mention that sack-backs are by definition armchairs, and so it would be redundant to call one a "sack-back armchair."

91. Armchair. English, c. 1750. (Design Council)

Figures 94 through 97 all represent the sort of sack-back Windsor that was exported in large numbers from Philadelphia. Figure 94 is branded *I. HENZEY* and is a good example of the simpler version of these chairs. It is a straightforward, no-nonsense, seven-spindle design with a crest rail that flattens out slightly as it enters the arm rail, and pleasing Philadelphia turnings. Figure 95, although not branded, is in its style and knuckle construction attributable to Henzey. Perhaps the chair is not branded because it was intended for domestic consumption. It is certainly a fancier chair with its nine spindles and good knuckles that curve outward. Both chairs have the typical Philadelphia oval seat, gently rounded on all edges and with a blunted pommel. In these two chairs we get our first glimpse of a stylistic and construction motif that seems to have been adopted almost as an ironclad rule by the sack-back chairmaker: the seven-spindle chairs have four short

94. Armchair. Philadelphia, 1765–1780. Branded I. [Joseph] HENZEY. *Painted green. Crest rail, arm rail, and spindles, hickory; arm supports, legs, and stretchers, maple; seat, poplar. SW 22″, SD 16½″, SH 18″, OH 38″. (Independence National Historical Park)*

spindles, two in front and two behind the point at which the crest rail attaches into the arm rail; while the nine-spindle sack-backs have six short spindles, four in front, and two behind, the crest rail.

Like figure 95, figure 96 is a fine Philadelphia sack-back but with some subtle differences. The knuckles of figure 96 are thinner. The legs have less splay but more taper, as do the arm supports. The spindles of figure 96 are also quite fat below the arm rail but taper as they penetrate it and rise to the crest rail. This chair is branded *F. TRUMBLE*, and such spindles are characteristic of many of the sack-backs from Trumble's shop.

While only a seven-spindle sack-back, figure 97 is in some ways the best of the lot. In addition to many of the qualities of the other chairs its arm supports are very bold and have a long taper to the seat. The seat itself is better as well, with a more pronounced pommel. Finally, the patina of the chair is wonderful, including nineteenth-century yellow paint decorated with dark green stripes, over an earlier red which covers the original green. This is a very desirable chair for the collector.

The chair in figure 98 is so similar to the Philadelphia product that, if it were not branded by Wilmington, Delaware craftsman

95. (left) *Armchair. Philadelphia, 1765–1780. Refinished. Crest rail and spindles, hickory; arm rail and knuckles, oak; arm supports, legs, and stretchers, maple; seat, poplar. SW 21¾", SD 15¾", SH 17", OH 38¾". (Privately owned)*

96. (above) *Armchair. Philadelphia, 1765–1780. Branded F.[rancis] TRUMBLE. Nineteenth-century black paint over the original brown. Crest rail, spindles, and arm rail, hickory; arm supports, legs, and stretchers, maple; seat, poplar. SW 21", SD 16", SH 17", OH 38". (Independence National Historical Park)*

98

97. (left) Armchair. Philadelphia, 1765–1780. Nineteenth-century yellow paint with dark green striping, over red, over the original green. Crest rail and spindles, hickory; arm rail and knuckles, oak; seat, poplar; legs and stretchers, maple. SW 21½", SD 16¾", SH 16¼", OH 34½". (See color plates XVI and XVII.) (Privately owned)

98. (right) Armchair. Wilmington, Delaware, 1775–1795. Branded S.[ampson] BARNET. Nineteenth-century dark brown paint over the original green. Crest rail, arm rail, spindles, and arm supports, hickory; seat, pine; legs and stretchers, maple. SW 21¼", SD 15½", SH 16½", OH 37½". (Charles G. Dorman)

Sampson Barnet, one would naturally attribute it to Philadelphia. The crest rail of this chair is nicely shaped where it meets the arm rail, and the spindles are well-tapered with a progressive outward curve.

A rare Philadelphia sack-back is shown in figure 99, certainly not the sort of chair that was made in large numbers. We can see from the oval seat shape that the chair was intended to be in the sack-back style, yet the design, with its sawed arms and arm crest, is in the comb-back style as exemplified by figure 40. Furthermore, the chair has a turning pattern identical to many Philadelphia comb-backs with the same arm construction. Perhaps the chair was produced as a sack-back companion to the comb-backs, or perhaps it was made by a shop that specialized in this type of arm.

A marvelous and equally rare New England version of this type of sack-back is shown in figure 100. The knuckle arms of this chair are stylishly rakish and beautifully undercut, projecting further beyond the point of attachment of the arm supports than on the Philadelphia example. The heavily chamfered, shield-shaped seat, although derived from the seats of such chairs as figure 44, is, I think, even better. The concave turning at the bottom of the legs is indicative of Rhode Island, but the chair may very well have been made in the Boston area.

99. Armchair. Philadelphia, 1765–1780. Refinished. Crest rail and spindles, hickory or ash; arm crest and seat, poplar; arms, oak; arm supports, legs, and stretchers, maple. SW 21⅜", SD 16⅛", SH 16", OH 35". (Barbara and Eugene Pettenelli)

As might be expected, Windsor makers in Lancaster County, Pennsylvania, had their own idea of what a sack-back should look like, and several of these often astonishing pieces are shown in figures 101 through 105. If for nothing else, figure 101 would be remarkable for its elaborately turned and unusually long arm supports. Other features of note are the crest rail, which narrows and then thickens before meeting the arm rail, and the front legs. The front legs taper the same way the rear legs do, but the taper runs into a wide collar, and the leg ends in a blunt-arrow foot— an unusual but effective design. As I have noted previously, the use of the blunt-arrow foot in the front and the tapered leg in the rear is a common feature of Windsors from Lancaster County, and this chair is surely one of the best of them. I have little doubt that figure 101 was made in the same shop as figure 35 because, except for the obvious differences in the front legs, both have extraordinarily similar turning patterns and seat shapes; in addition, the woods used in both are the same. That the sack-back and the comb-back styles were being made simultaneously in the same shop is something to keep in mind when dating Windsors.

Figure 102 is a lovely chair from top to bottom and, from the seat up, better than figure 101. The crest rail flattens out long

100. (above) Armchair. Probably Rhode Island, 1770–1800. Black paint over traces of the original green. Crest rail and spindles, ash; arm crest, arms, arm supports, legs, and stretchers, maple; seat, pine. SW 19⅛", SD 15¼", SH 16¾", OH 40⅜". (Colonial Williamsburg)

101. (right) Armchair. Lancaster County, Pennsylvania, 1765–1790. Nineteenth-century black paint over original green. Crest rail, arm rail, and spindles, hickory; arm supports, legs, and stretchers, maple; seat, pine. SW 20½", SD 15¼", SH 16½", OH 35". (Independence National Historical Park)

102. (left) Armchair. Lancaster County, Pennsylvania, 1765–1780. Crest rail, arm rail, and spindles, hickory; arm supports, legs, and stretchers, maple; seat, poplar. SW 21″, SD 15½″, SH 16½″, OH 37″. (Independence National Historical Park)

103. (below) Armchair. Lancaster County, Pennsylvania, 1765–1780. Traces of green paint. Crest rail, spindles, and arm rail, hickory; knuckles, arm supports, seat, legs, and stretchers, maple. SW 21″, SD 16½″, SH 16¾″, OH 37″. (Privately owned)

before it meets the arm rail, and at that point it takes a graceful forward curve. The spindles are nicely tapered, and the knuckles bold. The seat is deeply scooped and sharply chamfered in the best Lancaster County tradition. All of the turnings are exceedingly fine and sharp. The side stretchers have a characteristic slight bulge at either end, as does the medial stretcher, and you would hunt long and hard to find a Windsor with a medial stretcher of this type with a better turning than this one. The front legs are very interesting in that the turnings on either side of the cylinder are true mirror images of each other, a nice touch that very few Windsors have.

In spite of all that lavish praise, I think the chair in figure 103 is even better; indeed, it is a Windsor masterpiece. It is a fine example of how the rural craftsman often retained early features in the base of a chair—the blunt-arrow feet front and back and the Queen Anne medial stretcher—and combined them with an "updated" sack-back top. The crest rail of this chair is tall and

105. (below) Armchair. Lancaster County, Pennsylvania, 1765–1790. Original black paint. Crest rail and spindles, hickory; arm rail, hickory or oak; arm supports, legs, and stretchers, maple; seat, poplar. SW 21½″, SD 16½″, SH 16¾″, OH 43½″. (Mr. and Mrs. Richard Flanders Smith)

104. Armchair. Pennsylvania, possibly Berks County, 1770–1790. Traces of green paint. Crest rail and spindles, hickory; arm rail, oak; arm supports, stretchers, and legs, maple and curly maple; seat, poplar. SW 19½″, SD 15″, SH 19″, OH 38″. (The Metropolitan Museum of Art; gift of Mrs. Russell Sage, 1909)

somewhat pointed, and all the spindles are perfectly spaced. The delicate knuckles lunge forward, far beyond the edges of the seat. The arm supports are set well back and their extreme splay emphasizes the thrust of the arms and echoes the splay of the legs. The seat comes to a marvelously sharp edge and has an obvious pommel; the sharpness of the seat is due in large part to the fact that it is made of maple. The turnings are very crisp and precise with astonishing thicks and thins in the foot. The feet themselves are remarkably beautiful, rounded and tapered into a teardrop-shape in such a way that the chair seems poised like a toe-dancer, ready to spring into action. The balusters of the medial stretcher are a perfect reflection of the teardrop feet. In overall harmony of design and sheer beauty no American Windsor surpasses this delicate sack-back. And, needless to say, Windsors of this quality are great rarities.

Figure 104 is a fine example of a Lancaster County chair without blunt-arrow feet. Actually the chair may be from neighboring Berks County, as similar chairs have been found in the area of Sinking Spring, Pennsylvania. That, in turn, may account for its differences from the Lancaster style. Noteworthy features of this chair include the nearly vertical back spindles, the extremely stylized arm supports, and the sculptured saddle seat. The legs are quite simple in comparison to the arm supports, and the medial stretcher's three sausage-like bulges echo the shape of the arm supports. The side stretchers, although distinctive, seem to be an uncompleted idea, and one wonders why they do not have more thins. In any case the chair exemplifies the springiness and tension of rural Pennsylvania chairs as opposed to those from Philadelphia.

With its tall crest rail, figure 105 is a very rare type of Lancaster County sack-back. Although a chair of great dignity—probably intended for an important person—it still retains all the vitality of the best Lancaster County Windsors. Chairs of this type all have similar features and may have been made by the same shop; perhaps a shop that also made comb-backs, for the overall height of these chairs is virtually the same as Lancaster County comb-backs. The crest rails of these chairs tend to be squarish. On this particular chair, the crest rail is fluted on its entire leading edge. The pinched waist of the crest rail emphasizes the fact that it is

107. Armchair. New York, 1765–1780. Nineteenth-century brown varnish over the original green paint. Crest rail and arm rail, oak or hickory; spindles, hickory; arm supports, legs, and stretchers, maple; seat, poplar. SW 20½", SD 16⅜", SH 16½", OH 36". (Privately owned)

106. (left) Armchair. Probably Rhode Island, 1770–1790. Painted green; feet restored. Crest rail, spindles, and arms, hickory; arm supports, legs, and stretchers, maple or birch; seat, pine. SW 21", SD 15½", SH 17", OH 45¼". (The Metropolitan Museum of Art; gift of Mrs. Russell Sage, 1909)

set farther back on the arm rail than is customary on sack-backs. Indeed, the crest rail is set so far back that the maker broke the "rule" of seven-spindle sack-back construction mentioned earlier: the crest rail mortises into the arm rail behind, rather than between, the two short spindles.

Figure 106 shows an excellent New England high-bow sack-back, equally as rare as those from Lancaster County. The crest rail and the spindles of this chair are gracefully tapered. Rather than detracting from the design, the gap between the back spindles and the crest rail enhances the airiness of the piece, which, I think, would not be the case if the crest rail were shorter. The leg splay is also very good. This is a well-conceived design made by a fine craftsman.

The Windsor makers of New York produced some of the most beautiful sack-backs, and figures 107 and 108 show two of them, the former a nine- and the latter a seven-spindle design. In figure 107, note the fine taper of the crest rail, which flares into a flat shoulder before mortising into the arm rail. Note also how the rear legs are positioned quite far in from the back edge of the seat; the tops of the rear legs are also close together, and this results in

103

108. Armchair. New York, 1765–1780. Nineteenth-century black paint, over red, over the original green. Crest rail and spindles, hickory; arm rail, oak; seat, poplar; arm supports, legs, and stretchers, maple. SW 20½", SD 15¼", SH 17¾", OH 36½". (Mark and Marjorie Allen)

104

109. Armchair. Possibly Boston, 1780–1800. Old black paint over the original green; seat has remnants of red paint over the original green. Crest rail and spindles, ash; arm supports, legs, and stretchers, maple; seat, pine. SW 21¾", SD 15⅞", SH 20", OH 43¼". (Colonial Williamsburg)

a great splay to the legs. Such pleasing features are often found on New York sack-backs, but, as you have no doubt noticed, perhaps their best and most characteristic features are the turnings of the legs and arm supports.

Figure 108 shows a good and slightly different view of these New York turnings, emphasizing their boldness, their thicks and thins, and the almost spherical shape of their balusters. This is an extremely sophisticated turning pattern with an organic, elastic quality rarely found on chairs from other regions.

Figure 109 is a large and powerful design, a chair not likely to have been made in large numbers. The knuckles are beautifully executed. The extremely well defined rings punctuate rather than merely adorn the arm supports and legs; and their angularity is repeated in the unusual balusters, in the flatness of the leg just below the final, thick ring turning, the unusual ringed side stretcher, and even in the sides of the seat, which are cut away vertically, and then diagonally, rather than simply being rounded off. The great leg splay adds impact to the total design of this superb chair.

Figures 110 and 111 are two remarkably fine sack-backs. Figure 111 is often called a *triple-back* because of the comb extension of the back spindles. Indeed, if you examine these two chairs closely, you will see that, except for the comb on figure 111, the chairs are identical. Neither chair is signed, but, in my opinion, they

111. Armchair. Connecticut, 1770–1790. Refinished. First crest rail, arm supports, and legs, maple; second crest rail, spindles, arm rail, and knuckles, oak; stretchers, chestnut; seat, elm. SW 19⅜″, SD 15″, SH 16¼″, OH 45⅜″. (Mr. and Mrs. R. W. P. Allen)

110. Armchair. Connecticut, 1770–1790. Crest rail, oak or hickory; arm rail, spindles, seat, and side stretchers, chestnut; arm supports, legs, and medial stretcher, maple. SW 19½″, SD 15″, SH 16″, OH 35¼″. (Chloe and Anthony Leone)

are from the shop of Ebenezer Tracy. A few of the Tracy features of these chairs, known from branded examples, are the seat made of chestnut or, occasionally, elm with the legs not running through, the seat's shape, the lack of a rain gutter, the bulbous spindles, the very English-style crest rail on figure 111 (compare figure 11), and the turnings at either end of the side stretchers. The double ring on the lower portion of the arm supports is another Tracy feature. The knuckle handholds are wonderfully bold and fistlike. Tracy's son-in-law, A. D. Allen, made and branded similar chairs, but they do not have the same side stretchers.

With regard to figure 111, triple-back chairs are quite rare; rare or not, their success or failure largely depends on the design of their combs. This chair has a strong, dramatic upper crest rail that spans the entire back of the chair. Because the back spindles fan out, the chair seems more like a comb-back with a double arm rail than like a sack-back with an added crest rail.

112. Armchair. Massachusetts, 1770–1790.

113. (right) Armchair. New England, possibly Connecticut, 1770–1790. Dark green paint, over white, over the original green. Crest rail and arm rail, probably oak or hickory; spindles, hickory; arm supports, legs, and stretchers, probably maple; seat, pine. SW 20″, SD 15½″, tail piece 3″, SH 18″, OH 38¼″. (Mr. and Mrs. R. W. P. Allen)

114. (below) Armchair. Rhode Island or Massachusetts, 1770–1790. Traces of old black paint.

Figure 112 is in one way an even rarer triple-back because its comb is composed of seven spindles instead of the more usual three or five. This chair is successful for a different reason. The turnings are slim and understated, like those found on fan-back armchairs. The leg taper is very long and, without the comb, the chair might look like a sack-back whose legs were too tall. The comb makes the design harmonious, and the chair very desirable.

Figure 113 in many ways exemplifies the astonishing stylistic variety of American Windsors, given the inherent limitations of a furniture form that is little more than a plank of wood with sticks stuck in it. Almost everything about this sack-back is different, and it may be a unique chair. First, the spindles bend backward as well as outward. The seat is unusual, being cut away from the arm supports to form, visually, a stepped platform into which the arm supports and spindles are socketed. The turnings are "normal" until one looks below the second baluster; there one finds closely spaced double rings repeated on each leg and arm support and twice at the ends of each stretcher. As if that were not enough, the chair has two bracing spindles in the back, and this is the only sack-back I have ever seen with this arrangement. To be sure, such bracing spindles are a nice touch, but they are purely a design flourish, unnecessary for support because the arm rail serves that purpose. Where could such a chair be from?

115. (left) Armchair. Connecticut, 1770–1790. Original dark olive-green paint on the legs and stretchers; the remainder unfinished. Crest rail, hickory; spindles, chestnut; arm rail, sycamore; handholds and arm supports, beech; seat, pine; legs and stretchers, maple. SW 26″, SD 19¼″, SH 15¼″, OH 39″. (Also see color plate II.) (Mr. and Mrs. R. W. P. Allen)

116. (below) Armchair. Lancaster County, Pennsylvania, 1780–1800. Original brown paint; feet shortened and replaced. Crest rail, small bows, and spindles, hickory; arm rail, oak; arm supports, legs, and stretchers, maple; knuckle and seat, poplar. SW 21″, SD 16½″, SH 16⅝″, OH 42″. (Philadelphia Museum of Art; Titus C. Geesey Collection)

Connecticut, I think. Add up the features: the slight bulge in the spindles; the lack of a rain gutter on the seat; and the general seat shape. Add to those features the curious, rounded shoulder on the legs and arm supports just below the final ring turnings. This makes the overall design a kind of double baluster and reel, a turning pattern similar to that of the front stretchers of many slat-back, rush-bottom chairs found in Connecticut. Indeed, we have already seen a similar rounded shoulder on two other Connecticut Windsors: figures 86 and 88. The uniqueness of this chair and its exuberance should pique the interest of any collector.

Figure 114 has ram's-horn arm supports, which are quite unusual on sack-backs. The seat and the turnings are excellent. A similar turning pattern can be found on figure 56, especially with regard to the "extra" turning at the very top of the leg before it sockets into the seat. This turning pattern seems to have been popular in Massachusetts and Rhode Island.

Figure 115 is entirely original from top to bottom and may be unique. I, at least, have never seen another Windsor of its kind.

117. *Armchair. Probably New England, 1790–1810. Nineteenth-century dark red paint, over white, over the original green. Arm supports, two legs, and stretchers, maple; seat and two legs, chestnut. SW 20⅜″, SD 16″, SH 16″, OH 37″. (Mr. and Mrs. R.W.P. Allen)*

118. *Armchair. Rhode Island, 1780–1800. Early nineteenth-century black paint over the original grayish green. Made entirely in chestnut. SW 21½″, SD 14¼″, SH 16″, OH 35¾″. (Privately owned)*

Let me explain why. The legs and stretchers of this chair retain their original, dark olive-green paint. But the seat and all the parts above it, including the bow and spindles, have never been painted or shellacked or finished in any way. In addition tack holes may be found around the sides, under the front and back, and around the crest rail. This is excellent evidence that the chair was completely upholstered from the seat up, very much like a wing chair. Further evidence can be found in the fact that there are now two separate arm pieces—original to the chair but

now nailed under the seat for safekeeping—that fit over the arms to make them wider to accommodate the stuffing. Finally, the great width of this interesting sack-back leads me to conclude that the upholstery was not just an afterthought.

Figure 116 shows at least one sack-back that did at one time have a cloth sack pulled over it to shield the sitter from drafts. There are tack holes around the back of the seat to help hold the sack in place. The auxiliary bows at the top of the crest rail are original to the chair and, when covered, would have given this

119. Armchair. Lancaster County, Pennsylvania, 1780–1800. Refinished. Crest rail, spindles, and arm rail, hickory; arm supports, legs, and stretchers, maple; seat, poplar.

Windsor the appearance of a wing chair. I must point out here that this chair has suffered a bit of damage over the years. Among other things, one entire knuckle and half of the other are missing. Also, the legs have been pieced out; the cylinder was originally longer, and the front and rear legs once resembled the front legs of figure 105. However, this is a later chair than Figure 105, as evidenced by the bamboo turnings of the short spindles, arm supports, and medial stretcher.

Figures 117, 118, and 119 show three late (possibly turn-of-the-century) sack-backs, each highly stylized and interesting. Figure 117 is a country chair whose successful design depends mostly on the arching, angled treatment of its crest rail. It is a graceful chair, with its spindles tapered at both ends, a very well carved seat, and simplified but harmonious turnings. Its all-original condition adds greatly to its value.

Figure 118 is an innovative Rhode Island design and unusual for a sack-back. First, it is unusual to find an American sack-back with all its back spindles turned and a D-shaped seat with a pronounced pommel. Furthermore, what the maker has succeeded in doing on this chair is create a stretcher pattern that is a direct interpretation of the asymmetrical arrow-and-block stretcher pattern of high-style New England Queen Anne chairs (see also drawing 2). The asymmetrical turning pattern is carried through to all the turned parts of the chair. The maker has used late bamboo turnings, certainly, but in a highly original way. This is a Windsor that might not suit everyone's taste, but to me it is a marvelously individualistic piece.

Figure 119 is a sleek Lancaster County sack-back with late, but very good, bamboo turnings. Such turnings are found on other chairs, but not executed in this stylized manner. For example, the base of the arm supports is a knob rather than a narrow taper, and the turnings are, in general, more bulbous than one would expect to find on bamboo chairs from other regions. The tall, flat crest rail and the simplified, roll-over knuckle design, which still retains the side scrolls, are very pleasing features. This is a good example of the sort of chair that, while giving way to style trends, creates an idiom of its own.

CHAPTER FIVE
Continuous-arm Chairs

THE CONTINUOUS-ARM Windsor chair is one of the great innovations of American furniture design, one that literally put a new twist into the techniques of steam-bending wood. The backs of these chairs are formed by a steam-bent strip of white oak or hickory that is about an inch wide and three-quarters of an inch thick. This strip, when given a second bend on each side, continues forward to form the arms of the chairs. The arm supports rake forward to counterbalance the weight of the sitter against the back spindles—a concept not unlike that used in a suspension bridge. The resulting design, when combined with bulbous turnings, a shield-shape seat, and well-splayed legs, is one that practically quivers with life and movement. Continuous-arm chairs with oval seats are generally less successful.

To my knowledge the continuous-arm concept is not found south of New York, with one exception in the Lancaster area, which I have not seen. Nor does it seem to have been produced in Europe, making it a uniquely American design. In New York City the chairs were very popular. Indeed, the continuous-arm chair seems to have been to New York what the sack-back was to Philadelphia: a type of Windsor that became, more or less, a standard pattern that was produced in great numbers. Perhaps in their fervor to compete with the Philadelphia craftsmen, the New York chairmakers simply did them one better. The influence of the design filtered north from New York through New England rather than vice versa. The New York City chairs are frequently found branded or labeled with such names as MacBride, Bloom, and DeWitt and Sprosen; in Kingston, New York, we find Hasbrouck; in Connecticut, Tracy and Allen; and in Salem, Massachusetts, Tuttle. These are but a few of the Windsor makers to brand their continuous-arm chairs.

If these chairs were made in relatively large numbers, then one might well ask why they are not very numerous today. The answer, I think, lies in a flaw in the design: the sharp bend where the bow becomes the arms is a weak point. Many continuous-arm chairs have been found cracked or broken at that point, and no doubt many of them have been lost because they were discarded after breaking, as a break in the arm is devilishly difficult to repair properly.

Figures 120 and 121—two fine, braced continuous-arm chairs—are known to have been made in New York City and Lisbon, Connecticut, respectively, because they are both branded by makers who worked in those two places—John Sprosen (figure 120), who worked in Philadelphia from 1783 to 1788 and then moved to New York City; and Ebenezer Tracy (figure 121), who worked in Lisbon, Connecticut, from around 1764 until his death in 1803. I place these two chairs together in order to emphasize graphically their stylistic differences, as many collectors seem to have difficulty distinguishing New York chairs from Connecticut chairs. The following points of comparison are not hard-and-fast rules but generalizations that usually hold true.

We can see immediately that figure 120 has a shorter and visually broader bow than figure 121, and, indeed, New York chairs do tend to be broader than those from Connecticut. The spindles of figure 120 have a very slight bulge in their centers, but those of figure 121 have a definite small bulb, typical both of Tracy and of Connecticut Windsors in general. In the New York chair the spindles are more vertical, which creates a gap between the short and long spindles. The seat of the New York chair, while well-shaped, is broader than that of the Connecticut chair. The underside of the back edge of the New York chair is more rounded, the latter more clipped and flat. The New York chair's seat also has a rain gutter, while the one from Connecticut does not, and the waist of the seat of the Connecticut chair is more pinched. The circular depression in the seat of the Connecticut chair is more typical of Tracy than of Connecticut chairs as a class.

The turnings of the two chairs are also a point of comparison. We have seen turnings like those of figure 120 before—in figures 107 and 108. In addition to their distinctive thicks and thins the balusters are almost spherical. The Connecticut chair's turnings, although similar, are more attenuated, which is especially noticeable in the balusters directly below the arms and seat. Also, Tracy did not use two small rings at either end of the medial stretchers of his chairs, but New York chairmakers used them often. However, some Connecticut chairs do have the extra rings.

Both chairs are, of course, excellent Windsors, but the Tracy

120. (above) *Armchair. New York City, 1790–1800. Branded I. [John] SPROSEN. Nineteenth-century red paint over the original green. SW 22″, OH 35½″. (Israel Sack, Inc.)*

121. (right) *Armchair. Lisbon, Connecticut, 1770–1803. Branded EB: [Ebenezer] TRACY. Maple, ash, hickory, and chestnut. SW 20⅞″, SD 17½″, OH 38⅝″. (Yale University Art Gallery; Mabel Brady Garvan Collection)*

chair—although it has a lovely beaded crest rail with a characteristic cutout just before the arm bend—has a curious design quirk. Typically, Tracy has used an even number of spindles in the back of his chair, and there is no dead-center back spindle. Consequently, there is a gap in the back of the Tracy chair, which the bracing spindles do not adequately fill. This is not the only braced Tracy chair to have this quirk, and one wonders why a craftsman of his genius did not choose to fill the gap with another spindle.

Figure 122 is a continuous-arm chair that takes the Connecticut style to a somewhat spidery extreme, yet on its own terms the chair is very delicate and pleasing. The crest rail is tall for a chair of this type. The spindles are, well, *spindly*, and the bracing spindles are set rather close together in the tailpiece. Nonetheless, the total effect is open and airy. The arm supports could be a bit more substantial, but they are consistent with the weight of the spindles. The seat is typically Connecticut with very sharp edges, the movement of which is echoed in the sharp scrolling of the handholds. The leg turnings are perhaps slightly too bold for

123. Armchair. Probably Rhode Island, 1775–1800. Original black paint with gilt decoration. Crest rail and spindles, hickory; arm supports, legs, and stretchers, maple; seat, pine. SW 16½", SD 17", SH 17½", OH 37". (Abington Antiques)

122. (left) Armchair. Connecticut, 1775–1800. Painted light green. Crest rail, oak; spindles and arm supports, ash or hickory; legs and stretchers, maple; seat, poplar. SW 15¼", SD 17", SH 17½", OH 38½". (Museum of Art, Rhode Island School of Design; gift of the estate of Mrs. Gustav Radeke)

the rest of the chair. The end result is a chair that is more or less "normal" from the seat down but a bit too willowy above it. Judging from the thinness of the top components, the chair was probably made closer to 1800 than to 1775.

Some of the finest continuous-arm chairs were produced in Rhode Island, and figure 123 shows one such chair. From the seat up, this chair bears a strong resemblance to the best New York and Connecticut products. It is only in the base that we see the very popular Rhode Island leg turning pattern of a final, thick ring that overlaps the top of the leg almost in the center, and the concave, seemingly hollowed-out leg taper. The turnings on this particular chair are exceptionally good, with great thicks and thins, compressed balusters, and a fine movement to the leg beneath the overlapping ring—inward, outward, and then inward again. The original black paint with gilt decoration makes this a very desirable chair.

Figure 124 shows an even better Rhode Island chair that has,

124. Armchair. Rhode Island, 1775–1800. Bluish green paint over traces of the original red. Crest rail and spindles, ash; arm supports, legs, and stretchers, maple; seat, pine. SW 16¾", SD 17", SH 16½", OH 37". (Colonial Williamsburg)

125. (above) Portrait of a gentleman. Probably Rhode Island, 1790–1810. (Isobel and Harvey Kahn)

126. (below) Armchair. New England, probably Massachusetts, 1775–1800. Refinished. Crest rail, oak; spindles and arm supports, ash; legs and side stretchers, maple; medial stretcher, chestnut; seat, yellow pine. SW 17½", SD 17¾", SH 18". (William Oliver)

unfortunately, lost about an inch of its leg taper. This is the ultimate in Rhode Island continuous-arm chairs, the same type that is shown in the folk portrait (figure 125), which, by the way, apparently has an upholstered back—a very unusual feature on Windsors. Figure 124 has even bolder turnings than figure 123. In addition the back spindles are decoratively turned, a fairly common feature on Rhode Island Windsors but uncommonly well executed on this example. The crest rail is exceptionally well shaped, with a gentle bend for the arms. The flowing movement of the crest rail and arms is accentuated by double beading, which is continued in the rolled handholds nailed to the underside of the ends of the arms.

Figures 126 and 127 show two New England continuous-arm chairs with the attractive extra feature of knuckle handholds. Figure 126 is the less stylish of the two, being a bit too straight in the back and with too short a leg taper. Made in one piece, the knuckles seem rather thin. The chair has merit, but it is simply not so good as figure 127 with its braced back, better seat, and better turnings. Furthermore, the knuckles are bolder because they are formed by the addition of wood to the undersides of the handholds.

Figures 128 and 129 both originally sported upholstered seats, which accounts for what one earlier writer has called the "thick plank shapeless" seats on some otherwise superior Windsors; for if the edges of the seats had been finely chamfered, there would have been no room for the decorative brass upholsterers tacks, the holes from which are quite evident on the seats of both chairs. On figure 128 a bit of green wool still adhering to the seat suggests that this was the original upholstery material. The seat has never been painted or even smoothed off and it still retains quite obvious tool marks. Apart from the rare feature of its having been upholstered and its excellent proportions, this chair is interesting for several other reasons. First, it is part of a set of two armchairs and three side chairs. Three of the chairs still retain the label of their maker and read *JOHN DEWITT / WINDSOR CHAIR MAKER, /NO. 47, WATER-STREET, NEAR / COEN-TIES SLIP, NEW YORK.* The label also shows a woodcut of a

127. (left) Armchair. *New England, possibly Connecticut, 1775–1800.*

128. (above) Armchair. *New York City, 1797. Label under the seat reads, "JOHN DE WITT / Windsor Chair Maker, / No. 47, Water-Street, near / Coenties Slip, New York." Old black paint over the original green. Crest rail and spindles, hickory; arm supports, legs, and stretchers, maple; seat, poplar. SW 16¾", SD 17¼", OH 35¼". (Colonial Williamsburg)*

115

128A. (left) Armchair. Detail of chair maker's label.

129. (below) Armchair. Lisbon, Connecticut, 1780–1803. Branded EB: [Ebenezer] TRACY. Old blueish green paint. Crest rail, spindles, arm supports, and stretchers, oak; seat, chestnut; legs, maple. (Greenfield Village and Henry Ford Museum)

continuous-arm chair (figure 128A). Second, one of the chairs in the set retains the label of its upholsterer and reads *WILLIAM W. GALLATIAN / UPHOLSTERER & PAPER-HANGER / NO. 10, WALL-STREET, NEW YORK.* It is always significant when one finds such labels on early furniture, but beyond that, the labels fix exactly the year in which the chairs were made. First, the *New York Directory* lists John DeWitt as working at his 47 Water Street address only during 1796 and 1797; in 1798 he is listed at 442 Pearl Street. Second, Gallatian is listed at his 10 Wall Street address only during 1797. Furthermore, the date *May, 1797* is printed on the bottom half of the Gallatian label—conclusive evidence not only of the chairs' year of manufacture but of the month that they were upholstered. Contrary to what one might think, then, Windsors turned in the bold style of the 1770s were still popular and were being made at the turn of the eighteenth century.[24]

Figure 129 is branded *EB: TRACY* and manifests Tracy's design ideas especially in the turnings of the arm supports and the legs. Apart from being deeply incised, the bamboo turnings are interesting for their double score marks at the second bulge and the fact that Tracy has retained the feeling of the earlier baluster-and-ring turnings by positioning the stretchers below, rather than at, the score marks. This is a fine late chair, and I think I would have it re-upholstered in red leather if it were mine.

CHAPTER SIX
Bow-back Chairs

BOW-BACK Windsors have backs formed by a continuous, bowlike, steam-bent crest rail that is mortised into the back of the seat. On bow-back armchairs the arms are mortised directly into the bow. As a class of eighteenth-century Windsors, bow-backs are more numerous than any other, especially as side chairs. However, bow-back armchairs with baluster-and-ring turnings are rather rare. Shield-shaped seats are the rule on bow-backs. The more ordinary types may sometimes be found in sets. Figure 130 is a fine document of an early nineteenth-century Rhode Island interior showing two late bow-backs—one arm- and one side chair—placed near the walls of the room against the chair rail. Interestingly enough, both chairs appear to be upholstered.

Most Philadelphia bow-backs that we find today have the bamboo turnings of the 1780s and later. Thus, for a Philadelphia bow-back, figure 131 is somewhat rare because it has baluster-and-ring turnings. This type of chair is sometimes called a *balloon-back* because of the bow's pinched waist, which was intended to imitate the Hepplewhite style in chairs. Figure 131 is branded *I. HENZEY* (see figure 131A), and I speculate that such chairs may have been produced as side-chair companions to the sack-back chairs of the period, for example, figure 94, also branded by Henzey. Figure 131 is a very good chair. The back is especially stylish with its elaborately fluted bow and nine spindles. As I have pointed out before, the real flaw in these chairs is that their stretchers are too close to the floor, another way of saying that there is not much leg taper. However, the chair's rarity, in part, compensates for that.

It is also rare to find Lancaster County bow-backs with blunt-arrow feet, but figure 132 shows one such chair. The bow has a typically squarish shape and flares out slightly at the base, very much like the bow of figure 105, and the back retains the same general feeling of figure 105 and, somewhat, of figure 71. All

130. North parlour of Dr. Whitridges' Tiverton R.I. 1814. (*The Whaling Museum*)

131. (left) Side chair. Philadelphia, 1765–1780. Branded I. [Joseph] HEN-ZEY. Refinished; traces of green paint. Crest rail and spindles, hickory; legs and stretchers, maple; seat, poplar. SW 17¼″, SD 16″, SH 17¾″, OH 37″. (Privately owned)

131A. (above) Side chair. Detail of Henzey brand.

told, this is another fine example of Pennsylvania German crafts-manship.

New York and New England bow-backs with excellent bulbous turnings were produced from around 1770 until the end of the eighteenth century. Figure 133 is an example of New York Wind-sor craftsmanship at its best. On this chair we see the great New York leg turning pattern we have seen before on such chairs as figure 120. However, figure 133 has an even greater leg taper. The seat of this chair is wonderfully saddled, its front edges chamfered to an extraordinary sharpness. The nine spindles, fat at the base and well-tapered, are in keeping with the boldness of the leg turnings. Note the short back of this chair, a characteris-tic not only of New York bow-backs but also of continuous-arm chairs like figure 120.

Figure 134 is a rare New York bow-back armchair, and it has many of the same fine qualities and regional characteristics of

132. (below) *Side chair. Lancaster County, Pennsylvania, 1770–1790. Nineteenth-century black paint with gilt decoration. Crest rail and spindles, hickory; legs and stretchers, maple; seat, poplar. SW 18½″, SD 15″, SH 16¾″, OH 37″. (Mr. and Mrs. R.W.P. Allen)*

133. (right) *Side chair. New York, 1770–1780. Branded D. COUTONG. (Thomas K. Woodard Antiques)*

figure 128. The flat arms are also characteristic of these chairs. But, for a New York chair, figure 134 is in many ways fairly conventional, and it is interesting to compare it with the unconventional figure 135. This is a braced bow-back armchair that was found in Ulster County, New York. I hope you will be able to ignore the contraption attached to the chair, which I shall discuss in chapter twelve, and for the moment concentrate on the chair alone. As you can see, the back of this chair in shape, size, and beading is very much like that of figure 134, and the arm supports are turned in the best New York pattern. But the seat is unusual. It has a distinctly English quality about it in both its D-shape and lack of rain gutter (compare with figure 91). The legs, too, are turned in an English pattern, as in figure 11, but with a significant difference: the baluster turning of the leg directly beneath the seat, although it has no ring beneath it, is shaped very much like those of the more conventional figures 133 and 134. Precisely why figure 135 was made in this pattern I do not know, but as with this chair, figure 10, and many others, English design features seem to have had a stronger, more permanent influence on certain New York State and Connecticut Windsors. In any case, the overall design of figure 135 is, I think, quite effective.

Figure 136 shows a very fine Connecticut bow-back side chair that is branded *A. D. ALLEN*. Amos Denison Allen was appren-

134. (above) *Armchair. New York, 1770–1800.*

135. (right) *Armchair. Long Island, New York, 1770–1790. Eighteenth-century straw-color paint over the original green. Crest rail and spindles, hickory; arms, chestnut; arm supports, legs, and stretchers, maple; seat, pine. SW 18¼", SD 15", tail piece 3", SH 18", OH 36". (Olenka and Charles Santore) (Complete chair is shown in Figure 235.)*

136. (left) Side chair. Norwich, Connecticut, 1796–1810. Branded A.[mos] D.[enison] ALLEN. Original black paint with gilt decoration; three inches additional taper added to original legs. Crest rail and spindles, hickory; legs, maple; stretchers, chestnut; seat, pine. SW 15″, SD 43″, SH 19⅞″, OH 39″. (Privately owned)

137. (below) Side chair. Connecticut, 1770–1790. Traces of salmon red paint. Crest rail and spindles, oak; legs, maple; stretchers, maple and chestnut; seat, sycamore. SW 17″, SD 17″, tail piece, 3″, SH 16½″, OH 38″. (Mr. and Mrs. R. W. P. Allen)

ticed to Connecticut Windsor maker Ebenezer Tracy in 1796 and ultimately became his son-in-law, so it is little wonder that figure 136 manifests the influence of the Tracy style. Compare this chair with, for example, figure 121 and I think you will see the great similarities in the shape and height of the bow, in the bulbs in the spindles, in the seat shape and the lack of a rain gutter, and in the leg and stretcher turnings. Indeed, A. D. Allen probably made, in whole or in part, Windsors that bear the Tracy brand. Figure 136 has its original black paint and is decorated with gilt stripes and circles on the legs and spindles; other Allen Windsors I have seen have similar decoration. I should mention that this particular chair has had about three inches added to the bottoms of the *original* legs, and you will have to cover those additions to view the chair as Allen intended it.

Figure 137 is another Connecticut bow-back, and a fascinating one. The box stretcher arrangement with a baluster-and-reel front stretcher is common on the rush-bottom chairs of the period but is almost never found on early Windsors. Indeed, the only

other chair of this type that I have seen is in Colonial Williamsburg and is an identical mate to this chair. Like other chairs we have already examined, this chair has many Tracy features, including an even number of back spindles and a gap in the back, as in figure 121—and Tracy-style stretchers. Tracy was certainly innovative enough to have created this chair. Perhaps he made it for a customer who demanded a Windsor with the stretcher arrangement of a rush-bottom chair, to fit in with the other rush-bottoms in his house.

Two Rhode Island braced bow-backs are shown in figures 138 and 139. The former is a chair of the highest quality. The beading that runs around the entire bow of this chair is also continued on the tops of the arms and around the handholds.

138. (left) *Armchair. Rhode Island, 1780—1800. Black paint over the original green. Crest rail and spindles, ash; arms, mahogany; arm supports, legs, and stretchers, maple; seat, pine. SW 17⅛″, SD 19¾″, SH 17½″, OH 38¾″. (Colonial Williamsburg)*

139. (below) *Side chair. Rhode Island, 1785—1800. Mahogany-color paint over the original green; part of the original green wool upholstery still attached to seat; center stretcher replaced. Crest rail and spindles, hickory; legs and stretchers, maple; seat, pine. SW 17¾″, SD 18¾″, SH (including upholstery) 18″, OH 38¼″. (Colonial Williamsburg)*

The turnings are excellent and very distinctive. For example, the balusters of the legs directly under the seat are diminutive when compared with those of figure 124, yet they harmonize with the overall leg turning, and the arm supports echo their shape perfectly. The seat is very well sculptured. This is an elegant and stylish chair, and the fact that it has unpainted mahogany arms no doubt enhanced the chair's appeal in the eyes of the purchaser.

Figure 139 is not quite the classic that figure 138 is. Although very good, the turnings are simply not on the same level of definition and movement (note that the medial stretcher is a replacement). However, as you have undoubtedly noticed, figure 139 has the uncommon feature of seat upholstery. The seat still retains part of the original green wool upholstering material, which is stuffed with horsehair and straw. While the chair is very good in its own right, the upholstery makes it rare and desirable.

Figure 140 has many of the same features of figure 138. It even has mahogany arms. But the turnings are quite different. On the legs the turning just below the first baluster is not so much a ring as a simple, upward-flaring platform. Also, the final, thick ring does not overlap the leg in Rhode Island fashion. A previous owner apparently decided that the chair should have "Rhode Island features," so he shaved the bottoms of the legs to make

140. (left) *Armchair. Massachusetts (North Shore) or Rhode Island, 1780–1800. Nineteenth-century black paint with gold striping over the original red. Crest rail and spindles, ash; arms, mahogany; arm supports, legs, and stretchers, maple; seat, pine. SW 16½", SD 18", SH 16½", OH 36½". (Privately owned)*

141. (above) *Portrait of* William Whetcroft (d. 1789) *by Charles Willson Peale (1741–1827). Oil on canvas. (Yale University Art Gallery; the John Hill Morgan Collection)*

them concave, but this shape is not correct, and originally the legs were cylindrical and untapered (see figure 60). The stretchers with their six ring turnings and accentuated central bulb are also unlike the Rhode Island product. However, those turning patterns I have mentioned are found on chairs from Massachusetts, and I think this may be a Massachusetts Windsor maker's idea of a Rhode Island design.

Figure 140 is also an instructive example of how a Windsor with physical faults may still be desirable. The back spindles protrude through the bow, but that is merely an indication of age—that is, wood shrinkage—and is not at all uncommon. Those wire rods running from the arms to the seat are called *carriage bolts* and were often used in the late nineteenth century

142. *Armchair. Philadelphia, 1780–1800. Black paint over the original straw-color paint. Crest rail and spindles, hickory; arms, oak; legs and stretchers, maple; seat, poplar. SW 20″, SD 18″, SH 17″, OH 37″. (Descendants of the Wistar family)*

to strengthen Windsors that the owners thought worth preserving. The left arm is secured to the bow with a metal brace, and the seat, which split sometime during its life, has been repaired on the underside with a heavy iron brace. Finally, the chair has lost about an inch in height. Nevertheless, the chair's parts are entirely original and well-executed, and it has a mid-nineteenth-century coat of gilt-striped black paint over the original red. In my opinion the chair should be left untouched, early repairs and all, for they only add interest to an already interesting piece of Americana.

Figures 142, 143, and 144 show three bow-back armchairs of a type that, both as armchairs and side chairs, were called *oval-back* chairs in Philadelphia and became all the rage there at the beginning of the Federal period. These chairs with their rolled arms and ram's-horn arm supports are of the type in which William Whetcroft, an Annapolis, Maryland, silversmith, is shown sitting in his portrait by Charles Willson Peale (figure 141). This is the earliest painting I know of that depicts anyone sitting in one of these chairs. Whetcroft died in 1789, so the style predates his death, but I think we can safely say that the style was first made around 1780.

Figure 142 is one of the best and earliest of these bow-back armchairs. Although it is not branded, the turnings are identical to those of chairs branded by Joseph Henzey. Now covered by a coat of black paint, the chair was originally painted a straw color that was quite popular. The seat retains the shield shape of the comb-back and fan-back chairs of the 1770s. On some of these chairs the arms and even the arm supports are mahogany. On the earlier chairs of this type with thin arms the arms are attached to the arm supports with an open mortise. The curved arms are mortised into the bow in such a way that they look like an extension of it. This illusion is emphasized by the fact that the beading on the bow is continued over the tops of the arms but not on the bow beneath the arms. There we see a bamboo ring that is aligned with those of the spindles, which makes the bow beneath the arm appear almost as though it were another spindle. The illusion of a continuous arm is further enhanced by the arm's being the same thickness and width as the bow and even being cut in the same semi-round shape on its bottom surface. Although the construction is different from that of the continuous-arm chair—a style, as I have mentioned, that does not seem to have been produced in Philadelphia—the visual effect is similar, and I think it is possible that these bow-back armchairs, with their stronger back construction, were intended to compete with the continuous-arm chairs made north of Philadelphia. This is certainly one of the best Philadelphia chairs of its type, and the bamboo turnings are quite pleasing.

143. (left) *Armchair. Philadelphia, 1785–1800. Punch marks of William Cox (see text). Black paint over the original green. Crest rail, oak; spindles, hickory; arms and arm supports, probably oak; legs and stretchers, maple; seat, poplar. SW 19⅛″, SD 17½″, SH 16⅜″, OH 36″. (Barbara and Eugene Pettenelli)*

144. (below) *Armchair. Philadelphia, 1780–1800. Punch marks of William Cox (see text). Original yellow paint over red filler. Crest rail and legs, oak; spindles, hickory; arms and arm supports, mahogany; seat, poplar; stretchers, maple. SW 21″, SD 18¾″, SH 17¾″, OH 43¾″. (State-in-Schuylkill)*

145. (right) *Armchair. Pennsylvania, 1785–1800. Nineteenth-century black paint, over red, over the original green. Crest rail, hickory or oak; spindles, arm supports, legs, and stretchers, maple; seat, poplar. SW 19″, SD 17⅝″, SH 16½″, OH 36″. (Privately owned)*

Figure 143 shows what happened to this style as it became standardized. Although it still is a good chair, the bow, the arms, and the arm supports have become thicker and less gracefully curved. The seat is not as well shaped, nor are the legs as well turned. One interesting feature of this chair is that, while the seat is not branded, it does show on its underside a series of small, circular punch marks not unlike the touch marks used by silversmiths. I have seen these punch marks on similar chairs, one of which had both the punch marks and the brand of Philadelphia Windsor maker William Cox. Figure 144 is a variant of this form and also has the punch marks of William Cox. In this chair no attempt was made to create the illusion that the bow flows directly into the arms. Note the simplified design of the cylindrical leg—which must have been fairly easy to turn—and compare it with that of figure 236.

A marvelous provincial interpretation of these bow-back armchairs is shown in figure 145. With few exceptions, the Philadelphia product seems standardized, but this chair has a robustness in all its parts. The arms and arm supports have dynamic reverse curves; indeed, the arm supports wind back so far that they almost butt against the short spindles below the arm. The thick spindles accent this robustness and "fill" the back. The seat is vigorously saddled, and the bamboo turnings bold. This is another example of how the nonurban craftsman often made the conventional unconventional and exciting without making it aberrant.

The next chairs, figures 146, 147, and 148, are rare versions of the type just discussed. Of course, the primary difference lies in the ladderlike slat arrangement of the backs. These designs are no doubt derived from such late Philadelphia ladder-back Chippendale chairs as those produced by Thomas Tufft, Jacob Wayne, and Daniel Trotter (figure 149).[25] A set of these ladder-back Windsors ranged around a dining table must have been an elegant sight indeed! Near the turn of the century, a few American bow-backs were produced with such intricate patterns, but such adaptations were far more common on bow-backs in England of the same period.

Figures 146 and 147 are very similar to other chairs branded by John Letchworth and may have been made by him. The two chairs are also similar to each other, but figure 147 has a seat that is carved, it would seem, to simulate an upholstered seat. Even

146. *Armchair. Philadelphia, 1785–1800. Refinished. Crest rail, hickory or oak; slat supports, hickory; slats, walnut; arms, mahogany; arm supports, oak; legs and stretchers, maple; seat, poplar. SW 23¼", SD 15¾", OH 37". (The Henry Francis du Pont Winterthur Museum)*

147. *(right) Side chair. Philadelphia, 1785–1800. Refinished. SW 17¾", SD 16", OH 37⅜". (The Henry Francis du Pont Winterthur Museum)*

rarer than these two chairs is the one in figure 148, branded by John B. Ackley. Apart from its uncommon back, it is unusual in its plainness: there are no short spindles below the arms; the legs and medial stretcher have no bamboo scoring at all; and there is only a slight taper to the legs below the stretchers. Also highly unusual is the use of poplar for the legs and stretchers instead of, for example, maple. All of those features make for a chair of great lightness, both in weight and in appearance.

The chair in figure 150 is branded *I. LETCHWORTH*. Although Letchworth was one of the most successful and prolific of the Philadelphia Windsor makers, I do not think this style of bow-back armchair can hold a candle to examples like figure 142. With a thick bow, less shapely arms, and simple bamboo arm supports, the chair exudes sobriety and does not "sing." The leg turnings, while indifferent, clearly reveal an interesting feature of the later Philadelphia product: in figure 150 one can see how the tops of the legs are rounded before they enter the seat. (The same is true for the arm supports before they enter the seat, but that feature is not as clear in the photograph.)

Made about the same time as figure 150, figure 151 has the often astonishing exuberance of the provincial Windsor. Note the wonderfully exaggerated bamboo leg turnings, the finely saddled shield-shape seat, and the beading on the outer edge of

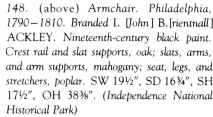

148. (above) Armchair. Philadelphia, 1790–1810. Branded I. [John] B.[rientnall] ACKLEY. Nineteenth-century black paint. Crest rail and slat supports, oak; slats, arms, and arm supports, mahogany; seat, legs, and stretchers, poplar. SW 19½", SD 16¾", SH 17½", OH 38⅜". (Independence National Historical Park)

149. (left) Side chair. Philadelphia, made for Stephen Girard by Daniel Trotter, bill dated May 3, 1790. (Girard College; The Stephen Girard Collection)

150. (right) Armchair. Philadelphia, 1795–1810. Branded I. [John] LETCHWORTH. Painted green. Crest rail and spindles, hickory; arms, mahogany; arm supports, legs, and stretchers, maple; seat, poplar. SW 20", SD 17½", SH 18½", OH 38½". (Independence National Historical Park)

the crest rail that continues along the outer edge of each serpentine arm. The scoring on the spindles is not intended to imitate bamboo but to accent the spindle turnings. The lower score marks are aligned with each other, but the upper score marks step up to a peak and then step down, enhancing the illusion of height in the back. This is a well-designed and exciting piece of Windsor furniture.

The bow-back side chair in figure 152 is interesting because of the method by which it was originally upholstered. Note the beading on the upper and lower edges of the seat. This demonstrates that the leather or fabric used in the original upholstery was not intended to cover the front of the seat and be tacked in place there. Many upholstered Windsors were finished in that way, but many were also finished with the brass tacks along the top edge of the seat, as shown here.

Figure 153 shows a bow-back side chair branded by Sampson Barnet of Wilmington, Delaware. While not a terribly inspiring

152. Side chair. Philadelphia, 1785–1800. Painted red; reupholstered in black leather. Crest rail and spindles, hickory; legs and stretchers, maple; seat, poplar. SW 17″, SD 16″, SH 18″, OH 37″. (Independence National Historical Park)

151. (left) Armchair. Probably Maryland, 1790–1810. Two coats of original white paint; later green paint on the seat. Crest rail, probably oak; spindles, hickory; arms, arm supports, legs, and stretchers, maple; seat, pine. SW 20″, SD 18½″, SH 15″, OH 38″. (Mr. and Mrs. R.W.P. Allen)

153. (right) Side chair. Wilmington, Delaware, 1795–1800. Branded S.[ampson] BARNET. Early nineteenth-century red paint over the original buff. (Philip H. Bradley Antiques)

154. Side chair. New England, probably Massachusetts or Rhode Island, 1780–1800. Traces of old black paint. Crest rail, oak; spindles, hickory; legs and stretchers, maple; seat, pine. SW 18″, SD 16½″, SH 18″, OH 37¼″. (Mr. and Mrs. R.W.P. Allen)

piece, the chair does have well-turned spindles and a nicely shaped, pinched bow. However, the leg turnings leave a bit to be desired.

As was the case with figure 146, a Windsor chair may have one rare feature that makes it interesting and sets it apart from the crowd. Figures 154 through 156 show three such chairs. Figure 154 is noteworthy for its cross-stretcher arrangement, a feature that is conceptually similar to that of such Rhode Island chairs as figure 59 and that came to America by way of England. The stretchers of figure 154 are more simply constructed than those of figure 59 in that there is no lap joint where the stretchers cross; instead, one stretcher merely passes through a hole in the central bobbin of the "host" stretcher. The seat and the bow of this chair are nicely shaped, and all of the chairs with this cross-stretcher that I have seen—all side chairs and all with the unusual three-ring turning on the bobbin of the host stretcher—are so similar to each other that I think they must have been produced in the same shop. That, in turn, is no doubt why they are rare in the first place.

Figures 155 and 156 are also rare and unusual for their so-called spoke stretchers, and possibly for other reasons as well. This spoke stretcher was infrequently used in America but is very common in England, where it was used on all manner of Wind-

155. Side chair. New England, possibly Connecticut, 1790–1810. Nineteenth-century white paint, over mustard-color paint, over a red ground. Crest rail, spindles, and curved stretcher, hickory; legs and straight stretchers, maple; seat, pine. SW 17″, SD 16¼″, SH 16½″, OH 36⅜″. (Virginia Aceti)

sors, mostly bow-backs and sack-backs. In America the device is used only on late bow-back Windsors. The front part of the stretcher is a piece of bent oak or hickory that is socketed into the front legs; into the bent stretcher are socketed two maple stretchers that radiate outward like spokes and are socketed into the rear legs. In addition, the American version has two bulbs on the bent stretcher and one on each of the straight stretchers, no doubt intended to imitate Sheraton design motifs. This makes an excellent design, because the bent stretcher echoes the shape of the bow below the seat and relieves the angularity of the normal H-stretcher arrangement below the seat.

Figure 155 differs from other known examples of spoke-stretcher Windsors in that the bulbs on the stretchers are fully round, not flattened as on the more "normal" chair in figure 156. A more minor difference is that the spindles have only two slightly bulbous turnings at the point of the bamboo rings, whereas other known spoke-stretcher chairs have three rather attractive, wavy bulbs—again, like figure 156. The reason for these differences may lie in the fact that figure 155 was made in Connecticut, the home of innovative Windsors; in any case the seat has a definite Connecticut flavor (compare, for example, figure 89). You will notice that figure 156 has an even number of back spindles—eight, in fact. That, too, is not unusual for a spoke-stretcher chair. How, then, does figure 156 differ from other spoke-stretcher Windsors? In a seemingly inconsequential way: it has arms. This is the only American spoke-stretcher armchair that this writer has ever seen, and it may be unique.

156. Armchair. Probably Massachusetts, 1790–1810. Refinished; traces of green paint; straight stretchers were rotated 90 degrees when curved stretcher was repaired. Crest rail and curved stretcher, oak; spindles, chestnut; arms, arm supports, legs, and straight stretchers, maple; seat, pine. SW 18¼", SD 18¾", SH 17½", OH 38". (Privately owned)

CHAPTER SEVEN
Rod-back Chairs

"'NEWFASHIONED' Windsor chairs with square tops"—that is how one craftsman described what we now call the rod-back Windsor, and it is perhaps the best general definition; for the more or less squarish back is the style's most distinctive and consistent feature. Whether you view it as Hepplewhite or Sheraton, the square back on rod-back Windsors is a direct interpretation of the formal Federal furniture of the 1790 to 1815 period.

Other generalizations about the style can also be made. First, the bases of the chairs have bamboo turnings. When the chairs have a box-stretcher arrangement—that is, four stretchers each connecting two legs around the perimeter of the base—the legs will have three bamboo rings. These three rings are generally echoed in the back post and back spindles. The front and rear stretcher are attached to the legs at the middle bamboo ring, and the side stretchers are attached at the bottom ring. Although the earlier H-stretchers are sometimes used on rod-back chairs, when the box stretcher is present, it indicates a date of no earlier than around 1790. The seats of these chairs are usually somewhat "degraded," meaning that they lack the saddling, pommel, and sharp chamfering of earlier Windsors; the legs are often less splayed, again a Federal influence; the arms of armchairs are frequently straight.

Although rod-backs are undeniably simplified versions of the classic American Windsor style and although they point the way to a general, often serious, decline of the form, nonetheless rod-backs can be exceptionally interesting and beautiful. Paint surface, hand-painted decoration, unusual form, or historical significance—such qualities can make a rod-back chair desirable to the collector or admirer of early American furniture. And some of those qualities can be seen in the exquisite folk portrait of a young girl (PLATE VI). In a companion portrait, her mother sits in which is called a "duck-bill" armchair because of the way the arms and arm supports come to a point (Figure 157). In the portrait of the daughter we can see the side-chair version of the mother's chair. Painted a reddish brown, the chair has what is called a "stepdown" crest rail with an attractive, hand-painted floral motif. Both the portraits and the chairs date from around 1820.

Figure 158 shows what might be called a good, typical rod-back side chair. Known as a "double-bowed" Windsor in the nineteenth century because of the secondary crest rail, today such chairs are called "birdcage" or "chicken-coop" Windsors because of the three spindles projecting through the secondary crest rail. This is a pleasing chair with an excellent patina of pale green nineteenth-century paint over the original dark green. The steam-bent crest rail gives us our first view of a common feature of rod-backs: where the crest rail and the back post meet, there appears to be a miter joint, but this is an illusion created by a bamboo ring at that point. If you look closely at the left-hand back post just below the top, level with the bottom of the crest rail, you will see a thin, flat line that is the actual joint (see also drawing 11). Although the miter joint is not real, the actual joint is much more difficult to make accurately than it might at first appear.[26] The seat of this chair is vaguely shield-shaped, and although plankish in appearance—the top is barely scooped out and there is no chamfering to create the illusion of a thin front edge—the effect is softened by two lines of beading on the front flat surface that continue around the side of the seat. This chair is branded *BURDEN*, showing that it was made in Philadelphia.

Figure 159 is a better chair. It has a molded back that curves out and arches nicely in the Sheraton style, and the seat has a more interesting, modified shield shape. The bamboo turnings are somewhat better as well. Note that this chair, unlike the majority of rod-backs, has the earlier H-stretcher arrangement and only two bamboo rings on the legs. This is a type of chair that seems to have been made only in the Pennsylvania region.

Figure 160 is an even better chair. It retains its original light green paint with gilt decoration in a delicate vine-and-asterisk pattern on the crest rail, back posts, and spindles, while the bamboo ringing and seat are trimmed in yellow. The crest rail is arched and the entire back bends nicely to the rear. The well-shaped seat is beaded along its sharp front edge and about an inch in from the edge. (Compare this design with that of the stool, figure 246.) This is a lovely, delicate rod-back.

Figure 161 is perhaps the best of all and was made by Windsor craftsman James Chapman Tuttle of Salem, Massachusetts. This chair is in its original green paint with ivory leaf decoration, but, of course, what makes it even more desirable is its beautiful and

157. (above) Portrait of a woman seated in a step-down, decorated Windsor. American, c. 1820. (Also see color plate VI.) (Catherine and Howard Feldman, also for color plate VI.)

158. (left) Side chair. Philadelphia, 1790–1815. Branded BURDEN. Nineteenth-century pale green paint over the original green. Crest rail and spindles, hickory; back posts, legs, and stretchers, maple; seat, poplar. SW 17″, SD 16″, SH 16½″, OH 33½″. (Barbara and Eugene Pettenelli)

159. *Side chair. Pennsylvania, 1780—1800. Refinished. Crest rail and back posts, oak; spindles, hickory; legs and stretchers, maple; seat, poplar. SW 18″, SD 16″, SH 18″, OH 35½″. (George Ireland)*

160. *(far right) Side chair. New England, 1800—1820. Original green paint with gilt decoration. Made of beech except for the pine seat and the front stretcher which is maple. SW 16½″, SD 15¾″, SH 17½″, OH 35″. (Also see color plate XI.) (Privately owned)*

unusual serpentine crest rail. Note, too, that all of the back spindles penetrate the secondary crest rail, a nice conceit. Quite possibly the design of this chair was influenced by the chairs of Samuel McIntire of Salem, a notable maker of sophisticated Federal furniture and a contemporary of Tuttle. The seat is carved in an interesting attempt to simulate the padded look of upholstered, formal Federal furniture. The design, condition, and provenance of figure 161 place it in the highest category of rod-backs. As though that were not enough, it is one of a set of four.

Figures 162 through 164 are a series of rod-back armchairs, two of which have a so-called butterfly medallion between the two crest rails. Figures 162 and 164 have three bamboo rings on their back posts and spindles, whereas figure 163 has only two. However, figure 163 has interesting arms: they have bamboo ringing behind the first short spindle, then flatten out as they move forward to become handholds. Figure 164 has the uncommon feature of curved, mahogany arms. This is one of a set of five chairs in their original mustard-color paint with the labels of Robert Taylor on the undersides of their seats. The bamboo ringing and the seat are accented in black, and there is a memori-

162. Armchair. Philadelphia, 1790–1810. Branded Ths. ASHTON. Nineteenth-century brown paint over original green. Crest rails and spindles, hickory; back posts, arms, arm supports, legs, and stretchers, maple; seat, pine. SW 19″, SD 17½″, SH 17″. (Stenton Mansion)

161. (left) Side chair. Salem, Massachusetts, 1800–1810. Branded I. [James] C.[hapman] TUTTLE. Original green paint with ivory decoration. SH 18″, OH 37″. (Patricia Ann Reed)

163. Armchair. Pennsylvania, 1810–1820. Refinished. Crest rail, arms, arm supports, and front stretcher, maple; spindles, back posts, legs, other stretchers, hickory; seat, poplar. SW 21″, SD 17″, SH 18″, OH 39¼″. (Privately owned)

al urn surrounded by laurel leaves painted on the butterfly medallion. These are quite fashionable rod-backs and are said to have been made for the First Bank of the United States in Philadelphia.

Figure 165 is a noteworthy rod-back armchair, one of a set of eight. These chairs were made by Frederick and Jacob Fetter for Masonic Lodge No. 43 of Lancaster, Pennsylvania, around 1811. We know this because of an existing bill for the chairs from the Fetters. There is even a bill for "ornamenting and Varnishing" the chairs in 1811 from one James Williams. The chairs are still owned by Masonic Lodge No. 43. They still have their original red paint with gilt and paint decoration of Masonic insignia. The oval spindles and stretchers—all decorated—the good knuckles,

164. (above) Armchair. Philadelphia, 1795–1810. Original mustard-color paint. Label under seat reads "Robert Taylor / Windsor and Fancy Chair Maker." Crest rail and spindles, hickory; arms, mahogany; arm supports, legs, and stretchers, maple; seat, poplar. SW 19″, SD 17″, SH 17½″, OH 35″. (Independence National Historical Park)

165. (right) Armchair. Lancaster, Pennsylvania, c. 1811. Made by Frederick and Jacob Fetter; decorated by James Williams. Original red paint with gilt and paint decoration. Crest rail, oak; spindles, maple and hickory; back posts, arms, arm supports, legs, and stretchers, maple; seat, poplar. SW 19⅝″, SD 17½″, SH 18¾″, OH 41″. (Also see color plates IX and X.) (Heritage Center of Lancaster County and Lancaster Masonic Lodge No. 43)

166. *Armchair. Pennsylvania, probably Philadelphia, 1790–1810. Painted black. Crest rail, oak; spindles and back posts, hickory; arms, mahogany; arm supports, legs, and stretchers, maple; seat, pine. SW 23¼″, SD 19½″, SH 17″, OH 45½″. (Privately owned)*

plus the indisputable provenance make these important rod-back Windsors.

Figure 166 is a very unusual rod-back armchair, and I have seen only one other like it. It has the D-shaped seat, crest rail, and knuckles of earlier comb-back Windsors, but it must be dated around 1790 because it has bamboo turnings and a box stretcher. Furthermore, if you compare the back of this chair with that of figure 159, you will see that figure 166 is merely a variation of the Pennsylvania Sheraton Windsor style. I think that the early and late styles have been blended quite successfully in this very large and commanding armchair.

Figure 167 is also quite unusual. It is a very elaborate interpretation of the bamboo rod-back; stylish and well conceived. The maker has succeeded in creating a chair that retains all the fine qualities of earlier Windsors—tapered back posts and spindles, a heavily chamfered, well-shaped seat, thicks and thins in the legs and stretchers, good leg splay—yet transforming them into a marvelous personal statement. Note, for example, the interesting crest rail, which echoes the bamboo turnings of the back posts and projects beyond them. This is a chair that any collector would be proud to own.

To call figure 168 "unusual" would be the height of understatement, so let us call it "exuberantly eccentric"—the product of the unfettered imagination of a country Windsor maker who was creating a chair for a special person or occasion. If we can look past the plethora of spindles for a moment, we shall see that the chair is very well made. The bamboo turnings are deeply incised and have great thicks and thins. The back spindles have an excellent taper. The oval seat is nicely chamfered and saddled, and the legs splay well. The overall design is, of course, completely aberrant—using spindles as though they were Christmas-tree ornaments. But the design does work according to a strict internal logic, with the birdcage of the back echoed in the arms and in the undercarriage. I find the raked arm supports that penetrate the seat and socket into the first side stretchers especially appealing—a design that is called a "double-bearing" arm and that is usually found only on rush-bottom New England armchairs. This probably one-of-a-kind rod-back is nothing less than Windsor folk art, and I think it is wonderful.

167. Side chair. Probably Easton, Pennsylvania area, 1790–1810. Spindles, crest, hickory; legs, back posts, ash or birch; seat, white pine. SW 16″, SD 15″, SH 16¾″, OH 34″. (Earl Jamison)

168. (far right) Armchair. American, 1800–1810. (Greenfield Village and Henry Ford Museum)

CHAPTER EIGHT
Writing-arm Chairs

THE WRITING-ARM Windsor chair is undoubtedly one of the most practical forms of furniture ever invented. Made in all the styles discussed in the previous chapters, these chairs are distinguished by a flat, paddlelike piece of wood that forms the right arm of the chair, which is, of course, intended to be used as a writing surface. Actually, I should have said "*usually* forms the right arm," for rare examples of left-handed writing-arm Windsors are known, as the folk portrait in figure 169 demonstrates (this happens to be a bow-back writing-arm chair). In addition to the writing arm and adding to the practicality of the chairs, they may be equipped with two storage drawers and/or a candle slide beneath the writing paddle and another drawer beneath the seat.

The addition of the large writing-arm paddle to a Windsor chair makes the design inherently clumsy and unbalanced, and it was the rare Windsor maker who had the ingenuity to overcome these obstacles to create a truly beautiful chair in this mode. Nevertheless, writing-arm chairs are today one of the single most sought-after forms of Windsors and are thus guaranteed to bring top-dollar for their age and condition.

Not many Philadelphia writing-arm chairs are known—none, as far as I am aware, from as early as, say, 1750. The chair in figure 170, with its tapered legs, rounded seat edges, and tapered spindles, dates from no earlier than around 1765. Yet the chair retains an early style of arm support, so it was probably made closer to 1765 than to 1780. In any case the writing paddle is certainly attached to the chair in the simplest possible way: a wrought-iron thumbscrew holds the paddle to the arm rail between the third and fourth spindles, and the paddle rests on a conventional arm beneath it. Of course, with this arrangement one could swing the paddle out of the way or toward oneself, or even detach it completely, if necessary.

169. Rebecca Jaquis Aged 79 Years, painted in the Year 1841 *by Jacob Maentel.* H 17¾". *(Abby Aldrich Rockefeller Folk Art Center)*

170. *Writing-arm chair. Philadelphia, 1765–1780.*

Of the Philadelphia writing-arm chairs that do exist, many were made by craftsman Anthony Steel. Figure 171 shows one such chair: a knuckle-arm, low-back Windsor. On this chair the writing paddle is constructed in the more conventional way: it is an integral part of the rest of the arm rail. The paddle is braced by three turned arm supports, which in turn are socketed into two tongues that project from, and are an integral part of, the seat. Steel has included two nice touches on this chair: a drawer with a bowed front beneath the paddle that conforms to the shape of the paddle; and, attached to that drawer, an oblong candle drawer that slides between the two front arm supports. Overall, the chair exhibits that conservative quality that we have come to expect in the later Philadelphia product.

The two excellent comb-back writing-arm chairs in figures 172 and 173 illustrate the dynamic qualities of the New England product as compared with, for example, the Steel chair just discussed. The splay of the arm supports and legs, the seat shape, and the turning pattern—all of those are better than in the Steel chair, although the latter is quite good. In addition, figures 172 and 173 afford us an opportunity for some stylistic detective work.

Although figure 172 is not branded, the stylistic details of the chair "brand" is as one made by Ebenezer Tracy, far and away the most prolific known maker of writing-arm Windsor chairs (compare, for example, figure 262, a branded Tracy writing-arm

171. *Writing-arm chair. Philadelphia, 1780–1790. Branded* A.[nthony] STEEL. *Refinished. Arm crest, arm supports, legs, and stretchers, maple; arms, oak; writing paddle, pine; spindles, hickory; seat, poplar. SW (overall) 25½″, SD 17″, SH 17½″, OH 30½″, writing paddle W 17″. (Museum of Art, Rhode Island School of Design)*

chair). The crest rail has a pleasing Tracy shape with small "horns" at the top edge. The turnings are superb and executed in a Tracy pattern. The seat shape, especially the pommel and the extreme curve at the edge before the arm supports, are also Tracy characteristics. Beyond all that the chair is on its own terms exceedingly fine. The writing paddle is braced by only two turned arm supports.

Figure 173 shows another very fine comb-back writing-arm chair, also from Connecticut and very similar to figure 172, but made by a craftsman influenced by Tracy, not by Tracy himself. The crest rail has the general shape of that of figure 172, but the horns are far more pronounced, a pattern not known to have been used by Tracy. The comb is also quite tall, a full one inch

172. (left) *Writing-arm chair. Connecticut, 1765–1780. Green paint over the original green. Crest rail, arm crest, arms, arm supports, and legs, maple; spindles and stretchers, hickory; writing paddle and seat, pine. SW (overall) 26″, SD 18″, OH 46½″, writing paddle 26″ × 21″. (Also see color plate IV.) (The Metropolitan Museum of Art; gift of Mrs. Screven Lorillard, 1952)*

173. (above) *Writing-arm chair. Connecticut, 1770–1790. Nineteenth-century black paint, over red, over the original green; drawers, early replacements. Crest rail, arm crest, arms, arm supports, legs, and stretchers, maple; spindles, hickory; writing paddle, oak; seat, oak or chestnut. SW (overall) 26½″, SD 17″, SH 16″, OH 47½″, writing paddle 18¾″ × 26¼″. (Privately owned)*

173A. Writing-arm chair. Detail of seat tongues and turned writing tablet supports.

142

174. (left) *Writing-arm chair. Connecticut, 1780–1800. Early nineteenth-century yellow grained paint over the original green. Crest rail, arm rail, and spindles, oak; arms supports, legs, and stretchers, birch; seat, poplar; drawers and candle slide, pine. SW (overall) 34¾", SD 15½", SH 17¼", OH 42", writing paddle 15½" × 22½". (Colonial Williamsburg)*

175. (below) *Writing-arm chair. Connecticut, probably Lyme-Westbrook area, 1770–1790. Original green paint. Crest rail, arm supports, legs, and stretchers, maple; arm rail, birch; writing paddle and seat, pine. SW 21", SD 17", SH 17½". OH 40", writing paddle 17" × 29". (Privately owned)*

taller than that of figure 172. Whereas the latter has slightly bulbous spindles, those of figure 173 have a very pronounced bulb that "steps up" progressively as it reaches the center of the back, and then "steps down." The arm supports are both turned in a similar pattern, but those of figure 173 have a less distinctive baluster shape. The front edge of the seat of figure 173 is quite different from that of figure 172. The former has two distinct curves that come to a point in the center of the seat; furthermore, the edges do not curve around the arm supports. In addition, figure 173 has a one-quarter inch groove carved along the top, outer edge of its seat and a chamfer on the bottom edge of the seat; the seat of figure 172 is flat. Finally, the legs of figure 173 are turned in an excellent Connecticut pattern, but not one that Tracy used on his writing-arm chairs. So, figure 173 is made in the Tracy style, but not, I think, by Tracy himself.

I hope that you are still with me and that this attention to small details has not blurred your vision, for I have one more detail to point out. As you can see from the close-up photograph (figure 173A), the chair has two projecting seat tongues, and, with the drawer removed from the underside of the writing paddle, you can see quite clearly how the supports are socketed into the paddle (which, by the way, is formed by two pieces of oak, doweled together lengthwise). Note also that the arm sup-

port in the background and the one in the right foreground are shorter than the support in the left foreground. That, of course, is a feature necessary for the construction of the chair, but what is interesting here is that the bases of the two shorter arm supports have double score marks just below the final baluster, whereas the longer arm support has a single score mark (the double score marks are most apparent in the background arm support). I believe that these double and single score marks were used by the turner to differentiate between the short and long spindles for the person who assembled the chair, thus avoiding an error in construction. For once the arm supports were socketed into the seat, it would have been a difficult and time-consuming job to pry them loose and correct the mistake.

While less of an achievement than the two chairs just discussed, figure 174 is nevertheless a charming Connecticut writing-arm chair. Although its proportions are not graceful and its turnings not the finest, the maker has paid attention to details. For example, the medial stretcher is decoratively turned, and there is a nice little candle slide under the arm drawer. Two of the arm supports are merely spindles, not decoratively turned. But the folksy quality of the turnings and the proportions are greatly enhanced by the early nineteenth-century grained paint over the original green, and comb-back writing-arm chairs are rare in this original, untouched condition.

176. (above) *Writing-arm chair. New England, possibly Vermont, 1790–1810. Nineteenth-century buff paint striped with green. Crest rail, arm rail, arm supports, legs, and stretchers, chestnut; spindles, hickory; writing paddle, pine. SW 22″, SD 16¼″, SH 18″, OH 37″, writing paddle 17½″ × 29″. (Philip H. Bradley, Antiques)*

177. (right) *Writing-arm chair. Possibly eastern Long Island or Connecticut, 1810–1830. Original red and black grained paint. SW (overall) 33″, SD 35″, OH 47¼″. (Israel Sack, Inc.)*

177A. (left) Writing-arm chair. Detail of swivel writing tablet.

178. (above) Writing-arm chair, New England, 1815–1840. Grained paint.

Figure 175 (in addition to the cover photo) is quite simply one of the finest writing-arm Windsors one could hope to find. The crest rail is wide, deeply curved, and shaped to a knife-edge on its top surface. The large, backward-thrusting comb perfectly balances the forward thrust and visual weight of the paddle. The paddle itself rests on a flattened, squared-off extension of the arm rail that does not look like the finished right-hand arm. The oval seat is well-scooped and heavily chamfered. The turnings are superb and, combined with the very long leg taper, put this chair in a class by itself. I should note also that figure 175 never had drawers, a loss with respect to practicality but a definite gain for beauty and harmony of design.

The lack of great beauty in figures 176 and 177 is compensated for by other qualities. Figure 176 is a late sack-back with quite simplified turnings. Two of the paddle supports are nothing more than spindles, and the maker has rather cleverly shaped the left-hand corner of the seat to a corner to accommodate those spindles. The chair is all original and covered with a buff-color paint striped in green. The total effect is quite pleasing.

The surface of figure 177 is entirely covered in exuberant red and black grained paint, which enhances its appeal and value tremendously. Without the paint we would be left with what amounts to a conglomeration of horizontal and vertical rectangles—the shapes of the crest rail, the drawers, the ends of the arm crest and right-hand arm, and of the "negative spaces" between the weakly turned spindles. Even the projecting tongues on the left-hand side of the seat, while rounded, have a rectangular quality. The wavy grain paint is a perfect foil for that rectangularity, and without the paint the chair would seem rather silly, especially as the maker has chosen to make a comb that merely perches on the arm crest and is not formed by a continuation of the back spindles. A feature of this chair that is not immediately apparent but that also enhances its value, is the fact that the writing paddle is hinged at the back and swings out to allow easy access to the seat (see figure 177A).

Made around 1830, the chair in figure 178 combines an American Empire crest rail with Sheraton arrow-shape back spindles. The chair is a common and basically undistinguished example of a late Windsor style that was quite popular in most regions of America. But with the addition of grain painting and a writing arm, it becomes unusual, and I place it here for that reason.

145

CHAPTER NINE
Rocking Chairs

WINDSORS that were originally constructed as rocking chairs—as opposed to those that have had rockers added at a later date—are something of a rarity, and that goes doubly for chairs with fine proportions and fine turnings. But such chairs were produced in the late eighteenth century, which can in part be documented by the fact that Northampton, Massachusetts, craftsman Ansel Goodrich advertised in the *Hampshire Gazette* for September 16, 1795, that he

has on hand and keeps constantly for sale all kinds of windsor chairs, viz.—Arm Chairs, Dining, do. of all kinds, Fanbacks, do. Fanback Foretails, Rocking Chairs, [and] Settees.[27]

Figure 179 shows a Windsor rocking chair that is certainly the best one could hope to find and it would be a marvelous chair even if it were not a rocker. The crest rail tapers nicely into the arm rail, and the knuckles are very well carved. The spindles below the arm rail are accented with wonderful little bulges. The seat is well chamfered and scooped out, and all the turnings are precise and beautiful. The medial stretcher even has an "extra" turning at either end. Finally, the rockers are pleasingly scrolled and notched where they socket into the legs. As evidenced by the brand (figure 179A), the chair was made by William Seaver of Boston, and even for him it is unusual because of its idiosyncratic, stylized turnings.

But, you may be asking, how can we determine that the rockers are original to the chair and that they were not added at a later date? There are several ways to do this. First, consider the paint history of the chair. The top layer of paint is black with gilt decoration on the spindles, arm supports, legs, stretchers, and rockers. Beneath that is the original paint, a pale grayish blue also covering the entire chair, including the rockers. Thus, the rockers have the same paint history as the rest of the chair, and the rockers must have already been attached to the chair when it received its first coat of gray-blue paint. Second, consider the fact that the bottom portion of the legs of this chair are not tapered but are cylindrical (figure 179B). Normally, of course, one would expect to find a tapered leg on such a chair, but because the chair

179. Rocking chair. Boston, 1790–1800. Branded [William] SEAVER. Black paint with gilt decoration over the original grayish blue. Crest rail and spindles, hickory; arm rail, oak; arm supports and legs, maple; stretchers, rockers and seat, chestnut. SW 19¼", SD 15", SH 19½", OH 38". (Wayne Pratt)

179A. *Rocking chair. Detail of Seaver brand.*

179B. *Rocking chair. Detail of leg and rocker construction.*

was intended to be a rocking chair, the turner purposely made the leg in a straight cylinder so that the mortise in the leg would have plenty of wood around it and not break from the strain of rocking and the hole made for the wooden pin would weaken the area. Finally, consider the fact that the legs of this chair already splay out tremendously, and that if they were any longer they would extend far beyond the edges of the seat; thus, the legs were not at some point in time cut down to accommodate the rockers, but were made the length they are on purpose. Such evidence makes quite a convincing case for the fact that the chair is all original.

Figure 180 shows a comb-back rocking chair that also is completely original. As is the case with many late Windsors, the original paint—in this case, black with gold decoration—makes the chair quite attractive. Although the turnings of this chair are simplified, the crest rail and the seat are nicely shaped.

A late arrow-back Windsor rocking chair is shown in figure 181. This chair has its original dark red paint and is fairly elaborately decorated with gilt leaves and, on the two flat crest rails, black plums. Note that the side stretchers have been eliminated, the maker apparently having decided that the rockers serve the same purpose. Although the chair is late, the maker has shown a nice sense of design in bending the three arrows of the back toward the rear of the chair and the three arrows of the comb toward the front, giving the back as a whole a pleasing S-shape. Paint decoration plus design add up to a charming piece of late country Windsor furniture.

147

180. (left) Rocking chair. Probably New England, 1800–1820. Original black paint with gilt decoration. SW 20″, SH 14″, OH 40½″. (Mr. and Mrs. Howard Feldman)

181. (right) Rocking chair. Probably Pennsylvania, 1820–1830. Original dark red paint decorated with gold and black. Seat and legs, poplar. SW 20″, SD 18½″, SH 16″, OH 45⅞″. (Howard Szmolko)

CHAPTER TEN
Settees

IN 1928, the pioneering American antiquarian Wallace Nutting said that Windsor settees "in all forms and any period ...are much sought after," and that statement is just as true today as it was then. Technically, a settee is any piece of unupholstered seating furniture that has a back and that can accommodate two or more people; settees that can accommodate *only* two people are often called love seats; and *any* Windsor settee may also be called a Windsor bench. As you might expect, Windsor settees have the same basic styles of the Windsor chairs of the period in which they were made, but settees were apparently not made in every region during all periods. For example, I have never seen a full-length settee in the early, classic, Philadelphia comb-back style, nor have I see one in the middle-period Philadelphia style. Most Windsor settees have arms, but occasionally one sees what I suppose might be called a "side settee" that never had arms. Because settees are wider than chairs, they presented unique design problems to the Windsor craftsman, and I will discuss those problems and their solutions as this chapter progresses.

Figure 182 shows a Philadelphia low-back settee. Such comparatively small, six-leg settees in this early style with full blunt-

182. Settee. Philadelphia, 1760–1780. Refinished. Arm crest, arm supports, legs, and stretchers, maple; spindles, hickory; arms, oak; seat, poplar. SW 53¾" SD 17", OH 30½". (The Metropolitan Museum of Art; gift of Mrs. J. Insley Blair, 1947)

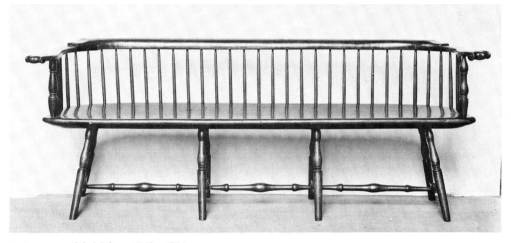

183. Settee. Philadelphia, 1765–1790.

184. Settee. Philadelphia, 1760–1780. Painted green. Arm rail, hickory; spindles, arm supports, legs, and stretchers, maple; seat, poplar. SW 75½", SD 22", SH 18", OH 29½". (Independence National Historical Park)

arrow feet are extremely rare. They are almost never found with knuckle handholds. Once in a great while one may turn up badly in need of repair (usually the balls of the feet have rotted off, among other things). Even rarer than the settee shown are those that are similar but that have the Queen Anne medial stretcher. I should mention that settees like figure 182 were very successfully reproduced in the early twentieth century. Many of these reproductions have acquired some age, and they may fool even the experienced eye, especially when they are covered with several coats of paint. Of course, figure 182 is authentic and beautifully proportioned. Note, for example, that the turnings of the stretchers have been "stretched" nicely to compensate for the wider distance than that which is found on a comparable Philadelphia low-back chair.

Longer low-back settees with eight or ten legs seemed to have become popular around 1765. They hardly ever have such early features as blunt-arrow feet or Queen Anne medial stretchers, but they frequently have knuckle handholds. Figures 183 and 184 show two of these wider settees. The bold knuckles of figure 183 add much to its classic, conservative Philadelphia design. The arrow-shape turnings at the ends of the medial stretchers add interest to the undercarriage and help fill some of the wide spaces

185. (left) *Settee. Philadelphia, 1790–1800. Branded [John] LETCH-WORTH. Traces of red paint; medial stretcher possibly replaced; knuckles missing. Crest rail, spindles, and arm supports, hickory; legs and side stretchers, maple; seat, poplar. SW 42″, SD 19″, SH 17¼″, OH 30″. (Colonial Williamsburg)*

186. (below) *Settee. Philadelphia, 1790–1810. Branded A.[nthony] STEELE. Painted brown; scrolled handholds missing. Arm rail and spindles, hickory; arm supports, legs, and stretchers, maple; seat, poplar. SW 42½″.*

between the legs. Note that the outer legs of this piece splay outward while the middle legs do not; as a result, the two outer medial stretchers are longer than the central medial stretcher. Nevertheless, the maker has turned each stretcher to the proper proportions, so that the differences in the length of the stretchers is barely noticeable to the casual observer.

Figure 184 is constructed differently from figure 183. The arm rail of figure 184 is a single piece of steam-bent hickory, and each spindle penetrates the arm rail and is wedged from above, which is conclusive evidence that the piece did not originally have a comb that was cut off. This settee has a very good undercarriage, often a weak point in settee design. By using ten legs on this settee, the maker was able to use stretchers that are less attenuated than they might be on an eight-leg settee. The undercarriage is thus more graceful and rhythmic than those usually seen. Also, the turnings of the legs and arm supports of this piece are as fine as one can find on Philadelphia Windsor furniture from the 1760 to 1780 period, and the side stretchers include an attractive extra ring at each end.

Figures 185 and 186 are two somewhat late low-back settees. Figure 185, although unfortunately damaged—the knuckle handholds are missing and the medial stretcher is probably a replacement—is still interesting for its square back and the fact that it is branded by John Letchworth, who chose to combine bamboo-turned legs with baluster-and-ring arm supports. To make the piece square, Letchworth attached the arms to the back rail with lap joints. In spite of these interesting features, the piece seems to cry out for an extra set of legs in the center.

Of approximately the same length as figure 185, figure 186 is a more satisfying design because it does have the extra legs, and all

the legs are turned somewhat better. The arm rail of this piece is constructed of two pieces of steam-bent hickory, joined at the back with a long, diagonal lap joint. Branded A. STEELE, this little bench has very pleasing proportions and lines. In the photograph you should be able to see fairly clearly the definite bulge and rounding off of the tops of the front legs before they enter the seat—a characteristic, as I have mentioned, of Philadelphia bamboo-turned Windsor furniture.

187. Settee. New England, probably Connecticut, 1770–1800. Painted green. Crest rail, spindles, and arm rail, hickory; arm supports, legs, and stretchers, maple; seat, pine. SW 37″, SD 20″, OH 42½″. (Greenfield Village and Henry Ford Museum)

Chairs in the sack-back style are very common, but, strangely, just the opposite is true of sack-back settees. Figures 187 through 190 show a series of such settees. The first, figure 187, is a very rare, small form. In addition to its fine turnings and proportions, the seat is exceptionally nice. The maker has carved the seat to delineate two separate oval seating surfaces, and he has included a scallop in the center of the seat above the middle front leg. The turning pattern, the seat shape, and the small bulbs at each end of the medial stretchers indicate a probable Connecticut origin.

Figure 188 is a Philadelphia product that, while quite fine, has a few problems. The back, although intact, appears to have a few "teeth" missing where the crest rail curves around to meet the arm rail. Furthermore, the crest rail appears a bit short. By contrast, the New England maker of the settee in figure 189 has solved those problems. First, he has filled the spaces in the back with a spindle on each side (a later carriage bolt can also be seen in the corner of the crest rail) and he turned all the spindles with the bulbs near the bottom. Second, he has made the back taller so that the arm rail appears to split it approximately in half. The leg turnings, while slim, are rather elegant. If this piece has a flaw, it is in the medial stretchers, which should have a ring at either end to help fill the wide spaces in the undercarriage.

Figure 190 is the ne plus ultra in sack-back settees, and, being incomparable, it would be unfair to refer to the preceding examples. Branded repeatedly on the seat bottom by Ebenezer Tracy and reputedly made for his own home, this tour de force should lay to rest any lingering doubts about whether or not Tracy was a genius—at least when it came to making Windsor furniture. The crest rail of this settee is nearly as thick as the arm crest. It narrows as it swoops down to meet the arm crest, and then, remarkably, ends in little carved paws that seem to stand on the arm rail. Resembling the carved feet of trifid-foot tables, these paws point the way toward the great knuckle handholds, whose outward curve is repeated in the flaring front edges of the seat. The stretchers have a marvelously fat bulge in their centers and two rings at either end. The first ring is as wide as the central bulge; the second, at the extreme ends of the stretchers, flares somewhat and echoes the flaring collars of the superb and typical Tracy-style turnings of the legs and arm supports. This is by no

188. Settee. Philadelphia, 1760–1780. Painted green. Crest rail, arm rail, and spindles, hickory; seat, pine; legs and stretchers, maple. SW 78″, SD 18½″, SH 15¾″, OH 34″. (Independence National Historical Park)

means a subtle piece of American Windsor furniture, but it is certainly among the most sublime.

Windsor settees with bamboo turnings can also be quite remarkable, as the two possibly unique pieces in figures 191 and 192 demonstrate. Although they in some ways defy definition, I shall call them fan-back settees for the sake of convenience. Branded J. BALCH, JR., figure 191 is a wonderful, probably Philadelphia, product that combines early and late features very successfully. The early-style crest rail with carved ears is an inspired addition, and one wonders why other makers did not use it on their settees more often. The back posts have the earlier baluster-and-ring turnings, and there is a central back post in the same pattern which, because of its location, would not interfere with anyone's comfort. The arms and arm supports are well scrolled in the manner of Philadelphia bow-back armchairs. The

189. (above) *Settee. New England, 1760–1790. Black paint. Crest rail, arm rail, and spindles, hickory; arm supports, legs, and stretchers, maple; seat, pine. SW 76″, SD 20½″, SH 19½″, OH 37¼″. (Abington Antiques)*

190. (below) *Settee. Lisbon, Connecticut, 1770–1803. Branded EB: [Ebenezer] TRACY. SW 85″, SD 25⅝″, OH 41″. (The Henry Francis du Pont Winterthur Museum)*

153

legs and stretchers have the best Philadelphia style bamboo turnings. The three, as opposed to two, bobbins in the medial stretchers indicate a date closer to 1780 than to 1800.

Although totally bamboo-turned and somewhat similar in style, figure 192 is even better than figure 191. The crest rail is exceptionally beautiful with its tall central arch and deeply carved ears—the equal of the finest Rhode Island designs. The construction of the back is ingenious, combining the fan-back style with that of the low-back. The turnings are excellent, and the side stretchers have a typical Rhode Island squarishness. The entire design is exceedingly graceful and dignified, and I do not think it is an exaggeration to say that the piece seems to wear its crest rail like a crown, deservedly.

Figure 193, a bow-back settee, is another piece that successfully combines early and late features. The fluid, serpentine arms, which are socketed and wedged into the seat, are intended to imitate upholstered Federal sofas whose serpentine arms continue downward and become the legs. Note again, as on the Balch settee, the middle stretchers. On this piece the maker has chosen to use baluster-and-ring legs with bamboo-turned stretchers, but

191. (above) Settee. Probably Philadelphia, 1780—1800. Branded J. BALCH, JR. Painted black. Seat, pine. SW 75¾", SD 17¼", OH 35". (Frank S. Schwarz and Son)

192. (right) Settee. Probably Rhode Island, 1780-1800. Spindles, stiles, stretchers, arm supports, and arm rail, hickory; legs possibly ash; crest, walnut or butternut, original green paint; seat, pine. SW 49¾", SD 17½", SH 15¾", OH 35".

193. *Settee. Philadelphia, 1780–1800. Nineteenth-century brown paint over the original white with blue decoration. Crest rail, spindles, and arms, hickory; legs and stretchers, maple; seat, poplar. SW 78″, SD 22¾″, SH 17½″, OH 37″. (Stenton Mansion)*

155

this concession to the Federal style is not jarring. All told, this is an unusual and elegant piece of Philadelphia furniture.

Figures 194 through 196 are somewhat more conventional settees of the early Federal period. One of a pair made by John Letchworth, figure 194 is a piece that is quite charming in this small size. The close spacing of the back spindles, legs, and stretchers seems just right and would not be nearly so effective on a full-size settee in this Philadelphia "oval-back" style. Figure 195 is also made by Letchworth and has mahogany arms. As you have probably gathered by this point, much of the total success of a settee depends on whether or not the long medial stretchers are well-realized, that is, whether or not their turnings can disguise or even enhance their actual length. The legs and side stretchers of figure 195 are good, but the medial stretchers are, I think, disappointingly weak. Figure 196 compensates, to some degree, for that same weakness by having an interesting crest rail that manifests the influence of high-style Federal sofas: a square back with a raised medallion in the center. The maker was no doubt imitating the work of such Philadelphia craftsmen as Henry Connelly and Ephraim Haines, who were producing furniture for Philadelphia's most affluent families. The curved section in the corners of the back are separate pieces of wood and quite unusual and attractive. Although the side stretchers are pleasingly fat, it is unfortunate that the maker did not execute the medial stretchers and for that matter, the legs, more expertly.

194. (above left) *Settee. Philadelphia, 1785–1810. Branded I. [John] LETCHWORTH. Painted black. Crest rail, hickory or oak; spindles, hickory; arms and arm supports, mahogany; legs and stretchers, maple; seat, poplar. SW 40½", SD 17", SH 16¼", OH 36". (Independence National Historical Park)*

195. (left) *Settee. Philadelphia, 1785–1810. Branded I. [John] LETCHWORTH. Painted green. Crest rail and spindles, hickory; arms, mahogany; arm supports, legs, and stretchers, maple; seat, poplar. SW 72", SD 22½", SH 18", OH 38". (Independence National Historical Park)*

196. Settee. Philadelphia, 1790–1800. Refinished. Crest rail, spindles, and legs, hickory; arms and arm supports, oak; seat, poplar. SW 72¼", SD 19¼", SH 17", OH 36". (Independence National Historical Park)

The success of the birdcage, rod-back settee in figure 197 can be found in its elegant back. The maker has used forty-one closely spaced and nicely articulated bamboo-turned spindles in this rectangular Sheraton design. The arms are unusual in that they repeat the birdcage design of the back. This is a very long settee, and whereas the design of the back takes that factor into account, the undercarriage does not. The wide spaces between the legs seem to accentuate the rather uninspired bamboo turnings of the legs and stretchers. With rod-back pieces such as this one, it begins to be difficult to place the Windsor chairs and settees of the period into regions. Stylistic differences tend to blur, and one must depend increasingly upon the kinds of wood, paint, and decoration used. In the case of this piece I think one might place it in New England because of the waviness of the back spindles.

Windsor love seats are rare from any period, and figure 198—a birdcage example with "butterfly" medallions in its back—is no exception. For so late a piece, it is really quite good. Noteworthy features include the central back post, the repetition of the bamboo ringing on each turned part, and the fact that the double crest rail curves into the back posts. In this piece the rounding of the tops of the legs and arm supports gives it a Philadelphia or Pennsylvania provenance.

Figure 199 has what is called a step-down crest rail. The seat is nicely shaped, having a sharp edge rather than one that is rounded off. It is beaded about an inch in. But why did the maker design a base that is more like two separate chairs with box

197. Settee, New England. 1800–1815. Painted black. Hickory, maple, and pine. SW 83". (Greenfield Village and Henry Ford Museum)

157

198. Settee. Pennsylvania, 1795–1810. SW 41″, SD 17″, SH 18″, OH 34¾″. (C. L. Prickett)

199. Settee. New England, 1810–1830. Hickory, maple, and pine. (Greenfield Village and Henry Ford Museum)

158

stretchers than like a conventional settee? I do not think that he did it because he did not know any better, for too many settees with conventional designs had already been produced that could have been used as models. Probably the piece was designed for a specific purpose or to fit a particularly awkward indoor or outdoor floor or ground situation. In any case most Windsor settees have a public rather than a domestic design feeling for me, but this one projects a familial feeling. I can picture mama and papa sitting at either end, two youngsters swinging their legs in the center, and the family hound curled up beneath the seat.

Figure 200 has an unusual rod-back design. All of the parts above the seat have a vertical or horizontal groove cut in them that one sometimes sees in the spindles of New England Windsor chairs. The piece at first gives the impression of a cradle with one side missing, but we can determine that it was made this way purposely due to the fact that the back posts have buttonlike finials and are turned quite differently from the arm supports (the left-hand one of which, by the way, has been broken off at the top). This settee seems to have been made more to contain its occupants than merely to support them, rather like a wagon seat. In any case the legs and stretchers are very well turned, and although a bit odd, this is nonetheless an attractive piece of Windsor furniture.

The duck-bill settee in figure 201 is a beautifully realized, astonishingly contemporary design of the late bamboo period. The Sheraton medallions repeated on all of the back spindles and on the front stretchers are effective features, and one hardly cares that the traditional bamboo rings have all but shriveled up. To me, the piece is reminiscent of fancy, painted furniture produced in Baltimore after 1800, and perhaps that is where it originated.[28] Surely this piece was originally paint-decorated, and it is a shame that we do not know what it looked like when it was first painted.

200. (above) Settee. New England, 1800–1820. Nineteenth-century brown paint with gilt striping over the original white. Crest rail and spindles, hickory; back posts, arm rail, arm posts, legs, and stretchers, maple; seat, pine. SW 36″, SD 16½″, SH 17″, OH 30″. (Privately owned)

201. (left) Settee. Possibly Baltimore, 1810–1830. Refinished. Crest rail and spindles, possibly ash; back posts, arms, arm supports, legs, and stretchers, maple; seat, pine. SW 36″, SD 18″, SH 17″, OH 33″. (J. and S. Schneider)

159

CHAPTER ELEVEN
Children's and Scaled-down Furniture

SOME OF THE MOST delightful examples of American Windsor furniture were made for children. Of course, the size of this furniture gives it a unique charm. But beyond that, children's Windsor furniture demonstrates time and again that small can be beautiful. In addition to children's Windsors, there is a type that, while obviously scaled-down in size, was nonetheless apparently not intended for use by children. This type of Windsor furniture is very rare, but a few examples are shown in this chapter. Both children's and scaled-down Windsor furniture presented the craftsman with special design problems, which I will discuss throughout this chapter.

Children's comb-back chairs are rare. Two such chairs are shown in figures 202 and 203. The best children's Windsor furniture retains as much horizontal bulbousness in the turnings as possible while diminishing vertical spaces so that the piece will fit a child. Put another way, if the size of the turnings are reduced in exact proportion to the reduction in height, something always looks wrong. The piece will become, as it were, too toylike and will take on the appearance of dollhouse furniture. Both figures 202 and 203 retain a nice bulbousness in the turnings. A carping critic might ask for one more spindle in the back of figure 202, but I, at least, admire the airy quality of the back of this fine little chair.

Figure 203 is, I believe, a good New England interpretation of a Philadelphia comb-back chair. The maker has retained the Philadelphia verticality in the wonderfully tall comb. Note, too, that the ears are scrolled the "wrong" way. The comparative lack of splay to the arm supports and legs has a Philadelphia quality as well, yet the deeply chamfered pine seat is one we would expect to find on a New England chair. In any case this is a beautifully realized piece.

The fan-back side chair in figure 204 is branded *E. TRACY*. As you can see, the chair is superbly designed and turned, with all the parts in the proper proportion. The addition of a patina of mustard-color paint over the original green makes this chair most desirable. The fact that the rockers are not original to the chair

202. *Armchair. Philadelphia, 1765–1780. Nineteenth-century black paint over the original green. Crest rail, oak; arm rail and spindles, hickory; arm supports, legs, and stretchers, maple; seat, pine. SW 16¾", SD 14", SH 12⅜", OH 29½". (Privately owned)*

203. Armchair. New England, 1770–1800. Black paint with gold striping over old red. Arm rail and spindles, hickory; arm supports, legs, and stretchers, maple. SW 14¾″, SH 11″, OH 27¼″. (Museum of Art, Rhode Island School of Design; gift of Mrs. Henry Vaughan)

really does not diminish it at all, in my opinion. Indeed, the rockers are themselves dated quite early.

Two sack-back children's chairs are shown in figures 205 and 206. The first has remarkably fine proportions. In addition, it is quite rare to find a Philadelphia sack-back of *any* size with the early cylindrical leg and ball foot. Notice the cylindrical turning of the arm supports just below the arm. Highchairs are sometimes found with this style of arm support: a hole is drilled through each cylinder, and, once the child is seated, a wooden rod would be inserted through the holes to prevent the child from falling (or climbing!) out of the chair (see, for example, figure 225). The arm supports of figure 205 could easily have been used on a highchair, but as this is not a highchair, no holes have been drilled. I should mention that the outside and bottom portions of the knuckle handholds of this chair are missing.

Figure 206 is marvelously bold—almost chubby. The leg and stretcher turnings are especially fine. Unfortunately, the arm supports are a letdown and far too crude for such a generally sophisticated chair with knuckle arms. One might think that the arm supports are replacements, but in fact they are not; they have the same surface appearance of age and the same paint history as the rest of the chair. One must simply accept such occasional design faults in an otherwise excellent piece of Windsor furniture. As Henry Fielding put it in *Tom Jones*:

> There is, perhaps, no surer mark of folly than an attempt to correct the natural infirmities of those we love. The finest composition of human nature, as well as the finest china [and, in this case, Windsor furniture], may have a flaw in it; and this, I am afraid, in either case, is equally incurable; though, nevertheless, the pattern may remain of the highest value.

Figures 207 through 209 show three excellent bow-backs. Figure 207 has turnings that are very compact and bold and perfectly scaled. This is an exceptionally good piece of children's Windsor furniture. The chair in figure 208 has baluster-and-ring leg turnings but a bamboo-turned medial stretcher. It is not peculiar to find such a combination of styles or other similar combinations, such as baluster-and-ring arm supports with bamboo legs, or baluster-and-ring arm supports and legs with bamboo

204. Side chair. Connecticut, 1770–1790. Branded E. TRACY. Nineteenth-century mustard-color paint over the original green; rockers not original, attached with handmade screws. Crest rail and rockers, maple; back posts and spindles, hickory; seat, legs, and stretchers, chestnut. SW 14″, SD 14½″, OH 31″. (Privately owned)

205. Armchair. Philadelphia, 1760–1770. Nineteenth-century black paint over the original green. Crest rail, spindles, and arm rail, hickory; arm supports, legs, and stretchers, maple; seat, poplar. SW 15½″, SD 11″, SH 12″, OH 27¾″. (Privately owned)

206. Armchair. New England, 1770–1790. Black paint over the original green. Crest rail, spindles, and arm rail, hickory; arm supports, legs, and stretchers, maple; seat, pine. SW 15½″, SD 11″, SH 10″, OH 23½″. (Colonial Williamsburg)

207. (left) *Armchair. Connecticut or Rhode Island, 1780–1800. Traces of the original green paint. Crest rail and spindles, hickory; arms, arm supports, legs, and stretchers, maple; seat, poplar. SW 12", SD 10¾", SH 13½", OH 27¾". (Mr. and Mrs. R. W. P. Allen)*

208. (below left) *Side chair. Connecticut or New York, 1780–1800. Nineteenth-century buff paint with blue striping over the original green. Crest rail and spindles, hickory; legs and stretchers, maple; seat, pine. SH 12½", SW 12½", OH 27". (Also see color plate XII.) (Privately owned)*

209. (below) *Side chair. Philadelphia, c. 1787. Branded I. [Joseph] HEN-ZEY; inscribed ISL—1787. Painted dark brown. Crest rail and spindles, hickory; legs and stretchers, maple; seat, poplar. SW 14⅞", SD 13", SH 11½", OH 24". (Colonial Williamsburg)*

spindles. In any case, the bamboo medial stretcher places this fine little chair in the 1780 to 1800 period. In addition to its design the chair is enhanced by nineteenth-century sand-color paint with blue striping over the original green.

Figure 209 is no doubt a unique bow-back child's side chair. As you can see, the ends of the bow have been decoratively turned as though they were the back posts of a fan-back chair. This is a great conceit, and I have never seen it used on any other bow-back side chair. Another interesting detail is the pyramiding design made by the single bamboo ring on each spindle. The chair is branded by Joseph Henzey and, interestingly, is dated 1787. Henzey must have made this child's Windsor for someone very special because few Windsors are dated.

Although less spectacular than the preceding, figures 210 through 213 show three lovely bamboo-turned bow-back side chairs, each with good proportions. Figure 210 is branded by John B. Ackley. The bamboo leg turnings on this chair are somewhat different from those one ordinarily encounters: the upper section of the leg is almost straight down to the first ring; below that ring, the leg becomes slightly concave, swells to the stretcher joint, then takes a fairly sharp, quick taper.

I like the chair in figure 211 especially for its pinched bow. The particular shape of this one—the bow narrowing and then entering the seat in an almost straight line—gives the chair a Lancaster or Chester County, Pennsylvania, provenance. The chair in figure 212 is quite small and could just as easily be a doll's chair as a child's chair. It is well-proportioned and detailed for such a small piece, right down to its nicely pinched bow, beading on the

212. Side chair. Philadelphia, 1800—1820. Three or four coats of white paint over original white. Crest rail, hickory or oak; spindles, probably hickory; legs and stretchers, maple; seat, poplar. SW 9¼", SH 9", SH 7", OH 18". (Robert Stewart)

front, bottom edge of the seat, and single, rather than double, bamboo ringing on the legs. The name *Perot* is carved in the seat bottom. This is a fine little Windsor.

The rockers on figure 213 are original to the chair. They have the same paint history as the other parts, including the original green, and they are mortised into a slot in the leg and pinned with square wooden pegs. The entire construction appears correct, and the shape of the rockers themselves seems right for the 1780 to 1800 period. Note also that, compared with figures 210 and 211, the first bamboo leg rings on figure 213 are much closer to the seat. I believe the maker designed the chair in this way to compensate visually for the relatively short taper at the bottom of the legs, necessary because of the rockers.

With figure 214 we move on to chairs in the rod-back style. This little chair is interesting because it combines the late rod-back crest rail and bamboo-turned back posts with the earlier, shield-shaped seat, baluster-and-ring legs, and H-stretchers. The crest rail is, I think, a bit too simplified, but on the whole the chair is quite good.

Figure 215 shows a very fine example of a child's duck-bill rod-back armchair. The back appears to be higher than it is because the arms have been positioned below the center point of the back posts. The bamboo turnings are well-defined, and the seat is

213. Rocking chair. Pennsylvania, 1785—1800. Underside of seat inscribed Maria Williams. 1792. Mahoganized paint over original green. Crest rail, oak spindles, hickory; legs and stretchers, maple; rockers, probably maple; seat, poplar. SW 16", SD 14", SH 13¾", OH 29½". (Privately owned)

214. (far right) Side chair. Probably New England, 1800—1810. Refinished. Crest rail and seat, sycamore; spindles, ash; back posts and side stretchers, maple; legs, beech; medial stretcher, chestnut. SW 12½", SD 12¾", SH 9", OH 24½". (Privately owned)

215. (far left) Arm chair. New England, possibly Wolfeboro, New Hampshire area, 1790–1810. Late nineteenth-century black paint, over red, over the original yellow. SW 14½", SD 12", SH 9", OH 24¼". (Ross Levett, Antiques)

216. (left) Side chair. Philadelphia, 1800–1815. Original brown paint. Crest rail, back posts, spindles, and stretchers, hickory; legs, maple; seat, poplar. SW 13½", SD 13½", SH 12", OH 24". (Leon Stark)

217. (below) Side chair. Pennsylvania, 1815–1830. Nineteenth-century black paint. Crest rail, legs, and stretchers, maple; back posts and spindles, hickory; seat, poplar. SW 14½", SD 14", SH 13", OH 28½". (Leon Stark)

nicely chamfered. Of course, the marvelous thing about this chair is the tremendous splay to the arm supports and the legs. Since the chair still has the H-stretcher arrangement, it probably dates closer to the 1790 to 1800 period than to the first quarter of the nineteenth-century.

Figures 216 and 217 are two of the more typical children's rod-backs from a somewhat later date. Both are quite simplified, but pleasing enough. Figure 216 has a seat shape that strongly resembles similar chairs branded by Thomas Ashton. The problem with such late children's or full-size Windsors is, indeed, their plainness, and, as I have mentioned more than once, the paint surface or decoration can often compensate for comparatively uninspired design. For example, in figure 218 we see a folk portrait from around 1816 of Henrietta Frances Cuthbert at about three years of age, her hand resting on her own rod-back side chair. The chair is painted red and decorated in gilded floral designs and striping. Figure 219 shows a similar chair that is wonderfully paint-decorated in white with gold decoration and lettering. The maker has used the same technique on this chair as the maker of figure 215 used to make the back appear taller; that is, he has lowered the arms. Rebecca Roup must have loved her chair very

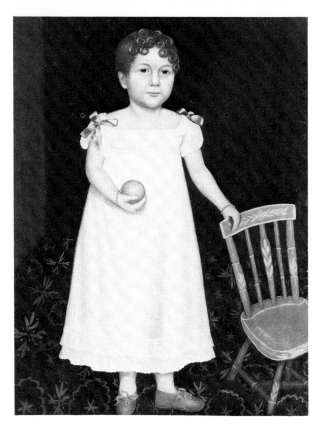

218. Portrait of Henrietta Frances Cuthbert (b. 1813), c. 1816. (Abby Aldrich Rockefeller Folk Art Center)

220. Armchair. Possibly New Jersey, 1840–1850. Original cream-yellow paint with gilt, red, and black decoration. Pine. SD 12″, SH 10″, SW 11¾″, OH 18½″. (See color plate XV.) (Privately owned)

219. Armchair. Pennsylvania, 1812. Original white paint with gilt decoration. Crest rail, back posts, arm supports, legs, and side stretchers, maple; spindles, oak; arms and medial stretcher, hickory; seat, poplar. SW 11½″, SD 11½″, SH 8½″, OH 22″. (Judy and Alan Wexler)

221. Settee. Pennsylvania, 1810–1820. Original mahoganized paint. Crest rail, spindles, and stretchers, hickory; back posts, arms, arm supports, and legs, maple; seat, poplar. SW 16½", SD 7¾", SH 6⅝", OH 14". (Privately owned)

much, as would any collector. Even figure 220, a very late, so-called firehouse Windsor that many collectors might ignore, is transformed into a desirable piece of Windsor furniture because of its remarkably preserved paint. The chair is a creamy yellow with gold leaf and red and black borders. The child's name on the arm crest, *Louie*, is also in gold leaf with a black border. The "potty seat" cutout is original to the chair.

Children's Windsor settees are extremely rare. Figure 221 shows a wonderful arrow-back example that might have been used for dolls as well as for small fry. The step-down crest rail is an unusual series of scallops. And note the interesting shape of the arm supports: two bulbs separated by a bamboo-turned ring. The shape of the ends of the medallion front stretchers is echoed in the sharp leg taper. Finally, the seat is nicely beaded on the front edge. All the features of this piece—scallops, spindles, knoblike finials, arrows, medallions, and beading—add up to a playful, whimsical piece of children's Windsor furniture that is far more than merely a pedantic scaling-down of a full-size piece.

Highchairs presented a double problem for the maker: not only the scaling down of the upper part of the chair but a scaling "up," as it were, of the undercarriage. The two superb, early Philadelphia comb-back highchairs shown in figures 222 and 223 solve these problems quite well. Figure 222 is a more vertical, narrow chair, both in its back and its lack of leg splay. Although its leg turnings are somewhat better than those of figure 223, the latter is on the whole a better chair because of its good leg splay and it certainly *looks* a lot more stable than figure 222. Note the Queen Anne medial stretchers of the type found on the earliest of Philadelphia comb-backs. Few collections, public or private, possess early children's Windsors of this quality.

A highchair like the one in figure 224 is surpassed only by the two preceding examples, and that is saying quite a bit. This is a slightly later comb-back highchair, and so the Queen Anne stretcher has been replaced by a simpler bobbin. The shape of the arm supports is an excellent scaling down of Philadelphia comb-backs from the 1760s. The detail photograph (figure 224A) shows this arm support and the hole drilled through it to receive the wooden restraining rod.

222. *Highchair. Philadelphia, 1750–1760. Nineteenth-century black paint over the original green; foot rest restored. Crest rail, spindles, and arm rail, hickory; arm supports, legs, and stretchers, maple; seat, pine. SW 14¾", SD 10½", SH 20¾", OH 40¼". (Colonial Williamsburg)*

223. (left) Highchair. Philadelphia, 1750–1770. Early nineteenth-century yellow paint with brown striping (to simulate curly maple) over original green. Crest rail, oak; spindles and arm rail, hickory; arm supports, legs, and stretchers, maple. SH 21½", SW 14⅞", SD 10½", OH 40". (Mr. and Mrs. Howard Feldman)

224. (above) Highchair. Philadelphia, 1760–1780. Original dark brown paint over red ground. Crest rail, arm rail, and spindles, hickory; seat, poplar; legs and stretchers, maple. SW 15", SD 10½", SH 21¾", OH 39½". (Descendants of the Wistar family)

224A. (below) Highchair. Detail of arm support showing hole drilled for child's restraining rod.

225. (right) Highchair. Philadelphia, 1765–1780. Refinished; foot rest missing. Crest rail, arm rail, and spindles, hickory; restraining rod, hickory with maple knobs; legs and stretchers, maple; seat, poplar. SW 15¼", SD 10¼", SH 20⅜", OH 35". (Mr. and Mrs. R. W. P. Allen)

Figure 225 is an excellent Philadelphia sack-back highchair. It is highly unusual for a chair to retain its original restraining rod, but this one does, and we can see the nicely turned end knobs. I have mentioned that sack-back chairs usually have oval seats, but this one is D-shaped. Sack-back highchairs often did have D-shaped seats. The maker used a D-shape to make it easier to position the arm supports at the front corners of the seat, thus allowing room for both the child and the restraining rod. The turnings on this chair are very vigorous. The footrest is missing from the leg just below the first ring turning, but that allows us to see that the maker thickened the leg slightly at that point to strengthen it and to accommodate the supports for the footrest.

A continuous-arm highchair of the very highest caliber is shown in figure 226. Virtually everything about this chair is masterful. The leg turnings are remarkably beautiful with great thicks and thins and an astonishingly high taper. Because the chair is a New England design with a compressed turning pattern, compared with the preceding examples, the maker was able to join the footrest into the thick second baluster turning of the leg, rather than into the thinner, upper part of the leg. This is a

226. (above) *Highchair. New England, probably Connecticut, 1770–1800.*

227. (right) *Highchair. New England, probably Connecticut, 1780–1810. Foot rest restored. Spindles, hickory; arms, possibly cherry; arm supports, legs, and stretchers, maple. (Greenfield Village and Henry Ford Museum)*

228. Highchair. Philadelphia, 1790–1810. Early nineteenth-century mahoganized paint over the original green. Crest rail and spindles, hickory; arms, oak; arm supports, legs, and stretchers, maple; seat, pine. SW 13¾″, SD 13″, SH 18¾″, OH 34″. (Philip H. Bradley, Antiques)

229. Highchair. Pennsylvania, 1800–1820. White, blue, and green paint over the original red. Made entirely in maple except for the seat which is poplar. SW 12½″, SD 10½″, SH 22¾″, OH 34″. (Privately owned)

230. Highchair. New England, 1810–1825. Original olive-green paint. Crest rail, back posts, arms, arm supports, legs, and stretchers, maple; spindles, hickory; seat, pine. SW 12½″, SD 11¾″, SH 21″, OH 33½″. (Philip H. Bradley, Antiques)

practical, as well as an attractive solution to both making the chair strong and integrating the footrest into the overall design. Because of the rearward placement of the arm supports, no restraining rod was used on this piece.

The bow-back highchair in figure 227 has good turnings that are slightly too attenuated, and I think the back might do with an extra spindle. However, the seat is very well saddled with a high pommel, and the long leg taper is effective. Figure 228 is a bow-back highchair from a later period. It has lost a great deal of panache in comparison with the two preceding examples—the arms are straight and the legs, quite simplified bamboo turnings—yet the seat shape is good and the legs have a relatively high taper. Furthermore, the nineteenth-century mahoganized paint over the original green has left an attractive patina.

Figures 229 through 231 are highchairs in the rod-back style. Figure 229 is a Pennsylvania piece, which we can recognize from the poplar seat; the heavy gauge of the bamboo-turned legs, back posts, and spindles; the rounded tops of the arm supports and legs; and the quick taper to the foot. The chair has white, blue, and green paint over the original red, and, consequently, a pleasing patina. Figure 230 is a New England rod-back with a much higher leg taper, turnings of a narrower gauge, and tapered tops to the legs and arm supports. The back bends rearward nicely, and the seat has a better shape than the preceding chair, and also the bamboo ringing does not appear above the seat, but both are really quite comparable. Figure 231 has a pleasing tall back and a good seat shape. The maker has cleverly supported the footrest with a vertical brace.

Figure 232 is an extremely rare form of highchair: a two-seat version probably intended for twins. Note that the chair's front stretcher has been lost. This type of rod-back is sometimes called a "thumb-back" because of the thumblike shape of the tops of the back posts. The piece is very desirable not only because of its rare form but also because of its original paint decoration: black splashed with red and accented with a gold floral design and striping.

Although figures 233 and 234 may at first appear to be children's chairs, they are not. A fan-back side chair, figure 233 has a seat and back that are only slightly less than adult size, but the seat height from the floor is only nine and one-half inches as

232. Double-seated highchair. New England, 1810–1840. Original black paint splashed with red and with gilt decoration; footrest and front stretcher missing. Made entirely in birch except for the white pine seat. SW 24⅝", SD 11¾", SH 20½", OH 33¼". (Colonial Williamsburg)

opposed to the average seventeen inches. The legs are very well turned but they have been miniaturized and show no evidence of ever having been cut down. The construction and turnings are in the best Philadelphia tradition—indeed, the chair stylistically resembles examples made by Francis Trumble—which leads me to believe that the general distortion of the chair was no accident of an inept maker.

Similarly, the seat and back of figure 234 are the same width and height that one would expect in a full-size Philadelphia sack-back Windsor. This chair, I believe, was made by Joseph Henzey and bears comparison with figure 94. Like figure 233, figure 234 has a seat that is built close to the floor. Indeed, the arm supports of this interesting chair are longer than the legs, and the latter show no evidence of having been cut down. I believe that this chair was simply a special order, perhaps made to be a "slipper chair," that is, a chair used in the bedroom to change one's shoes.

And what of figure 233? It is a chair designed for a person with an almost normal torso but with stunted legs. My conclusion: figure 233 is a dwarf's chair!

231. Highchair. Probably New England, 1800–1820. Painted red. Crest rail, spindles, arms, arm supports, legs, and stretchers, maple; seat, pine. (Greenfield Village and Henry Ford Museum)

233. Side chair. Philadelphia, 1765–1780. Old black paint, over buff, over the original green. Crest rail, oak; back posts and spindles, hickory; legs and stretchers, maple; seat, pine. SW 17″, SD 15½″, SH 9½″, OH 27½″. (Privately owned)

234. Armchair. Philadelphia, 1765–1780. Late eighteenth-or early nineteenth-century black paint with yellow striping over the original salmon red. Crest rail, hickory or oak; spindles, hickory; arm rail, oak; arm supports, legs, and stretchers, maple; seat, poplar. SW 21¼″, SD 15¼″, SH 13¼″, OH 35″. (Privately owned)

176

CHAPTER TWELVE
Other Forms
of Windsor Furniture

AN "other form of Windsor furniture" is one that, while it is not a Windsor chair or settee, nevertheless incorporates the stylistic motifs and usually the construction methods of a Windsor chair or settee. For example, in this chapter we shall take a look at such objects as stools, tables, and cradles, all obviously Windsor in appearance and usually in construction as well, and many of them rather innovative.

Having mentioned all that, I shall begin this chapter with two pieces that do not strictly conform to my definition. Certainly figures 235 and 236 are Windsor chairs but with a definite difference: they both have extraordinary foot-operated fan contraptions attached to them.

Figure 237 shows a schematic drawing of such a Windsor "fan chair" along with a handwritten explanation of same. This drawing was accompanied by a letter dated July 31, 1786, from American artist and inventor Charles Willson Peale to Dr. Benjamin Rush. The letter reads, in part:

> Inclosed I send you a drawing of the Fan-Chair, which the very Ingenous [sic] Mr. [John] Cram (Musical Instrument Maker) Invented and made for me. The movement being simple and easy, I hope [the chair] will be found very useful to the studious and others that are obliged to sit at their employments, for while their hands are busily employed, a small motion of the foot, will move the Fan in such a manner, as to keep themselves cool, and with some cuttings of paper attached to the fan, will prevent the Flies from being troublesome. How far this simple machine may be conducive to the health of the Sedentary I leave to you who by Profession and Inclinations are lead [sic] to study and relieve the distresses of human nature.

As you might expect, Windsor fan chairs are exceptionally rare. Figure 235 is, with one minor exception (a single screw), in

235. Fan chair. Chair, Long Island, New York, 1780–1790. Fan apparatus, probably Philadelphia, after 1786. All original except for one replaced screw. Painted straw-color; fan decorated with gilt and paper cutouts. Fan, pasteboard; strap, leather; back support and treadle, pine; large dowel, yellow pine; treadle supports, walnut. Treadle L 34¼", OH 77½". (Also see color plate XIV.) (Olenka and Charles Santore)

236. (right) *Fan chair. Chair, Philadelphia, 1786–1790. Fan apparatus, probably Philadelphia, after 1786. Painted dark brown; fan, gilded and paint decorated. OH 77". (New Haven Colony Historical Society)*

237. (below) *Drawing of a fan chair with an explanation of the mechanism by Charles Willson Peale. Philadelphia, 1786. (American Philosophical Society Library)*

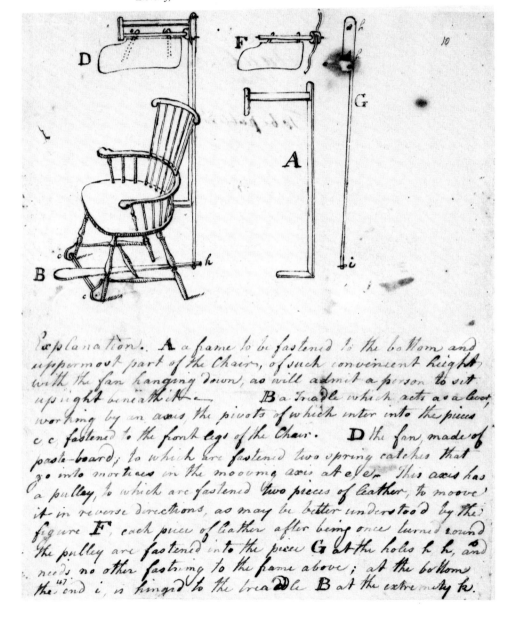

entirely original condition. A coat of straw-color paint was applied to the entire chair when the fan apparatus was attached. The chair has its original green paint under the straw paint (for a closer view of the chair, see figure 135). Apart from its appearance and the fact that it is in perfect condition, what is also remarkable about figure 235 is how similar it is to figure 236.

Of course, the two Windsor chairs themselves are different. One is a bow-back armchair from New York, the other a sack-back from Philadelphia. But the fan contraptions are virtually identical in every way except for their color, the decoration on the fans, and the fact that someone has added roundhead brads to the treadles of figure 236. Indeed, even the chairs have one interesting similarity: the front legs of both are rather thick where the protruding S-curve braces for the treadles are screwed into them. Figure 235 achieves this thickness because the legs are in the English style and not tapered; figure 236 achieves it because the legs have purposely been turned without a taper where one would normally expect it (compare with figure 144). In any case the effect is the same. Because the front legs are thick where the

screws pass through them, they are less likely to crack at that point than conventional tapered legs.

What does all this mean? First, of course, that the chairs were purposely selected, or purposely made, for the attachment of a fan contraption. But the chairs are, in fact, stylistically different from each other while the fans are the same. For that reason I speculate that, although the chairs were made in two different regions, the *fans* were made in the same place, that is, Philadelphia, home of inventor John Cram, mentioned in Peale's letter. In fact, I think that Cram, who was not a chairmaker, but a musical instrument maker, probably made the fan contraptions himself, perhaps as kits. Cram could then have shipped the kit to the buyer, or the buyer could have purchased the kit while in Philadelphia. Later, the buyer could paint and decorate the chair and fan in any way he chose, which accounts for the differences in decoration and color of the two fans.

Now we shall move on to other forms of Windsor furniture that better fit my definition. Windsor tall stools with baluster-and-ring turnings such as the one shown in figure 238 are very rare.

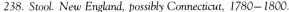

238. Stool. New England, possibly Connecticut, 1780–1800.

239. Tall stool. Probably New England, 1800–1815. Branded W. C. P. Traces of the original red paint. Legs, maple; stretchers, hickory; seat, pine. Seat 16½″ × 14¾″, OH 27¾″. (Mr. and Mrs. R. W. P. Allen)

179

On this particular piece the turnings are somewhat simplified, so it was probably made during the 1780 to 1800 period. One would be more likely to find a bamboo-turned Windsor stool like figure 239, but they are by no means common, especially tall stools that are as well-proportioned and well-turned as this one. The beading on the seat surface is a nice touch. Figure 240 is a tall stool that is unusual for its three legs, staggered stretcher arrangement, and footrest. The footrest is reminiscent of Windsor highchairs, but this stool was probably used by a clerk who sat at a high desk. The surface of the footrest is nicely worn.

Windsor footstools are more common than tall stools, but not those of the quality and early date of figure 241. This is a very well turned piece, much better, for example, than figure 238. Figure 242 is unusual for its English-style turnings, rather like those of the legs of figure 135, for example. This footstool shows no evidence of ever having been painted or stained. The legs are darker in color than the top from natural exposure. The top itself has tack holes around the flat edge. Furthermore, the bottom

241. (above) Footstool. New England, 1760–1790. Traces of black paint. Top, pine; legs and stretchers, maple. Top diameter 11″, OH 11″. (Phyllis and Louis Gross)

242. (below) Footstool. American, 1760–1790. Top, pine; legs, maple. Top 9½″ × 10″, OH 8½″. (Privately owned)

240. Tall stool. Philadelphia, 1790–1810. Stained dark brown. Foot rest, pine; legs and stretchers, maple; seat, poplar. Seat diameter 15″, OH 30¾″. (Independence National Historical Park)

surface of the top is slightly darker in color than the upper surface. All that is evidence that the upper surface of the top was always upholstered.

Figures 243 through 247 are a series of bamboo-turned footstools. Figure 243 is desirable for several reasons. First, it is nicely turned. The comparatively elaborate beading on the edge of the seat is attractive and shows that the seat was turned on a lathe. An especially desirable feature is the painted decoration. It is gray and black and in a style called *smoke decoration*, occasionally used on furniture of the nineteenth century. The effect is achieved by holding a freshly painted piece over a smoking candle. An interesting construction feature of this stool is a three and one-quarter inch batten, visible at the front edge of the top, that is inserted in a slot under the top. The batten runs perpendicular to the grain

of the top and was inserted before the top was turned, as is evidenced by the fact that the beading on the edge of the top continues across the edge of the batten.

It is very unusual to find such a matched pair of Windsor footstools as are shown in figure 244. They are quite well turned and have nicely dished tops. In addition these stools are important because, as Dean F. Failey has pointed out, they "bear the conjoined *HPD* brand (see figure 244A) of their original owner, Henry Packer Dering (1763-1822), first customs officer and postmaster of Sag Habor. . . . These stools were undoubtedly made in one of the several chair-making or cabinetmaking establishments in Sag Harbor."[29]

Figures 245 through 247 show a bit more of the variety of bamboo-turned Windsor stools. The box stretcher examples are

243. Footstool. Pennsylvania, 1780–1820. Original gray and black paint. Top, poplar; legs, maple. Top diameter 11½", OH 12½". (Privately owned)

244. *Pair of footstools. Long Island, New York, probably Sag Harbor, 1800–1820. Branded HPD [Henry Packer Dering]. Top diameter 12¼", OH 12⅝". (Society for the Preservation of Long Island Antiquities)*

244A. *Pair of footstools. Detail showing owner's initials.*

245. (above) Footstool. Philadelphia, 1780–1800. Old black paint over the original red. Top, poplar. Top 10″ × 11″, OH 10¼″. (Leon Stark.)

247. Footstool. Possibly Pennsylvania, 1790–1810. Top, poplar; legs, chestnut and maple; stretchers, maple. Top 10½″ × 11″, OH 10¾″. (Mr. and Mrs. R. W. P. Allen)

246. (below) Footstool. Pennsylvania, 1800–1820. Nineteenth-century dark red paint over the original green. Top, poplar; legs, maple. Top 9½″ × 15″, OH 11½″. (Privately owned)

probably later than figure 245. Figure 246 has an especially nice oval top that is well-chamfered to a sharp edge and is beaded about an inch in from the edge (see figure 160). Figure 247 is a square-top example.

A very unusual folding campstool with a linen seat is shown in figure 248. Although this piece is necessarily constructed differently from the stools shown thus far, it nonetheless retains a Windsor quality in the shape of its legs. On the top of the seat, the name *F. Tuckerman* is lettered in ink, adding interest to the piece.

Of all American Windsor furniture, tables and stands are the rarest. Figure 249 shows a type of table that is often called a "Windsor" table. How such tables acquired their Windsor label I do not know, since there is nothing particularly Windsorlike about them. Distinctly non-Windsor features of such tables include their turning patterns, their rodlike stretchers, and their lack of leg splay. Furthermore, the construction method used in these tables and their general style are far more like that of rush-bottom chairs being made during most of the eighteenth century than that of Windsor chairs.

Perhaps someone will think up a better name for these attrac-

248. (above) *Camp stool. Possibly Pennsylvania, 1800–1825. Seat signed "F. Tuckerman." Maple and linen. SW 11", OH 10¾". (Privately owned)*

249. (below) *Table. New England, possibly New Hampshire, 1775–1800. Top, pine; legs, pine; stretchers, ash. Top 18⅜" × 25¼", H 28½". (Privately owned)*

250. *Table. Pennsylvania, probably Philadelphia, 1760–1780. Original dark green paint. Top, pine; legs and stretchers, hickory or ash. Top 23" × 23½", OH 26¾". (David Pottinger)*

tive and rare tables (chairmakers' or turners' tables?). Until then, let's stop calling them Windsor tables.

I have seen examples of real Windsor tables and stands made entirely of walnut, or mahogany, or maple, or curly maple, as well as of a combination of woods. The two basic construction methods used in these tables are legs that penetrate the top and are wedged from above, as in a Windsor chair, or a triangular batten nailed or screwed to the underside of the top into which the legs are socketed.

Figure 250 shows a Windsor table with the latter construction method; figure 251, the former. Both have fine Philadelphia Windsor turnings. Note, too, that the stretchers are staggered so that the socket holes will not weaken the legs. Figure 252 is another Philadelphia Windsor table, this one with a dished top. Perhaps this piece falls more into the category of a candlestand. Certainly figure 253 does. This exquisite piece comes about as close to high-style furniture as Windsor furniture ever does. The legs are gracefully turned, and the dished top with its molded and rounded edge is as beautifully realized as the base. This candlestand is made entirely of mahogany, and the stretchers are pinned to the legs with wooden pegs. Almost all of the tripod stands and

251. (left) *Table. Philadelphia, 1765–1790. Traces of green paint. Top poplar; legs, hickory; stretchers, maple. Top 23¼″ × 24⅜″, OH 24½″. (The Metropolitan Museum of Art; gift of Mrs. J. Insley Blair, 1947)*

252. (above) *Table. Philadelphia, 1765–1790.*

tables from this early period that I have seen are, I feel, Philadelphia pieces despite the fact that many of them were found in Chester County. Wealthy Philadelphia Quaker families had country homes in Chester County, and later settled there.

The table in figure 254 is from a later period but nevertheless is Windsor in concept. Note the double-bobbin leg turnings and the double scoring near the tops of the legs, the latter feature echoing the beading on the lower edge of the apron. Those features combined with the leg splay make this a piece of Windsor furniture. As for construction details, the top and the legs are pinned to the apron with wooden pegs. This is a very good, late piece and a comparatively rare one.

Windsor cradles are a refreshing change from the coffinlike form of conventional cradles. Lying in a Windsor cradle, an infant would no doubt have better air circulation, and the child's parents would be better able to keep an eye on him since no part

253. *Candlestand. Pennsylvania, 1770–1790. Made entirely of mahogany. Top 10″ × 10⅜″, OH 26⅜″. (Mr. and Mrs. R. W. P. Allen)*

254. *Table. Pennsylvania, 1790–1810. Dark brown stain over original red paint. Made entirely of poplar. Top 18¾″ × 21″, OH 28¼″. (Barbara and Eugene Pettenelli)*

255. *Cradle. Philadelphia, 1780–1800. Made entirely of mahogany except for the pine bottom, which is framed in mahogany. 13″ × 36½″, foot H 17⅞″, head H 27″. (Stenton Mansion)*

256. *Cradle. Pennsylvania, 1790–1810. Made entirely of mahogany; three hood spindles replaced. 20¼″ × 44¼″, foot height 19¼″, head height 30¾″. (Robert Stewart)*

of the cradle would block their view of the interior. All of the Windsor cradles I have seen seem to be from the late eighteenth and early nineteenth centuries. Perhaps earlier Windsor cradles exist. If they do, they would be even rarer than the already uncommon later cradles.

Figures 255 through 257 show three Windsor cradles that, in their conventional form, would be called hooded cradles. Except for its pine bottom, figure 255 is entirely mahogany. The Sheraton influence is evident on this lovely piece in the molded rails forming the terminus of the spindles of the front, sides, and top; the general form resembles the back of the Windsor chair in figure 159. Figure 256 is similar to the preceding, but the bold arch of the hood is more in keeping with the design of the foot and accentuates the height of the piece. However, when compared with those of figure 255, the moldings of figure 256 appear too heavy and thick, and the rockers are less refined. The spindles of figure 256 are interesting in that they taper from bottom to top, but they, too, are thick and the overall feeling is one of less airiness. Both are fine and rare pieces, but perhaps each could have "learned" something from the other.

187

257. Cradle. Philadelphia, 1790–1810. Branded I. [John] LETCH-
WORTH. Original brown paint. All bent parts, hickory; spindles, maple;
bottom, pine framed in walnut; rockers, oak. 17¼″ × 39½″, OH 19¾″.
(Chester County Historical Society)

258. Cradle. Probably New England, 1800–1820. Painted green. Hickory, maple, and pine. L 40¾". (Greenfield Village and Henry Ford Museum)

The bottom of figure 257 is branded by John Letchworth. This is a remarkably innovative design in which all of the rails are formed by steam-bent pieces of hickory. As in figure 255, the bottom is composed of a single board that is framed, in this case with walnut. The shape of the rockers of the two pieces is also quite similar.

Figures 258 and 259 show two cradles in a different, low-sided style. Figure 258 is very well turned, with bamboo ringing all around and the same birdcage style at the head that we have already seen on many rod-back Windsors. The bottom is a single, scooped-out pine board. Figure 259 is the more graceful of the two. Apart from the handsome finials, one of the most attractive features of this piece is that it retains the molded edges and H-stretcher pattern of the Windsor chair. Once again, the bottom is a single pine board.

259. Cradle. Pennsylvania, 1780–1810. Refinished. Crest rails, legs, medial stretcher, and rockers, chestnut; corner posts, ash; spindles, hickory; side stretchers, maple. 11½" × 33", OH 24". (Privately owned)

Figure 260 is quite different in that its ends are both identically rounded, and it is tall enough to be rocked by someone sitting in a nearby chair. The legs have a distinctly English design feeling, and the piece is probably from New England.

Figure 261 is certainly one of the most unusual Windsor forms, and I have never before seen anything quite like it. It seems to be a drying stand or cloth rack of some sort. It is quite a small piece. The horizontal spindles are thicker on one end and taper to a pencil thinness at the other. To me, this strongly suggests that these spindles were actually existing chair spindles that were used on this piece by the maker instead of on a chair. Although this may be a cloth rack, the spindles show no wear on their original paint, which would have been the result of hanging and removing cloth or fiber over a long period of time. And so I shall have to end the main chapters of this book on a note of mystery.

260. (left) Cradle. Probably New England, 1780–1810. Top rail and stretchers, hickory; spindles and legs, maple; bottom, pine. (Greenfield Village and Henry Ford Museum)

261. (above) Rack. American, 1800–1825. Original blackish green paint. Spindles, uprights, and legs, hickory; base, poplar. L 15¼", OH 29½". (The Bohn's)

CHAPTER THIRTEEN
Questions and Answers about Windsor Furniture

THE FOLLOWING are my responses to questions frequently asked about Windsor furniture. It is my hope that this appendix will help to clear up any points of confusion you may have about the pieces illustrated in this book and similar pieces that you may run across.

Q. How does one date a Windsor chair?
A. By its latest stylistic feature. This is a matter that I have discussed at length throughout all the chapters of this book.

Q. Is a nine-spindle Windsor chair better than a seven-spindle Windsor?
A. First, let me explain what we mean when we speak of nine- and seven-spindle Windsors. This refers to the number of long spindles in the back of a given chair. The number of spindles does not in and of itself determine the quality of a Windsor. Indeed, some fine Windsors have six or eight spindles in their backs. What is important is how the spindles are spaced in relation to themselves and to the other parts of the chair, especially the seat. For example, a small seat with too many spindles may look like a mouth with too many teeth. Furthermore, the quality of a Windsor does not depend on any single feature such as the spindles. Quality is a function of how well each part is executed, how well the parts relate to each other, and how well the chair as a whole is constructed.

Q. Are brace-back Windsors more desirable than those without braced backs?
A. Given two Windsors of similar design, one braced and one not, the braced chair will usually be more desirable because of the added design interest in its back and because brace-back Windsors are rarer.

Q. Is a signed, labeled, or branded Windsor more desirable than an anonymous chair?
A. That depends. To museums, curators, and collectors who specialize in regional furniture or who collect the work of a particular craftsman, signed Windsors have top priority. But as far as I am concerned, the design quality and the paint surface of a chair are more important factors. Obviously, if you have the choice between two Windsors of the same style and quality, and one is branded or labeled, you should choose the branded example even if it is more costly. However, if you are offered two Windsors priced the same and of the same style, and one is branded but weaker in design, then the more beautiful, anonymous chair should be your choice.

Q. Are baluster-and-ring turned Windsors more desirable than those with bamboo turnings?
A. Generally speaking, yes. The former were made during the golden age of American Windsor craftsmanship and they exhibit a definite eighteenth-century design. The simpler bamboo-turned chairs are often the product of stepped-up manufacturing and shortcuts in craftsmanship. There are exceptions, of course, as I have discussed in the text, but on the whole the chairs in the earlier style are more highly valued.

Q. Were Windsor chairs made in sets?
A. Yes. Some late eighteenth-century bills of sale and account books list sets of chairs. Judging from the prices charged, these were usually side chairs. Sets of late eighteenth- and early nineteenth-century Windsors occasionally turn up for sale. But one must make certain that these are true sets of identical chairs and not assembled sets of nearly identical chairs, assuming that one is paying the price for an authentic set.

Q. Were Windsors always painted?
A. Almost always. But I have seen Windsors that never had a coat of paint or even varnish. And there is evidence in shipping orders and in bills for Windsors sold "in the white," that is, unfinished and ready to be painted by the customer.

Q. Should a refinished Windsor be repainted?
A. Usually a Windsor that was stripped of its paint in the 1920s and 1930s and was finished with shellac or varnish has by now mellowed to a pleasing color. Such a chair is better left alone.
Most chairs were stripped and refinished when a broken part was replaced. The advantage of leaving such a chair alone is that

it is easier to see any problems the chair might have. It is also easier to determine if the chair is entirely original. Once a chair has been repainted, the age of the chair, or parts of the chair, may be completely obscured. From the antiquarian's and the collector's point of view, the value of a repainted chair will have been diminished, and such a chair may arouse questions about why it was repainted in the first place, even if the original intentions were honorable. For those reasons, I never repaint a Windsor that has been refinished.

Q. If a Windsor with baluster-and-ring turned parts also has bamboo turnings, is that a reason to suspect replacements?
A. No. As I have mentioned in the text, many Windsors of the 1780s and 1790s have parts turned in more than one style. Generally this was done in an attempt to make the chairs fashionable or, perhaps in an attempt to utilize existing chair parts at a time when new patterns were being introduced. The most obvious sign of a replaced part is when, for example, just *one* side stretcher or *one* arm support is bamboo-turned.

Q. Are the seats of Windsor chairs always made from a single board? What about the seats of settees?
A. In almost all period Windsors the seats are made from a single board. But I have seen a handful of chairs that are unmistakably original in which the seat was made from two pieces of wood, mortised-and-tenoned together and then saddled and shaped. As for settees, every one that I have seen has had a seat made from a single board.

Q. Do all authentic Windsors have definite plane marks on the undersides of their seats?
A. No. On all the Windsors I have seen from the 1750s and 1760s, plane marks are clearly visible (and can be felt) on the undersides of the seats. However, the seats of many New England Windsors of the 1770s and 1780s were cut from planks and show little or no marks of the plane. That applies doubly to late chairs in the bamboo-turned style.

Q. Are Windsor seats always made of pine or poplar?
A. No. I have seen seats made of such diverse woods as oak, maple, chestnut, walnut, basswood, and butternut, to name a few. Nonetheless, the majority of the seats of American Windsors are made of pine or poplar.

Q. Is a pine seat an indication of New England origin and a poplar seat of Pennsylvania origin?

A. No. Although the majority of New England Windsors have pine seats and the majority of Pennsylvania Windsors poplar, both woods were used in both regions.

Q. Are such turned parts of Windsors as the legs, stretchers, and arm supports always made from the same wood?
A. No. On most Windsors they are, but I have seen many (some of them shown in this book) that are all original but that have legs of maple and another wood such as oak or birch; and the stretchers may be chestnut or hickory. There is really no hard-and-fast rule about this, but I would estimate that about fifty percent of the chairs made during the 1740 to 1780 period, especially in urban areas, have turnings made of the same wood. On later chairs, as production methods became standardized, the likelihood increases to eighty or ninety percent that the turnings will be made of the same wood.

Q. Were nails used in the construction of Windsors?
A. Not in the joints of Windsors. But it is not unusual to find nails used to fasten the handholds of Windsors to the ends of the arms. In some New England fan-back armchairs the arms are fastened to the back posts with large nails driven in from behind.

Q. Does one ever find a Windsor chair whose spindles seem to have been shaved at the top to fit into the crest rail?
A. Yes. I have, on occasion, seen all-original Windsors in which the tops of the spindles were shaved, as opposed to running smoothly into the crest rail. This should be a cause for concern only if there is additional evidence that the crest rail has been replaced by a new crest rail, or if there is evidence that the original crest rail has been removed and then replaced, perhaps because the original spindles broke off at the top and, because of their taper, had to be shaved down to fit into the holes in the original crest rail.

Q. Why are so many Windsors found with legs that have been cut down?
A. This is really a function of rapidly changing nineteenth-century fashion trends. As the popularity of Windsors waned (to be revived, of course, in the early twentieth century), the chairs were relegated to the position of second-class citizens. The chairs were cut down so that they could be used as slipper chairs in bedrooms, so that children could use them, or so that they could be turned into rocking chairs. Sometimes they were simply left in barns or dirt-floor basements, where their feet rotted off. Later, the rotted wood was cut off, and the legs appear today to have

been purposely cut down. Finally, Windsors are found today with the rear legs cut down but the front legs intact; this was probably done for the sake of comfort. The chair leans back like a lounge chair.

Q. How can one determine if the legs of a Windsor have been pieced, or ended, out?

A. That is not always easy to do. If the chair has been stripped, and the legs have been pieced out, it should be obvious where the new wood begins; its color and grain quality will be different. Even if the new parts have been painted, one should be able to see the break in the leg through the paint. However, sometimes a clever craftsman will replace the entire leg taper of the chair and hide the break in the turning, so that it is not immediately apparent. If the chair is then repainted, it may be almost impossible to detect the repair. There will be several points to check. First, you should be aware of the fact that wood shrinks across its grain as it ages; as a result, the originally round (in cross-section) turnings on a Windsor will have become ovoid with time. But the new feet will still be round. Some experts use calipers to check for differences in roundness in the turnings of early furniture. Second, check the paint history of the legs to see if it jibes with that of the rest of the chair. Third, check to see if the wear on the bottoms of the feet is identical; if not, one or more legs may have been pieced out. Of course, if all the legs have been pieced out, they will have more or less the same appearance. Fourth, check to see if the bottoms and tops of the legs line up properly. Fifth, check to see if the tool marks left by the turner's chisels are apparent on both the bottoms and tops of the legs; these marks will appear as a series of spiral grooves, which are often quite evident on the turnings of Windsor furniture. Finally, the grain of the wood should be consistent, and be able to be traced from the top of the leg to the bottom.

Q. Should I purchase a Windsor that has been extensively restored?

A. No. Of course, some restoration is acceptable in a chair that is 200 years old or more. For example, one new leg, a few new spindles, a new knuckle or stretcher, or even two new stretchers might be acceptable depending on the price, age, and rarity of the chair. But a chair with an entirely new undercarriage, or a new seat, or new back spindles and a crest rail is not acceptable. Ask yourself the question: is the chair an old one with a few restored parts, or is it a new chair with a few early parts? In the latter case you may be better off purchasing a good reproduction.

Q. How much does a potty-seat cutout detract from an otherwise good chair?

A. Of all the various problems a period Windsor can be plagued with—such as broken or replaced legs, stretchers, spindles, crest rail, or knuckles—a potty seat is the least serious. For if the potty seat is, or has been, repaired properly, that is, if the original contours of the seat are retained, the design of the chair will be in no way compromised.

Q. What is the best way to restore a potty seat?

A. Basically, there is only one proper way to restore a potty seat without diminishing the value of the chair, and that is to fill the potty-seat hole and only the hole. This should be done with a round or square piece of wood that is as close to the size of the hole as possible and that leaves as much of the original seat intact as possible. The wood should be the same type as that of the seat, of approximately the same thickness, and the grain should run in the same direction as that of the seat.

The wrong way to restore a potty seat is to cut out the middle section of the seat from left to right, completely across the width of the diameter of the hole. This method is often used because the repair is almost invisible. But twice as much of the original seat must be eliminated as you are attempting to replace; and the seat is that much less original. Furthermore, while lowering the value of the chair, this method has the disadvantage of being more time consuming and expensive, usually requiring the restorer to work with the spindles on each side of the seat and then to reshape the contours on both sides.

Q. Should a broken leg, stretcher, or arm support be replaced on a period Windsor, or should it be repaired?

A. Preferably, the latter. The rule is always to save as much of the original chair as possible, and that means repairing parts not replacing them.

Q. Along these same lines, when is it worthwhile to purchase a Windsor that needs restoration?

A. That is a complex question with no easy answer. Whether or not it is worthwhile to purchase a Windsor that needs restoration depends on several interrelated factors, primarily: the inherent value of the chair as is; the extent of the necessary restorations; the cost of these restorations; and the value of the chair after the restorations compared with a similar chair that needs no restorations.

For example, figure 262 shows a very fine writing-arm chair that is branded by Ebenezer Tracy. For many years I had seen similar Tracy chairs and noted that the spindles penetrated the

arm crest. That was unique to my experience, and I thought these chairs were certainly comb-backs on which the combs had broken off. Finally I examined one of these Tracy chairs very closely: I discovered that the paint on the arm crest, around and in the spindle holes, was identical in color and quality to the paint on the rest of the chair, and that the spindles that penetrated the arm crest were correctly wedged and were in original condition. Apparently Tracy, and perhaps a few other makers, made low-backs with spindles that penetrated the arm crest. Had I owned the chair, and had I been rash enough to "restore" the comb, I would later have discovered that I had made a costly and foolish error.

But suppose for a moment that the chair in figure 262 is in fact a cut-down comb-back. Is the chair worth purchasing? Most assuredly. It is an exceptionally good chair, with or without the comb, and would undoubtedly be quite expensive. Should we restore the comb? I wouldn't. Even if the chair were a cut-down comb-back, it now looks exactly like Tracy's other low-back writing-arm chairs. Furthermore, only the most ingenious crafts-person could restore this chair to its original appearance. In short, I would leave well enough very much alone.

Now look at the chair in figure 263. The bow is broken and three spindles are missing. Is this chair worth purchasing and restoring? In my opinion, yes—with the important provisos that the chair did not cost much to begin with (it did not); that the work will be done by someone who knows what he is doing; and that the total cost of the chair plus the restoration will be quite a bit less than the cost of such a chair in all-original condition. I feel that the expense is justified because the chair has fine turnings, a very well-shaped seat, and its original gray paint under the white.

What about the chair in figure 264? This is a good example of a Windsor that, except for the fact that it is branded, is of little value to the collector, restored or not. The chair simply has too many problems to correct, and the expense of doing so would far exceed the value of the chair. One leg and one spindle are replacements; all four legs have been cut down so that the stretchers almost rest on the floor; the seat is split; and the finish is gone. Such bamboo-turned bow-back side chairs were made in great numbers at the end of the eighteenth century and are not difficult to find. Unless you are going to use this chair exactly as it is, you would be better off purchasing a similar chair in better condition.

Q. How can one guard against purchasing a fake or reproduction Windsor chair sold as authentic?

A. There is only one way, and that is to know what an authentic Windsor looks like with respect to age and style.

Check to see if the chair is constructed in a method consistent with early craftsmanship. Are there tool marks where one would expect to find them, especially on the turnings? Is the seat made in one piece (it almost always is on authentic Windsors)? Are there any modern nails? Are wedge joints or mortise-and-tenon joints used in the proper places? Do similar turned parts exhibit variations in size and shape because of hand craftsmanship? Is the chair worn in a logical way? For example, do the handholds and feet show wear from use? Are the turned parts out of round because of shrinkage? Similarly, if the chair is a comb-back or a fan-back, can you feel the bulges of the spindles where they come through the crest rail as you run your fingers along either edge, this also because of shrinkage? Does the surface as a whole look properly worn? Has old paint been faked? Has the chair really been stripped of its paint, or was the *original* finish simply varnish or shellac, a possible indication of a reproduction? The list of such questions could go on, but I think you get the idea.

As for style, certain twentieth-century quirks almost always creep into the design of fake or reproduction Windsors, and you must be alert to such quirks. For example, consider the two chairs

264. Side chair. Philadelphia, 1780–1800. Branded F.[rancis] TRUMBLE. (See text for condition.) (Privately owned)

195

in figures 265 and 266. Both were made in the early twentieth century, and stylistically both are quite incorrect (compare them with such authentic pieces as figures 20 and 223. On figure 265, the crest rail is rounded along the upper front edge, a feature not found on authentic early Pennsylvania Windsors. Also incorrect are the tapered short spindles beneath the arms; the tapered long spindles; leg turnings that are far too precise and voluptuous; and a seat that is too rounded on its outer edges for an early chair with a Queen Anne medial stretcher. Figure 266 suffers from similar problems: the crest rail is rounded on its upper front edge; the spindles all taper; the seat is incorrectly shaped along its chamfered front edge (it should be flat); and the balusters of the leg turnings are exaggerated (however, the arms supports and the medial stretcher are well-done). Neither chair shows any early tool marks on the turnings, and the turnings are too precisely identical to each other. The crest rail of neither chair shows any signs of shrinkage, nor do the turnings. By the way figure 266 is a Wallace Nutting reproduction that was advertised in Nutting's 1930 catalogue; and the old paint surface has been rather poorly faked on this chair, and the Nutting label has been removed from the underside of the seat. The chair was in fact once sold and purchased as an authentic piece of eighteenth-century American furniture.

265. (above) Armchair, modern. Original reddish brown stain. Crest rail, chestnut; spindles, maple; arm rail, oak; arm supports, seat, legs, and stretchers, birch. SW 24½″, SD 17½″, SH 17″, OH 45¼″. (John and Joanne Conti)

266. (right) Highchair, modern. Made by Wallace Nutting (label removed); advertised 1927. Painted green. Crest rail, spindles, and arm rail, hickory; arm supports, legs, and stretchers, maple; seat, pine. SW 15″, SD 10½″, SH 22″, OH 41″. (Privately owned)

APPENDIX I:
THE CONSTRUCTION
OF WINDSOR CHAIRS

Throughout the chapters of this book I have mentioned various construction methods used in the making of Windsor furniture. Here I present, in condensed form, some additional information on the subject, intended primarily for those of you who have some knowledge of furniture construction. Entire books and sections of books have been written on the construction of early American furniture, and I do not wish to rehash the entire subject here. For a good, general treatise, see Moreton Marsh, *The Easy Expert in American Antiques* (New York: J.B. Lippincott, 1978).

Additional information on Windsor construction is provided in question-and-answer form in chapter thirteen of this book. Data about the different woods used in the various parts of Windsors is given within the captions for the illustrations herein.

Seats. The seat of a Windsor chair is almost always made from a single, originally unseasoned board about two inches thick. The board has either been riven from a log or cut into a plank from a log. It was then further cut, planed, shaved, carved, and smoothed to the proper shape. Seat woods are usually relatively soft, easily worked varieties such as pine, poplar, or chestnut. When harder woods such as maple are found, the entire chair is often made in that wood. Holes were drilled partway or, more often in the early period, all the way through the seat to accept the legs, back posts, and arm supports; the holes for the spindles usually do not penetrate the seat.

Legs, stretchers, back posts, arm supports, and spindles. These parts are usually turned on a lathe. However, it is not unusual to find early Windsors with spoke-shaved spindles. The stretchers are socketed into each other and into the legs; on rare occasions the stretchers are also pinned to the legs and to each other with hardwood pegs. The socket holes in the legs and stretchers are formed by a bit with a rounded nose; consequently, the interior of the hole on authentic Windsors will have a rounded end (figure 267). Sometimes a special sort of bit was used that could cut a hole that is wider on the inside than on the outside. The ends of the stretchers were then turned with a flaring shape, and when the stretchers were pounded into the legs and each other, the joint formed was extremely tight.

More often than not, the legs of Windsors penetrate the seat through holes drilled about three or four inches in from the seat's outer edge. The legs are held fast in the following way: a split is cut in the top of each leg, and a hardwood wedge is driven partway into the split; the tops of the legs are then worked into the holes in the seat, and, when the legs are properly aligned, the protruding hardwood wedges are driven home, flush with the top of the seat. The effect of this is to expand the tops of the legs in the seat, making for a tight joint. Two other points about this method of construction should be made. First, the wedges were aligned to be more or less at right angles to the direction of the grain of the seat wood; the effect of this was to exert tremendous pressure on the seat wood around the wedged joint without splitting the wood along the grain. Second, because the seat was made

267. *Cutaway view of a late Windsor-chair leg showing the interior of a stretcher hole made with a round-nose pod bit. Twentieth-century reproduction Windsors usually have holes drilled with high-speed bits, which leave flat ends.*

of unseasoned wood and the legs were not, the seat would tend to shrink as the wood dried out, thus holding the legs even tighter.

On some Windsors, usually those with hardwood seats, the legs do not penetrate the seat. In that case they are merely socketed into the seat and sometimes glued. In the past some writers have mentioned a joining method that utilizes what is called a *blind*, or *fox*, wedge. In this construction the wedge was supposedly driven partway into a split in the tops of the legs, and, when the legs were pounded home and forced against the base of the hole, the wedge was automatically driven into the tops of the legs, expanding them and holding them fast. However, I have never seen such a blind-wedge joint used on any Windsor—either in the seat or in the stretchers—and that makes me doubt the existence of such a joint. Furthermore, I have discussed the subject of blind joints in Windsors with four master craftsmen: Michael Dunbar, Robert Whitley, Allen Miller, and Howard Szmolko, and an expert dealer-collector, Roy Allen. Their experience in repairing, restoring, and creating Windsors totals about seventy years. None of them has ever seen a blind joint used on any part of a Windsor.

The back posts and arm supports of Windsors usually penetrate the seat. They are then wedged from below in the manner of the legs. Sometimes the base of the arm supports or back posts may be pinned through the side of the seat with wooden pegs.

With the exception of fan-backs and comb-backs, at least a few of the spindles of any Windsor chair are either wedged from the top where they penetrate the arm rail or crest rail, or they are pinned through the side of the seat and the arm rail (as, for example, in certain Rhode Island low-back and fan-back chairs). If the chair is a low-back with an arm crest, the spindles do not penetrate the arm crest; if they do, the chair is almost certainly a comb-back with its comb cut off. The one exception to this rule that I have seen are low-back writing-arm chairs made by Ebenezer Tracy, in which the spindles do penetrate the arm crest and are wedged from the top.

The spindles on certain early Windsors, such as Pennsylvania comb-backs, were formed with a spokeshave. However, on the majority of Windsors the spindles were formed on a lathe. Unless the spindles are quite thick, they are usually made from a wood with high tensile strength, such as hickory.

Arms. Chairs with thin arm rails—comb-backs, sack-backs, and continuous-arm chairs—have steam-bent arms. With the exception of continuous-arm chairs all other styles of Windsors may also have sawed arms. The arms are attached to the arm supports with either wedge joints or with wooden pegs. They are attached to the back of the chair in the same manner or with nails. Generally speaking, the handholds are formed from one or two extra pieces of wood nailed or pinned to the ends of the arms.

Crest rails. Bowed crest rails are mortised into the arm rail or seat and are then wedged from below or held fast with wooden pegs. In the crest rails of comb-back and fan-back chairs the spindles are socketed into the crest rails part-way. The crest rails are then almost always held fast with at least two wooden pegs, attached through the crest to secure the outer spindles on each side.

APPENDIX II:
THE RE-CREATION OF THOMAS JEFFERSON'S
SWIVEL WINDSOR

Shown in figure 268 is a re-creation of the swivel Windsor chair in which Thomas Jefferson is said to have composed the first draft of the Declaration of Independence while living at the house of Jacob Graff in Philadelphia in 1776. The original chair, greatly altered, is shown in figure 3. The latter descended to Jefferson's daughter, Martha Jefferson Randolph. In 1836 she gave the chair to Judge J. K. Kane, who in 1838 donated it to the American Philosophical Society in Philadelphia.

It is quite possible that this swivel Windsor was made to Jefferson's specifications while he was in Philadelphia. Later he had it shipped to Monticello, where he used it in his bedroom chaise-lounge-style in combination with a bamboo-turned Windsor couch, which was in turn spanned by a writing table with a rotating top. Jefferson used this three-piece writing arrangement to relieve pressure on his rheumatic back.

I first became involved with the original swivel Windsor when Charles G. Dorman, a curator at Independence National Historical Park, asked me to examine it for a planned re-creation of the chair to be used in the re-created Graff House in Philadelphia. From my examination of the original chair, I was able to determine several things. First, the seat of the original chair is absolutely round and shows no evidence of legs ever having been attached to it. That led to the obvious conclusion that the chair had always been a swivel chair; the chair rotates on a central iron spindle and on rollers made of window-sash pulleys set in a groove between the two seats. Second, the writing paddle is a later addition, made in a style consistent with the mid- to late 1830s, about the time the chair was given to the American Philosophical Society by Judge Kane. Further evidence that the writing paddle is an addition was found in the fact that the arm supports of the original chair had been moved back one space on each side and that the arms had been appropriately shortened in the back. This was done on the left-hand side to allow space at the front of the chair for the additional writing-paddle supports and, on the right-hand side, to allow room for someone to climb into the chair in the first place.

The base, however, is another story. The alterations here were probably made soon after the chair arrived at Monticello, and, indeed, the base is entirely new. Whether the original base had been lost or destroyed I do not know. In any case a new base had to be made for the swivel Windsor. Furthermore, the new base had to be made to an appropriate height so that the swivel chair could butt up against the Windsor couch, whose end is cut in a semicircle to accept the round edge of the chair seat, and the legs had to match, stylistically, those of the couch.

It was my opinion that the new base for the original chair had been made from an existing bamboo-turned Windsor chair, probably one already at Monticello. The seat had been cut off of this bamboo Windsor chair, and the tops of the legs were then attached to a new, round, secondary seat on which the upper seat could swivel. Because of the increased height

268. (above) *Swivel armchair, modern. Painted black. Designed by the author; made by Robert Whitley.*

269. (above right) *Sketch of the Thomas Jefferson swivel Windsor as it probably looked originally.*

of the added seat, on this new base the *tops* of the legs had been cut down considerably before the round secondary seat was attached, and this seat was quite flat. Indeed, the chair you see in figure 3 has had the *tops* of the legs restored two and three-quarter inches; but the chair used to be that much shorter so that it could be used with the Windsor couch, and so there would be room for Jefferson to fit under the table as he wrote.

I felt that the re-created Jefferson swivel chair should have a base that was stylistically consistent with other fine Philadelphia comb-back Windsors of the 1770s. And so, while Charles Dorman waited in my studio, I made a rough sketch of the way I thought the chair originally looked—with a new base in the Philadelphia style, the arm supports returned to their original position, and the writing paddle eliminated (figure 269). Master craftsman Robert Whitley made the re-creation shown in figure 268, and the chair is now in the re-created Graff House. I think the new Jefferson swivel Windsor is quite successful and probably faithful to the original design.

APPENDIX III:
THE BRANDS OF EBENEZER TRACY

In the past it has been suggested by various writers that there were two Windsor makers with the surname Tracy working in Connecticut: Ebenezer Tracy and Elisha Tracy. The former, it was said, branded his chairs *EB: TRACY,* while the latter used the brand *E. TRACY.*

Details of the life and work of Ebenezer Tracy are fairly well known, but those of Elisha Tracy are another matter. That he existed seems certain; that he made Windsor chairs, however, has never been based on any evidence apart from the fact that the *E. TRACY* brand is found on chairs with Connecticut features, and that the *E. TRACY* brand is different from the *EB: TRACY* brand.

Based on certain pieces of physical evidence, it is my belief that *EB: TRACY* and *E. TRACY* are one and the same person. Consider the two representative brands shown in figures 270 and 271. First, both are in the same style of type, and in both, the serif is missing from the lower right-hand side of the *T* in *TRACY.* Second, both of the chairs on which these brands are found are stylistically the same. Third, the woods used in both chairs are the same, right down to such important details as maple crest rails, chestnut seats, and chestnut side stretchers. Finally, the construction details are the same, for example, the legs do not penetrate the seats and the back posts are pinned through the seats with squarish wooden pegs. The only difference between the two chairs is the fact that the *B* is missing from one of the brands.

I suggest that both of the chairs were made in the shop of Ebenezer Tracy, who used two different brands.

270. (far left) EB: TRACY brand on seat bottom of a fan-back side chair.

271. E. TRACY brand on seat bottom of fan-back side chair.

NOTES

1. Although the painting depicts an event that took place in 1776, the painting itself was begun in 1784, completed after Pine's death in 1788, and Pine himself was not an eyewitness to the event. It is for this reason that the chairs in the painting have bamboo-turned legs, a feature of Windsor chairs that is more in keeping with the time the painting was executed than with the time of the actual event. Philadelphia Windsor-chair maker Francis Trumble supplied twelve Windsor chairs to the State House on May 31, 1776, and as the only sack-back chairs known to bear Trumble's brand have the earlier baluster-and-ring turnings, the Trumble sack-back shown in figure 96 is probably a more accurate example of the sort of chair Ben Franklin, *et al,* sat in when voting Independence.

2. For an accurate picture of the way the chair originally looked and for a discussion of same, see figure 268 and Appendix II.

3. William Macpherson Hornor, Jr., *Blue Book of Philadelphia Furniture—William Penn to George Washington* (Philadelphia: privately printed, 1935; Washington, D.C.: Highland House, 1977) p. 296.

4. To give but one example, the "Micropaedia" of the current *Encyclopaedia Britannica* tells us that the name *Windsor chair* "is said to derive from the fact that on one of his many excursions into the homes of his humbler subjects, George III was so captivated by this type of chair that he immediately ordered several made for Windsor Castle." But in the very next sentence, the article writer discredits the legend: "The name, however, was in use before George III was born; indeed, the Royal Household Accounts for 1729 contain a reference to '2 Mahogany Windsor Chairs richly carved.'" This confusion is not cleared up by still another *Britannica* article that says the name *Windsor* was apparently first used in England in 1731.

5. I must mention here that in Gordon's inventory the final letter of the word *Windsor* in the entry "Five Windsor Chairs" has been somewhat obscured, and that the letter may be either an *r* or a *w*. Nevertheless, the first six letters of the word are most certainly "Windso." What I am suggesting here is the possibility that the compiler of the inventory may have intended "Five Window Chairs" rather than "Five Windsor Chairs." In any case, the experts to whom I have shown photocopies of the Gordon inventory unanimously agree that the word is *Windsor,* not *window,* and I concur with that judgment. Furthermore, Windsors at this time sold for between ten and fifteen shillings, and the chairs in the Gordon inventory are appraised at eleven shillings six pence each,

lending weight to the idea that the chairs were in fact Windsors. Presumably, window chairs would have been fancier and would have cost more than Windsors, which were relatively inexpensive.

6. Simon Jervis, "The First Century of the English Windsor Chair, 1720-1820," *Antiques* (February 1979): p. 366.

7. Quoted in Jervis, p. 364. In this and the following three paragraphs I draw in part on information provided by Jervis. I should add here that for many years the date 1708 has been given in various publications as the earliest mention of a Windsor chair—in America, at that—but with no reference to where this mention occurs. I have traced the reference to Esther Singleton, *The Furniture of Our Forefathers* (New York: Doubleday, Page & Co., 1924; first edition 1900), p. 88. Here the author refers to one John Jones, a Philadelphia "gentleman of great wealth," whose inventory at his death in 1708 contained among other things a Windsor chair. Jones did die in 1708, but his inventory, while it lists Windsor curtains, makes no mention of Windsor chairs. Apart from the 1736 Gordon inventory discussed in note 5, the inventory of Hannah Hodge, who died in Philadelphia in 1736, contains the earliest definite American mention of a Windsor chair that I have been able to uncover.

8. The chair in figure 8 may well have been made by early Philadelphia Windsor maker Thomas Gilpin. See my discussion of the Gilpin chair, figure 26.

9. For other chairs and even a stool in this book with similar leg turnings, see figures 59, 135, 242; for a Connecticut Windsor with a similar crest rail, bulbous spindles, and stretcher turnings, see figure 111.

10. See Dean F. Failey, *Long Island Is My Nation* (Setauket, N.Y.: Society for the Preservation of Long Island Antiquities, 1976), pp. 68-76. Failey himself gives the Floyd chair a provenance of "probably Philadelphia," because Floyd "spent a considerable amount of time in Philadelphia, beginning in 1774, as a representative from New York to the Continental Congress." However, as Failey points out in another context (p. 75), "understandably, Connecticut and eastern Long Island chairs are often of similar design." Although the Floyd chair may have been intended to look English, Connecticut features have inevitably crept into its design.

11. There is an earlier advertisement from someplace other than Philadelphia that is quoted in Marion Iverson Day, *The American Chair,*

1630-1890 (New York: Hastings House, 1957), p. 80, which appeared in the *Virginia Gazette* for November 28, 1745: "Richard Caulton, Upholsterer, from London, gives the Public Notice . . . He makes and mends Easy-chairs, Dressing Chairs, Windsor Chairs, Settees, Pin Cushion Chair seats, couches. . . ." The advertisement, however, is somewhat ambiguous, as it concentrates on upholstered furniture. American Windsors, as I point out later in this chapter, do not seem to have been upholstered before round 1785. Furthermore, it is unclear whether Caulton actually made American Windsors or merely repaired upholstered English chairs. In any case, from the tenor of the advertisement, he was not a turner.

12. Quoted in Nancy A. Goyne Evans, "Francis Trumble of Philadelphia: Windsor Chair and Cabinetmaker," *Winterthur Portfolio One* (1964), p. 229.

13. *Ibid.*, p. 228.

14. Quoted in Irving W. Lyon, *The Colonial Furniture of New England* (Boston: Houghton, Mifflin, 1891), p. 177.

15. Harold E. Gillingham, "The Pennsylvania Windsor Chair and Its Journeyings," *Pennsylvania Magazine of History and Biography* 55 (1931):316.

16. Even as late as the 1820s, a Windsor-chair maker named Richard Hand advertised in Bridgeton, New Jersey, that he made "fancy and windsor chairs equal to those made in Philadelphia."

17. Quoted in Marshall B. Davidson, *The American Heritage History of Colonial Antiques* ([New York]: American Heritage Publishing Co., 1968), p. 289.

18. From the official report of the ceremonies, quoted in J. Thomas Scharf and Thompson Wescott, *History of Philadelphia* (Philadelphia: L. H. Everts and Co., 1884), vol. 1, p. 450. It is interesting to note that among the group of "Cabinet- and Chair-Makers" was a "Mr Jedediah Snowden, with the rules of architecture." As late as 1773 Snowden was advertising himself as a "cabinet maker and Windsor chair maker." Snowden apparently thought of himself as more of the former than of the latter, as he was not marching with his fellow Windsor makers.

19. Quoted in Goyne, "Francis Trumble," pp. 233, 239.

20. Quoted in Dean A. Fales, Jr., *American Painted Furniture 1660-1880* (New York: Duttton Paperbacks, 1979), p. 89.

21. A pair of Philadelphia Queen Anne side chairs made by Solomon Fussell for Benjamin Franklin (bill dated 1748) show the pronounced scrolled ears on either end of the yoke-shaped crest rail, which are echoed on Philadelphia comb-back Windsors. Fussell was also a maker of rush-bottom chairs and closely associated with turners. Perhaps he made Windsors himself.

22. Ethel Hall Bjerkoe, *The Cabinetmakers of America* (New York: Doubleday & Co., 1957), p. 166.

23. Charles F. Hummel, *With Hammer in Hand: The Dominy Craftsmen of East Hampton, New York* (Charlottesville, Va.: The University Press of Virginia, 1968), p. 252.

24. For further discussion of these chairs, see Joe Kindig III, "Upholstered Windsors," *Antiques* 62 (July 1952):52-53.

25. It is interesting to note that there is at least one bill from Daniel Trotter to Philadelphia merchant John Girard, dated 1787, charging Girard for "6 Windsor Chairs." Unfortunately, there is no way of determining whether Trotter, generally considered a maker of high-style furniture, actually made the Girard Windsors in his own shop—perhaps in the style of figure 168—or merely subcontracted for them, a not uncommon practice. At any rate, in addition to Windsors, Trotter was not adverse to supplying both John Girard and his more well-known brother, Stephen, with such distinctly mundane items as ironing boards, parrot stands, pine tables, rulers, and packing crates.

26. Conversation with expert contemporary Windsor maker Michael Dunbar.

27. Quoted in Leigh Keno, "The Windsor-Chair Makers of Northampton, Massachusetts, 1790-1820," *Antiques* (May 1980):1102.

28. For an example of what I mean, see Fales, *American Painted Furniture 1660-1880*, figure 221. Perhaps this sort of settee is what Baltimore Windsor makers John and Hugh Finlay referred to in their 1805 advertisement for, among other things, "new pattern . . . Windsor Chairs and Settees."

29. Failey, *Long Island Is My Nation*, p. 170, figure 198.

SPECIAL NOTE
Addition to Windsor Makers Checklist. Just discovered before publication.

STOW, J. Philadelphia. Working last quarter of the eighteenth century. The only example of a heretofore unknown Philadelphia chairmaker. Fan-back side chair branded: "J. STOW, PHILA. *fecit.*"

INDEX

The Windsor Style in America
1730–1840
Volume II

To Olenka

Contents

Foreword

When I first read *The Windsor Style in America*—the book by Charles Santore that preceded the present volume—I was delighted. I felt that never before had a writer done such an interesting, thorough job of recounting the history and analyzing the design of a single form of early American furniture.

Now we have *The Windsor Style, Volume II*, and once again I am delighted.

This book, a comprehensive supplement to the first, is not so much a history of the Windsor style as it is a compendium of regional comparisons and influences. Santore shows us hundreds of examples of Windsor chairs from various regions and points up their similarities and differences; he shows how similar pieces from different regions and from within the same region may have influenced each other; and he discusses the aesthetic qualities of each one.

Santore also poses some thoughtful questions about Windsors: Why were most writing-arm Windsors made in Connecticut? Why were fan-back Windsors produced in quantity in Pennsylvania but infrequently in New York? Why was the continuous-arm chair so popular in New York but not in Pennsylvania? Those questions and others are answered intelligently and perceptively.

This informative, authoritative book is one that collectors, curators, and dealers will treasure, not only for ready reference but for the pure pleasure of browsing through its handsome pages.

Dr. Robert Bishop
Director
Museum of American Folk Art
New York City

Preface

Not long after I delivered to Running Press the final manuscript, photographs, and drawings for my first book, *The Windsor Style in America 1730–1830*, I began to feel another book coming on! The primary reason was that Windsor chairs I had never seen before kept turning up—chairs I felt should have been included in the book.

My editor, Tom Voss, and my publishers, Lawrence and Stuart Teacher, said, "Stop! No more! *Fini!* You've made your point!"

I reluctantly agreed. But then I would discover yet another new example and say to myself, "Look at that chair. It has an arm support (or a comb-piece, or a leg) that I've never seen before. Windsor collectors should know about this."

The variety of chairs seemed endless, the list of chairmakers grew, and new variations of styles kept emerging.

The opportunity to organize a Windsor loan exhibition for the University Hospital Antiques Show in Philadelphia in 1982 brought me into contact with yet another group of fine Windsors, many never before seen publicly. And the publication of *The Windsor Style in America* began to prove very rewarding to me in a way I had not anticipated: until then, I had had to ferret out as best I could most of the Windsor forms and related information I compiled. After the book's publication, collectors, dealers, and antiquarians began sending me photos of Windsors and information they thought would interest me, sharing what they knew as well as asking for my opinions.

Far and away, though, the majority of the letters and phone calls were about forms of Windsors that did not appear in *The Windsor Style*, or in Wallace Nutting's *American Windsors*, or in Thomas Ormsbee's *The Windsor Chair*. The only response I could make to these inquiries was to write a new book about it all—the book you are holding in your hands.

Nutting, Ormsbee, and I—in attempting to cover the evolution, variety, and basic types of Windsors—had been forced to select examples of chairs that emphasized striking differences among Windsors from period to period and from region to region. In order to show these differences graphically, we had to skip over the many similarities and the more subtle differences that could fill in the gaps of our Windsor vocabulary. In this volume I have included many Windsors that are similar in turning patterns, construction, and general impact. I believe that in doing so I have been able to paint more clearly a realistic picture of the Windsor panorama in America.

The more American Windsors I see, the more I am convinced that American chairmakers followed the English tradition more closely than previously believed. In England, particular types or styles of chairs are frequently named after the places of their production. Thus we have Yorkshire, Lancashire, Mendelsham, and High Wycombe Windsors—to name a few.

I've noted in *The Windsor Style* that virtually every type of American Windsor, with the interesting exception of the continuous-arm chair, was first produced in England, and there seems to be universal agreement that the first American Windsors were influenced by the English products. But then—so goes the common wisdom—our own ingenuity took over.

I'm now convinced that the practice of identifying a particular style or type of Windsor with a particular city or region was as common here as it was in England. This notion has probably been overlooked because, with the exception of the "Philadelphia chair," we did not *name* our chairs after their places of origin. But if we were not as quick as the English to speak for our chairs, the chairs will speak for themselves. And what they tell us is that there is a pattern in Windsors produced in different regions, from Maine to Virginia, between 1730 and the mid-nineteenth century.

Why does one very prolific and sophisticated center of Windsor chairmaking—New York City—produce virtually no comb-back or fan-back chairs, types already made popular by another prolific chairmaking center—Philadelphia? On the other hand, why does Philadelphia produce no continuous-arm chairs—a type that originated in New York City and influenced Windsor design in most of the colonies? Why do at least 60 to 70 percent of all Windsor writing-arm chairs come from a single region—Connecticut—and the majority of those from a single shop—that of E. B. Tracy?

The evidence seems to indicate that chairmaking centers were content with, and probably proud of, the Windsor styles they sold the most of, and that they simply conceded the other types to their respective centers. Thus, although a style was seldom named after the place of its greatest production and popularity, it went without saying that its place of origin was synonymous with its design.

Such patterns are most evident in the large, urban chairmaking centers. The influence of these centers on their neighboring communities might, in turn, spread to another small community that had already been exposed to yet another chairmaking center, and so on. The end result was stylistic specialization in the urban centers and stylistic proliferation in the provinces.

By studying the similarities and differences among Windsors, one can see how aware American craftsmen were of developments around them, and how quickly they incorporated external influences into their own Windsor vocabulary. It is only by studying the products of these prolific craftsmen that we can understand their intentions, aesthetic sense, business sense, and their attitude toward their craft.

Birth, death, and marriage records, bills of lading, street directories, and advertisements—all of these are important in helping us to understand the Windsor story in America. But those documents notwithstanding, the most revealing document of all is the product—the Windsor chair itself.

As much as possible, I have tried in this book to let the chairs speak for themselves, allowing their own organic development to dictate the organization and content of the book. I hope that this format will be another valuable tool for collectors, dealers, auctioneers, and Windsor scholars.

CHARLES SANTORE

Acknowledgments

I learned, during my experience with the first volume of this book, that it is impossible to produce a book of this type without the interest and help of a great many people. So it comes as no surprise that the present volume has also been a joint effort, and I would sincerely like to acknowledge the support, concern, and assistance of those individuals who contributed their time, expertise, and collections in making this book a reality.

First, I would like to thank Tom Voss and Bill Holland for their collaboration on this project. I have come to rely on their vision and insight, and this book, like our last, is better because of their participation. More important, we are still friends.

A special thanks is due to Dr. Robert Bishop for his interest, concern, and enthusiasm for this project.

Many knowledgeable collectors and Windsor-lovers graciously opened their collections to me, unhesitatingly offering their cooperation and advice. For their invaluable assistance, I would like to thank Roy and Carol Allen, Claude and Alvan Bisnoff, H. Richard Dietrich, Jr., William K. du Pont, Steven and Helen Kellogg, Don and Joan Mayoras, Mr. and Mrs. John C. Price, and Tom and Nancy Tafuri.

I am extremely grateful for the expertise and unflagging support of Sam Bruccoleri, James and Nancy Glazer, Wayne Pratt, and David Schorsch. They are always on the alert for new Windsor discoveries, and they have my respect, admiration, and deepest thanks.

I would like to include a very special mention of my gratitude to my publishers, Lawrence and Stuart Teacher, whose personal interest in early American furniture and Windsors in particular was so evident in publishing *The Windsor Style* and which is now reaffirmed in this book; and to Elizabeth Zozom and the entire design department at Running Press: I'm very proud of our relationship. To Nancy Steele, my editor at Running Press whose guidance and careful scrutiny in every detail of this book was so critically important, my deepest respect and gratitude.

I have always felt fortunate to be so close to Independence National Historical Park. Having access to its superb collection of Philadelphia Windsors has been a wonderful opportunity, and I owe a debt of gratitude to all the staff of INHP. I would like to thank particularly former Park Superintendent Hobart Caywood, Chief of Museum Operations John C. Milley, Supervisory Curator Doris Fanelli, Assistant Curators Jane Coulter and Robert Ganini, and staff members Ricardo Hutchinson and Gloria McLean.

For their valuable assistance and generosity I am deeply grateful to Lynne Anderson, Rosemary Beck and Ed Rogers, Barry Blum of Blum's Antiques, Charles E. Bolton of Federation Antiques, Richard A. Bourne Co., Inc., Philip H. Bradley Antiques, James Brooks, Tom Brown Antiques, Richard

Chalfant, Skip and Lee Ellen Chalfant, Richard Champlin, Marianne Clark, The Clokeys, Barry Cohen, Michael Cook, Suzanne Courcier and Robert Wilkens, Elizabeth R. Daniel, Charles G. Dorman, Hazel Douglass, Nancy Druckman, Joseph Dumas, Howard and Kathy Feldman, Burton and Helaine Fendelman, Amy Finkel, Kenneth Finkel, Morris Finkel, Paul and Rita Flack, Stephen L. Fletcher, Kyle and Doris Fuller, Frank R. Gaglio and Kathleen Molner, Albert F. Gamon, Elizabeth R. Gamon, Stephen H. Garner, Ralph Giguere, Peter and Janie Gross, Tom and Karen Helm, Don and Trish Herr, Marjorie Hooper, Charles Miller and Charlotte Hornberger, Robert W. Hughes, Charles W. Huntress, William C. Jennens, Victor and Joan Johnson, Elizabeth Kannan, Maribeth Keene and Wayne Pratt Antiques, Mr. and Mrs. Gary Koenig, Leigh Keno, Leslie Keno, Doug and Kendra Krienke, Ed and Audrey Kornowski, Richard F. Kozar, Allan and Joan Lehner, Anthony Leone, Bernard & S. Dean Levy, Sarah Lippincott of Lippincott Antiques, Mr. and Mrs. Gary W. Lipton, Michael McCue and Mike Rothstein, Chris and Corinne Machmer, George S. Manger, Kenneth and Ida Manko, Mr. and Mrs. Craig Mayor, Christine Meadows, Dr. and Mrs. Donald McHarl, John Mecray, Alan Miller, Mr. and Mrs. Richard Alan Mones, Kathleen Mulhern, Charles Muller, John C. Newcomer, Sam Pennington, M. M. Pernot, Eugene Pettinelli, Michael Pillagalli, Frank and Barbara Pollack, David Pottinger, Deborah McCracken Rebuck, Jean and John Renshaw, Frank Rentschler, Gregory and Barbara Reynolds, Marguerite Riordan, William Schwind, Jr., Antiques, Mr. and Mrs. Steven Score, William Stahl, Lita Solis-Cohen, Barbara and Chuck Soltis, Robert Stallfort, Charles Sterling, Mason Stewart, Tom Strofelt, Howard Szmolko, Nancy and Alan Tessler, Robert Trent, Ruth van Tassel, Mrs. Jo Ann Wagner, Mark and Kathy Winchester, Edwin Wolf, Stephanie Wood, and Richard Worth. Wayne Pratt's photographs are courtesy of John J. Courville.

I am also grateful for the assistance of "The Arts and Antiques Review" of the *Newtown Bee;* The John Bartram Association; Margaret Bleecker Blades at The Chester County Historical Society; The Burlington County Historical Society; Christie's; Colonial Williamsburg; The Concord Antiquarian Society; The Dietrich American Foundation; The Library Company of Philadelphia; Ludens, Inc.; *Maine Antique Digest;* Elizabeth Mankin Antiques; The Metropolitan Museum of Art; Mount Vernon; The Mount Vernon Ladies Association; The Museum of Early Southern Decorative Arts; The New Hampshire Historical Society; The Pennsylvania Historical Society; Pook & Pook, Inc.; David and Marjorie Schorsch, Inc.; The Redwood Library and Atheneum; Skinner, Inc.; Sotheby's; Waynesborough; Whistler Gallery, Inc.; The Peter Wentz Farmstead; The Henry Francis du Pont Winterthur Museum; The Yale University Art Gallery.

To all of the aforementioned, I am deeply indebted. Thank you.

A Portfolio of Drawings

1. Philadelphia and New England bamboo-turned legs and stretchers.

Top to bottom: medial stretcher, Boston, 1790–1796; medial and side stretcher, Philadelphia, 1780–1793.

Left to right: rear leg, Philadelphia, 1780–1793; front leg, Boston, 1790–1796.

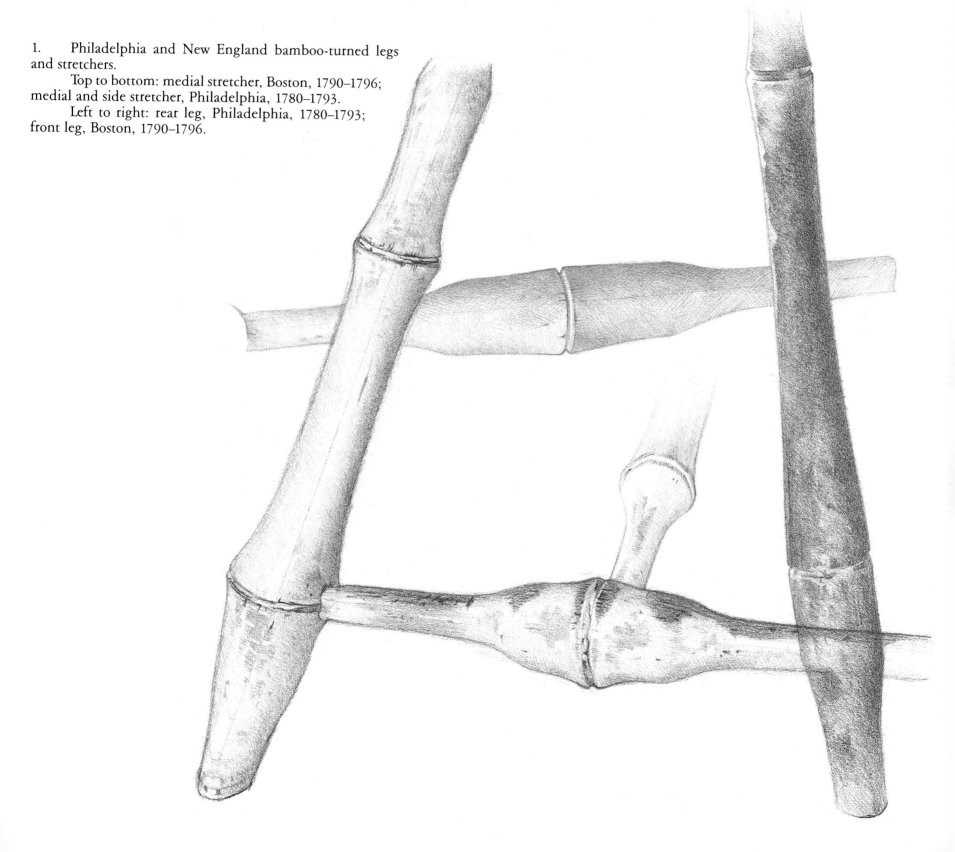

2.   New England and Philadelphia leg and back
post turnings for children's fan-back side chairs.
    Left to right: front leg and back post, Lisbon,
Connecticut, 1790–1800; back post and front leg,
Philadelphia, 1765–1780.

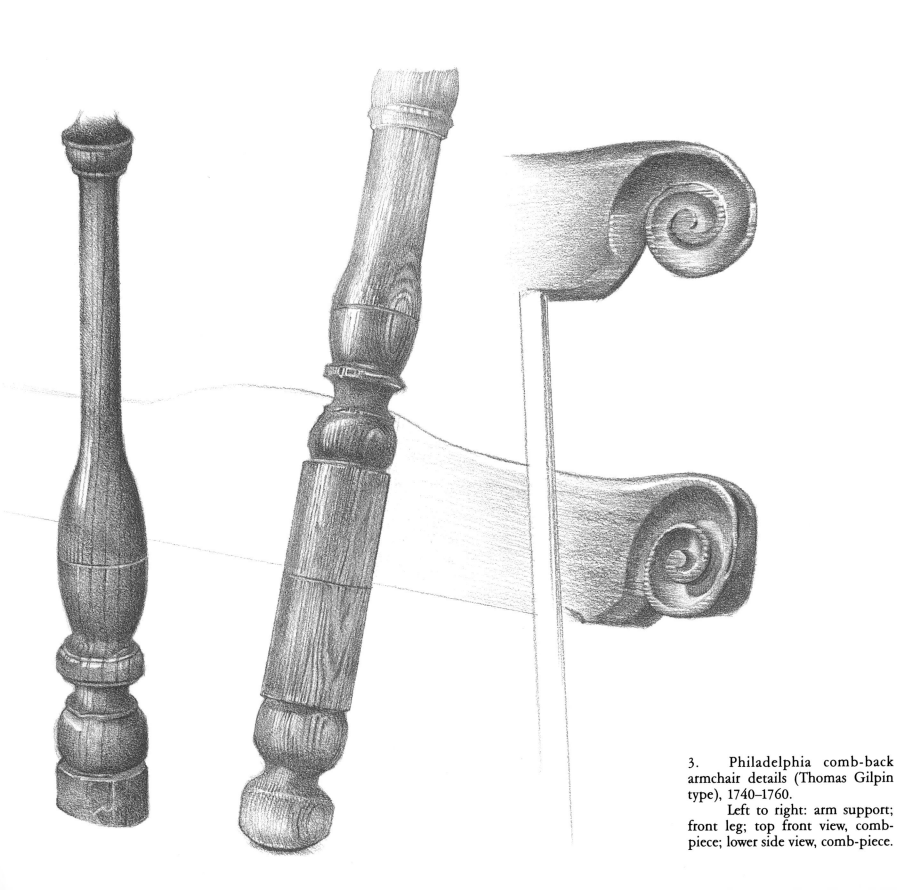

3. Philadelphia comb-back armchair details (Thomas Gilpin type), 1740–1760.

Left to right: arm support; front leg; top front view, comb-piece; lower side view, comb-piece.

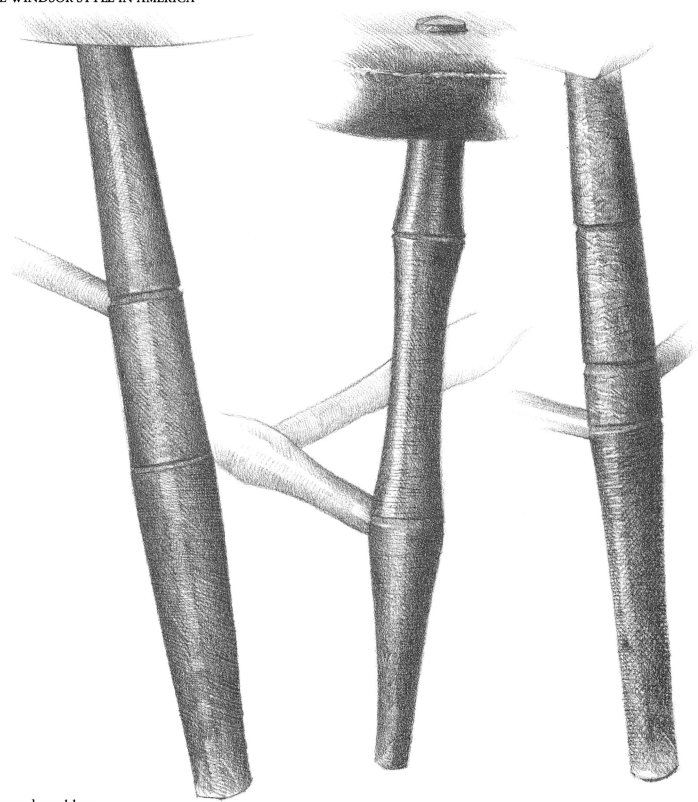

4.   New England bamboo-turned stool legs.
      Left to right: box stretcher type, Massachusetts, 1800–1820;
medial stretcher type, New England, 1790–1800; box stretcher type,
New England, 1800–1820.

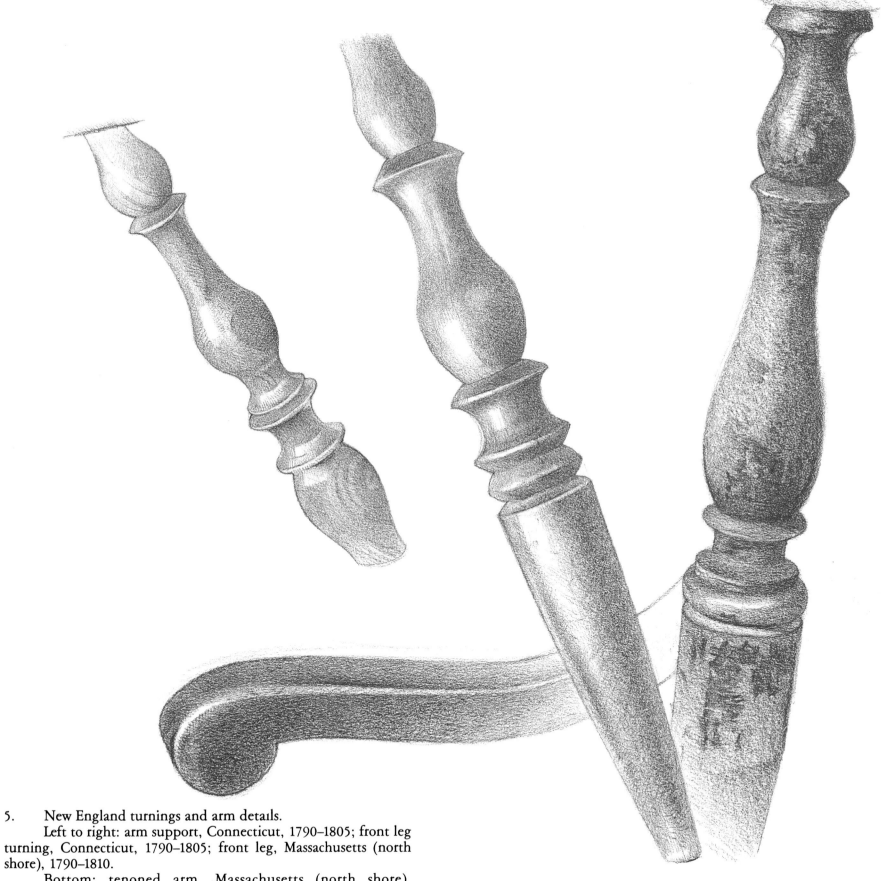

5.	New England turnings and arm details.
	Left to right: arm support, Connecticut, 1790–1805; front leg turning, Connecticut, 1790–1805; front leg, Massachusetts (north shore), 1790–1810.

	Bottom: tenoned arm, Massachusetts (north shore), 1790–1810.

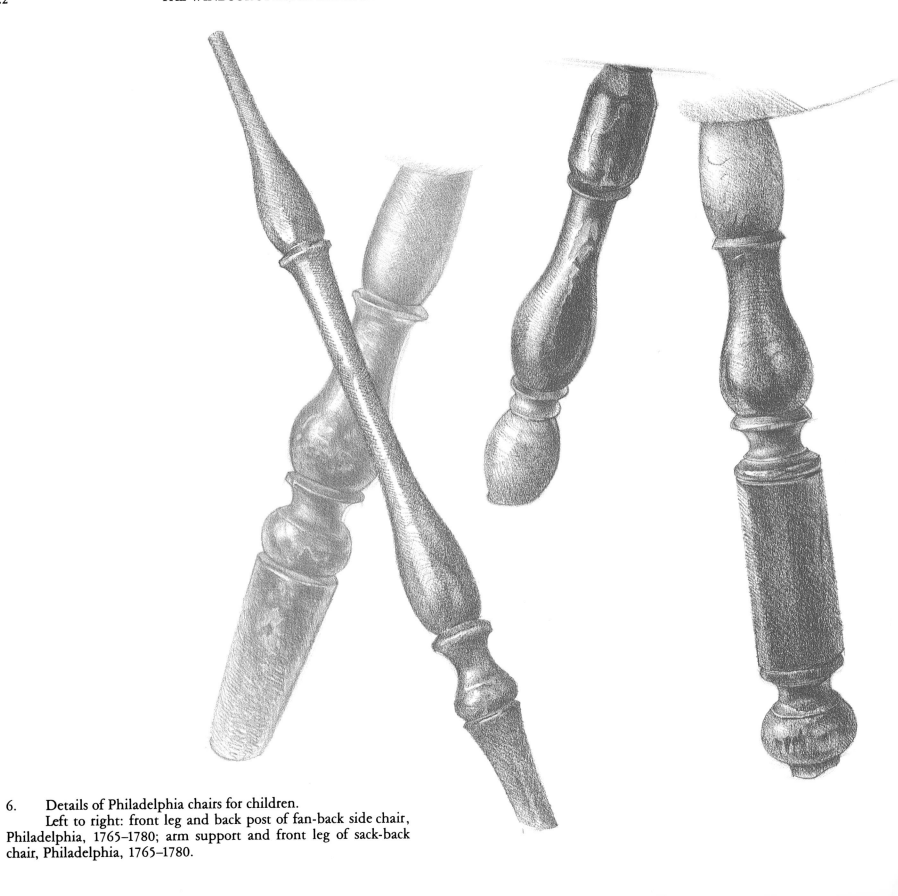

6.   Details of Philadelphia chairs for children.
       Left to right: front leg and back post of fan-back side chair,
Philadelphia, 1765–1780; arm support and front leg of sack-back
chair, Philadelphia, 1765–1780.

© Charles Santore 1981

7. Philadelphia Windsor chair details.

Top to bottom: comb-piece, 1745–1770; comb-piece, 1765–1780; handhold of steam-bent arm, 1740–1770; knuckle handhold and turned arm support, 1765–1780; arm and crest rail of low-back chair, 1750–1770.

Lower left to right: medial stretcher, 1740–1760; leg, 1765–1780; leg, 1745–1760; arm support, 1745–1760.

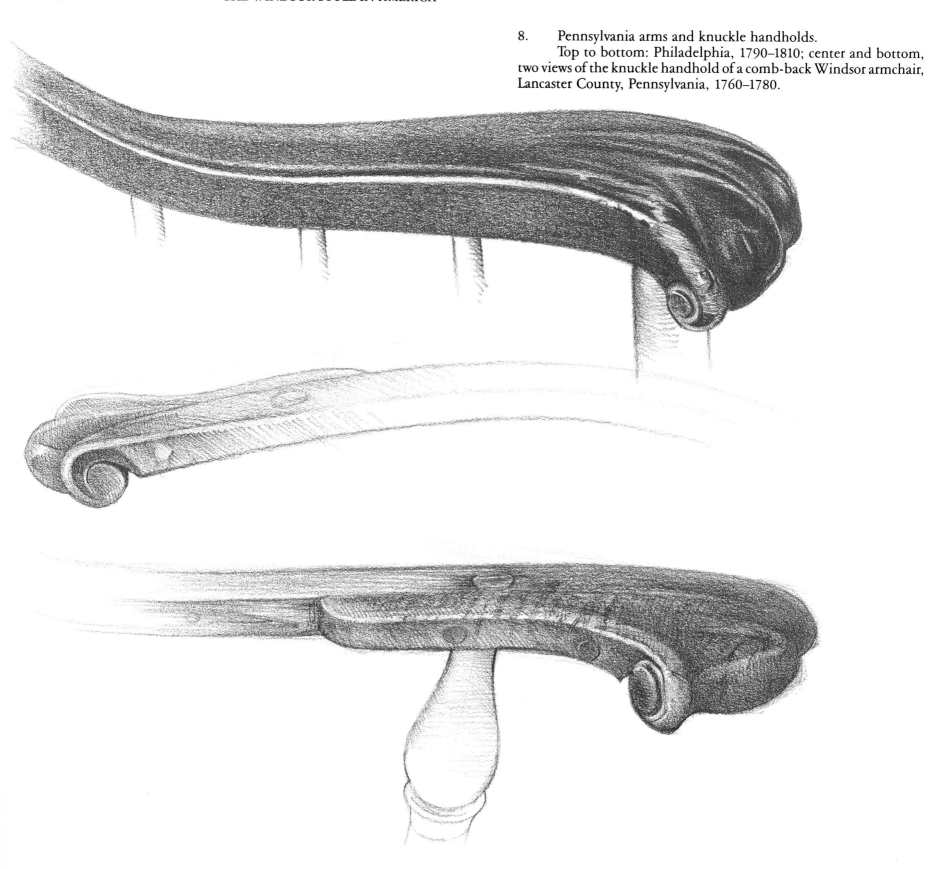

8.   Pennsylvania arms and knuckle handholds.
Top to bottom: Philadelphia, 1790–1810; center and bottom,
two views of the knuckle handhold of a comb-back Windsor armchair,
Lancaster County, Pennsylvania, 1760–1780.

A Study of Windsor Surfaces

Plate I.   Portrait of a mother and child, probably by Jacob Maentel; probably Lancaster County, Pennsylvania; early nineteenth century. Watercolor on paper. 10″ × 15″. (Barry Cohen)

The paint colors of the Windsor chairs shown in this picture—apple green with yellow, and some red, decoration—were very fashionable in the first quarter of the nineteenth century. Note that, although the chairs have been painted to match, the high chair does not have arrow-shaped spindles; thus the chairs were probably not part of a set.

Plate II. Armchair. Originally painted dark
green, this is a good example of a Windsor chair
dating from the third quarter of the eighteenth
century that was "updated" in the early nineteenth century with the same fashionable combination of apple-green paint with red, blue, and
gilt striping and decoration seen in Plate I. The
flaking here and there of the newer paint, exposing the original paint, creates a marvelous surface
quality. (Also see figure 76.)

Plate III. Armchair. While this master-piece of Philadelphia Windsor chair-making of the 1765–1780 period has a coat of late eighteenth- or early nineteenth-century reddish-brown grain paint over its original green paint, the chair as it stands is in untouched condition. Since absolutely nothing would be gained by attempting to remove the second coat of paint by dry-scraping, the chair should be left exactly as it is, with its undisturbed paint history intact. (Also see figures 16 and 16A.)

Plate IV. Armchair. I have seen many early Windsors with paint histories like that of this chair: nineteenth-century red paint over earlier nineteenth-century buff, over the original eighteenth-century green. As is common in these examples, the hickory spindles, which do not hold paint very well, are pleasingly mottled, revealing the different levels and colors of paint.

On such a chair, the patina becomes as important as the structure, making the piece a rare—and, from the collector's point of view, exciting—historical document. However, while this chair is very desirable, it is slightly less so than the previous two examples because it has three, rather than two, coats of paint. (Also see figure 3.)

Plate V. Candlestand. So often we speak of "original green paint" on Windsor furniture. Here is what it comes to look like when it is completely undisturbed for more than 200 years (in this case, laid over a salmon-color ground). For a piece of Windsor furniture to have survived so long in this pristine condition—without having been overpainted—is remarkably rare. (Also see figure 249.)

Plate VI. Armchair. The yellows used to paint Windsors were usually soft in tone—ochres or straw colors, for example. This fine and typical rod-back of about 1800, with its original cadmium yellow and black ringing, is almost startlingly bright. The color seems perfectly appropriate for a bamboo-turned Windsor and certainly brings the chair to life. (Also see figure 162.)

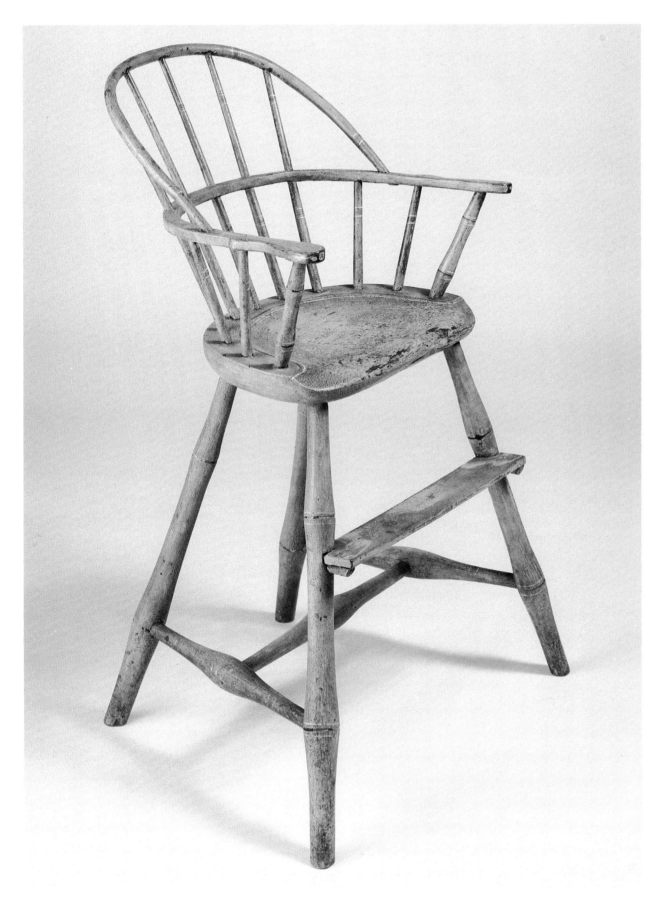

Plate VII. High chair. Here is one of those instances when a second coat of early paint—in this case, over the original green—makes a piece more interesting and exciting than it would have been had it been left in its original color.

While this is a well-proportioned sack-back high chair with good bamboo turnings, it is not of the best style. Yet its second coat of nineteenth-century yellow paint with white, ringed with white and red, makes this piece sing. This is an excellent example of how important a bright paint history is to a successful Windsor statement. (Also see figure 231.)

Plate VIII. Pair of side chairs. Massachusetts, 1790–1810. Early nineteenth-century mustard-yellow paint over the original green paint. (Collection of David A. Schorsch)

Additional examples of Windsors that have been enhanced by a second coat of paint, these eighteenth-century fan-backs now sport a top coat of bright nineteenth-century yellow paint over the original green. Painted this way, these chairs have a more graphic architecture.

Plate IX. Armchair. Probably South Windham, Connecticut; 1796–1805. Probably by Amos Denison Allen (it descended in the Amos Denison Allen family). Original blue paint. Crest rail, spindles, and arms, hickory; arm supports and seat, butternut; legs and stretchers, maple. SW 19¾″, SD 15″, SH 16½″, OH 33″. (Collection of David A. Schorsch)

Many of the Windsor chairs known to have been made by Amos Denison Allen were originally painted black with gilt decoration. Probably made by Allen, this chair is a rare find because it has its original blue paint and has never been overpainted.

Plate X. Armchair. This beautifully proportioned Rhode Island continuous-arm chair is about as fine and graceful a piece of Windsor furniture as one could hope to see.

When found, the chair had been overpainted with black and striped decoration, probably of mid-nineteenth-century vintage. Fortunately, the black paint had thoroughly dried out and was literally falling off in spots. What was emerging beneath it was a coat of early nineteenth-century teal-blue paint over the original eighteenth-century green.

In this case, the place to stop removing the paint was obvious. The blue paint was in excellent condition and would never separate from the original green as easily as the black paint separated from the blue. There would be no point in going to the trouble of removing the blue paint anyway, because the chair is wonderful just as it is! (Also see figure 160.)

Plate XI. Side chair. Dry-scraping—usually done with a spoon or a dull knife—is a tedious process, yet it is the only tried-and-true method of removing old crystallized paint from a Windsor chair without disturbing the undercoats.

In this photo, we see the results of dry-scraping a coat of early twentieth-century black paint from an upholstered Philadelphia bow-back side chair. The results are quite dramatic: the original white paint, mellowed by time, has been revealed, and the bamboo turnings can now be seen and appreciated. Note the splotches of black paint over the original white still in evidence on the underside of the seat where the legs are socketed. This is a good place to look when trying to determine the paint history of a Windsor chair. (Also see figure 120.)

Plate XII.   Here we see a continuation of the dry-scraping process on
the bow and spindles of the chair pictured in Plate XI. On the bow,
or crest rail, you can see that where the black paint has already been
removed, not much original white paint remains. Close examination
reveals that the white paint had been worn away before the chair was
painted black. Since the raw oak of the bow was exposed, the black
paint was absorbed by the open wood grain, making removal of the
black paint extremely difficult. The spindles are a different matter:
most of the original white paint was still intact when the chair was
overpainted black. The paint bond was weak, and the black paint can
now be easily chipped and scraped away.

Plate XIII. A detail of the wonderfully original crest rail of figure 179 is shown here. The chair retains its original early nineteenth-century brown paint.

Note how the paint is worn along the top of the crest rail, exposing the wood beneath—a telltale sign of age. Such areas of exposed wood on painted Windsors should never be touched up. They are imperfections, yes, but the various smooth spots, bare spots, cracks, scrapes, and scratches are an integral part of the character of a venerable old Windsor. They add up to patina, not just paint color. After all, 200 years ago brown paint was not much different from brown paint today; what's important is how and where the years have affected that paint.

On the other hand, a chair with paint that is crazed on every inch of its surface would be unnatural: one would have to suspect that the "patina" had been manufactured. Similarly, if the quality of the wear were exactly the same on all the chair's surfaces, one would have to check carefully to make certain that the wear had not been faked.

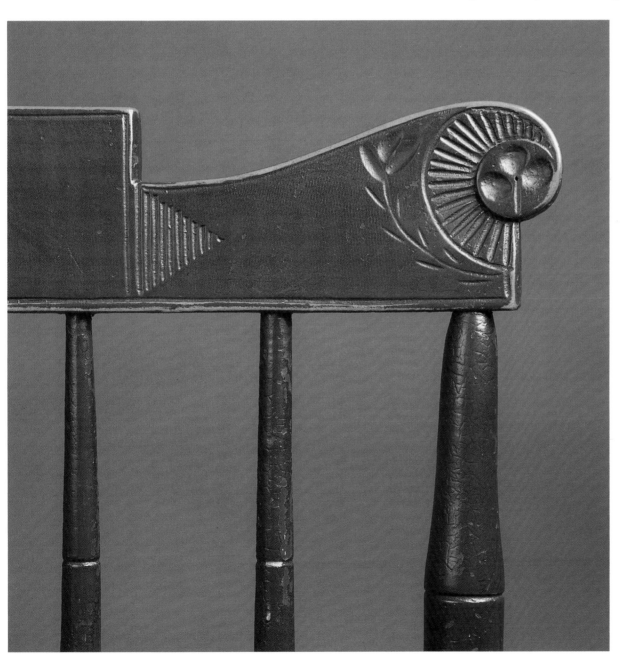

Plate XIV.   The ear of a Connecticut fan-back side chair is shown in this detail. Instead of carved volutes, the ears have a rosette pattern—a kind of stylized floral carving common to Connecticut furniture. Note how, due to use and age, the high spots on the carving have been worn through the paint to the bare wood beneath. Note, too, that the original black paint is thickest and most crazed in the low spots of the carving. When it was first applied, the paint served to decorate, unify, and protect the piece. With time, however, the paint on a piece of early furniture becomes part of its architecture, and the changes in the color and texture of the paint begin to explain and emphasize the piece's form. (Also see figure 61.)

Plate XV. Armchair. A remarkable miniature Windsor chair only 7¼″ tall, this piece retains its original green paint with gilt decoration on the crest rail, front edge of the seat, and turnings. The paint decoration has been scaled down to match the scale of the construction, making the chair a completely successful miniature. (Also see figure 245.)

COMB-BACK

~

CHAIRS

The comb-back chair is almost certainly the earliest style of Windsor produced in America and is synonymous with Philadelphia. The form probably saw the light of day in that city circa 1730 and was fully realized by 1750. During the 1750–1790 period, the comb-back accounted for a substantial part of Philadelphia Windsor production. But even in Philadelphia, the comb-back seems to have been favored by only a handful of shops, judging by the relative frequency with which these branded and stylistically identifiable examples turn up.

If Philadelphia was the hub of comb-back Windsor chairmaking, its outlying areas were the spokes. For example, many marvelous, highly stylized comb-backs have come out of Lancaster County, Pennsylvania, as well as Chester, Berks, and Bucks counties. Wilmington, Delaware, produced comb-backs, but these chairs are heavily influenced stylistically by the Philadelphia product.

In major chairmaking centers outside the Philadelphia area, very few comb-backs were produced, the other makers apparently choosing not to compete with Philadelphia makers. The two significant exceptions are the cross-stretcher comb-backs in the English taste made in Newport, Rhode Island, and the much smaller comb-backs with long, tapering legs from various areas of Connecticut. The Hartford area produced quite a number of small comb-backs, generally attributable to John Wadsworth during the 1793–1796 period, but the great Connecticut Windsor-making dynasty headed by E. B. Tracy seems to have made few comb-back chairs. New York chairmakers ignored the form in favor of sack-backs, bow-backs, and continuous-arm chairs. And coastal Massachusetts makers seem to have preferred the fan-back armchair to the comb-back type.

The comb-back form is powerful, classic, and difficult to surpass. Some of the finest American Windsors ever produced were made as comb-backs.

1.   Armchair. Philadelphia, 1740–1750. Branded T. GILPIN under seat pommel. Early nineteenth-century black paint over the original red paint. Crest rail, oak; spindles, hickory; arms, possibly ash; arm supports, chestnut; seat, poplar; legs, oak or chestnut; stretchers, hickory or chestnut. SW 21″, SD 15″, SH 15½″, OH 40½″. (Privately owned)

Thomas Gilpin (1700–1766) is the earliest Windsor maker whose branded chairs have survived. Indeed, the chairs of no other maker of the early period seem to have been branded. Thus branded Gilpin chairs are a rarity, and this one is rarer still because of its relatively small size. Still, the chair has all the Gilpin characteristics, among them: ears whose contour does not rise at the ends; a comb-piece that is thick on the bottom, allowing the ears to be deeply carved; arm supports with urn-shaped turnings at the top; two short spindles under each arm; and a decoratively turned medial stretcher. Note, too, that the medial stretcher is not socketed in the center of the side stretchers but is "stepped back," a feature of the earliest Philadelphia comb-backs as well as of low-backs.

1

NOTE: *In this book, dimensions are given in inches and are abbreviated as SW (seat width), SD (seat depth), SH (seat height), and OH (overall height).*

2.   Armchair. Philadelphia, 1740–1750. Dark reddish-brown paint over the original green paint. Crest rail, probably oak; arms and arm supports, ash; spindles, hickory; seat, pine; legs and stretchers, chestnut. SW 24″, SD 16″, SH 17¼″, OH 45″. (James and Nancy Glazer)

While not branded as is figure 1, this chair has all the Gilpin characteristics. The chair never had scrolled handholds, which gives it a rather English feeling.

3.   Armchair. Philadelphia, 1750–1770. Nineteenth-century dark red paint over a buff-color ground, over the original green paint. Crest rail and arms, oak; spindles, hickory; arm supports, legs, and stretchers, maple; seat, poplar. SW 24½″, SD 16¾″, SH 17″, OH 42½″. (Also see color plate IV.) (James and Nancy Glazer)

This is a typical, classic, early Philadelphia comb-back. Note-worthy features include its scrolled ears with two full spirals; nine untapered spindles; three short spindles under each arm; a steam-bent arm rail with scrolled handholds; a medial stretcher in the Queen Anne style; and ball feet (with some loss on this particular chair).

4. Armchair. Philadelphia, 1750–1770. Ball feet missing. Late nineteenth-century brown paint over traces of the original green paint. Crest rail, arm supports, legs, and stretchers, maple; spindles, hickory; arms, ash; seat, poplar. SW 23¾″, SD 15¾″, SH 14½″, OH 41″. (Burlington County Historical Society)

Similar to figure 3, this chair has a crest rail with more emphatic curves; ear volutes with more chamfer; less bulbous arm supports with an extra reel before the baluster turning; and a more bulbous medial stretcher with smaller ring turnings. Note the slight concavity in the leg turning, a feature sometimes seen on these chairs. The rolled shape of the seat and the more gently shaped side stretchers indicate a slightly later date for this chair than for figure 3.

5. Armchair. Pennsylvania, possibly Lancaster County; 1750–1770. Original black paint. Crest rail and arms, oak; spindles, hickory; arm supports, legs, and stretchers, maple; seat, pine. SW 24½″, SD 16″, SH 17″, OH 42″. (Tom Brown)

This chair has a Lancaster County ear and medial stretcher, but the chair as a whole is based on a Philadelphia type (compare with figure 3). Note the interesting block turning at the top of the leg before it enters the seat.

4

5

7.   Armchair. Philadelphia, 1765–1780. Refinished; traces of the original green paint. Crest rail, oak; spindles and arms, hickory; handholds, oak; arm supports, legs, and stretchers, maple; seat, poplar. SW 24¾″, SD 17″, SH 17″, OH 45¼″. (Mr. and Mrs. R. W. P. Allen)

With this chair, we move to a somewhat later, middle-period Philadelphia-style comb-back. The chair has the same generous comb-piece as the earlier chairs, but the turnings have become less distinctive. For example, the legs have a long, rigid baluster and a tapered foot rather than a ball foot. And the baluster-and-ring medial stretcher is later than the Queen Anne stretchers of the earlier chairs.

6.   Armchair. Philadelphia, 1750–1770. Legs pieced out incorrectly; should have ball feet. Early nineteenth-century putty-color paint with black, brown, and green decoration over the original green paint. Crest rail, arms, and handholds, oak; spindles, hickory; arm supports, legs, and stretchers, maple; seat, poplar. SW 24⅝″, SD 16¾″, SH 17¼″, OH 44¾″. (John Bartram Association)

Though it possesses an ample seat, a nicely spread nine-spindle comb, and the same general characteristics as figure 3, this chair does not make as strong a statement. The comb-piece is tamer than that of figure 3, the arm supports not as bulbous, the seat not as deeply saddled.

8.   Armchair. New York City, 1765–1780. Nineteenth-century dark brown paint over the original green paint. Crest rail, arm supports, legs, and stretchers, maple; spindles, hickory; arms and handholds, oak; seat, pine. SW 23¾″, SD 17½″, SH 17½ ″, OH 43½″. (James and Nancy Glazer)

At first glance, this chair might be taken for a Philadelphia or Pennsylvania comb-back, but the shape of the crest rail, the arm supports, and especially the leg turnings—with their short baluster and long taper—suggest to me that the chair is one of those rare examples of a New York City comb-back influenced by the Philadelphia style.

9.   Armchair. Philadelphia, 1765–1780. Old refinish. Crest rail, oak; spindles and arm rail, hickory; arm supports, legs, and stretchers, maple; seat, poplar. (Wayne Pratt)

From the seat up, this chair has the general characteristics of comb-backs from the early period. For example, the arm supports are quite similar to those of figure 3, although slimmer. However, the medial stretcher is no longer double-baluster-and-reel turned but has a more generic single bobbin; the side stretchers have been turned symmetrically to accommodate the medial stretcher (i.e., the medial stretcher is not stepped back); and the seat is rounded off at its edges.

10

10.   Armchair. Philadelphia, 1765–1780. Bottoms of handholds missing. Brown varnish over old red paint, over traces of the original green paint. Crest rail and arms, oak; spindles and handholds, hickory; arm supports, legs, and stretchers, maple; seat, poplar. SW 21½″, SD 16¼″, SH 16½″, OH 40¾″. (John Bartram Association)

A comb-back version of the sack-back chairs produced in Philadelphia at that time, this is a well-balanced, well-proportioned example of the later Philadelphia comb-back style. The elliptical seat—a feature of sack-back Windsors—has soft edges and is not as severely carved as the earlier D-shaped seat. The tapered spindles fan outward slightly, and the ears have a relatively small contour with deep carving. Because the arm supports are set back, they can rake forward, and the turning of the bottom of the arm support echoes the concave turning of the leg taper.

The turnings are very vigorous for a Philadelphia chair of this period, and the leg taper is as long, if not longer, than the baluster—just one example of what we mean when we speak of the balance of the turnings.

11

12. Armchair. Philadelphia, 1765–1790. Bottoms of knuckles missing. Refinished. Crest rail and arms, oak; spindles, hickory; arm supports, legs, and stretchers, maple. SW 21¼″, SD 16″, SH 17¾″, OH 43¼″. (Mr. and Mrs. R. W. P. Allen)

Here is another example of a middle-period Philadelphia comb-back. Its most unusual feature is its remarkable number of spindles—fifteen in its back, as opposed to the usual nine, and five under each arm where three would be expected.

12

11. Armchair. Philadelphia, 1765–1780. Bottoms of handholds missing. Very old mahogany varnish over a light ground, over traces of the original green paint. Crest rail, arm supports, legs, and stretchers, maple; spindles and arms, hickory; seat, poplar. SW 21½″, SD 16½″, SH 17″, OH 43″. (Historical Society of Pennsylvania)

This chair is in essentially the same style as figure 10, and its ears are well carved. Yet the chair as a whole is less strong than figure 10. The arm supports are more attenuated. The seat has the same basic elliptical shape but is more vaguely carved. The leg turnings, although typical of the Philadelphia style, are quite slender, and their baluster is longer than their taper, creating the illusion that there is too much distance from the seat to the stretchers.

13

13.   Armchair. Philadelphia, 1765–1790. Branded I. [Joseph] HENZEY. One of a pair. Late eighteenth-century mahoganizing over the original green paint. Crest rail, oak; spindles, hickory; arm crest and seat, poplar; arms and knuckles, mahogany; arm supports, legs, and stretchers, maple. SW 21″, SD 15¾″, SH 17″, OH 42¾″. (Peter Wentz Farmstead)

    Though superficially similar to figure 11, this Henzey chair shows certain distinctive structural differences. For one thing, Henzey chose to make the chair with a sawed arm joined by an arm crest—a device not normally associated with Henzey. Furthermore, it is rare to find a Windsor chair of this period that combines a heavy arm crest with an elliptical seat, arm crests usually being found on chairs with shield-shaped seats. It's quite possible that this chair was a special order, made to match a set of other chairs with elliptical seats. Adding weight to this possibility is the fact that the chair has mahogany arms and knuckles, which might also have been specially ordered. (To date I have seen only a few chairs of this type with mahogany arms and knuckles.) The turnings of this chair are better developed than those of figure 11, but they are still not as well balanced as those of figure 10 because, once again, the leg taper is shorter than the second baluster turning.

14

15

14.   Armchair. Philadelphia, 1765–1780. Medial stretcher and one side stretcher are early replacements. Early nineteenth-century mahoganizing over a salmon-color ground, over the original green paint. Crest rail and arms, oak; spindles, hickory; arm crest and seat, poplar; arm supports, legs, and stretchers, maple. SW 20½″, SD 17″, SH 16½″, OH 42″. (Independence National Historical Park)

Because this chair has a shield-shaped seat, it is more typical of Philadelphia comb-backs of the period with this arm construction. This chair has nine back spindles, although chairs of this type usually have seven spindles in their backs and two short spindles under each arm. The use of the shield-shaped seat not only allows the arm supports to be stepped back quite far but also allows them to have a rakish angle. At the same time, the arms and knuckles appear to have a more dramatic projection than those of most other types of Windsors.

15.   Armchair. Philadelphia, 1765–1780. Bottoms of knuckles missing; far right spindle replaced. Black paint over traces of the original green. Crest rail and arms, oak; spindles, hickory; arm supports, legs, and stretchers, maple; seat, poplar. SW 20¼″, SD 16″, SH 16½″, OH 41″. (Independence National Historical Park)

A more typical seven-spindle fan-back with a shield-shaped seat, this chair exhibits a slightly different turning pattern from that of figure 14. Note the thickness of the arm supports as they enter the seat. The leg turnings would be better if they were a bit less rigid.

16.

16.   Armchair. Philadelphia, 1765–1780. Early nineteenth-century brownish-red paint over the original green. Crest rail and arms, oak; spindles, hickory; arm crest and seat, poplar; arm supports, legs, and stretchers, maple. SW 19¾″, SD 16¾″, SH 17¾″, OH 41½″. (Also see color plate III.) (Privately owned)

This chair is the finest example I have ever seen of a Philadelphia comb-back Windsor with a shield-shaped seat, arm crest, and turned arm supports. It is also the most formal Windsor I have encountered, and I believe it should be considered a masterpiece of its period and of its type. Furthermore, I have seen only one other chair of this type that also has blunt-arrow feet.

So often one can point up excellent details of a particular chair, while other parts can be criticized. Throughout this chair, however, not only are all the individual parts virtually perfect, but they also fit together in perfect harmony. For example, the slightly longer cylinder of the legs supporting a slightly shorter baluster emphasizes the leg splay; and the slightly elongated blunt-arrow feet lift the chair as though on toes. Did the chairmaker intentionally set out to create a perfect Windsor, or did he do it by chance and instinct? I do not know. There is no theory of perfect Windsor chairmaking; there is only the *practice* of chairmaking. And in my experience with hundreds of comb-back armchairs and thousands of Windsors, I have never seen Windsor chairmaking practiced better than in this chair.

16A. Armchair. A side view, showing the dramatic carving of the seat. The angle of the splayed legs emphasizes the rake of the arm supports, and the outward flare of the knuckles reflects the contour of the side of the seat.

16A

17

17.   Armchair. Massachusetts, 1770–1800. (Wayne Pratt)
Here is a New England interpretation of what by then had become a very popular Philadelphia style. A heavy arm crest and sawed arms are used, but the two arm pieces are joined in the Rhode Island manner, with a mounted crest. Unlike the knuckles of Philadelphia chairs, these knuckles are carved directly on the ends of the arms, which makes them appear a bit skimpy. This is a pleasing chair with nice splay and balance, but the seat carving and turning patterns are not as dynamic as those of better New England comb-backs. The ears of the comb-piece are smaller than those of comparable Philadelphia chairs, but more exaggerated. Note how the arched, carved contour below the ear is echoed in the carving behind the knuckle.

18. Armchair. Pennsylvania, possibly Philadelphia; 1765–1780. Refinished. Crest rail, legs, and stretchers, maple; spindles, hickory; arm crest and seat, poplar; arms and arm supports, oak. SW 17¼″, SD 16⅛″, SH 15⅜″, OH 39½″. (Privately owned)

A variant of figure 16, this chair has ram's-horn arm supports in the English style. It is a well-proportioned chair with crisp turnings and an interesting medial stretcher. Note the slightly flaring cylinders above the ball feet. The carved ears are beautifully executed but have somewhat longer necks than would ordinarily be found on a Philadelphia product.

19. Armchair. Massachusetts, 1780–1800. Medial stretcher replaced. Refinished. Crest rail and spindles, hickory; arm crest, arms, arm supports, legs, and stretchers, maple; seat, pine. SW 21¼″, SD 15″, SH 17¾″, OH 41″. (Joan and Don Mayoras)

Once again, we see a New England version of a Philadelphia-style comb-back with sawed arms and an arm crest. However, this is a highly stylized chair with a wonderfully flaring comb-piece, nicely carved ears, and spindles with great fanning and taper. Although the knuckles are carved directly on the ends of the arms, and hence are quite thin, they are also rather wide, which compensates for their thinness. The arm supports and legs, though slender, are crisply turned, and the side stretchers are more elaborate than one would expect on such a chair. Note the heavy scoring on the turnings, added as a decorative device. The seat is boldly saddled.

20.   Armchair. Massachusetts, 1780–1800. Very old crackled orange shellac over the original green paint. Crest rail, arm supports, legs, and stretchers, maple; spindles and arms, hickory; seat, pine. SW 21″, SD 15½″, SH 18½″, OH 45½″. (Richard Kozar)

This is a simple but elegant comb-back with crisp, graceful turnings and a well-carved seat. Note that the ears have gouge marks instead of the usual volutes. Over the years I have seen this motif used on several fan-back side chairs, and in every case, the chair's comb-piece has been made of maple. However, I have never seen another comb-back armchair with this motif.

21.   Armchair. New England, probably Massachusetts; 1780–1800. Original black paint. Crest rail and arms, oak; spindles, hickory; arm supports, legs, and stretchers, maple; seat, pine. SW 21″, SD 14¾″, SH 18″, OH 42½″. (Mark and Kathy Winchester)

Almost a study in tapers, this chair has well-defined turnings and a comb-piece with an exceptionally deep bend. All in all, a very dramatic Windsor statement.

20

21

23.   Armchair. Connecticut, 1780–1800. Nineteenth-century black paint with gilt striping over the original gray paint. Crest rail, maple; spindles, hickory; arms, oak; arm supports, legs, and stretchers, maple; seat, pine. SW 20⅛″, SD 14¾″, SH 18″, OH 41″. (Sam Bruccoleri)

The fine comb-piece of this chair—typical of certain Connecticut Windsors—has uncarved, neckless ears that turn upward and have an almost knife-edge thinness at the top. Other typical Connecticut features include the slightly bulbous spindles and the bulbous, high stretchers that narrow before they enter the legs. The heavily chamfered elliptical seat has a sharp pommel. This is a pleasing country product.

22.   Armchair. Rhode Island, 1780–1800. Refinished; traces of dark brown paint. Crest rail, spindles, and arms, hickory; back posts, arm supports, legs, and stretchers, maple; seat, yellow pine. SW 20″, SD 15¼″, OH 38¾″. (Museum of Early Southern Decorative Arts, Winston-Salem, N.C.)

Instead of the conventional tapering spindles, this chair has short, baluster-turned spindles on either end of the comb-piece—a feature occasionally found on Rhode Island Windsors. The effect is the same as that of Rhode Island bow-backs with so-called pipestem spindles (see figure 137). The turning patterns on this chair are typical of Rhode Island.

24. Armchair. Connecticut, probably the Westbrook area; 1780–1800. Nineteenth-century black paint with gilt striping over the original green paint. Crest rail, probably oak; spindles and arms, hickory; arm supports, legs, and stretchers, maple; seat, pine. SW 20½″, SD 15″, SH 18⅛″, OH 40″. (Kathleen Mulhern)

This is a more successful chair than figure 23 in practically every way except for the seat carving and the medial stretcher. The turning pattern is influenced by New York City Windsors.

25. Armchair. Connecticut, 1780–1800. Painted red. Crest rail and arms, ash; spindles, hickory; arm supports, legs, and stretchers, maple; seat, pine. SW 16¾″, SD 17½″, SH 17″, OH 37¾″. (Joan and Don Mayoras)

Judging by the large number of Connecticut comb-backs in this style that have been discovered, this type of chair must have been nearly as popular in Connecticut as the sack-back was in Philadelphia. Characteristically on the small side, these chairs usually have narrow ears that flare up; bulbous, tapering spindles; an arm rail with tiny handholds that echo the shape of the ears; and a shield-shaped seat. On this example, the seat seems a bit too thick for the small size of the chair. The baluster turnings are nicely done and seem to be influenced by New York City Windsors.

26. Armchair. Hudson River Valley or southern Connecticut, 1780–1800. Painted olive green. SW 21″, SD 15½″, SH 15¼″, OH 39″. (The Robert Wagner Collection)

This is an extremely interesting chair with arm-support and leg turnings like ones I have seen in other Windsors from the Hudson River Valley area. Possibly there is a Dutch influence at work here, since at least one other chair with similar turnings is branded HERRCK (see figure 91). Another similarity to figure 91 is the seat carving. Figure 94, a Connecticut sack-back, also has a similar seat carving. Note the pinwheel design on the ears and handholds—a favorite Connecticut motif. The piercing of the comb-piece is an unusual design feature. The comb-piece is basically Connecticut in style because of its upturned ears, reflecting the strong English influence on many Connecticut Windsor crest rails.

27. Armchair. Pennsylvania, 1790–1810. Seat upholstery is a later addition to cover potty cutout. Painted pale green, with arm supports painted orange, over the original dark green. Crest rail, arms, and legs, oak; spindles, hickory; arm supports and stretchers, maple; seat, pine. SW 20″, SD 15½″, SH 18½″, OH 44½″. (Eugene Pettinelli)

The legs and medial stretcher of this chair have bamboo-turned double bobbins, but the side stretchers and arm supports are baluster-turned. The bamboo leg turnings are typical of Pennsylvania. The chair is sturdy and well proportioned for such a late Windsor.

26

27

LOW-BACK
~
CHAIRS

L ike comb-back Windsors, low-backs are mainly identified with Philadelphia. When they were produced in other areas—as they seldom were—they were usually heavily influenced by the Philadelphia product.

Most of the Philadelphia examples display such early characteristics as untapered spindles, D-shaped seats, scrolled handholds, Queen Anne medial stretchers, and cylinder-and-ball feet. The only low-back form that stands apart is the Newport, Rhode Island, low-back, with its cross-stretchers and basically English design. (Those chairs, by the way, are often made of a single wood, such as maple or chestnut.)

By the 1770s, only a small proportion of Philadelphia low-back Windsor chairs reflected the latest fashion in Windsor design.[1] However, it is interesting to note that while few Windsor low-back chairs were produced during the bamboo period in Philadelphia (1785–1800), many Philadelphia low-back settees with bamboo turnings were made.

The low-back continued to be produced in smaller and smaller quantities during the first years of the nineteenth century. But the form was never part of the mainstream of Windsor fashion, and was always to remain a mid-eighteenth-century style.

---

28. Armchair. Philadelphia, 1740–1760. Nineteenth-century black paint over red, over the original green. Arm crest, arm supports, legs, and stretchers, maple; spindles, hickory; arms, oak; seat, poplar. SW 24¾″; SD 17⅛″; SH 17″; OH 28½″. (David Miller)

This is a classic Philadelphia low-back Windsor of the early period. The double-baluster-and-reel medial stretcher—sometimes called a Queen Anne stretcher—is socketed into the side stretchers with abrupt ball turnings. Here we also see the classic Philadelphia leg, with the top baluster buried midway into the underside of the seat; the elongated baluster turnings below that, over a reel and ring; and then a cylinder and the characteristic Philadelphia ball foot.

Note especially the turning pattern of the arm supports. There is a baluster turning right below the arm rail—very characteristic of the early chairs—which is turnip-like. It sits on a flaring collar, followed by a narrow cylinder, then an abrupt baluster, a thin neck, a wide ring, a thin neck, and, finally, a ring made to look like a ball buried deep in the seat.

The seat is characteristically D-shaped, with sharp, angular chamfering. The spindles are vertical, with no taper.

29. Armchair. Philadelphia, 1750–1770. Medial stretcher probably an early replacement; end piece of arm crest missing on right side. Nineteenth-century red paint over the original green. Arm crest and seat, poplar; spindles, hickory; arms, oak; arm supports, legs, and stretchers, maple. SW 25″, SD 17⅛″, SH 16¼″, OH 27½″. (Philip Bradley Antiques)

Although this low-back has many of the characteristics of figure 28, it is probably somewhat later because the turning pattern has been toned down, which is especially evident in the side stretchers. The paint surface and overall condition are good for such an early chair.

28

29

30.   Armchair. Philadelphia, 1765–1780. Branded R-B. One of a pair. Late nineteenth-century black paint, over red, over the original green. Arm crest and seat, poplar; spindles, hickory; arms, white oak; arm supports, legs, and stretchers, maple. SW 24⅝″, SD 17⅜″, SH 16¼″, OH 28¾″. (Independence National Historical Park)

Here is a good example of a slightly later version of the Philadelphia low-back. We can see the turnings beginning to change: the balusters have become much more gentle in their flow; the turnip-like turning at the top of the arm support has become smaller and not as bulbous; the collar above the reel at midleg has a rounded shoulder and is not as high and crisp. Note that the medial stretcher has a bulbous baluster turning with a ring on either side. The side stretchers, although similar to those of figure 29, no longer have the abrupt center ball turnings of figure 28.

The R-B brand is probably the identification mark of an owner. The chair has a New York State history, and owners' brands seem to have been common there.

31.   Armchair. Philadelphia area, 1765–1780. Refinished. Arm crest, poplar; spindles, ash; arms, oak; arm supports, legs, and stretchers, maple; seat, pine. SW 23⅞″, SD 17″, SH 17¼″, OH 29″. (Burlington County Historical Society)

The feet, legs and spindles of this chair offer additional evidence of how turning styles change over time. First, this chair has blunt-arrow feet, as opposed to ball feet. The balusters and medial stretcher are like those found on chairs in such outlying areas of Philadelphia as Bucks and Chester counties. Note also the slight taper of the spindles, an indication of lateness on these chairs. In this photograph, the decorative score marks on the tops of the arms can be seen clearly.

32. Armchair. Philadelphia, 1765–1780. Marked A.C.J. PAINTER 1888 on the seat bottom. Medial stretcher bobbin broken in the center. Late-nineteenth-century grain-painted to imitate rosewood, over a salmon-color ground, over the original green paint with yellow decoration. Arm crest and seat, poplar; spindles, hickory; arms, oak; arm supports, legs, and stretchers, maple. SW 24¾″, SD 16¾″, SH 17″, OH 28¾″. (Claude and Alvan Bisnoff)

Note the slight concavity of the leg cylinders, a feature of some Philadelphia low-backs and comb-backs. The side stretchers are unusually bulbous for this sort of chair. In addition to being a fine example of its type, this chair is also interesting for its late nineteenth-century paint decoration, used to update a Windsor form that had come back into fashion as a so-called captain's chair.

33. Armchair. Philadelphia area, 1765–1790. Old refinish. Arm crest, poplar; spindles, hickory; arms, chestnut; arm supports, legs, and stretchers, maple; seat, pine. SW 23¾″, SD 16″, SH 15¾″, OH 27½″. (Burlington County Historical Society)

A provincial copy of a Philadelphia form, this chair is not as sophisticated as previous examples. Thick throughout, the arm rail and arm supports seem a bit clumsy. The leg turnings are not well proportioned, and the cylinders are too wide and too long for the size of the balusters. The abrupt bulb in the medial stretcher makes the ends of the stretcher seem sticklike.

32

33

34

34.   Armchair. Philadelphia, 1765–1780. Refinished; traces of white paint over the original green. Arm crest and seat, poplar; spindles, hickory; arms and arm supports, oak; legs and stretchers, maple. SW 18⅜″, SD 17″, SH 17¾″, OH 29⅜″. (Eugene Pettinelli)

The fact that this is a Philadelphia low-back in the English or High Wickham style, as opposed to a comb-back, makes this an extremely rare form—and indeed, it is the only such chair I have seen. Nevertheless, there is no doubt that this chair was originally made as a low-back and is not simply a comb-back that has lost its comb. First, the spindles do not penetrate the arm crest; second, the arm crest itself rolls over in the back, as it would not do on a comb-back.

Its English features include the ram's-horn arm supports and the shovel-shaped seat, which is squared off on the back edge and which has no "rain gutter."[2] The chamfering on either side of each scrolled arm is unusual, but the blunt-arrow feet and the stretchers are typical Philadelphia products.

35.   Armchair. Newport, Rhode Island, 1764. Made for Newport's Redwood Library and Atheneum in 1764, probably by Timothy Waterhouse. One of 12. Black paint over several other coats of paint, over the original bottle green. Made entirely in maple, except the pine seat. SW 22″, SD 15⅛″, SH 16″, OH 27½″. (The Redwood Library and Atheneum)

Based on physical evidence of the Windsors I have seen over the years, I am increasingly convinced that very few Windsor chairs were produced in New England prior to the end of the Revolutionary War. Before that time, New England residents were saturated, and apparently satisfied, with the exported products of Philadelphia Windsor makers. However, in Newport, Rhode Island—a center of high-style furniture—the type of low-back Windsor shown here was produced almost in isolation before 1776. The Redwood Library and Atheneum has documentation indicating that this particular chair—part of a set of 12—was purchased in 1764.

As far as we know, this is the earliest type of Windsor produced in New England, and it shows a strong English influence in the turning patterns of its arm supports and legs. The back construction and cross-stretchers are quite similar to those of formal Newport cabriole-leg corner chairs of the period. Note especially the small arrows at the ends of the stretchers just before they enter the legs. Also shown clearly in the photo is the back construction: the arm crest sits atop the sawed arms, which meet in the back of the chair in a butt joint. (In Philadelphia low-backs, the arm crest is attached with a lap joint.) Similar Rhode Island Windsors exist, but they are provincial-looking and were probably not made in Newport. This is another example of how Windsor chairmakers interpreted more formal designs of the period.

35

36. Armchair. Pennsylvania, 1765–1790. Refinished; traces of white paint and the original green paint. Arms, arm supports, seat, legs, and stretchers, poplar; spindles, ash. SW 20⅝″, SD 16⅝″, SH 18″, OH 28¼″. (Corinne and Chris Machmer)

This is the only low-back Windsor of its type that I have ever seen. However, while it may be unique, it is related to a group of three low-back settees in the same style, two of which are shown in figures 208 and 209 and which were found in the Pennsylvania-Maryland border area. The leg turning and stretchers of this piece are identical to those of figure 209. Unlike most low-backs, this chair does not have a separate arm crest; instead, the arms with their false crest are made in two pieces that are joined in the back with a large dovetail joint.

The elliptical seat, with its pronounced pommel and heavy chamfering, as well as the stretcher turnings, are like those found on Lancaster County, Pennsylvania, fan-backs and sack-backs. Also, the seat is quite thick (about three inches), another provincial characteristic. Although the spindles are not decoratively turned, as they are on figures 208 and 209, they do angle progressively outward from the center until the outermost spindles match the angle of the arm supports. Overall, this is a very fine and interesting chair that, unfortunately, has been refinished.

37. Armchair. Probably New Jersey; early nineteenth century. Crackled dark brown varnish, probably original. Arm crest, probably maple; spindles, hickory; arms, oak; arm supports, legs, and stretchers, maple; seat, poplar or pine. SW 25″, SD 16″, SH 16⅞″, OH 27″. (Privately owned; courtesy of Federation Antiques, Inc.)

I have seen several comb-backs with turnings similar to those of this chair that have come from the Trenton, New Jersey, area. They were probably produced in the same shop during the first quarter of the nineteenth century. The legs are reminiscent of the work of a spinning-wheel maker.

37

36

FAN-
BACK

~

CHAIRS

Fan-back side chairs were produced in large numbers, not only in Philadelphia but also in New England. The armchair variety seems to have been most popular in coastal Massachusetts, including Nantucket—whose craftsmen were probably influenced by the small quantity of Philadelphia fan-back armchairs produced and exported. In Philadelphia, the fan-back armchair was made in both the blunt-arrow and later tapered-leg style, whereas in coastal Massachusetts the tapered-leg style dominated.

Oddly enough, the fan-back chair seems to have been largely ignored by the New York City chairmakers. Over the years I have seen only a handful that might have been produced in New York, and none that I would judge to be unequivocally New York in origin.

Like the Massachusetts fan-backs, those from Rhode Island often display a Philadelphia influence. Perhaps half of the Connecticut fan-backs use a comb-piece with uncarved, turned-up ears reminiscent of English, rather than Philadelphia, models. The bulk of the Connecticut, the Rhode Island, and the Massachusetts fan-backs have ears that turn down and have carved volutes. Generally speaking, when carved volutes are used, the ear contour turns down; when the ears are plain, the contour turns up. The plain, upturned comb-piece does show up in the simpler Philadelphia versions. In New England, this plain comb-piece often appears in certain otherwise quite elaborate fan-backs, especially those from Connecticut.

38.   Armchair. New England, probably Newport, Rhode Island; 1765–1780. Original greenish-black paint with gilt striping and decoration. Crest rail and arms, oak; back posts and spindles, hickory; seat, pine; arm supports, legs, and stretchers, maple. SW 19¾", SD (including tailpiece) 20½", SH 17", OH 41½". (Bernard & S. Dean Levy, Inc.)

An elegant example of a New England fan-back armchair, this type was first produced in Philadelphia and modeled after English chairs.[3] Particularly fine features include the arm scroll, reminiscent of Philadelphia low-back Windsor handholds, and the beautifully turned blunt-arrow feet, which retain their full height. Interestingly, in the English fashion, the legs of this chair do not penetrate the seat, which is practically full-round with the wood grain running on the diagonal so that the tailpiece can be cut directly from the seat plank. In Philadelphia, this type of chair always seems to be a brace-back. Other typical Philadelphia characteristics include five long, almost perpendicular spindles; back posts that fan out; and bracing spindles filling the space between the back posts and back spindles.

38

39. Armchair. Philadelphia, 1765–1780. Early nineteenth-century black paint over the original olive green. Crest rail, back posts, arm supports, legs, and stretchers, maple; spindles, maple or hickory; arms, oak; seat, poplar. SW 19″, SD 17″, tailpiece 3⅞″, SH 17″. (Chester County Historical Society)

Although this fan-back armchair is generally constructed like the one in figure 38, an obvious difference is the crest rail, which is similar to the arm crest of a low-back Windsor. The back posts have a long baluster above the arm, and the scrolled arms end abruptly and look like unfinished knuckle handholds—a not uncommon feature of these chairs. The medial stretcher has no rings, and the legs do penetrate the seat.

39

40. Armchair. New York, 1770–1790. Nineteenth-century black paint with yellow striping and decoration over the original green. Crest rail, oak; spindles and back posts, hickory; arms, arm supports, legs, and stretchers, maple; seat, poplar. SW 18¾", SD (including tailpiece) 19¾", SH 17¼", OH 43½". (Suzanne Courcier and Robert Wilkins)

The basic style of this chair is that of Philadelphia. Similarities include the ringed back posts, the flaring, scrolled ears, and abruptly ending arms. But the leg turnings are quite different, and typical of New York City in their bulbousness and long taper. The seat, though round, has not been carved well from underneath to create the illusion of thinness, suggesting that the chair may be provincial and not from New York City. Similarly, the arms have a provincial thickness. Such chairs were produced mainly in Philadelphia and Massachusetts, and it is rare to find one with New York turnings.

41

40

41. Armchair. Pennsylvania, 1770–1790. Very old black paint with gilt striping over the original black. Crest rail, oak; spindles, hickory; arms, arm supports, legs, and stretchers, maple; seat, pine. SW 18", SD 16", SH 16", OH 40". (Tom Brown)

Over the years this type of chair has come to be called a "lady's chair" because of its narrowness. It is an unusual form, and probably a provincial example of a much more sophisticated Philadelphia type. The chair has the blunt-arrow feet of the earlier 1750–1770 period, but the tops of the legs and the arm supports are in a later style. The seat is nicely sculpted but a litte too thick, making the undercarriage appear too small. The necks of the ears are long and rather quaint, and, interestingly, the volutes are only painted on, not carved. The center back spindle has been turned to echo the shape of the arm supports. Every time I have seen a similar center spindle on a fan-back Windsor, the chair has not been a brace-back; it is as though the added "back post" gives the chair enough extra strength to make back bracing unnecessary.

42. Side chair. Philadelphia, 1780–1800. Branded J[ohn] STOW PHIL.^A *fecit*. Refinished. Crest rail, oak; spindles and back post, hickory; seat, poplar; legs and stretchers, maple. (Independence National Historical Park)

This is a "garden variety" nine-spindle fan-back of its period, but it is interesting because it is the only known chair branded by John Stow. Furthermore, it is very unusual to find a Philadelphia product with the words *fecit Phila.*, or "made in Philadelphia," branded in Latin or in any other language.

43. Side chair. Philadelphia, 1765–1780. Branded I. [Joseph] HENZEY. Very old black paint over the original green. Crest rail, oak; spindles and back posts, hickory; seat, poplar; legs and stretchers, maple. SW 18½″, SD 17″, SH 18″, OH 38″. (Privately owned)

In comparison with figure 42, this is a very ambitious chair in the highest style. It has crisp turnings, beautifully scrolled ears, and a broad, well-saddled seat.

42

43

44

44.   Side chair. Philadelphia, 1765–1790. Label reads: "Maker of Windsor and rush bottom chairs/Made and sold by/William Widdefield [sic]/in Spruce St. below the drawbridge/Philadelphia." One of a pair. Very old black paint over the original green. Crest rail, probably oak; spindles and back posts, hickory; seat, poplar; legs and stretchers, maple. SW 17½", SD 17", tailpiece 4", SH 18", OH 39¼". (Mr. and Mrs. Victor Johnson)

Far more elegant than the typical Philadelphia product, this chair betters even the one in figure 43. Here we see all of the brilliant design and proportions of the best Connecticut and Massachusetts fan-backs. The long taper of the legs, for example, is quite graceful and rarely found on Philadelphia Windsors. The back is taller and more narrow-waisted than those of most Philadelphia chairs, the shape of the comb-piece has a more distinctive roll, and the seat is more deeply saddled. Furthermore, this is a brace-back chair, and most Philadelphia fan-backs were not made this way. Perhaps Widdifield, known to be a Philadelphian, had studied New England Windsors and was influenced by their designs.

45. Side chair. Philadelphia, 1780–1800. Branded L[awrence] ALLWINE. Reupholstered. Nineteenth-century black paint, over the original moss green, over a red ground. Crest rail and back posts, oak; spindles, hickory; seat, poplar; legs and stretchers, maple. SW 18″, SD 15½″, SH 18½″, OH 36½″. (James Brooks)

Because the seat of this chair was carved to be fitted with upholstery, it is not saddled. On the front of the comb-piece, spindles, legs, and stretchers is ornamental gouge carving, which was probably executed in the early nineteenth century to update the chair and make it fit in with the then fashionable "fancy" chairs.

46. Side chair. Pennsylvania, possibly Philadelphia; 1770–1790. Original dark mustard-color paint, oxidized to a dark brown. Crest rail, oak; back posts, ash; spindles, hickory; seat, poplar; legs and stretchers, maple. SW 17⅜″, SD 15½″, tailpiece 2″, SH 18″, OH 36½″. (Nancy and Tom Tafuri)

This chair is something of a puzzle. The seat and leg turnings are finely executed and have a Philadelphia look, but the medial stretcher and the comb-piece seem provincial. Also, Philadelphia chairs of this type usually have shorter backs and uncarved ears. Thus it is difficult to pinpoint the origin of this piece. The original paint has oxidized nicely to a deep brown.

48. Side chair. Richmond, Virginia, 1780–1800. Label reads: "Made and Warranted by William Pointer." Refinished. Crest rail, legs, and stretchers, maple; back posts, ash; spindles, hickory; seat, poplar. SW 16⅞", SD 16", SH 16⅜", OH 35⅜". (Museum of Early Southern Decorative Arts, Winston-Salem, N.C.)

William Pointer was a Virginia chairmaker who was apparently influenced by Windsors made in Philadelphia. This is a pleasing chair, but it does not have the authority of the Philadelphia product.

47. Side chair. Philadelphia, 1770–1790. Nineteenth-century reddish-brown paint over traces of the original green. Crest rail, oak; back posts and spindles, hickory; seat, poplar; legs and stretchers, maple. SW 17¾", SD 16¼", SH 18", OH 35¾". (Eugene Pettinelli)

A very well-proportioned fan-back, this is the type of chair that was exported by the thousands from Philadelphia by Stephen Girard and other shippers and chairmakers.

49. Side chair. Chester County, Pennsylvania, 1780–1800. Branded J[esse] CUSTER. Late nineteenth-century black paint over the original green. Crest rail, oak; back posts, legs, and stretchers, maple; spindles, hickory; seat, poplar. SW 17¼″, SD 16⅛″, SH 17″, OH 37″. (Lori and Craig Mayor)

Because of the slender taper of its legs, which Custer seems to have used in most of his leg turnings, this is a very elegant side chair—more graceful than most Pennsylvania side chairs. The chair would be even better if it had carved ears.

49

50

50. Side chair. Lancaster County, Pennsylvania, 1760–1780. Early nineteenth-century dark red crackled varnish. Crest rail, back posts, and spindles, hickory; seat, poplar; legs and stretchers, maple. SW 19¼″, SD 15¼″, SH 17″, OH 37″. (Privately owned)

Here is certainly one of the most beautiful examples of this type of Lancaster County Windsor. The comb-piece is of the finest design that can be found in Lancaster County. And note the blunt-arrow feet: they are wider in diameter than the rest of the legs. This means that the maker turned the legs narrower than the feet, chiseling away the extra wood—an extremely unusual technique for a Windsor chair. This technique requires extra work and is much like the method used in making certain early Pennsylvania slat-back chairs which have ball feet that are wider than the rest of the legs.

51

51.   Side chair. Lancaster County, Pennsylvania, 1780–1800. Reddish-brown paint with blue striping over the original green paint. Crest rail and spindles, hickory or ash; back posts, ash; seat, poplar; legs and stretchers, maple. SW 19″, SD 15″, SH 16½″, OH 37½″. (Marjorie Hooper)

This is another superb example of Lancaster County Windsor-making with the same Germanic feeling as figure 50. In fact, the design seems akin to certain Moravian chairs with stick legs and plank seats. The ears are higher than those of figure 50, the comb-piece is wider, and the back posts are more elaborately turned. On the other hand, the slimmer turnings of figure 50 make the seat look taller and the chair as a whole more stately. It's a toss-up as to which chair is better. Note how the back of figure 51 does not seem to fan out but simply leans backward; this is a common feature of many Lancaster County fan-backs.

52.   Side chair. Lancaster County, Pennsylvania, 1770–1790. Traces of original green paint. Crest rail, back posts, and spindles, hickory; seat, poplar; legs and stretchers, maple. SW 16¾″, SD 15½″, SH 14″, OH 34″. (Frank Rentschler)

Note the modified blunt-arrow leg design on this chair. The cylinder has been shortened above the foot to achieve a low overall height for the chair. With this type of leg—as opposed to the tapered leg—the maker had to custom-reproportion the length of the cylinder to make the chair higher or lower; with the tapered leg, all he had to do was cut the leg to the desired length. Short chairs like this are often called "slipper chairs." This one has all the characteristic Lancaster County features except an imposing comb-piece.

52

53.   Side chair. Probably Lancaster County, Pennsylvania; 1775–1790. Refinished. Crest rail, back posts, and spindles, hickory; seat, poplar; legs and stretchers, maple. SW 19″, SD 14¾″, SH 17″, OH 36″. (Robert Stallfort)

This is a very simplified chair with generic back posts and legs in the Philadelphia style. The seat shape, however, is typical of Lancaster County. Note the similarity to the crest rail of figure 52.

53

54

54.   Side chair. Connecticut, 1790–1810. Branded S. McCORMICK. Nineteenth-century beige paint over red, over black, over the original green. Crest rail, hickory; back posts, legs, and stretchers, pine; spindles, ash; seat, poplar. SW 15⅝″, SD 16¼″, tailpiece 2⅜″, SH 16¼″, OH 35⁵⁄₁₆″ (Steven and Helen Kellogg)

It is very unusual for the turned parts of a Windsor chair to be made of pine, as they are in this chair. Because pine is relatively soft, the legs, stretchers, and back posts are not turned as crisply as they might have been. Overall, the chair has a country look.

55.   Side chair. Connecticut, 1790–1810. Early nineteenth-century black paint, ringed and striped with gilt, over the original green paint. Crest rail, ash; back posts, hickory or ash; spindles, hickory; seat, pine; legs and stretchers, maple. SW 15″, SD 15½″, SH 15¼″, OH 35¼″. (Melissa and Gary Lipton)

The sides of the seats of Connecticut chairs are usually heavily chamfered, as here. The back posts have an interesting long taper, and the legs are unusual because there is no turning on them before they enter the seat. Note the decorative leaf carving on the ears—another unusual feature.

56.   Side chair. Probably New York City; 1780–1800. Refinished; weathered surface. Crest rail, oak; back posts, chestnut; spindles, hickory; seat, pine; legs and stretchers, maple. SW 17″, SD 16⅛″, SH 16¾″, OH 37″. (Philip Bradley Antiques)

Sack-backs, bow-backs, and continuous-arm chairs from New York City are quite common, but fan-backs are almost nonexistent. Nevertheless, this chair may be one of those rarities. The thicks and thins of the turnings are remarkably like those of other known New York City Windsors. Note the beautifully carved ears with very short necks. If the chair is from New York City, it may explain why the necks are so short in comparison with similar chairs from nearby areas such as Connecticut.

55

56

57

58

58. Side chair. Connecticut, possibly the Westbrook area; 1780–1800. Early nineteenth-century dark red paint striped with gilt over the original blackish-green paint; seat has a coat of black varnish. Crest rail, oak; back posts, legs, and stretchers, maple; spindles, ash; seat, pine. SW 15½″, SD 17¾″, SH 17½″, OH 36⅞″. (Nancy and Tom Tafuri)

This is a very vigorously turned fan-back typical of Windsors from the Westbrook area of Connecticut. Note the nicely sculpted seat and the high taper of the back posts.

57. Armchair. Probably Connecticut; 1780–1800. Early blue-green paint over original salmon ground. Crest rail and spindles, hickory; back posts, arms, arm supports, legs, and side stretchers, maple; seat, pine; medial stretcher, chestnut. SW 23½″, SD 16″, SH 18″, OH 48½″. (Privately owned; courtesy of James and Nancy Glazer)

An exceptionally tall chair with an almost fully vertical stance, this is a good example of a tenon-arm fan-back without bracing spindles. The crest rail is beautifully scrolled, like that of figure 56, and the spindles show a kind of Connecticut swelling. The back posts are modestly turned, with the most complex parts right below the crest rail. The legs and stretchers are typical of the type found on many Connecticut Windsor fan-backs. However, it is unusual to find a Connecticut Windsor with a D-shaped seat—a seat shape that almost dictates vertical arm supports with no rake.

59. Side chair. Connecticut, 1790–1810. Nineteenth-century varnish over the original green paint with gilt striping. Crest rail, back posts, and spindles, hickory; seat, pine; legs and stretchers, maple. SW 14⅛″, SD 15¾″, SH 16½″, OH 36½″. (Nancy and Tom Tafuri)

Connecticut seems to have produced endless examples of very good, stylized provincial chairs, of which this is one. The crest rail rolls in almost to the first spindle, and the seat is heavily chamfered. Note the double baluster-and-reel medial stretcher, which is also found on Connecticut furniture made in styles other than Windsor.

60

59

60. Side chair. Connecticut, 1780–1810. Nineteenth-century black paint striped with gilt over earlier red paint. Crest rail and spindles, hickory; back posts, legs, and stretchers, maple; seat, pine. SW 14¼″, SD 17″, SH 14¼″, OH 34¼″. (Privately owned)

This relatively small "youth" chair is, in the Connecticut tradition, highly idiosyncratic. The crest rail is V-notched, and the contour of the seat on the front edge is nearly round. The turning pattern of the medial stretcher can also be found on certain Connecticut rush-bottom chairs.

61. Side chair. Connecticut, Roxbury area, 1780–1810. Nineteenth-century black paint over the original salmon red. Crest rail, back posts, and stretchers, chestnut; spindles, hickory; seat, pine. SW 17¼″, SD 16″, SH 17″, OH 36½″. (Also see color plate XIV.) (Charles Sterling)

Here is another charming, zany example of the imagination of Connecticut Windsor chairmakers. Note the crest rail with its pin-wheel carving—a motif found on all sorts of Connecticut furniture. The seat, with its cleft front, is an exaggerated form of the traditional shield-shaped seat. By comparison with the rest of the chair, the legs and stretchers seem rather tame, but such inconsistencies are normal on provincial Windsors.

61

62. Side chair. Connecticut, 1780–1810. Original black paint over a gray ground. Crest rail, back posts, spindles, and stretchers, hickory; seat, pine; legs, maple. SW 17″, SD 14½″, tailpiece 3¾″, SH 16″, OH 37¼″. (Bernard & S. Dean Levy, Inc.)

The cupid's-bow crest rail is a wonderfully idiosyncratic conceit, and very "Connecticut." The terminations of the ears are reminiscent of so-called statehouse Windsors from the Hartford area. The bulbous spindles and the arrows at the ends of the stretchers are also Connecticut features, but the turning pattern is quite individualistic, as is the rotated H-stretcher arrangement. Note that the tailpiece is part of a spline that runs from the front to the back of the seat; the front edge of the spline can be seen in the photograph.

63

63. Armchair. Coastal Massachusetts, possibly Nantucket; 1780–1800. Mid-nineteenth-century red paint over the original green paint with salmon striping. Crest rail, oak; back posts, arm supports, legs, and stretchers, maple; spindles, hickory; arms, birch; seat, pine. SW 21⅞″, SD 16¼″, tailpiece 4⅜″, SH 15¾″, OH 41¾″. (Steven and Helen Kellogg)

This type of tenoned knuckle-arm Windsor always seems to emphasize the design of the back and arms over the design of the undercarriage. The back of this particular chair is the finest of its type, and the back posts are extraordinary. So often in these chairs all the decorative turnings of the back posts occur above the arms, but on this chair the back posts are also turned below the arms. The crest rail, with its small scrolled ears and long necks, is very well designed. The tailpiece is a separate piece of wood that is mortised into the seat, as is usual in chairs of this type.

64.   Armchair. Coastal Massachusetts, 1780–1800. Old shellac finish over traces of yellow paint, over a gray ground. Crest rail, oak; back posts and spindles, hickory; arms, arm supports, legs, and stretchers, maple; seat, pine. SW 22⅜", SD 17⅞", SH 17½", OH 43¾". (Mr. and Mrs. R. W. P. Allen)

Fan-back armchairs, although relatively rare, seem to turn up in the coastal Massachusetts area more often than anywhere else, including Philadelphia. They usually have certain characteristics—with, of course, variations in detail. As in this case, the seats are elliptical and the tailpiece is usually a mortised-on addition. This chair has very sensuous arms and knuckles. The elaborately saddled seat has a great overhang in relation to the legs. This is a particularly handsome chair, albeit a bit more conservative than the one shown in figure 63. Here, the back posts seem to keep themselves much more in place as back posts, complementing rather than upstaging the leg turnings. The medial stretcher with its waferlike rings is characteristic of this Windsor. Note the simplified ear volutes compared with Philadelphia examples (see figure 44).

65. Side chair. Massachusetts, 1780–1800. Nineteenth-century black paint striped with gilt over the original gray-green paint. Crest rail, hickory or oak; back posts, legs, and stretchers, maple; spindles, hickory; seat, pine. SW 17″, SD 16½″, SH 18″, OH 37½″. (Sam Bruccoleri)

The leg turnings of this beautiful Massachusetts fan-back are perfectly balanced, and the vigorous turnings of the back posts, which can sometimes be spindly on these chairs, are in this case a match for the legs. The crest rail is quite nice, with a fine flourish to the ears.

66. Side chair. Massachusetts, 1780–1800. Traces of old black paint over traces of the original green. Crest rail, back posts, legs, and stretchers, chestnut; spindles, hickory; seat, pine. SW 17¼″, SD 16½″, SH 17¾″. (John Bartram Association)

Compared with figure 65, this chair seems delicate. Yet the crest rails and the seats of the two are almost identical.

67.   Side chair. Massachusetts, 1780–1800. Very old tobacco-brown shellac over traces of yellow paint, over traces of the original green paint. Crest rail, ash; back posts, legs, and stretchers, maple; spindles, hickory; seat, pine. SW 17¾″, SD 17″, SH 17½″, OH 35″. (Privately owned)

The crest rail of this beautifully turned and well-proportioned chair does not terminate in the usual turned volutes but in rosettes—a popular motif more common to bonnet-top highboys and other case pieces from Massachusetts, Connecticut, and Rhode Island. The seat is a very thick 2¾ inches.

67A.   Side chair. Detail of rosette terminating crest rail.

67A

67

68. Side chair. Boston or possibly Rhode Island; 1780–1810. Old varnish over the original gray paint. Crest rail, legs, and stretchers, maple; back posts and seat, chestnut; spindles, hickory. SW 16⅛″, SD 16″, SH 17¼″, OH 34″. (Philip Bradley Antiques)

Very stylized, this chair has fine leg splay and a well-carved seat. The seat is almost flat on the bottom and is carved on the top. The legs are Rhode Island in style. The crest rail is not as well realized as the rest of the chair. The back posts are idiosyncratic, and there are six back spindles instead of the more common seven.

68

69

69. Side chair. Rhode Island, 1780–1800. Branded U. TUFTS. Old green paint over lighter green. Back posts, legs, and stretchers, maple; spindles, ash; seat, walnut. (David A. Schorsch, Inc.)

This is quite simply one of the finest Rhode Island fan-backs, with extraordinarily bold, crisp turnings.

71. Side chair. Probably the Boston area; 1790–1810. One of four. Old blackish-green paint over the original brown; seat, buff color. Crest rail and spindles, hickory; back posts and legs, maple; seat, pine; stretchers, chestnut. SW 14¾″, SD 15½″, SH 17¼″, OH 36″. (Privately owned)

This is a small chair with a small seat. The thick bamboo spindles, which are almost as heavy as the back posts, are typical of chairs known to be from the Boston area, and their design compensates for the ordinariness of the undercarriage.

70. Side chair. Connecticut, 1780–1800. Nineteenth-century black paint with gilt striping over older white paint, over the original green. Crest rail, oak; back posts and spindles, hickory; seat, pine; legs, maple; stretchers, chestnut. SW 15″, SD 16¾″, SH 14½″, OH 35″. (Mr. and Mrs. Paul Flack)

For a chair of such small overall size, this chair has a high back. It was probably intended as a youth chair. Note the finely shaped spindles and boldly turned legs.

72.   Side chair. Connecticut, 1790–1810. Original black paint with late-nineteenth-century decoration. Crest rail, back posts, spindles, legs, and stretchers, hickory; seat, chestnut. SW 16¾″, SD 15⅞″, SH 18″, OH 36³⁄₁₆″. (Steven and Helen Kellogg)

The combination of bamboo legs and medial stretcher with baluster side stretchers and back posts turned in the Connecticut pattern is interesting. The crest rail is quite simple, but nicely realized.

73.   Side chair. Maine, 1790–1820. Original black paint with gilt and red decoration. Crest rail, ash; back posts and spindles, hickory or ash; seat, pine; legs and stretchers, maple. SW 13¾″, SD 15½″, SH 18″, OH 33⅞″. (Janie and Dr. Peter Gross)

Because the ears of its crest rail do not project upward, the overall feeling of this graceful chair is like that of a rod-back Windsor. The beautifully designed bamboo legs, with turnings balanced like those of the earlier vase-and-ring turning style, plus the high H-stretcher arrangement, equals an excellent design. The seven finely shaped back spindles, turned in a simple bamboo pattern, swell slightly.

74

74.   Side chair. Probably New England; 1800–1820. Refinished; crest rail repaired. Crest rail and spindles, chestnut; back posts, legs, and stretchers, maple; seat, pine. SW 16½″, SD 14½″, SH 17½″, OH 36″. (Mr. and Mrs. R. W. P. Allen)

As much folk art as it is furniture, this is one of those fan-back Windsor chairs that defies identification. I admit that I have never seen anything like it. The back posts, turned and carved in a wonderfully imaginative way, have a shape that generally echoes that of the seat contour. And the seat, carved as it is, gives the impression of being made of some sort of pliable material. Strangely, the bracing spindles, shaped like the back posts, are socketed right into the back of the seat, which has no tailpiece. The comb-piece is beaded on the bottom edge and has two horns on top. The only "normal" features of this quirky chair are its legs, stretchers, and spindles.

SACK-BACK

~

CHAIRS

Judging from the number of sack-back Windsors that have survived over the last two centuries, the form enjoyed great popularity. A closer look at the various types of sack-backs will shed some light on regional Windsor production in general.

Produced after 1760, the majority of sack-backs were made in Philadelphia and exported by the thousands to all the Colonies. Philadelphia sack-backs are so similar in design that it is difficult to attribute a chair to a maker unless the chair is branded. Many Philadelphia chairmakers worked for each other at one time or another, or worked in close proximity. From a purely business point of view, that was probably advantageous, since different shops could be called upon to fill a particularly large shipping order that one shop was unable to handle alone—without a noticeable difference among the products.

Philadelphia sack-backs influenced most Windsor-makers in other areas—primarily in one of three ways. First, in centers such as Boston and Wilmington, Delaware, many chairmakers made sack-back Windsors with turning patterns and bow shapes quite similar to those of the conservative Philadelphia Quaker sack-backs. Second, Windsor chairmakers in Connecticut embraced the sack-back design but made it their own, and in my experience the widest variety of sack-back patterns were produced in Connecticut. Finally, although New York did not produce nearly the quantity of sack-backs one might expect from such a large chairmaking center, the New York sack-backs, while similar to the Philadelphia model, almost always exhibit the wonderfully bulbous turning patterns also found on New York bow-backs and continuous-arm chairs. This seems to hold true for Rhode Island as well, although we do not have evidence of nearly as many Rhode Island sack-backs as bow-back armchairs. Like their Connecticut counterparts, Rhode Island chairmakers were servicing local needs, and their designs tended to take on characteristics that changed from county to county and even shop to shop within a small geographic region. For example, witness the wide-ranging influence of E. B. Tracy's designs on many Connecticut Windsor chairmakers.

As might be expected, as soon as a particular shop's designs caught on, other chairmakers would follow suit, producing what we would today call knock-offs of a similar design. Of course, the more successful a particular shop, the more apprentices it needs. Eventually, some of those apprentices go into business for themselves, taking with them the design and construction techniques they learned at the hand of the master craftsman.

75

75.   Armchair. Philadelphia, 1765–1780. Old shellac finish over traces of the original green paint. Crest rail and arms, oak; spindles, hickory; arm supports, legs, and stretchers, maple; seat, poplar. SW 21¼″, SD 15¾″, SH 17½″, OH 38½″. (James and Nancy Glazer)

We begin with this chair because it is the only sack-back Windsor I have ever seen with the cylinder-and-ball foot of the Philadelphia comb-back Windsor. That design fell out of favor when Windsors became a mass-market product, so we can speculate that this chair was a custom order. The piece shows all the characteristics of the designs of Joseph Henzey and was probably made by him (see figure 79).

76. Armchair, Philadelphia, 1765–1780. Nineteenth-century apple-green paint with red, blue, and gilt striping and decoration, over the original green. Crest rail and arms, oak; spindles, hickory; arm supports, legs, and stretchers, maple; seat, poplar. SW 21¾″. SD 16⁵⁄₁₆″, SH 17¾″, OH 38⅝″. (Also see color plate II.) (Privately owned)

This is a very fine, well-turned sack-back with a strong, heavy-gauge bow. The stocky leg turnings are like those found on Windsors branded by Francis Trumble. What makes the design work so well are the closely spaced spindles. The two short spindles behind the arm supports represent a feature almost always found on these nine-spindle chairs. Like most other Philadelphia chairs of the period, this one has two ring turnings on either side of the medial stretcher. The paint surface adds an extra dimension to the piece.

77

76

77. Armchair. Philadelphia, 1765–1780. Branded W[illiam] WIDDEFIELD. Original green paint. Crest rail and arms, oak; spindles and arm supports, hickory; seat, poplar; legs and stretchers, maple. SW 21⅝″, SD 16⅜″, SH 17½″, OH 37¾″. (Privately owned)

Here is a seven-spindle Philadelphia sack-back of the best quality. It has a scrolled, flat arm, as do most seven-spindle Philadelphia sack-backs, but it also has two short spindles behind the arm support, usually found only on nine-spindle chairs like figure 76. The teardrop-shaped turning at the base of the arm support is an attractive feature.

78. Armchair. Philadelphia, 1765–1780. Bow repaired. Nineteenth-century varnish over traces of the original green paint. Crest rail and arms, oak; spindles, hickory; arm supports, legs, and stretchers, maple; seat, poplar. SW 21¾″, SD 15¾″, SH 17″, OH 37″. (Anthony Leone)

A well-proportioned chair, this is one of the type that was produced by the thousands in Philadelphia and exported. It is a good, solid, conservative Quaker product, not as bold as the preceding chairs and lacking the extra short spindle behind each arm support. The turning pattern of the arm supports is much more typical of the Philadelphia product.

79. Armchair. Philadelphia, 1765–1780. Bottoms of knuckles missing. Dark green paint over the original green. Crest rail and arms, oak; spindles, hickory; arm supports, legs, and stretchers, maple; seat, poplar. SW 20⅞″, SD 15½″, SH 17″, OH 38⅝″. (Privately owned)

While this fine chair is not branded, it exhibits many details that mark it as a product of the shop of Joseph Henzey. Among these features: 1) there is a slight chamfer on either side of the bow about four to five inches before it enters the arm rail; 2) the bow enters the arm rail flush with the outside edges instead of in the center; 3) the outside scroll of the handholds is formed by the arm rail itself instead of being an applied addition; 4) double wedges instead of single are used in all wedge joints; 5) the second and third spindles from the left and right penetrate the bow; 6) the leg turnings have a long baluster and short taper; 7) the turnings are rather slender overall.

Regrettably, the bottoms of the knuckles have fallen off, a problem I have seen on many Henzey chairs. The reason is that the bottoms of the knuckles on these chairs are held in place only with glue and a single nail through the center, an unfortunately weak construction method. One more nail would have prevented this problem.

80

81

81. Armchair. Lancaster County, Pennsylvania, 1780–1800. One of six. Traces of the original green paint. Crest rail, spindles, and arms, hickory; arm supports, legs, and stretchers, maple; seat, poplar. SW 20¼″, SD 15½″, SH 17½″, OH 37″. (John Bartram Association)

One of a set of six, this chair has the typical Lancaster County seat with a heavy chamfer on the sides and a generally elliptical shape that is flatter in the front and rounder in the back than the seats of similar Windsor chairs. The front of the seat has been carved into a very distinctive pommel. The spindles swell slightly, the arm rail is thick, and the bow is a bit crude. The leg splay is good. Note the absence of the usual collar on the turnings where the baluster enters the ring.

80. Armchair. Philadelphia, 1765–1780. Branded I. [John] B. ACKLEY. Late nineteenth-century dark red paint over the original green. Crest rail and arms, oak; spindles, hickory; arm supports, legs, and stretchers, maple; seat, poplar. SW 21¼″, SD 16″, SH 17¾″, OH 39″. (James and Nancy Glazer)

All the earmarks of the style of Joseph Henzey can be seen here, yet this typical Philadelphia sack-back is branded by another Philadelphian, John Ackley—proving, perhaps, that chairmakers who work in close proximity may adopt each other's styles. The chair is not typical of the Ackley shop, which seems to have produced far more bamboo-turned than vase-and-ring-turned sack-backs like this one.

82.   Armchair. Philadelphia, 1780–1800. Branded L[ewis] BENDER. Bottoms of knuckles missing. Two coats of original green paint. Crest rail and arms, oak; spindles, hickory; arm supports, legs, and stretchers, maple; seat, poplar. SW 20⅜″, SD 15″, SH 17″, OH 36½″. (Lawrence Teacher)

At first glance this chair might seem to fully exemplify the Philadelphia style—but its medial stretcher has arrows at either end, in the Lancaster County style.

83.   Armchair. Bucks County or Lancaster County, Pennsylvania, 1780–1800. Nineteenth-century brown varnish, over an ochre ground, over traces of the original black paint. Crest rail, arms, and spindles, hickory; handholds, oak; arm supports, legs, and stretchers, maple; seat, poplar. SW 20¼″, SD 15¾″, SH 16½″, OH 44½″. (Mr. and Mrs. R. W. P. Allen)

With the same type of medial stretcher as figure 82, this chair is overall further removed from the Philadelphia style. The tall bow has a squarish shape. The front leg turnings are similar to those of the rear legs, and the four legs are tapered, whereas most Lancaster County Windsors have front legs with blunt-arrow turnings and tapered rear legs (see figures 84 and 85).

84.   Armchair. Lancaster County, Pennsylvania, 1765–1780. Refinished. Crest rail, spindles, and arms, hickory; handholds and seat, poplar; arm supports, legs, and stretchers, maple. SW 21¼″, SD 15⅞″, SH 15¾″, OH 42½″. (Privately owned)

This chair is much more typical of the Lancaster County product. However, sack-backs with such tall bows are a rare form. Many of them exhibit similarities, including the slightly pinched bow, which suggest that the chairs may all have been made in the same shop. The blunt-arrow foot, as opposed to a tapered foot, is a holdover from earlier Windsors. Lancaster County Windsors of this tall bow type usually have blunt-arrow front legs and tapered back legs; chairs with four blunt-arrow legs are more rare.

The Pennsylvania Germans were great cabinetmakers who loved to show, rather than hide, how their pieces were constructed. Thus, for example, the handholds are pinned in place with very large dowels. Note also the slightly swelling spindles.

84

85.   Armchair. Lancaster County, Pennsylvania. 1775–1790. Old refinishing with traces of the original green paint. Crest rail, oak; seat, poplar; spindles, hickory; arms, hickory or ash; handholds, arm supports, legs, and stretchers, maple. SW 21″, SD 15½″, SH 16½″, OH 35¼″. (Mr. and Mrs. Victor Johnson)

A well-proportioned Lancaster County Windsor, this armchair has exceptionally fine knuckles. The leg taper starts almost directly below the stretcher.

85

86

86.   Armchair. Lancaster County, Pennsylvania, 1760–1785. Old dark green paint over the original green. Top crest rail, hickory or oak; crest rail and handholds, oak; spindles and arms, hickory; arm supports, legs, and stretchers, maple; seat, poplar. SW 25½″, SD 23⅟₁₆″, OH 44⁹⁄₁₆″. (The Henry Francis du Pont Winterthur Museum)

This is a rare triple-back form of which I have seen only three Lancaster County examples. The top of the comb-piece echoes the wave beneath the comb. The leg and arm-support turnings are very crisply executed, and the turnings where the arm support enters the arm are narrow and delicate.

87. Armchair. New York City, 1765–1780. Old black paint over traces of the original green. Crest rail and arms, oak; spindles, hickory; arm supports, legs, and stretchers, maple; seat, poplar. SW 20⅝″, SD 16⅛″, SH 16¾″, OH 36⅛″. (Janie and Dr. Peter Gross)

New York sack-backs are relatively rare—not nearly as numerous as sack-backs from Pennsylvania or Connecticut, for example. With its nine spindles, wonderfully bold turnings, and great presence, this is one of the best New York City sack-backs. Most of these chairs have flat arms, no knuckles and seats with no distinct pommel.

88. Armchair. New York City or southern Connecticut, 1780–1800. Late-nineteenth-century green paint over the original salmon-color paint. Crest rail and arms, oak; spindles, hickory; arm supports, legs, and stretchers, maple; seat, pine. SW 21″, SD 15¼″, SH 18½″, OH 45½″. (Mr. and Mrs. R. W. P. Allen)

Highly stylized and unusual, this sack-back has typical New York City turnings on its legs, stretchers, and arm supports. The long back spindles are very delicate and flare out suddenly as they enter the seat, but the short spindles under the arms seem a bit heavy. The arm scroll is exaggerated, and the seat is imaginatively carved. Despite its New York turnings, the chair has an overall Connecticut look in its bow shape, arm rail, and the flat side of its seat.

87

88

89.   Armchair. New England, possibly Connecticut; 1790–1800. Branded O. NELSON. Varnish finish over green paint. Crest rail and spindles, hickory; arms, ash; arm supports, legs, and stretchers, maple; seat, pine. SW 20″, SD 13″, SH 17¼″, OH 38″. (Steven and Helen Kellogg)

The swell and sweep of this chair's bow can be found on other, similar Windsor chairs from Connecticut. This is an interesting, quirky piece with a very long reel on the leg turnings. Note how narrow the back spindles are at the seat and how they differ from the side spindles.

89

90.   Armchair. Connecticut, 1780–1800. Late nineteenth-century dark red paint over the original green paint, striped and decorated with gilt paint. Top crest rail and crest rail, oak; spindles and arms, ash; arm supports and stretchers, chestnut; seat, basswood; legs, maple. SW 20¼″, SD 16¼″, SH 17¼″, OH 44¼″. (Sam Bruccoleri)

Here is a great piece of Connecticut furniture and one very much like chairs that are known to come from the Westbrook area. Though the ears are typically Connecticut in design, all seven spindles penetrate the comb-piece, which is not typical. Another Connecticut feature is the fact that the medial stretcher has no double ring. The long taper of the arm supports is unusual. Although the legs have been notched out for rockers, this should not detract appreciably from the chair's value because the legs have not been cut down. The chair is decorated like mid-nineteenth-century "fancy" chairs.

91. Armchair. New York, Albany area, 1780–1800. Branded S. N. HERRCK. (Sotheby's, Inc.)

New York chairs with idiosyncratic turnings often come from the Albany area. Signed by a Dutch maker, this piece shows a strong Dutch influence in its turning patterns. There is a nice swell in the leg turnings where the stretcher enters. All told, this is a well-proportioned, good variation on the conventional Windsor design.

91

92

92. Armchair. Massachusetts, possibly Concord; 1790–1800. Early nineteenth-century green paint over the original salmon-color paint. Crest rail and arms, oak; handholds, cherry; spindles, hickory; arm supports, legs, and stretchers, maple; seat, chestnut. SW 21″, SD 16″, SH 18½″, OH 42″. (Nancy and Tom Tafuri)

In many ways, this chair is similar to figure 186. The seat is quite thick—3″—and well carved. The unusual leg turnings are also similar to those of figure 186. Oddly, the knuckle pieces are attached to the inside of the arms rather than the outside.

93.   Armchair. Connecticut, 1780–1800. Nineteenth-century red paint over the original green. Crest rail and arms, oak; spindles, hickory; arm supports, legs, and medial stretcher, maple; seat and side stretchers, chestnut. SW 21¼″, SD 15½″, SH 16¾″, OH 37″. (Nancy and Tom Tafuri)

This is a beautifully proportioned chair with great splay and a wonderful paint patina. The knuckles are very well carved and made from a single piece of wood. All the long spindles penetrate the bow. The legs do not penetrate the seat.

93

94. Armchair. Connecticut, 1790–1810. Early nineteenth-century black paint with gilt striping over blue paint, over the original green paint. Crest rail and arms, oak; spindles, hickory; arm supports, legs, and stretchers, maple; seat, pine. SW 20″, SD 15″, SH 17″, OH 37⅜″. (Nancy and Tom Tafuri)

Though simple in design, this chair has great provincial charm. The seat is very heavily chamfered, and the turnings are reminiscent of those found on certain tavern tables.

95

94

95. Armchair. Connecticut, 1790–1810. Very old dark brown paint over traces of the original gray-green. Top crest rail and stretchers, chestnut; crest rail and arms, oak; spindles and arm supports, hickory; seat, butternut; legs, chestnut (left side) and maple (right side). SW 21″, SD 14¾″, SH 16¼″, OH 51½″. (Kathleen Mulhern)

Both delicate and simple, this is an open, airy chair. The leg turnings—two balusters separated by a reel—are typical of Connecticut. The seat has been carved to almost a knife edge. Like that of figure 86, the bottom edge of the comb-piece conforms to the shape of the bow—a feature not always found on these chairs. (Compare the curve with that of figure 86.) The spindles penetrate the bottom of the seat. While the legs are turned from two different woods, they are original.

96

97

97. Armchair. Lisbon, Connecticut, 1790–1803. Branded EB: TRACY. Refinished. Crest rail and arms, oak; spindles, hickory; arm supports and legs, maple; seat and stretchers, chestnut. SW 19¾″, SD 15½″, SH 16¾″, OH 36½″. (Joan and Don Mayoras)

With this chair begins what was to become a Connecticut chairmaking dynasty with far-reaching influence. This Ebenezer Tracy Windsor differs from other Connecticut Windsors in its abruptly swelling spindles; its distinctive seat shape and leg turnings; its thin medial stretcher with arrows; its arm supports, whose turning pattern differs from that of the legs; its chestnut seat; and its bow, which does not flatten out as it enters the arm rail but merely tapers. While this is not a knuckle armchair, Tracy produced them—and when he did, the side stretchers often have arrows like that of the medial stretcher in this example.

96. Armchair. New England, possibly Connecticut; 1800–1810. Nineteenth-century salmon-color paint over the original green. Crest rail and arms, oak; spindles, hickory; arm supports, legs, and stretchers, maple; seat, pine. SW 21″, SD 15⅞″, SH 17¼″, OH 36½″. (Nancy and Tom Tafuri)

The leg turnings on this chair are quite simple, but that does not mean the chair is uninteresting. The chair has an unusually high stretcher arrangement that works quite well. The seat is not particularly well developed, with only a vague attempt at saddling. The legs do not penetrate the seat. The nineteenth-century salmon paint over the original green gives this piece a great deal of its charm.

98.   Armchair. Lisbon, Connecticut, 1795–1800. Branded E[lijah] TRACY. Refinished; traces of white, black, and the original green paint. Crest rail, oak; arms, ash; spindles, stretchers, and seat, chestnut; arm supports and legs, maple. SW 19½″, SD 15¼″, SH 16¾″, OH 35¾″. (Joan and Don Mayoras)

Out of the same shop as figure 97, this chair was possibly made by Ebenezer Tracy's son, Elijah. Overall, it is not quite as good as figure 97, especially in the arm supports.

99

98

99.   Armchair. Lisbon, Connecticut, 1790–1803. Original black paint with gilt striping. Crest rail, spindles, arm supports, and stretchers, hickory; arms, oak; seat, chestnut; legs, maple. SW 19½″, SD 15½″, SH 16″, OH 34¼″. (Steven and Helen Kellogg)

Though unbranded, this chair is so similar to the previous two examples that it almost certainly came from the Ebenezer Tracy shop. When Tracy used knuckles on his chairs, he also used side stretchers with arrow terminations, as in this chair; usually, when his chairs have flat scrolled arms, the side stretchers do not have arrows.

100

101. Armchair. Connecticut, 1796–1800. Early nineteenth-century mahoganizing over traces of the original black paint. Crest rail, spindles, and handholds, hickory; arms, oak; arm supports, legs, and side stretchers, maple; seat, chestnut; medial stretcher, birch. (Steven and Helen Kellogg)

This is a chair that may be attributable to A. D. Allen—but, I think, made after Allen left Ebenezer Tracy's shop to open his own. The chair retains the same basic design as figure 100, but the turning patterns have changed, the legs and stretchers no longer reflecting the Tracy design. For example, on each leg a rounded shoulder begins the taper below the ring. The turning pattern of the side stretchers flows more gradually, suggesting that Allen is now turning his own parts and not pulling them from the general Tracy stock. This chair also combines arrowed side stretchers with knuckle handholds, as does figure 99. While this is certainly a fine chair, the turnings are not the equal of Tracy's.

101

100. Armchair. Connecticut, 1796–1800. Branded A[mos] D[enison] ALLEN. Refinished. Crest rail, hickory; spindles, seat, and stretchers, chestnut; arms, oak; arm supports and legs, maple. SW 19½″, SD 15″, SH 16¼″, OH 35¼″. (Joan and Don Mayoras)

An apprentice to Ebenezer Tracy from 1790 to 1795, A. D. Allen eventually married Tracy's daughter Lydia and opened his own shop in 1796. In this chair we can see the influence of the Tracy style on Allen. There is a slight difference in the front of the seat: Allen carved his straight across, while Tracy undercut the seat from beneath. Like Tracy, Allen did not usually use arrows on the side stretchers of chairs with flat, scrolled arms.

102

103

102. Armchair. Connecticut, 1795–1800. Leather seat not original. Early nineteenth-century varnish with a salmon-color ground to simulate rosewood. Crest rail and arms, oak; spindles, ash; arm supports, chestnut; seat, pine; legs and stretchers, maple. SW 20½″, SD 16⅜″, SH 17″, OH 35⅝″. (Claude and Alvan Bisnoff)

Like the previous chair, this may also be an A. D. Allen product. On the other hand, it may only be a Tracy-influenced chair. The knuckles are very well executed. The seat shape is different from figure 101, and the stretchers have only rings, rather than the characteristic Tracy-Allen arrows at the ends. The leather cover of the seat is old, but not original. The knuckles on this chair are extremely bold.

103. Armchair. Massachusetts, 1780–1795. Original green paint over a gray ground. Crest rail and arms, oak; spindles, hickory; arm supports, chestnut; seat, legs, and stretchers, maple. SW 20¾″, SD 14⅝″, SH 17¾″, OH 38¾″. (Claude and Alvan Bisnoff)

The turnings on this chair are graceful, slender, and crisp. Note the tall back and how high the arm rail is from the seat.

104

105

105.   Armchair. Massachusetts, Boston area, 1780–1800. Branded [William] SEAVER. Original black paint over a gray ground. Crest rail and arms, oak; spindles and side stretchers, hickory; arm supports and medial stretcher, chestnut; seat, possibly maple; legs, maple. SW 19¾″, SD 14⅞″, SH 18¼″, OH 37″. (Claude and Alvan Bisnoff)

Some of the chairs made by William Seaver are wonderfully quirky. The abrupt bulbs in the spindles, the blocking in the legs before they enter the seat, and the medial stretcher with its ring-and-arrow design give this chair its stylistic personality.

104.   Armchair. Massachusetts, 1780–1800. Red varnish over late nineteenth-century red paint, over the original green paint. Crest rail and arms, oak; spindles, hickory; arm supports, legs, and stretchers, maple; seat, pine. SW 20½″, SD 15⅜″, SH 17″, OH 36½″. (Nancy and Tom Tafuri)

This chair is similar to figure 103, but has somewhat more vigorous turnings. In fact, the turnings are like those found on the great tenon-arm fan-back Windsor chairs from eastern Massachusetts (see figures 63 and 64). The back has a nice little shoulder where the bow enters the armrail.

106

106A. Armchair. Detail of knuckles. The strange groove cut behind the knuckles must have had some use, but its purpose has been lost.

106A

106. Armchair. Boston, 1780–1800. Refinished. Crest rail and arms, oak; spindles, ash; arm supports, legs, and stretchers, maple; seat, possibly butternut. SW 21¾", SD 15¾", SH 18", OH 41". (Joan and Don Mayoras)

Characteristic of a type of Boston product, this chair has a medial stretcher very similar to that of figure 105.

108. Armchair. Rhode Island, 1780–1800. Late nineteenth-century black paint with gilt striping. Crest rail and arms, oak; spindles, hickory; arm supports, legs, and stretchers, maple; seat, pine. SW 21¼″, SD 16″, SH 18½″, OH 38″. (Charles Sterling)

Here is a well-balanced sack-back with all the earmarks of the New York City influence on Rhode Island chairmakers. It does have a slightly softer turning pattern, and, of course, the typical Rhode Island leg taper.

107. Armchair. Rhode Island, 1780–1810. Green paint over nineteenth-century salmon-color paint, over the original green. Crest rail and arms, oak; spindles, hickory; arm supports, legs, and stretchers, maple; seat, pine. SW 20½″, SD 15½″, SH 18½″, OH 39½″. (James and Nancy Glazer)

This handsome chair has typically Rhode Island leg and medial stretcher turnings. Note how far back the arm support is positioned behind the front legs. It is unusual to find a sack-back in this form, which is much more common to bow-back armchairs or continuous-arm chairs from Rhode Island.

109. Armchair. Massachusetts or Rhode Island, 1780–1800. Old shellac refinish. Crest rail and arms, oak; spindles, ash; arm supports, legs, and stretchers, maple; seat, chestnut. SW 20″, SD 15⅛″, SH 18″, OH 38¼″. (Joan and Don Mayoras)

This chair seems to have a Connecticut influence, especially in its bow, seat carving, and arm supports. The finely executed legs are in the Rhode Island style, and the medial stretcher has a Massachusetts look. Perhaps the chair was made in Boston—influenced by Connecticut and Rhode Island.

110. Armchair. Massachusetts or Rhode Island, 1790–1810. Refinished; traces of old black paint. Crest rail, spindles, and arms, hickory; arm supports, legs, and stretchers, maple; seat, pine. SW 20″, SH 17″, OH 46″. (Privately owned)

The high, delicate bow and spindles of this chair make it a rare form.

109

110

111.

Original dark blue paint. Crest rail, spindles, and arms, hickory; arm supports, legs, and stretchers, maple; seat, pine. SW 20″, SD 13″, SH 16″, OH 32″. (Marianne Clark)

Perhaps this chair was made by a country craftsman who did not specialize in Windsors. The leg turnings resemble those of many New England tavern tables with their ball feet. The arm supports are turned in a pattern like the arm supports and leg turnings found on Rhode Island low-back Windsors, which are in the English taste. The spindles start with a very low taper. This is a very animated country Windsor.

112.

111.   Armchair. Rhode Island, possibly Newport; 1770–1800. Traces of red paint. Crest rail, oak; spindles, legs, and stretchers, chestnut; arm supports, maple and oak; seat, curly maple. SW 22″, SD 15″, SH 16½″, OH 36″. (David A. Schorsch, Inc.)

A strong English influence asserts itself in this chair, especially in the ram's-horn arm supports and Queen Anne medial stretcher. Such chairs are often mistaken for Pennsylvania products because of their D-shaped seats and blunt-arrow feet. This seat is made of curly maple. Newport chairs often are made entirely of one wood, and it is not unusual to find chairs in this style made completely from a single wood, often chestnut or maple. This is not so in Pennsylvania; the swelling in the spindles also is not found among Pennsylvania chairs.[4]

113. Armchair. Lancaster County, Pennsylvania, 1790–1810. Nineteenth-century black paint with gilt striping, over straw-color paint, over gray paint. Crest rail, hickory or oak; spindles and arms, hickory; handholds and seat, poplar; arm supports, legs, and stretchers, maple. SW 21½″, SD 16¼″, SH 18″, OH 41½″. (Wayne Pratt)

This is, in effect, a bamboo-turned version of many earlier Lancaster County sack-backs. Most interesting are the flared front feet, which follow the Lancaster County tradition of placing blunt-arrow feet in the front. In the typical late style, the knuckles are simplified and rolled over; they are made with three pieces added to the outside, inside, and underside. The second short spindle under each arm forms the same angle as the back spindles.

113

114

114. Armchair. Lancaster County, Pennsylvania, 1780–1800. Refinished; traces of the original green paint. Crest rail and arms, oak; spindles, hickory; handholds and seat, poplar; arm supports, legs, and stretchers, maple. SW 21⅜″, SD 16½″, SH 17¾″, OH 45¼″. (Mr. and Mrs. R. W. P. Allen)

Like figure 113, this is a bamboo-turned version of an earlier style. The chair has larger knuckles than those of figure 113. While the turning patterns of the legs and side stretchers can be found on many Philadelphia sack-backs—showing, perhaps, that the Lancaster chairmakers were paying attention to the Philadelphia products—the arm supports, high flat bow, slightly swelling spindles, and knuckle shape are pure Lancaster County.

BOW-BACK
~
CHAIRS

In much the same way that the comb-back and low-back chairs became identified with Philadelphia in the 1750s, the bow-back also was a Philadelphia first. Based on an Oriental design that spread via England, the bow-back was introduced into Philadelphia in the 1780s when that city's chairmakers began producing bow-backs with bamboo turning patterns. This stylistic innovation was an immediate success and quickly became the Philadelphia chairmakers' most popular Windsor product, both locally and for export. From the mid-1780s through the 1790s, the New York makers, rather than imitate the Philadelphia product, created bow-backs with their own extraordinarily fine versions of the earlier vase-and-ring pattern.

Judging by the number of surviving New York bow-backs and the remarkable similarity in turning patterns and overall design among chairs by different makers—the crisp-edged, shield-shaped seat with sliding corners, the slightly swelling spindles, the relatively short back, and the like—the bow-back must have been immensely popular and a best-seller in New York, despite design changes in other Windsor production centers. Apart from its general excellence, another reason for its popularity may have been the fact that the bow-back made a perfect side chair for another Windsor form identified with New York—the continuous-arm chair. To be sure, New York bow-back armchairs exist, but they are very rare and have a curiously experimental look about them, with their stubby arms that seem almost out of place. To me that implies two things: the bow-back form as a whole probably preceded the continuous-arm chair, and the experiment of the bow-back armchair in New York City was quickly abandoned in favor of the far more elegant continuous-arm chair.

The New York influence spread to chairmaking shops primarily in Connecticut and Rhode Island. The Rhode Island makers, also influenced by Philadelphia, produced some of the best bow-back armchairs and side chairs, some of which have distinctively turned baluster spindles.

Most of the bow-backs produced in other areas—such as the rest of New England and the South—seem to have been mainly influenced by the Philadelphia model, the bamboo-turned bow-back side chair and armchair with arms attached by mortise-and-tenon joints. Indeed, it is quite likely that the New York continuous-arm chair was designed to compete with the Philadelphia tenon-arm bow-back. I base this on the fact that I have never seen a continuous-arm chair from Philadelphia, nor have I ever seen a bamboo-turned tenon-arm chair from New York.

Such steadfast adherence to certain regional designs may well have been a reflection of an unwritten rule or deliberate choice among Windsor makers to acknowledge their competition in other cities and demonstrate their pride in creating their own Windsor idioms.

115. Armchair. Philadelphia, 1785–1800. Branded I. [John] B. ACKLEY. Traces of original mahoganizing. Crest rail, arms, and arm supports, oak; spindles, hickory or oak; seat, poplar; legs and stretchers, maple. SW 20¼", SD 17¾", SH 18", OH 37¾". (M. Finkel & Daughter)

If there were a typical Philadelphia bow-back armchair, this would be a good candidate to represent the many chairs of this style that were produced by most of the Windsor chairmakers of the period—including Henzey, Lambert, Trumbull, Pentland, Cox, and Allwine. This chair by J. B. Ackley is so similar to those produced by Henzey that it would be difficult to differentiate between them if the chair were not branded. The turning pattern of the side stretchers is especially typical of both Henzey and Ackley, although other makers used a similar pattern.

116

115

116. Armchair. Philadelphia, 1780–1800. Punch marks of William Cox. Original mahoganizing over straw-color ground. Crest rail, spindles, arms, and arm supports, oak; seat, poplar; legs and stretchers, maple. SW 19¼", SD 17½", SH 17¼", OH 37½". (Michael McCue)

Somewhat more conservative than figure 115, this is another typical Philadelphia bow-back design that is even more commonly found.

117. Armchair. Philadelphia, 1785–1795. Punch marks of William Cox. One spindle missing. Nineteenth-century mahoganizing over original mahoganizing; original horsehair-stuffed muslin seat cushion; outer upholstery missing. Crest rail, oak; spindles, hickory; arms and arm supports, mahogany; seat, poplar; legs and stretchers, maple. SW 20″, SD 18″, SH 17″, OH 39″. (Privately owned)

Its upholstered seat makes this an interesting variation of the Philadelphia bow-back—and, indeed, simply an upholstered version of figure 116. The seat has been stripped of its original leather covering, which was wrapped around and tacked in place, and we can see the inner muslin cover stuffed with horsehair and nailed onto the thick, unsaddled plank seat. This chair has mahogany arms and arm supports—fine features—but the leg and stretcher turnings are rather bland when compared with the crisp, bulbous leg and stretcher turnings of figure 115.

118. Armchair. Philadelphia, probably 1792. One of 12. Original mahoganizing over buff-color ground. Crest rail, hickory; spindles, probably hickory; arms, mahogany; arm supports, oak; seat, poplar; legs and stretchers, maple. SW 21″, SD 16½″, SH 18½″, OH 38⅛″. (The Library Company of Philadelphia)

The minutes of the Library Company of Philadelphia for December 6, 1792, mention a dozen chairs that were purchased from Joseph Henzey. A set of 11 Windsors still remains in the Library Company—of which this is one—and these are believed to be the chairs mentioned in the minutes. Aesthetically, this chair ranks between figures 115 and 117 as an expression of the Philadelphia bow-back.

117

118

119

120. Side chair. Philadelphia, 1785–1800. Branded LAMBERT. Old black paint over the original white; reupholstered. Crest rail, oak; spindles, hickory; legs and stretchers, maple. SW 18″, SD 16½″, SH 18″, OH 37″. (Also see color plates XI and XII.) (Privately owned)

Its upholstered seat makes this chair unusual, although it is similar to figure 115 in its legs and stretchers.

119. Armchair. Philadelphia, 1780–1800. Refinished; traces of original yellow paint. Crest rail, center posts, splats, and arm supports, oak; spindles, legs, and stretchers, maple; arms, mahogany; seat, poplar. SW 20¾″, SD 16″, SH 17½″, OH 37⅜″. (Mr. and Mrs. R. W. P. Allen)

This is a ladder-back Windsor of the so-called Trotter type, a very rare form that was made in limited sets. It is practically identical to the three previous examples, with the exception of its ladder-back slats, which are no doubt derived from Philadelphia Chippendale formal chairs made by Daniel Trotter, Thomas Tufft, and others. Chairs with this kind of back arrangement and these curved arm supports are very English in character. A side chair version also exists.

120

121. Side chair. Philadelphia, 1780–1800. Branded W[illiam] BOWEN. Refinished; traces of red paint over the original green. Crest rail and spindles, oak; seat, poplar; legs and stretchers, maple. SW 17″, SD 16″, SH 18″, OH 37½″. (Mrs. Hazel Douglass)

Similar to figure 120 but with less pronounced turnings, this is a typical Philadelphia bow-back product with bamboo turnings, nine spindles, and pinched bow.

122

121

122. Side chair. Philadelphia, ca. 1791. Branded C[hristian] HEINY. Refinished; traces of black paint over the original green. Crest rail, oak; spindles, hickory; seat, poplar; legs and stretchers, maple. SW 17¼″, SD 16½″, SH 18″, OH 37″. (Mrs. Hazel Douglass)

Like figure 121, this chair is very similar to the typical Philadelphia product, but the proportions of its legs are more pleasing. Note the extra flare on the leg turning before it enters the seat and the fullness at the bottom of the leg where the side stretchers are socketed. The back is better as well because the spindles are thicker. Heiny is known to have worked in Philadelphia in 1791.

123

123.   Pair of side chairs. Pittsburgh, 1780–1800. Branded T. RAMSEY/W. DAVIS/PITTSBURGH. Original black paint. Crest rails and spindles, hickory; seats, poplar; legs and stretchers, maple. SW 18″, SD 16″, SH 17″, OH 37″. (Tom Brown)

While Philadelphia chairmakers were producing bamboo turnings, Pittsburgh makers were still using vase-and-ring-turned legs and baluster side stretchers. However, the medial stretchers on these chairs are bamboo-turned. The backs, seats, and leg turnings are especially well executed. In fact, the chairs resemble those made by Henzey, but the balusters are shorter and the leg taper longer.

125. Side chair. Richmond, Virginia, 1790–1800. Label of Andrew and Robert McKim. Traces of black and yellow paint. Crest rail and spindles, hickory; seat, poplar; legs and stretchers, maple. SW 17″, SD 15¾″, SH 17¼″, OH 37½″. (Museum of Early Southern Decorative Arts, Winston-Salem, N.C.)

We know that many Windsors were shipped from Philadelphia to Richmond. Here is an example of a chair that was made in Richmond but which bears the unmistakable stamp of the Philadelphia stylistic influence in its seat shape, bamboo turnings, and the shaping of the bow. Compare this chair with figure 122, which has nine spindles, like most Philadelphia bow-backs.

124. Side chair. Philadelphia area, 1785–1800. Mid-nineteenth-century black paint with gilt striping, over earlier gray paint, over the original bronze-color paint. Crest rail, oak; spindles, hickory; seat, poplar; legs and stretchers, maple. SW 17¼″, SD 16½″, SH 16½″, OH 37⅜″. (Eugene Pettinelli)

Here is a provincial variant of chairs like figure 120. The chair-maker has attempted to turn the legs in proportion, but the result is somewhat clumsy. The tops of the legs are weak and club-shaped, and the seat saddling is vague. The back of the chair is more successful. Nonetheless, the chair is desirable because of its paint surface and its country charm.

126.   Side chair. Berks County or Lancaster County, Pennsylvania, 1780–1800. Old red paint over the original green. Crest rail and spindles, hickory; seat, pine or poplar; legs and stretchers, maple. SW 17¼″, SD 16″, SH 19″, OH 39¼″. (Marianne Clark)

Chairs of such idiosyncratic stylishness often are provincial products. The finely saddled seat of this chair has an almost sculptural quality, and the leg turnings are very beautiful. The stretchers are turned in a pattern typical of the area. The pinched waist of the bow is a nice touch.

126

127

127.   Armchair. Frederick-Hagerstown (Piedmont) area of Maryland, 1790–1810. Very old brown paint over the original red. Crest rail, oak or hickory; spindles and arm supports, hickory; arms, legs, and stretchers, maple; seat, poplar. SW 19⁵⁄₁₆″, SD 16¹¹⁄₁₆″, SH 15¾″, OH 35¼″. (Museum of Early Southern Decorative Arts, Winston-Salem, N.C.)

This chair descended in the Taney family of the Frederick-Hagerstown area of Maryland. The shaping of the arms and the carving of the knuckles is an exaggeration of the Chippendale style and a very lively conceit. Note the especially low seat (less than 16″), the severe bend in the "wrist" of the arm, and the pinched bow—the latter a motif seen much more often in side chairs than in armchairs. All these features appear on other Windsors found in the same area.

127A. Armchair. Detail of arm.

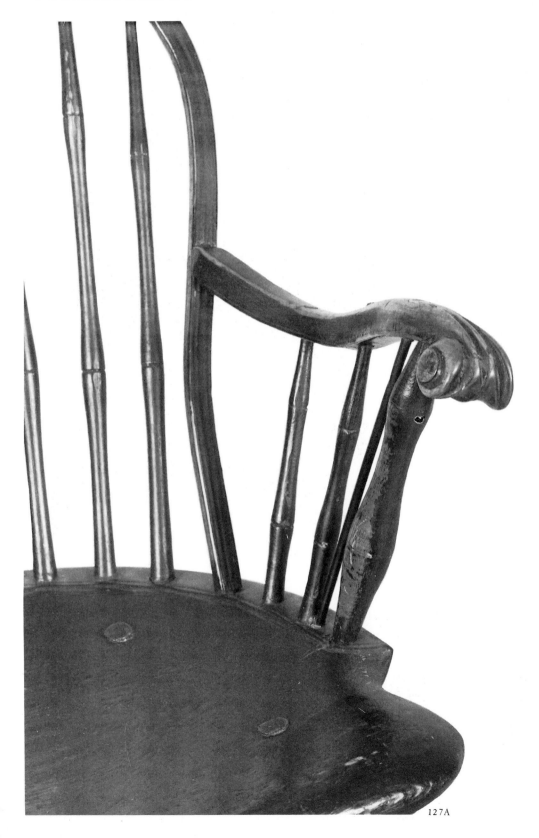

127A

128.   Side chair. Frederick-Hagerstown (Piedmont) area of Maryland, 1790–1810. Late nineteenth-century varnish over traces of the original white paint. Crest rail, probably oak; spindles, hickory; seat, pine; legs and stretchers, maple. SW 17¼″, SD 16⅞″, SH 16¼″, OH 36¼″. (Privately owned)

Overall, this chair is a marvelous regional variant of the bamboo-turned Windsors produced in Philadelphia. The turner incorporated the new bamboo motif into his turning patterns without completely dismissing the earlier baluster turnings. The seat is beautifully saddled, and the lower spindle turnings are echoed in the tops of the legs. I have seen several side chairs like this one, and all are relatively low to the ground—that is, not cut down.[5]

129

129. Armchair. New York City, 1780–1795. Nineteenth-century varnish over the original red paint. Crest rail and arms, oak; spindles, hickory; arm supports, legs, and stretchers, maple; seat, pine or poplar. SW 18¼″, SD 17½″, tailpiece 3¾″, SH 17″, OH 36″. (Privately owned)

In New York, and north into New England, bow-backs were still being made with vase-and-ring turnings rather than bamboo turnings at a rather late date. These New York and New England chairs often have braced backs, whereas Philadelphia bamboo-turned chairs almost never do. This is a very fine chair of a rare type with short, mortised arms. Indeed, the arms are like those one would expect to find on a sack-back Windsor, but cut off abruptly. Occasionally chairs like this one have flaring arms with well-carved knuckles, but they are an even rarer form. The vase-and-ring turnings shown here are very bold, and so typical of the New York City style.

129A. Armchair. Detail of seat. Also typical of the New York City style is the very pronounced shield-shaped seat, bolder in its contours than its Philadelphia counterparts.

130

130.   Side chair. New York City, 1780–1800. Label of Thomas and William Ash. One of a pair. Two coats of original green paint. Crest rail, ash; spindles, probably hickory; seat, pine; legs and stretchers, maple. SW 16½″, SD 17½″, tailpiece 3¾″, SH 18″, OH 38½″. (Privately owned)

The best turning pattern of New York City bow-back Windsors is beautifully exemplified in this chair. Most New York City bow-backs are braced and do not have pinched waists.

131. Side chair. New York City, 1780–1800. Nineteenth-century dark red paint over a salmon ground, over the original green paint. Crest rail, oak; spindles, hickory; seat, pine; legs and stretchers, maple. SW 16¾″, SD 17¾″, SH 18″, OH 38″. (Sam Bruccoleri)

Similar in expression to figure 130, this design features slightly bolder turnings.

132

131

132. Side chair. New York City, 1790–1800. Branded I. [John] SPROSON. Painted black. Crest rail and spindles, hickory; seat, pine; legs and stretchers, maple. SW 16¼″, SD 17¼″, tailpiece 2½″, SH 18″, OH 35½″. (Mr. and Mrs. R. W. P. Allen)

This is an excellent braced bow-back from New York City with the best turnings and a finely saddled seat. Although practically identical to figures 130 and 131, this chair has legs with a slightly longer taper (however, this is not because the legs of the others have been cut down, since all three chairs have a seat height of 18″). The back of this chair is shorter than those of figures 130 and 131, and the spindles fan out more. Since the bow of figure 130 is higher, its back has a more vertical feeling.

Unfortunately, this chair has been repainted. Figure 131 has a nineteenth-century dark red paint over a salmon ground over the original green, which is a more desirable surface because it is closer to the original. But figure 130 is in even more pristine condition, with two coats of original green paint in virtually untouched condition; thus in my opinion it is the most desirable of the three chairs because of its surface condition, its Ash label, its taller back, and the fact that it is one of a pair.

134.   Side chair. New York City, 1780–1800. Nineteenth-century dark red paint with gilt striping over the original moss-green paint. Crest rail, oak; spindles, hickory; seat, pine; legs and stretchers, maple. SW 17½″, SD 17½″, tailpiece 2⅜″, SH 15½″, OH 34¾″. (Janie and Dr. Peter Gross)

Although not quite as well proportioned as figure 133, this chair is a good example of the New York City Windsor style. The leg turnings are somewhat overpowered by the deeply carved saddle seat. Furthermore, its more interesting paint surface makes this chair desirable from a collector's point of view.

133.   Side chair. New York City, 1790–1800. Branded W[illiam] MacBRIDE/N-YORK. Refinished; traces of the original green paint. Crest rail and spindles, hickory; seat, pine; legs and stretchers, maple. SW 14¾″, SD 17¼″, tailpiece 3″, SH 17¼″, OH 36⅝″. (Bernard & S. Dean Levy, Inc.)

Here is another well-turned, rather typical New York City braced bow-back side chair. The turnings are bold and well defined, but unfortunately, the chair has been skinned and refinished.

135

136. Side chair. Connecticut, 1790–1800. Label of William Harris, New London. Refinished. Crest rail, oak; spindles, ash; seat, pine; legs and stretchers, maple. SW 15¾″, SD 16½″, tailpiece 2¾″, SH 18″, OH 36″. (Dietrich American Foundation)

This is a good example of the Connecticut version of the New York City bow-back chair. The seat is narrower than those of New York examples, and the top is a little light in relation to the undercarriage; this might be the result of its having seven spindles instead of the more usual nine. It's a nice chair, however, and a type that was more popular in New York City than in Connecticut, judging from the number of surviving examples with New York brands or labels.

136

135. Side chair. New York or Connecticut, 1780–1800. One of a pair. Two coats of green paint over nineteenth-century salmon paint, over the original green. Crest rail, oak; spindles, oak or ash; seat, pine or poplar; legs and stretchers, maple. SW 16⅛″, SD 17″, tailpiece 3⅜″, SH 17″, OH 36″. (Sam Bruccoleri)

The slight swelling of the spindles of this chair, which occurs gradually from bottom to top, seems to be a New York feature—differing from the abrupt, bulbous swelling of Connecticut Windsors (see figures 98, 99, and 100). The swelling spindles, strong turnings, heavy bow, and broad, fully sculpted shield-shaped seat could be viewed as an attempt by a Connecticut maker to create a New York-style bow-back Windsor. While this is a fine chair, it does lack the sophistication of figures 130, 131, and 132.

137. Armchair. Rhode Island, 1790–1800. One of a pair. Late nineteenth-century black paint over the original green, over a gray ground. Crest rail and spindles, hickory; arms, mahogany; arm supports, chestnut; seat, pine; legs and stretchers, maple. SW 18½″, SD 17¾″, tailpiece 2¾″, SH 17¾″, OH 39⅛″. (Claude and Alvan Bisnoff)

A beautiful example of Rhode Island chairmaking, this chair has typical Rhode Island turnings, pipestem spindles, a high back, and wonderfully curved mahogany arms. Its paint sequence is very common to Rhode Island Windsors.

137

138. Armchair. Rhode Island, 1800–1810. Refinished. Crest rail and spindles, ash; arms, mahogany; arm supports, legs, and stretchers, maple; seat, pine. SW 16½″, SD 16⅜″, SH 17¾″, OH 38½″. (Joan and Don Mayoras)

The most obvious evidence for this chair's late date is the bamboo-turned medial stretcher. It's not a replacement, since it has the identical heavy decorative scoring that appears on the legs and side stretchers. The side stretchers have a late baluster shape, and the seat is shaped like those found on rod-back Windsors—i.e., a simplified shield. The spindles are no longer of the pipestem variety. This is a nice chair, but not as well realized as figure 137, to which it is somewhat similar.

139. Side chair. Rhode Island, 1790–1800. Refinished. Crest rail and spindles, hickory; seat, pine; legs and stretchers, maple. SW 16½″, SD 16¼″, tailpiece 2″, SH 17¾″, OH 37½″. (Dietrich American Foundation)

This is a side chair version of figure 137. The undercarriage is quite beautiful, but without the pipestem spindles in the back, the top of the chair doesn't live up to the undercarriage.

140.   Side chairs. Newport, Rhode Island, 1790–1800. Three of a set of six. Nineteenth-century black paint with yellow, white, green, and gilt decoration over the original blue-green paint. Crest rails and spindles, ash; seats, pine; legs and stretchers, maple. SW 15¾″, SD 19¼″, SH 18½″, OH 39¼″. (David A. Schorsch, Inc.)
    More than any other bow-back Windsors, these chairs have backs that could be called balloon-shaped. Note how the spindles look like a unit in the center of the bow and how the pipestem turnings of the spindles are set high. The seats are thick but crisply carved and saddled. The legs and stretchers are turned in the best Rhode Island pattern. The medial stretchers are unusual.

141. Side chair. Massachusetts, probably Boston area; 1790–1810. One of six. Nineteenth-century varnish over traces of the original black paint. Crest rail and spindles, hickory; seat, pine; legs and side stretchers, maple; medial stretcher, chestnut. SW 16″, SD 16″, SH 18½″, OH 38½″. (Claude and Alvan Bisnoff)

The undulating spindles of this chair are a very interesting accomplishment, unifying the design of the undercarriage with the back of the chair. The leg turnings represent a variation of the Rhode Island style, and their vase-and-ring pattern blends nicely with the later style of the bamboo-turned spindles and medial stretcher because of the additional swelling in the center of each bamboo spindle.

141

142. Side chair. Boston, 1790–1810. Original yellow paint with black decoration. Crest rail, oak; spindles and bowed stretcher, hickory; seat, pine; legs and rear stretchers, maple. SW 17¼″, SD 16½″, SH 17½″, OH 37½″. (Mr. and Mrs. R. W. P. Allen)

The yoke stretcher arrangement of this chair, common on English Windsors, is a rarity among American Windsors and does not seem to have been popular in this country. It is most often seen among chairs from the Boston area, especially those made by Seaver and Frost, and seems always to appear on bow-backs, almost always side chairs. This chair is a graceful example of the type. Note how similar the spindles are to those of figure 141—bamboo turnings with an extra swelling between the two score marks. This is typical of many of these chairs from the Boston area.

143.   Side chair. Massachusetts, probably Boston area; 1790–1810. Old black paint over nineteenth-century red paint. Crest rail and spindles, hickory; seat, pine; legs and stretchers, maple. SW 18″, SD 15¾″, SH 21¼″, OH 40″. (Mr. and Mrs. R. W. P. Allen)

Exceptionally tall for a bow-back side chair, this chair may have been used for a particular purpose, perhaps as a musician's seat. Note the similarity in the leg turnings to those of figure 142—the blocking and the concavity below it—and the slight flaring of the spindles just before they enter the seat. The chair also has a pinched waist and the same form of shield-shaped seat.

144.   Side chair. Boston, 1790–1810. Branded S[amuel] J. TUCKE. Very old light blue paint, over beige paint, over the original green. Crest rail, oak; spindles, hickory or ash; seat, pine; legs and stretchers, maple. SW 15⅛″, SD 16″, SH 17¼″, OH 30″. (Privately owned)

The unfinished pine seat of this chair has the mellow color of wood that has never been painted, and it is peppered with tack holes—evidence that the seat originally was upholstered. The spindles flare slightly before they enter the seat, as in figures 142 and 143, and there also is a similarity in the block stretcher and leg turnings of figure 143.

The very short back and upholstered seat indicate, I think, that the chair originally was designed for the workplace, perhaps as a loom or spinning-wheel chair. In any case, the form is rare: I have seen only a handful of Windsors with such short backs.

143

144

145

145.   Armchair. Connecticut, 1790–1800. Late nineteenth-century dark red paint over the original green. Crest rails, spindles, and arm supports, hickory; arms, legs, and stretchers, maple; seat, poplar. SW 18″, SD 17″, SH 17¼″, OH 45″. (Privately owned; courtesy of Federation Antiques, Inc.)

Bow-backs with comb-pieces are rare. Sometimes the comb-piece, though always a welcome addition, seems to be merely a tacked-on afterthought; not so here. This bow-back has actually been designed to have a comb-piece. We can say that with some authority because, without the comb-piece, the back of this chair would appear too short; with the comb-piece, the proportions seem just right. In addition, the turnings are very well balanced. Unfortunately, the seat shows virtually no saddling.

146.   Side chair. New England, possibly Rhode Island; 1790–1800. Original black paint with gilt decoration over a white ground. Comb-piece, chestnut; crest rail, probably oak; spindles, hickory; seat, pine; legs and stretchers, maple. SW 16½″, SD 16½″, SH 17½″, OH 46¾″. (Privately owned)

The added comb-piece raises what might have been an ordinary chair to a high level of visual excitement. Note also that the maker chose to support the comb with six spindles instead of the usual three or five; thus the comb could be made wider and more imposing. This chair may be from Rhode Island because the ears of Rhode Island chairs usually have longer necks than those of chairs from other regions, as do these.

146

147.   Armchair. Philadelphia, 1785–1800. Refinished; traces of white paint. Crest rail and spindles, hickory; arms, mahogany; arm supports, legs, and stretchers, maple; seat, poplar. SW 19½″, SD 17¾″, SH 18″, OH 37¾″. (Privately owned)

Here we see a rare form—no doubt an attempt to emulate the shield-back formal chairs of the Hepplewhite style. This design would have been very successful had the back been made taller. As it is, we are left with the impression that the arms are set too high. Also, the legs and stretchers are a bit plain. Still, the rarity of the piece makes it desirable.

CONTINUOUS-ARM

~

CHAIRS

The continuous-arm Windsor chair has been something of a mystery in the world of early American furniture. While other Windsor forms—the comb-back, low-back, fan-back, sack-back, and bow-back—can be traced to English models from paintings, advertisements, inventories, wills, and surviving examples, the continuous-arm chair appears to have no English Windsor prototype in the eighteenth century, and has been called a true American invention.

Having thought about the matter for many years—and having done a little digging—I have now developed a theory of the origin of the form which identifies its prototype and its approximate time of development, and confirms that the form is, if not a totally American invention, at least an American innovation.

It was in the mid-1780s in New York City that several developments in furniture fashion probably inspired Windsor-makers there to create the continuous-bow armchair. First, although the Hepplewhite and Sheraton styles were the dominant forces in American furniture design from 1785 to 1800, the French taste was becoming popular in urban furniture-making centers. Boston, Philadelphia, and New York chairmakers were producing furniture in styles from Louis XVI designs to neoclassic designs inspired by French archaeological discoveries at the close of the eighteenth century. The fact that elliptical and circular shapes were mainstays in the vocabulary of these new French designs suggested new problems of construction for translating these flowing neoclassic styles into a back-and-arm construction for Windsor chairs.

The techniques of bending wood were not new to Windsor craftsmen, whose bow-back chairs were the height of fashion after 1780, particularly those chairs produced in Philadelphia with the newest simulated bamboo-style turnings. There had been a marked increase during the second half of the eighteenth century in patents for applying bent wood to manufactures, and Windsor craftsmen would naturally have been taking notice. In 1769 Joseph Jacob received an English patent for constructing wheel carriages "with hoop wheels."[6] One of the first recorded experiments in bending wood took place in Paris in 1778 at the shop of M. Migneron: observers saw "with astonishment" wood treated in some manner whereby it could be bent into different shapes and strengthened at the same time. M. Migneron's discovery was submitted to the Academies of Science and Architecture at Paris, Bordeaux, and Toulouse, and Benjamin Franklin was among the many distinguished inventors and artists to view this discovery.[7]

Similar ideas for the bending of wood soon appeared elsewhere. In 1791 a John Bevans took out a patent for "circular wooden sash frames, sashes and soffits; fanlight door mouldings and handrails for stairs" made from bent wood.[8] Samuel Bentham obtained an English patent dated April 23, 1793, for "giving curvature to wood by bending."[9]

Interest in these new wood-bending techniques was running high among the furniture craftsmen of New York, and among Windsor-chairmakers in particular, since they were then producing bow-backs and the earlier sack-back style, as were their Philadelphia counterparts. Competition between Windsor-chairmakers in New York and Philadelphia must have been keen, and I believe not without elements of regional pride. Whereas the simulated bamboo-turned bow-back accounted for at least ninety percent of the bow-back styles produced in Philadelphia, New York chairmakers seem to have ignored the style altogether; they seem to have preferred the turning patterns already in use on their earlier Windsor products. Nevertheless, the bow-backs of both New York and Philadelphia were basically the same: a steam-bent bow, socketed into the seat with seven or nine spindles.

It is when we look closely at the armchair versions of these New York and Philadelphia bow-backs that we see the greatest similarity and the greatest differences: similarity of purpose in the creation of an arm-and-back construction that achieves through design a continuity of line in keeping with the new classical influences; and differences in the way this design concept is achieved.

Philadelphia chairmakers were content to use a mortise-and-tenon joint to attach the arms to the bow. This form of arm-and-back construction, a traditional method, had been in use for formal Philadelphia chairs for some time. The illusion of the bow and arms of a bow-back Windsor being formed from a single piece of wood is created by using arms cut in the same thickness as the bow; by adding to the top surface of the arms a decorative beading that runs in a continuous line up onto the front facing of the bow; and by rounding the bow below the tenon of the arm and scoring it to resemble scored, bamboo-turned spindles.

There was a short-lived attempt among some New York City Windsor chairmakers to make a tenon-arm bow-back version of their own (see figure 129).[10] The design of these chairs was not very successful; there is no attempt to create the illusion of continuity between the bow and the arms, and the arms have a "stuck-on" look. Chairs of this type are quite rare. It does not appear that many of these tenon-arm chairs were produced; the design probably was quickly discarded in favor of a more successful and ultimately more popular design: the continuous-bow armchair.

New York City Windsor chairmakers succeeded in their attempt to bend the bow and arms from a single strip of wood, and for the first time outdid their Philadelphia competitors. Until the creation of the continuous-bow armchair, the New York City chairmakers were followers, producing sack-backs and other Windsor forms that already had been defined by the Philadelphia Windsor makers. Now, at last, a truly New York Windsor!

I think it is interesting to note that Philadelphia chairmakers did not produce continuous-arm Windsors, and New York City chairmakers as a rule did not produce the bow-back, bamboo-turned, tenon-arm counterparts. New York City Windsor-maker John Sproson, who made some of the finest continuous-arm chairs, did work in Philadelphia from 1783 to 1788, but he did not brand his chairs while working in that city. His branded continuous-arm chairs are New York in style and no doubt date from 1789 to 1798, when he had moved from Philadelphia and was living and working in New York City.

The identity of the first New York City Windsor chairmakers to produce a continuous-arm Windsor probably will never be determined with any certainty, but the brothers Thomas and William Ash probably are strong contenders for that honor. Born into a tradition of formal furniture-making, they were sons of Gilbert Ash (1717–1785), one of

New York City's most outstanding makers of Chippendale-style furniture, particularly chairs. Thomas and William Ash were both actively producing Windsors between 1785 and 1794. The following advertisement appeared in the *New York Packet* March 3, 1785:

> Thomas and William Ash, Windsor-chairmakers, No. 17 John Street . . . Now ready at the Ware-house, a great number of very neat chairs and settees, some of which is [*sic*] very elegant, being stuffed in the seat and brass nailed, a mode peculiar to themselves and never before executed in America.[11]

I have seen an example of an upholstered Ash continuous-bow armchair which, with the addition of brass nails, would indeed be very elegant and would bear a remarkable resemblance to a type of formal Federal upholstered armchair popular at that time known as a bergère-type chair. The similarities to a continuous-arm chair are especially noticeable in the flowing curve of the back into the arms. A labeled example of this type was produced in New York City in 1797 by John DeWitt and upholstered by William Gallatian.[12] Seven years earlier, in 1790, Thomas Burling, a New York City maker of formal furniture, produced a unique, swivel version of the bergère form for George Washington (figure 148). Thomas Jefferson, who had returned from his five-year mission to France the previous year, purchased a similar chair from Burling in 1790. America was closely affiliated with France at the close of the eighteenth century, and French-style furniture was popular with American political leaders. The fact that both Washington and Jefferson previously made other furniture purchases from Burling suggests Burling's prominence as a furniture maker.

The bergère form was very popular in formal furniture centers in Federal America. In 1797, George Bright of Boston produced thirty of these chairs, upholstered and brass-nailed, for the Boston State House.[13]

Could the Ash brothers, coming from a formal furniture background and armed with the most sophisticated recent information from abroad on wood-bending techniques, have seen the elegant bergère design as the best solution for putting arms on a bow-back Windsor chair? Mention has been made in the past of the stylistic similarities between one of the labels used by Thomas and William Ash and the label engraved for cabinetmaker Thomas Burling by Abraham Godwin of Paterson, New Jersey, who was trained in New York.[14] It is interesting to note that in accordance with their formal furniture background, Thomas and William Ash used labels rather than brands to identify their products, a practice not common among Windsor chairmakers in New York or Philadelphia.

The continuous-arm chair seems to have been an immediate success, and New England chairmakers soon were producing their own versions, but the New York influence is always evident in the turning patterns, the seat shape, and the overall rakish elegance of these chairs. With the development of this new Windsor form, New York City became as great an influence on the American Windsor market in the 1790s as Philadelphia had been in the previous decades.

148. Swivel armchair of the bergère type. New York, New York, 1790. Made by Thomas Burling for George Washington. Original upholstery. (Mount Vernon Ladies' Association)

148

149. Armchair. New York City, 1792. Branded [Abraham] HAMTON & [James] ALWAYS. Nineteenth-century dark green paint over the original green. Crest rail, oak; spindles, hickory; arm supports, legs, and stretchers, maple; seat, pine. SW 18″, SD 17½″, SH 18″, OH 36¼″. (Rosemary Beck and Ed Rogers)

A classic example of the highly sophisticated and ingenious continuous-arm chair first introduced by New York City chairmakers, this chair displays all the characteristic features, including bulbous, almost explosive turnings; a sharply chamfered, shield-shaped seat; a long leg taper; and nine nearly vertical spindles flanked by two short spindles.

149

150

151

151.   Armchair. New York City, 1785–1800. Branded W. Mac-BRIDE/N-YORK. Refinished; traces of the original blackish-green paint. Crest rail, oak; spindles, hickory; arm supports, legs, and stretchers, maple; seat, pine. SW 17″, SD 17½″, SH 17¾″, OH 38⅞″. (Bernard & S. Dean Levy, Inc.)

This handsome chair has more successfully turned arm supports than those of figure 150. The seat, while nearly identical, has a slight depression behind the pommel—a nice touch. The leg turnings are very well balanced and dynamic, and are matched by equally dynamic side and medial stretchers, which in figure 150 are something of a letdown. The greatest flaw in this chair is its highly refinished surface.

150.   Armchair. New York City, 1785–1800. Crest rail and spindles, oak; arm supports, legs, and stretchers, maple; seat, pine. SW 17¾″, SD 18″, SH 18¼″, OH 36¾″. (Joan and Don Mayoras)

Similar to figure 149, this New York armchair exhibits minor differences: the leg taper is not as long, so the chair is slightly less dramatic, and the top turning on the leg under the seat is a bit more bulbous—perhaps too bulbous.

152. Armchair. New York, possibly Albany area; 1790–1810. Painted black. Crest rail, oak; spindles, hickory; arm supports, legs, and stretchers, maple; seat, pine. SW 17½", SD 18", tailpiece 3¼", SH 18", OH 37½". (Mr. and Mrs. R. W. P. Allen)

At first glance, this braceback chair may seem to be a typical New York City product, but I think the slight rigidity of the leg turning pattern—without the thicks and thins of the previous examples—as well as a certain thickness in the front edge of the seat, and the heavy top baluster of the arm support, give the chair an air of provincialism. Nonetheless, it is a handsome piece. J. M. Hasbrouck produced similar chairs in the Albany area.

153

152

153. Armchair. New York, 1785–1810. Nineteenth-century black varnish over the original green paint with gilt striping. Crest rail, oak; spindles, hickory; arm supports, legs, and stretchers, maple; seat, pine. SW 17¾", SD 17⅛", SH 18¾", OH 37½". (Rosemary Beck and Ed Rogers)

Like figure 152, this chair lacks the sophistication of New York City continuous-arm Windsors. There is a slight thickness to the front chamfer of the seat, and the top balusters of the arm supports seem too small (just the opposite of figure 152). Also, the side stretchers are too bulbous for the thickness of the legs. This is a good attempt at a New York City chair, but it doesn't quite hit the mark. However, it does have a wonderful paint surface.

154.   Armchair. New York, 1785–1800. Late nineteenth-century
black paint with gilt striping over the original green paint. Crest rail,
oak; spindles, hickory; arm supports, legs, and stretchers, maple; seat,
poplar or pine. SW 17¾″, SD 17″, tailpiece 3″, SH 16⅛″, OH 34¼″.
(Philip Bradley Antiques)

    The turnings of this chair are beautifully executed, but the
chair as a whole has a quiet, almost passive quality. The seat carving
is a bit clumsy; the legs and arm supports do not splay very much; the
bow does not have much bend; and the handholds are not scrolled.
The chair does have a very pleasing paint surface.

154

155

155. Armchair. Probably Connecticut; 1790–1810. Early nineteenth-century white paint with gilt striping over the original green paint. Crest rail and spindles, ash; arm supports, legs, and stretchers, maple; seat, poplar. SW 16½″, SD 17″, SH 17″, OH 35½″. (David A. Schorsch, Inc.)

This is probably a Connecticut version of a New York City chair. The turnings do not have the thicks and thins typical of New York chairs, especially evident in the arm supports. The medial stretcher has no double rings. The handholds are quite thick and do not have chamfer on their underside, as New York chairs usually do. The seat is well saddled but not as heavily chamfered or refined as those of the New York City product. The bow is slightly more peaked than those of New York chairs. Overall, the chair has a wonderful stance, and its surface is enhanced by early nineteenth-century white paint with gilt striping over the original green.

156. Armchair. Connecticut, 1790–1800. Nineteenth-century dark brown paint over the original green. Crest rail and arm supports, oak; spindles, hickory; seat, pine; legs and stretchers, maple. SW 17¼″, SD 18″, tailpiece 3″, SH 18″, OH 40″. (Lori and Craig Mayor)

A far more typical Connecticut product than figure 155, this is similar to chairs made by Ebenezer Tracy[15] and clearly reveals the difference between the Connecticut and New York styles.

The general stance and splay are comparable, but the backs of Connecticut chairs are usually higher—in this case 40″, compared with New York chairs whose backs are usually 37″ or less in height. The Connecticut bow is narrower, and there is a more abrupt lift from the bend of the arm to the handhold. Connecticut chairs have spindles that distinctly swell about one-third their height from the seat. The Connecticut seat is different, as well: the legs do not penetrate the seat; the seat is usually made of a hardwood such as chestnut (although in this case the seat is pine); there is no scoring or "rain gutter" on the top back of the seat in front of the spindles, and the chamfering on the sides and front of the seat is usually very sharp and flat. The arm support and leg turning patterns tend to be slimmer but with a much wider reel than that of New York chairs. The medial stretcher has no ring on either side of its bulbous turning.

156

157.

158.   Armchair. Connecticut, 1790–1810. Feet repaired. Refinished. Top crest rail, arm supports, legs, and stretchers, maple; crest rail, oak; spindles, hickory; seat, pine. SW 17¾″, SD 18″, SH 16¾″, OH 44¼″. (Privately owned)

The bow of this chair is rather square, like that of figure 157; however, here the squareness seems appropriate because of the added and very appealing comb-piece, which is supported by the five longest spindles penetrating the bow. As is true of most Connecticut chairs, there is no double ringing on the medial stretcher. Overall, the chair has a pleasingly rustic quality.

157.   Armchair. Massachusetts, 1790–1810. Old varnish or shellac over traces of dark green paint. Crest rail, oak; spindles, hickory; arm supports, legs, and stretchers, maple; seat, pine. SW 17½″, SD 17½″, SH 17⅛″, OH 35⅞″. (Mr. and Mrs. R. W. P. Allen)

This is a highly idiosyncratic chair. It has blocked bamboo turnings like those found on certain other Massachusetts Windsors (see, e.g., figures 142 and 143). The bow has an interesting squareness. Knuckle handholds are very rare on continuous-arm chairs, and these are cut from a single piece of wood.

159. Armchair. Probably Massachusetts; 1790–1800. Late nineteenth-century black paint over the original green. Crest rail, ash; spindles, hickory; arm supports, legs, and stretchers, maple; seat, chestnut. SW 16½″, SD 17½″, SH 18″, OH 35½″. (Mr. and Mrs. R. W. P. Allen)

Both the New York and Connecticut styles seem to have influenced this interesting Windsor. The turnings resemble those of New York Windsors, except for the blocking of the stretchers. While the spindles do not swell like those of Connecticut chairs, the back does have eight spindles—a hallmark of many chairs produced by Connecticut maker Ebenezer Tracy. Like the seats of many Connecticut Windsors, this one is made of chestnut and has a Connecticut shape, but it retains the rain gutter, and the legs penetrate the seat.

160

159

160. Armchair. Rhode Island, 1785–1800. Late nineteenth-century black paint over blue paint, over the original green. Crest rail, hickory; spindles, probably hickory; arm supports, legs, and stretchers, maple; seat, pine. SW 17⅜″, SD 18″, SH 18″, OH 37½″. (Also see color plate X.) (Sam Bruccoleri)

Here is a fine example of a Rhode Island continuous-arm chair with vigorous turnings and long leg taper. The influence of the New York City style is evident in the arm supports, basic leg turning pattern, spindles, and double ringing on the medial stretcher. In contrast, the spindles have narrower bases than New York City Windsors, the seat rolls up more from the underside than the seats of New York chairs, the top baluster of the leg is different, and, of course, the concave leg taper is quite different. The painted surface of this chair is wonderful.

161

161.   Armchair. Rhode Island, 1785–1800. Branded P. N. W. One of a pair. Very early black paint over the original green. Crest rail and spindles, hickory; arm supports, legs, and stretchers, maple; seat, pine. SW 16¾″, SD 17″, SH 17″, OH 36½″. (Joan and Don Mayoras)

Compared with figure 160, this is a less successful example of a Rhode Island version of a New York continuous-arm chair. The leg turnings are much more Rhode Island in style—in the reel and baluster, for example, and in the very distinctive drooped collar just below the first baluster. The baluster terminations of the medial stretcher also are a Rhode Island feature. Note that all the spindles of this chair pierce the bow. Like figure 160, this chair has a very fine early black paint surface over the original green.

However, although this is a fine chair, it is not quite equal to figure 160. The turnings are a bit heavy in the legs, stretchers, and arm supports; and lack the wonderful extremes of narrow-to-bulbous that make figure 160 so elegant.

ROD-BACK

~

CHAIRS

First introduced in Philadelphia around 1800, the rod-back, or Federal, Windsor style seems to have been an immediate success. The style quickly spread to most chairmaking centers from Maryland to Maine, New York being one of the notable exceptions.

Earlier Windsors had been used in outdoor settings, but the rod-back achieved a full *integration* with such settings. With its trellis-like back and turning patterns simulating bamboo, the rod-back has the organic feeling of a garden. Quiet, simple, and frequently elegant, its style is one that I find generally delightful.

Often, the merits of the style have been judged in relation to earlier styles, such as the comb-back and the fan-back. In the past, I myself have been guilty of this. But there is no more value in such comparisons than in comparing a painter such as John Kensett with John Constable, or Winslow Homer with Charles Willson Peale. Different times pose different problems that result in new design solutions and expressions.

In the rod-back, I believe the Windsor chairmaker was finally able to unify all the various parts of the chair into a totality of design. In the past, the legs, stretchers, arm supports, and back posts were baluster-turned—a design holdover from the earlier William and Mary period. The parts of the chair were used in concert but never fused into a design whole. For the most part, turning patterns remained decorative.

With the bamboo rod-back pattern, introduced from England via the Orient, all the parts of the chair could be turned to resemble bamboo in various stages of growth—thicker for the legs, back posts, and crest rails, and thinner for the stretchers and spindles. The result was a unity and purity of design that had never before been achieved in a Windsor.

162

162.   Armchair. Philadelphia, 1800–1820. Nineteenth-century cadmium yellow paint with black striping over the original pale yellow paint. Crest rails and back posts, oak; crest medallion and seat, poplar; spindles, hickory; arms, arm supports, legs, and stretchers, maple. SW 19½″, SD 16½″, SH 18″, OH 33¼″. (Also see color plate VI.) (Mr. and Mrs. Paul Flack)

A typical Philadelphia rod-back Windsor of its period with a so-called butterfly medallion in its back, this chair has the characteristic rolled-shoulder turning pattern at the bottoms of the back posts, at the tops and bottoms of the arm supports, and at the tops of the legs. Note the triple ringing on the bamboo-turned tenoned arms. One might expect the maker to have socketed the arms into the back posts at the middle bamboo rings, but instead the arms are socketed above, at the centers of the back posts.

Usually, several back spindles of these chairs penetrate the lower crest rail and are socketed into the upper crest rail—giving the back a "bird-cage" effect—but here that is not the case.

163.

164.   Armchair. Philadelphia, 1800–1820. Branded I. [John] CHAPMAN. Old shellac finish. Crest rail, spindles, and back posts, hickory; arms, mahogany; arm supports, legs, and stretchers, maple; seat, poplar. SW 18½″, SD 16½″, SH 16¾″, OH 36½″. (Independence National Historical Park)

     This handsome rod-back has only a single crest rail. The arms, which form a nice cyma curve, are tenoned into the back posts just like the arms of bow-back armchairs. Thus the chair exhibits features of both periods.

163.   Armchair. Philadelphia, 1800–1830. Late nineteenth-century putty-colored paint over the original green. Crest rails and spindles, hickory; crest medallion, pine; back posts, arms, arm supports, legs, and stretchers, maple; seat, poplar. SW 18″, SD 16½″, SH 18¼″, OH 35¼″. (Eugene Pettinelli)

     The top crest rail and arms of this Philadelphia rod-back have been joined in the so-called duckbill pattern to resemble mitered corners. Actually, the "mitered" joints are an illusion created by extensions at the ends of the crest rail and arms. Note the double beading on the front edge of the seat.

164.

165.   Side chair. Exeter, New Hampshire, 1800–1820. Branded G. L. ILSLEY/EXETER N.H. (Elizabeth R. Daniel)

There are interesting regional differences between this "butterfly bird-cage" Windsor and figure 162. First, the edge of the seat in figure 162 rolls down, whereas here the seat has a fairly sharp, beaded edge as well as "rain-gutter" beading on top that is typical of the New England style. Also, in the leg-turning pattern of figure 162, the thickest part of the leg is just below the seat, and the leg gradually narrows toward the foot; here, the leg is narrowest at the seat and widest at the foot. Note, too, that the bamboo turnings of figure 162 are concave between the ringing, while those of this chair are convex.

The backs of these chairs are sometimes steam-bent to create an arched back. This occurs more often on New England chairs than on those from Philadelphia. And, of course, on this chair the second spindle on each side penetrates the lower crest rail and frames the butterfly medallion.

If this chair were not branded, it could as easily be attributed to Connecticut or Massachusetts as New Hampshire. Not having developed an indigenous Windsor style of their own, New Hampshire craftsmen seem to have been most influenced by Massachusetts and Connecticut Windsors.

166

165

166.   Armchair. Pennsylvania, 1800–1820. Original black paint with gilt striping. Crest rail, back posts, and spindles, hickory; medallion, pine; arms, arm supports, legs, and stretchers, maple; seat, poplar. SW 21½", SD 20", OH 59¼". (The Metropolitan Museum of Art; gift of Hazel Kirk Koepler and Virginia Lee Koepler, in memory of Olivia Hamilton Verne, 1975)

This remarkable ceremonial chair has a square pine insert in the top of its back on which is painted the Masonic symbol. The spindles are very well articulated. The arms are beautifully carved, with good knuckle terminations—a rare feature on rod-back Windsors. The piece is probably one of a kind.

167. Armchair. Connecticut, 1800–1820. Medial stretcher missing. Old red paint over black, over the original green. Crest rails, spindles, back posts, and arm supports, hickory; arms, legs, and stretchers, maple; seat, poplar. SW 20½″, SD 17¼″, SH 18¾″, OH 43½″. (Mr. and Mrs. R. W. P. Allen)

    Here is a very lovely but eccentric rod-back armchair. The back is beautifully realized: the distance between the first and second crest rails is especially effective and dramatic, emphasizing the four penetrating spindles. The graceful cyma curve of the arms echoes the arm style of earlier tenon-arm, bow-back Windsors such as figure 138, and the handholds are well scrolled. Note the interesting overlapping or stepped-down turning pattern of the arm supports, which is repeated on both crest rails. The seat is nicely carved, with sharp corners reminiscent of the shield-shaped seats of Hepplewhite-style formal chairs. The leg turnings are of the double-ringed bamboo type often found on Connecticut Windsors.

167

168

168. Armchair. Connecticut, 1800–1820. Nineteenth-century dark brown paint over the original green. Crest rail, back posts, arms, arm supports, and legs, maple; spindles and side stretchers, hickory; seat, pine. SW 17⅛″, SD 17″, SH 18″, OH 38⅛″. (Nancy and Tom Tafuri)

    Once again we see a chair that exemplifies the creativity of Connecticut Windsor-makers and their ability to spice up a potentially mundane product. The bamboo leg turnings of this chair are generally similar to those of figure 167, but they also have the feeling of tapered baluster-turned legs. The bamboo scoring is deeper than normal, and midway between the scoring is an unusual ring. The arms, arm supports, and medial stretcher precisely echo the shape of the legs, but the back posts and crest rail make only a vague attempt at it. The back posts end in nipple-like finials, and, oddly, the spindles have no bamboo scoring. The shield-shaped seat, normally found on Connecticut continuous-arm chairs, is unusual for a rod-back. Overall, this graceful chair creates an interesting visual experience.

169. Side chair. Pennsylvania, probably Bucks County or Chester County; 1790–1810. Probably cut down about 1½″. One of a pair. Nineteenth-century dark green paint, with orange spindles and stretchers, over the original white paint. Crest rail and back posts, oak; spindles, hickory; seat, pine; legs and stretchers, maple. (Howard Szmolko)

This is an example of the Philadelphia-style "Sheraton" rod-backs that were produced in Philadelphia and nearby counties. Such chairs usually have seats that are better articulated, and overall they can be much more sophisticated.

170

169

170. Side chair. Pennsylvania, possibly Easton area; 1790–1810. One of eight. Refinished; traces of green paint. Crest rail, spindles, back posts, legs, and stretchers, hickory; seat, pine. SD 14¾″, SH 17″, OH 36″. (Downingtown Antiques)

Chairs such as this one are known to have come from the Easton, Pennsylvania, area. The extreme serpentine crest-rail shape is repeated on the front edge of the seat, and the double beading of the crest rail can be found on the front edge and sides of the seat. The spindles are very effective, with one bamboo score mark and then a long taper to the top of the chair. The bamboo legs are graceful, with a well-placed H-stretcher arrangement.

171. Side chair. New Hampshire, 1800–1820. Branded J. R. HUNT. (New Hampshire Historical Society)
This simple rod-back clearly shows the false mitered corners where the crest rail meets the back posts, a feature of many rod-backs. The rather nondescript seat is not as nicely realized as the back.

171

172

172. Side chair. Philadelphia, 1810–1825. One of a pair. Original yellow paint with black striping. Crest rail, back posts, legs, and stretchers, maple; spindles, hickory; seat, pine. SW 16⅛″, SD 16¼″, SH 17¼″, OH 34½″. (Mr. and Mrs. Paul Flack)
Some rod-backs have solid, flat crest rails, like this one. The triple bamboo scoring, box stretcher, button back-post finials, and cushionlike Hepplewhite-style seat shape are frequently found on Pennsylvania rod-backs.

173. Side chair. Philadelphia, 1810–1825. Traces of old white paint over the original red. Crest rail, oak; spindles, hickory; back posts, legs, and stretchers, maple; seat, poplar. (John Bartram Association)

Similar to figure 172 in nearly every respect, this chair has a more elaborate step-down crest rail.

174. Side chair. Philadelphia, 1810–1830. Traces of the original white paint. Crest rail, back posts, legs, and stretchers, maple; spindles, hickory; seat, poplar. SW 16¼″, SD 15½″, SH 17½″, OH 33″. (John Bartram Association)

Although comparable to figures 172 and 173, this chair is somewhat later, as is evident from the seat design: a simple, squared-off plank with very little attempt at carving.

173

174

175

176

175.   Armchair. Philadelphia, 1810–1830. Nineteenth-century mahoganized grain painting. Crest rail and back posts, maple; arm supports, seat, legs, and stretchers, poplar; spindles, hickory; arms, pine. (Independence National Historical Park)
        This massive rod-back belonged to Bishop White of Philadelphia, the first American bishop consecrated by the Church of England and one of the two official chaplains of the Second Continental Congress. This chair has legs that fit into small wooden blocks with the same paint history as the rest of the chair. The purpose of these blocks is unknown.

176. Armchair. Massachusetts, probably Boston; 1820–1830. Original chocolate-brown paint decorated in yellow, red, green, and black with yellow striping. Crest rail, back posts, arm supports, legs, and stretchers, maple; spindles, hickory or white oak; arms, mahogany; seat, poplar. SW 19″, SD 19¼″, SH 17¾″, OH 48½″. (Collection of Melissa and Gary Lipton; courtesy of David A. Schorsch, Inc.)

Rod-backs with step-down crest rails were popular in New England at the beginning of the nineteenth century. Such chairs were produced around 1810, but the arms of this chair are its latest feature—more akin to those of the so-called Boston rocker of the 1825–1840 period. The comb-piece of this chair is simply a smaller version of the crest rail below it. The five supporting spindles of the comb-piece are socketed into the crest rail and are not extensions of the back spindles. This is a commode chair: the center section of the seat is hinged at the back and can be lifted.

177

176 A

176A. Armchair. Detail of crest, showing painted decoration.

177. Side chair. New England, probably Maine; 1810–1830. One of four. Original golden-yellow paint with red, black, and brown decoration. Crest rail and seat, pine; spindles, hickory; back posts, legs, and stretchers, maple. SW 15½″, SD 15″, SH 18¼″, OH 35″. (Claude and Alvan Bisnoff)

This chair may have been made by Windsor-maker and painter Daniel Stewart, who worked in Farmington, Maine, from 1812 to 1827, since it is remarkably similar in form and paint decoration to another chair which bears Stewart's label.[16]

178. Side chair. New England, 1815–1830. Original mustard-color paint with black decoration. Crest rail, back posts, legs, and stretchers, maple; spindles, beech; seat, pine. SW 15¾″, SD 16″, SH 17½″, OH 36″. (Marianne Clark)

A version of the step-down arrow-back Windsor, this chair has a rather ambitious crest rail that is carved up from the bottom to accentuate the top curve (unlike the previous two examples, which have crest rails with flat bottoms). The paint decoration is very elaborate, and the success of the crest rail's large rectangular panel depends upon its painted vine-and-fruit motif. From the seat down, the chair is a typical late New England rod-back design.

178

179

179. Armchair. Maryland, 1810–1830. Two coats of original brown paint. The entire chair is maple, except the poplar seat. SW 18¼″, SD 17″, SH 18½″, OH 35½″. (Also see color plate XIII.) (Charles Sterling)

The rolled knuckle arms of this chair are similar to those found on other chairs from Maryland, such as figures 127 and 127A. Otherwise, the chair is "normal" until we come to the crest rail, which is a tour de force. Actually, the crest rail is positioned like that of a fan-back chair. Its general contour is somewhat similar to the Lancaster County pattern, and the carving is highly individualized, with matchstick incised triangles flanking a central medallion, leaf patterns, and more matchstick incising on the ears. Note, too, that the matchstick carving is repeated at the tops of the handholds.

WRITING-ARM

~

CHAIRS

After having seen at least a hundred writing-arm Windsor chairs, I have observed that 60 to 70 percent of them were produced in Connecticut, and at least half of those were made by the E. B. Tracy shop. This conclusion is based on branded examples, woods used, construction methods, and turning patterns. Thus the form probably originated in Connecticut, perhaps with Tracy. However, no matter where writing-arm Windsors come from, they represent a rare form.

Almost no writing-arm chairs were produced in Philadelphia, with the exception of low-back versions made by Anthony Steel in the last decade of the eighteenth century; one Pennsylvania-style rod-back chair (branded ROSE) that I have seen; and a handful of writing-arm adaptations of "normal" Windsor armchairs. New York and Rhode Island also are notably lacking in examples of writing-arm Windsors. Massachusetts produced a few, but not many.

Basically, there are three ways to make them: from the ground up, as a unified, new design; as an adaptation of a normal Windsor, with a writing paddle substituted for the original arm; or with a writing paddle merely tacked on over the original arm.

The latter version usually is not particularly interesting, and perhaps it isn't really a writing-arm Windsor at all. The ground-up examples tend to be quite practical; they are usually more massive, with wider seats and extra space for drawers, candle slides, and the like. However, they are sometimes rather clumsy-looking because of their bulk. The writing-arm adaptations, on the other hand, are often quite graceful, especially the comb-backs.

180. Writing-arm chair. Philadelphia, 1765–1780. Back legs pieced out about one inch. Refinished. Crest rail and arms, oak; spindles, hickory; writing paddle and seat, poplar; arm supports, legs, and stretchers, maple; wing nut, wrought iron. SW 25⅛", SD 17", SH 17⅜", OH 44¾", writing paddle 12¾" × 23⅝". (Privately owned)

Although this chair was originally pictured in *The Windsor Style In America*,[17] I can now provide information about its woods and dimensions. I now feel that this rare Philadelphia chair probably is a product of the same shop that made the low-back settee shown in figure 201; the turning patterns of the arm supports, legs, and stretchers are virtually identical.

180

181. Writing-arm chair. Lisbon, Connecticut, 1780–1803. Branded EB: TRACY, with three hash marks under the seat and arm drawer. Black paint, over late nineteenth-century red, over yellow, over green. Crest rail and arms, maple; arm crest and writing paddle, pine; spindles, cross-braces, and stretchers, hickory; arm supports and legs, maple; seat, chestnut. SW 27⅛", SD 18⅞", SH 15¾", OH 46⅞", writing paddle 18¾" × 26½". (Steven and Helen Kellogg)

Considering the large number of Tracy writing-arm chairs that have turned up over the years, one could conclude that making such Windsors was a specialty of his. This is an excellent chair and a typical Tracy product in that it has one tongue and two supports to hold the writing tablet.

182. Writing-arm chair. Connecticut, 1800–1810; descended in a Burlington County, New Jersey, family. Nineteenth-century mahoganizing, over straw-colored paint, over the original blue-gray paint. Crest rail, arm crest, arms, and legs, maple; spindles, arm supports, and stretchers, hickory; seat and writing paddle, pine. SW 27⅛″, SD 18″, SH 17¼″, OH 46¾″, writing paddle 18¾″ × 25¼″. (Privately owned; courtesy of the Burlington County Historical Society)

This is a fine example of a late writing-arm chair produced by one of the Tracys. Stylistically and proportionally, the piece is simply a bamboo-turned, toned-down expression of figure 181. Note, for example, the similarities of the comb-pieces, the use of six tall back spindles, the arms, arm crests, front edges of the seats, stretchers, and the writing tablet construction—all unmistakable E. B. Tracy features that are found on all branded Tracy comb-back writing-arm chairs.

183

182

183. Writing-arm chair. Probably Lisbon, Connecticut; 1780–1803. The gallery around the writing surface is a nineteenth-century addition. Mid-nineteenth-century black paint with gilt striping over the original green paint. Arm crest, arms, arm supports, legs, and stretchers, maple; spindles, ash; writing paddle, pine; candle slide and drawer, chestnut; seat, possibly maple. SW 27¼″, SD 19″, SH 15½″, OH 27″, writing paddle 18¾″ × 25½″. (Steven and Helen Kellogg)

Because this chair is virtually identical to others that are marked with the brand of Ebenezer Tracy, we can attribute it to him. Like the others, this chair has one tongue and two writing tablet supports, and all the spindles penetrate the arm crest. The turnings are just like those of figure 181, but the legs have a bit more taper. A candle slide beneath the writing-arm drawer is always a welcome feature on a writing-arm chair.

184

184. Writing-arm chair. New Bedford, Massachusetts, 1800–1825. Branded SWIFT (probably Reuben & William Swift). Early green paint over the original green. Crest rail, spindles, arms, and arm supports, hickory; writing paddle, legs, and stretchers, maple; seat, pine. SW 27″, SD 16⅝″, SH 18″, OH 38½″. (Steven and Helen Kellogg)

Here we see early nineteenth-century double-bobbin turnings above the seat of this chair combined with earlier vase-and-ring turnings on the undercarriage. Indeed, the top of the chair is so simplified compared with the undercarriage that it suggests the maker was not terribly confident in his ability to make a writing-arm chair. Had he used vase-and-ring-turned arm supports, he would have had to turn them very precisely. Instead, he used a simple double-bobbin design, which allowed him to cut the arm supports any length he chose. In the photograph we can see that the three writing-arm supports, although turned similarly, are cut completely differently to compensate for the fact that they are three different lengths. Note also the leg turnings—typical of Rhode Island, but found in Massachusetts and Connecticut as well.

185. Writing-arm chair. Connecticut, 1780–1800. Original black paint. SW 20″, SD 14″, SH 17″, OH 36¼″, writing paddle 18″ × 26″. (Privately owned)

This is a very interesting variant of the well-known Tracy type of Connecticut writing-arm chair. This chairmaker, unlike Tracy, used knuckle handholds, two tongues, and three writing tablet supports. Also, note that the front edge of the seat is chamfered, but there is no attempt at saddling. The back is quite short for a chair of this overall size.

185

186. Writing-arm chair. Massachusetts, probably Concord; 1790–1820. Top writing paddle a later addition. Made in white pine, maple, and ash. SW 18″, SD 16⅜″, SH 16½″, OH 39¾″. (Concord Antiquarian Society)

According to the Concord Antiquarian Society, this chair was owned by the Rev. Ezra Ripley (1751–1841), who bequeathed it to his step-grandson, Ralph Waldo Emerson. It also was used by Nathaniel Hawthorne at the Old Manse between 1842 and 1845. The unusual leg turnings are nearly identical to those of figure 92. The original writing tablet is probably below the later addition, which was used to raise the height of the writing surface. The original writing arm probably had a drawer or candle slide. Like figure 185, this chair has an unusually short back.

187. Writing-arm chair. Probably Connecticut, 1790–1810. Old black paint over traces of the original green. Crest rail, hickory; spindles, hickory or chestnut; arms, arm supports, legs, and stretchers, maple; writing paddle, poplar; seat, pine; drawer, poplar with cherry divider. SW 24¾″, SD 18⅜″, SH 16¾″, OH 43³⁄₁₆″, writing paddle 17³⁄₁₆″ × 24″. (Philip Bradley Antiques)

This is a provincial chair. The double score marks on the arm supports are found on many Connecticut Windsors, and the comb is very "Connecticut" in style. All told, this is a pleasing, quaint attempt at building a stylish writing-arm Windsor chair.

187

188

188.   Writing-arm chair. Richmond, Virginia, 1802. Dated label of Andrew and Robert McKim. Restored black paint with yellow decoration. Crest rail and back posts, oak; spindles, arms, and arm supports, hickory; writing tablet and seat, poplar; legs and stretchers, maple. SW 24⅜″, SD 17⅞″, SH 18″, OH 37⅞″, writing paddle 18⅞″ × 29³⁄₁₆″. (Museum of Early Southern Decorative Arts, Winston-Salem, N.C.)

This type of rod-back Windsor chair—with its squared-off, beaded crest rail—usually is the most successful of the rod-back designs. The maker of this chair paid great attention to details not usually found on rod-backs: the crest rail is nicely shaped; the beading on the arms continues onto the back posts; the back posts are bamboo-turned; the writing tablet is beaded; the handholds are scrolled; the legs are boldly turned with good splay; the medial stretcher is baluster-and-ring-turned; and there are nine spindles in the back and four under each arm. This chair is no doubt based on a Philadelphia model such as figure 164—right down to the rounded shoulders at the tops of the legs where they enter the seat—and it would be difficult to determine its origin if it were not labeled.

189. Writing-arm chair. Philadelphia, 1800–1820. Nineteenth-century brownish-red paint, over straw-colored paint, over the original green. Crest rail, spindles, and arms, hickory; back posts, arm supports, and legs, maple; seat and writing paddle, pine; stretchers, hickory and poplar. SW 20¾″, SD 16¼″, SH 17¼″, OH 35¼″, writing paddle 17⅜″ × 23¼″. (Burlington County Historical Society)

Here we see what is basically a rod-back bird-cage armchair with a writing tablet added over the original arm. Since the writing tablet has the same paint history as the rest of the chair, it is not a later addition. The flat writing-tablet support dovetails into the writing tablet and the side of the seat.

Very few writing-arm chairs were made in Philadelphia, and even fewer as rod-backs. This chair is merely a late adaptation of a form that had waned in popularity.

189

190

190. Writing-arm chair. New Jersey, 1800–1820. Branded A. THAYER. Drawer under writing paddle missing. Nineteenth-century dark brown paint, over blue-gray paint, over the original green. Arm crest and arms, hickory; spindles, arm supports, legs, and stretchers, maple; writing paddle and seat, pine. SW 24″, SD 16¼″, SH 18½″, OH 33″, writing paddle 16¼″ × 23⅜″. (Dowingtown Antiques)

Very few low-back writing-arm chairs have steam-bent (as opposed to sawed) arm rails, which makes this piece unusual. Constructed in this way, the arm rail is pleasingly slender. The box-stretcher arrangement indicates a late date for this very simple but rather elegant piece. Note that the legs are turned with triple, rather than double, bobbins.

191. Writing-arm chair. Probably Southern, 1790–1810. (Museum of Early Southern Decorative Arts, Winston-Salem, N.C.)
   This very simplified provincial interpretation of a writing-arm chair has an almost homemade look. The bamboo-turned arms are a nice touch.

192.   Writing-arm chair. Connecticut, 1820–1840. Original yellow paint with green and red decoration. Crest rail, back posts, spindles, arms, and arm supports, maple; writing paddle, pine; seat, legs, and stretchers, chestnut. SW 23⅜″, SD 16¾″, SH 15½″, OH 31⅝″, writing paddle 18⅜″ × 27½″. (Steven and Helen Kellogg)

Although it is a late chair, this has a wonderful folk-art quality. Its earlier-style bamboo turnings contrast with the "latest" pattern in the arm supports and spindles. The front stretcher is interesting because it is flat on its face but full-round on its back.

As construction of Windsors became simpler, the paint decoration became more elaborate and important—in fact, the chairs were purposely designed to accommodate fancy painted surfaces that would highlight the architecture of the chairs. This particular piece has its original yellow paint with green floral decoration trimmed in red.

192

193.   Writing-arm chair. New England, 1800–1820. The drawer is a
later addition. Black paint over traces of the original white. Crest rail,
oak; back posts, spindles, legs, and stretchers, hickory; arm, writing
paddle, and seat, pine; arm supports, hickory and maple. SW 32⅝",
SD 20½", SH 17½", OH 32½", writing paddle 21½" × 33". (Bill
Jennens)

    Both the writing tablet and the arm of this chair were originally
upholstered in black pigskin. Rather than create a tongue to support
the writing tablet, the maker simply increased the seat width, giving
the chair the feeling of a loveseat. This proportion fits nicely with the
overall boxiness of the back and allows the chair to have 13 spindles.

193

ROCKING

CHAIRS

Windsor rocking chairs were produced in all the chairmaking regions throughout the second half of the eighteenth century, although they were few and far between until the end of the century. By the early 1800s, Windsor rockers had become extremely popular; one notable example in New England was the tall-backed "Salem rocker." But by the 1840s, Windsor rockers had been displaced by "fancy" rocking chairs such as the famous "Boston rocker."

As a rule, Windsor rocking chairs have relatively high backs and are often comb-backs rather than, say, bow-backs or sack-backs. They are usually armchairs, but side chairs do turn up. Elaborate paint decoration with striping and floral motifs is quite common, perhaps because the chairs were viewed as leisure, rather than formal, furniture.

While I have tried to limit this chapter to pieces that were originally created as rocking chairs, as opposed to those whose rockers were added later, the first example shown seemed too interesting to ignore.

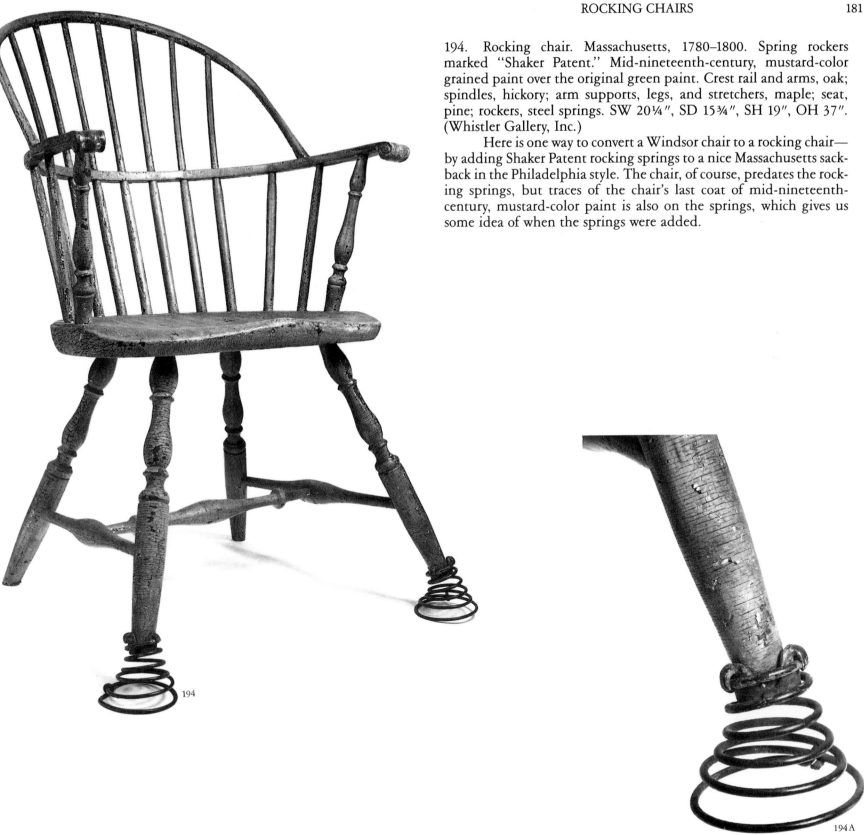

194. Rocking chair. Massachusetts, 1780–1800. Spring rockers marked "Shaker Patent." Mid-nineteenth-century, mustard-color grained paint over the original green paint. Crest rail and arms, oak; spindles, hickory; arm supports, legs, and stretchers, maple; seat, pine; rockers, steel springs. SW 20¼″, SD 15¾″, SH 19″, OH 37″. (Whistler Gallery, Inc.)

Here is one way to convert a Windsor chair to a rocking chair—by adding Shaker Patent rocking springs to a nice Massachusetts sackback in the Philadelphia style. The chair, of course, predates the rocking springs, but traces of the chair's last coat of mid-nineteenth-century, mustard-color paint is also on the springs, which gives us some idea of when the springs were added.

194A. Detail of Shaker Patent rocking springs.

195. Rocking chair. Probably Pennsylvania; 1800–1820. Nineteenth-century brown paint with gilt striping. Crest rail, oak; back posts, spindles, and side stretchers, hickory; seat, poplar; legs and medial stretcher, maple; rockers, walnut. SW 17¾″, SD 15¾″, SH 16″, OH 36″. (Privately owned)

  This is a good example of a Windsor rocking chair with legs purposely turned to accept rockers. The shape of the so-called "cheese-cutter" rockers is like that found on rush-bottom chairs that date from the middle to the end of the eighteenth century. The rockers are mortised into the legs and held in place with pegs. The fact that it has no arms makes this rocker uncommon.

195

196. Rocking chair. Probably New Jersey; 1810–1830. Original black paint with yellow decoration. Crest rail, possibly oak; spindles, arm supports, legs, stretcher, and rockers, maple; arms, ash; seat, pine. SW 20½″, SD 15¾″, SH 15″, OH 42¾″. (M. Finkel & Daughter)

  For this chair, the rockers serve a dual purpose: as rockers and as side stretchers. The medial stretcher is doweled into both rockers, and the thickness of the rockers allows the legs to be socketed into them as well. The design of the rockers is slightly later than the rocker design of figure 195.

  This chair was found in New Jersey and has the slim turnings of certain other New Jersey Windsors.

196A. Detail of rocker and leg construction.

196

196 A

197.   Rocking chair. Boston, 1790–1800. The name "Sanborn" is
marked in chalk on the seat bottom, possibly by chairmaker Reuben
Sanborn. Painted black. Top crest rail, arms, arm supports, legs, and
stretchers, maple; crest rail, oak; seat, pine; rockers, birch. SW 19½″,
SD 16¼″, SH 14½″, OH 43½″. (Mr. and Mrs. Thomas Helm)
      Although this chair is a Boston interpretation of a Philadelphia
bow-back form, the comb-piece arrangement we see here is never
found on Philadelphia Windsors.

197

198

198. Rocking chair. New England, 1800–1815. Original olive-green paint with yellow decoration. Top crest rail, legs, and stretchers, maple; crest rail, spindles, and arm supports, ash; arms, mahogany; seat, drawer, and rockers, pine. SW 20″, SD 18½″, SH 13½″, OH 42″. (David A. Schorsch, Inc.)

The top crest rail of this rocker is attached in an unusual way that creates nine "bird-cage" bars in the back of the chair. Also interesting is the "knitting drawer" under the seat that pulls out from the side.

Note how the legs are chamfered at the bottom where the cheese-cutter rockers are socketed.

199. Rocking chair. New England, possibly Connecticut or New Hampshire; 1820–1830. Original yellow paint with green-and-gilt sponge decoration. Crest rail, spindles, arms, arm supports, legs, stretchers, and rockers, maple; seat, pine. SW 17¾″, SD 17″, SH 17½″, OH 46⅜″. (Steven and Helen Kellogg)

For this chair, as for figure 196, the rockers also serve as side stretchers. This piece is very similar to rocking chairs of this type that were made by A. Wetherbee of New Ipswich, New Hampshire.

199

200.   Rocking chair. New England, 1830–1840. Original yellow paint
with red-and-black decoration. Crest rail, back posts, spindles, arm
supports, legs, and stretchers, maple; arms, mahogany; seat, pine;
rockers, chestnut. SW 19¼″, SD 18″, SH 14″, OH 42¼″. (Steven and
Helen Kellogg)
        Later Windsor rockers like this one are difficult to regionalize.
By the 1830s, they were almost identical in woods, construction, and
paint—especially rockers from Connecticut, Massachusetts, and New
Hampshire. This type of rocking chair may have been the forerunner
of the so-called Boston rocker.

200

SETTEES

CHAPTER TEN

Most of the earliest American Windsor settees—those from the 1750–1770 period—were made in Philadelphia and were low-backs, judging from surviving examples. Around 1765 or so, some sack-back settees were produced, but they apparently were never as plentiful as the low-backs—interesting, I think, because sack-back Windsor chairs far outnumbered low-back chairs.

The basic construction of the Philadelphia low-back settee was the same as that used for low-back chairs. Of course, the settees are longer, but their length did not weaken the construction of the back. This was not the case with the sack-back and the later bow-back settees. The necessary length of the spindles may be in part responsible for the fact that not many sack-back benches have survived intact; and the fact that the backs of these settees were not particularly sturdy may, in turn, account for the fact that not many were produced in the first place.

Bow-back, tenon-arm settees seem to have been made in larger numbers than sack-backs. Certain other forms were attempted, such as the continuous-arm settee, the tenon-arm fan-back settee, the armless bow-back settee, and the rare triple-back settee. However, it was the rod-back form of Windsor bench of about 1800 that was produced in the greatest numbers as well as in the greatest variety of color, decoration, and back design. During the first quarter of the nineteenth century, rod-back settees were produced as part of sets, often consisting of six side chairs, two armchairs, and a settee, all similarly paint-decorated. During this period two-person settees, or loveseats, also were popular.

As was true of chairs, the designs of settees were most conservative in areas such as Philadelphia and Boston, and most individualistic in Connecticut, Rhode Island, New Hampshire, and areas remote from the design centers. Interestingly, it is very rare to find a settee made in New York.

201.   Settee. Philadelphia, 1765–1780. Nineteenth-century crackled varnish over traces of red-and-green paint. Crest rail and seat, poplar; spindles, hickory; arms and handholds, oak; arm supports, legs, and stretchers, maple. SW 80″, SD 22½″, SH 17½″, OH 29½″. (Privately owned)

This is a very strong example of a Philadelphia low-back settee of the period. The turnings are robust and bulbous, probably a holdover design from the earlier blunt-arrow style. The arm supports are not vase-tapered, as they are in comb-backs, and are reminiscent of the work of Francis Trumble. The flaring seat edge conforms with the flare of the knuckles. This is one of the earliest examples of a vase-and-ring-turned settee. The seat is constructed of two boards. (Although the seats of settees are almost always made of a single plank, occasionally a two-board construction is used.)

201

202

203

202.   Settee. Philadelphia, 1765–1780. Old black paint over traces of the original green. Arm crest, chestnut; arms, possibly oak; spindles, hickory; seat, poplar; legs and stretchers, maple. SW 60¾″, SH 15½″, OH 29″. (Wayne Pratt)

Like figure 201, this piece has an early character, especially noticeable in the turnings of the arm supports. While both pieces have an overall height of 29″ or so, this piece has a seat height of 15½″, while figure 201's is 17½″; thus figure 201 has a more compressed design that could be considered better. Figure 201 also has more spindles in its back. On the other hand, this settee has a desirable feature that figure 201 lacks: ringed side stretchers. Thus the two pieces are quite similar expressions with some interesting differences.

203.   Settee. Philadelphia, 1765–1790. Branded I. [John] LETCHWORTH. Approximately one inch of foot lost. Shellac finish. Arm crest and seat, poplar; arms, oak; spindles, hickory; arm supports, legs, and stretchers, maple. SW 76″, SD 21″, SH 16¾″, OH 32″. (Independence National Historical Park)

This settee is slightly later than the previous two examples. Its later features include the vase taper where the arm support enters the seat and the general slimness of the turning patterns. Its overall height is three inches more than the previous two settees—and it would be even taller were some of the feet not missing. This settee also has a remarkable 48 spindles.

204.   Settee. Lancaster County, Pennsylvania, 1760–1780. Very old black paint over the original green. Arm crest, probably maple; spindles and arms, hickory; seat, pine; arm supports, legs, and stretchers, maple. SW 75″, SD 18¼″, SH 18″, OH 30″. (Privately owned)

Lancaster County settees are rare, and were no doubt made in smaller quantities than those from Philadelphia. These pieces have several distinctive characteristics, among them: a steam-bent arm rail; knuckles made in three pieces (with the sides and bottoms attached to the arm rail); slightly bulbous spindles; blunt-arrow feet on the front legs, and tapered rear legs; score marks on the balusters of the arm supports and legs; and ring-and-arrow turnings on the medial stretchers.

Another special characteristic of this settee and others with steam-bent arm rails (as opposed to those with sawed arm rails, such as figures 205, 206, and 207) is that the arm crest does not wrap around the top of the arm rail, and its width more or less corresponds to the distance between the outer back legs.

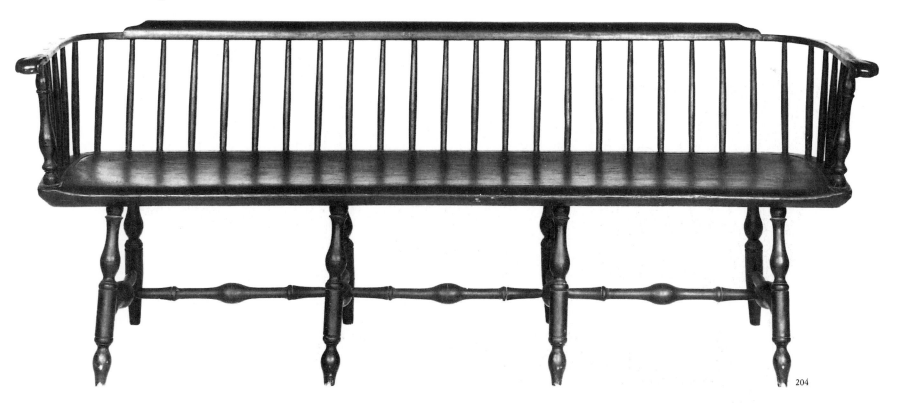

204

205.

205. Settee. Lancaster County, Pennsylvania, 1780–1800. Original blue-gray paint. Arm crest and seat, poplar; spindles and arms, hickory; handholds, walnut; arm supports, chestnut; legs and stretchers, maple. SW 77¾″, SD 23″, SH 18″, OH 31″. (Privately owned)

Here is another good example of a Lancaster County settee, though later than figure 204. Like figure 204, it has a steam-bent arm rail, three-piece knuckles, slightly bulbous spindles, and characteristic side stretchers. However, the legs of this bench are of the double-bobbin variety, with a flared foot at the front and a tapered foot in back. (This flared foot is often called a "goat foot" in the Pennsylvania Dutch country.) The design of this flared front foot, like that of figure 204, is a more elaborate design than that of the back foot. Even with the use of the later, simplified bamboo turnings, this provincial Windsor-maker created a powerful design.

206. Settee. Pennsylvania or Maryland, 1790–1810. Original paint. Arm crest, oak; spindles and arms, hickory; arm supports, legs, and stretchers, maple; seat, poplar. SW 84″, SD 22″, SH 17″, OH 32″. (Tom Brown)

This settee has several Lancaster County characteristics: a steam-bent arm rail; arm supports turned in the Lancaster style; and three-piece knuckles. But the bamboo leg turnings, the almost barrel-shaped side stretchers, and the double-bobbin medial stretcher are not in the Lancaster County style. They are, however, found on settees from Maryland near the Pennsylvania border.

Note the extreme overhang of the seat beyond the legs, and, because of it, how proportionately short the arm crest appears.

207. Settee. Pennsylvania or Maryland, 1790–1810. Nineteenth-century brown varnish over a putty-color ground, over gray-green paint, over the original green paint. Arm crest, handholds, and seat, poplar; arm supports, spindles, legs, and stretchers, hickory; arms, oak. SW 85″, SD 23¾″, OH 32½″. (The Henry Francis du Pont Winterthur Museum)

Though it appears similar to figure 206, this settee has an arm crest that is constructed differently. The arm crest is not a single, solid piece of wood, but has been created by nailing three separate strips of wood to the front, top, and back of the steam-bent arm rail, creating the illusion of a single piece of wood. As with the previous three examples, the knuckles of this settee are made in three pieces.

There are also several stylistic parallels to figure 206: the long seat overhang; the relatively short crest rail; the barrel-shaped side stretchers; the double-bobbin medial stretchers; the leg turnings (although these have a longer taper); the arm-support turnings; and the general shape of the knuckles. Of course, the one obvious difference is that the spindles of this settee are baluster-turned, which adds a great deal of visual energy.

206

207

208.   Settee. Pennsylvania, 1765–1780. Nineteenth-century crackled varnish. Arms, arm supports, legs, and stretchers, maple; spindles, maple and hickory; seat, pine. SW 76″, SD 19″, SH 18″, OH 30″. (Privately owned)

This is one of three known settees by this maker. It has a very unusual, dynamic design, with all spindles baluster-turned and with a rare bell-shaped cap that is echoed in the leg turnings. Only the center spindle is perpendicular, the others being progressively angled until the last spindle is parallel to the arm support. The bold knuckles (done in the Lancaster County style with a protruding center knuckle), shield-shaped seat (flared at the front edges), and baluster-like turning in the leg cylinder where the stretcher is socketed (where the leg would normally be straight) all mark this piece and the two others like it as the product of a single shop. At least one low-back armchair in exactly the same style is also known (see figure 36).

Note the beading on the front edge of the arm crest, which emphasizes an uncommon design feature of this piece: the arm crest, which in a Philadelphia low-back would overlap the arms, in this piece and the two other examples is actually cut from the same piece of wood—that is, there is a mortise-and-tenon joint rather than a lap joint. This is actually a stronger joint than those used on Philadelphia low-backs.

It is unusual for a settee to have a medial stretcher pattern like the one found here, which, in fact, is just like that found on certain Delaware Valley rush-bottom chairs. The side stretchers are in the English taste and in a pattern found among Philadelphia and Rhode Island Windsors.

The tall, turnip-like blunt-arrow foot adds a nice finish to the leg. Scribe marks on the underside of the seat of this piece mark the tentative leg-hole placement, but the holes were drilled elsewhere, suggesting that this may have been an experimental piece or a prototype.

208

209. Settee. Pennsylvania, 1765–1780; found in New Market, Maryland. Nineteenth-century mahoganizing over the original green paint. Arm crest and seat, poplar; spindles, arms, handholds, arm supports, legs, and stretchers, maple. SW 81⅝", SD 21¼", OH 32". (The Henry Francis du Pont Winterthur Museum)

Here is the second settee by the same hand as figure 208. The construction is identical, but the embellishments are different. The knuckles are better realized on this piece, with more flare in the Chippendale style. The spindle turning pattern is practically the same, but the baluster turning is better. Though the top half of the leg is like that of figure 208, from midleg down the bulging cylinder is longer and the flaring collar of figure 208 is replaced by the more traditional reel and ring. The foot is a ball with a long nipple. The medial stretchers are a type found on Lancaster County fan-back, sack-back, and bow-back Windsors.

Perhaps this piece is slightly later than figure 208 and the "final design" derived from the prototype.

209

210

211

210. Settee. Probably Lisbon, Connecticut, 1770–1803. Nineteenth-century black paint over red, over blue, over the original green. Arm supports and legs, maple; arms, spindles, and stretchers, oak; seat, chestnut. SW 81½″, SD 22¾″, SH 15¾″, OH 30⅛″. (Mr. and Mrs. Victor Johnson)

This piece is attributable to Ebenezer Tracy of Lisbon, Connecticut.[18] It is a most exuberant example of Connecticut furniture and shows Tracy at his best. The rake of the two inside legs is unusual and makes the settee look almost like two chairs. Tracy seems to have paid more attention to the base of the piece than to the top, and the large, waferlike rings on the stretchers mark the piece as special and undoubtedly a custom order.

211. Settee. Philadelphia, 1780–1800. Branded A[nthony]. STEEL. Old varnish over traces of gray paint. Arm crest and seat, poplar; spindles, hickory; arms, oak; arm supports, legs, and stretchers, chestnut. SW 78″, SD 20½″, SH 18″, OH 30½″. (Chalfant & Chalfant Antiques)

Something of a "transitional" piece, this settee has bamboo-turned legs but vase-and-ring-turned arm supports and baluster-shaped medial stretchers with bamboo scoring. Like many Philadelphia low-back settees of the bamboo period, this one does not have knuckles. It is a typically conservative expression of Philadelphia furniture-making.

212. Settee. Philadelphia, 1780–1800. Branded D[aniel]. CARTERET. Late nineteenth-century black paint over older blackish-green paint. Arm crest, arm supports, legs, and side stretchers, maple; spindles and medial stretchers, hickory; arms and handholds, oak; seat, pine. SW 77¾″, SD 21″, SH 17⅝″, OH 32″. (Bernard & S. Dean Levy, Inc.)

A similar expression to figure 211, this settee has vase-and-ring turnings and bamboo legs, yet retains the full knuckle. The better taper of the legs and the presence of knuckles sets this piece apart from the ordinary. However, it also has the more typical bamboo medial stretchers.

212

213. Settee. Philadelphia, 1780–1800. Original salmon-color paint with black decoration. Crest rail, oak; arm supports and spindles, hickory; arms, mahogany; seat, poplar; legs and stretchers, maple. SW 69⅝″, SD 23⅜″, SH 17⅝″, OH 38⅜″. (Claude and Alvan Bisnoff)

Tenon-arm construction of bow-back Windsors was very fashionable during this period, and this settee is much like the chairs of its period. The seat width and depth are unusually long in over-hang and extension.

213A. Settee. Side view showing seat width.

214.   Settee. Possibly Virginia; 1780–1800. Early nineteenth-century ochre paint over the original gray. Crest rail and spindles, hickory; arm supports and stretchers, possibly hickory; seat, poplar; legs, maple. SW 83″, SD 21½″, SH 17⅝″, OH 37½″. (Museum of Early Southern Decorative Arts, Winston-Salem, N.C.)

Based on the Philadelphia model of the period, this settee has the same general appearance as figure 213 but is much more detailed and elaborate. The piece is vase-and-ring turned throughout, and the arms are finely detailed, with beautiful knuckles. There are five sets of legs. The arms are mortised into the bow at a higher point than one would expect, making for a nice, flowing transition from bow to arm.

214

215

215.   Settee. New England, possibly New Hampshire; 1790–1800. Original dark red paint. Crest rail, oak; seat, pine; spindles, legs, and stretchers, hickory or chestnut. SW 48¾″, SH 17¼″, OH 36″. (Frank and Barbara Pollack)

A very rare form with no arms, this piece could almost be called a double-seat side chair. The bow is nicely pinched, and the form possesses a quiet elegance of design.

216.   Settee. Philadelphia, 1800–1810. Mid-nineteenth-century red grained paint, over a buff-color ground, over the original green paint. Crest rail, back posts, and spindles, hickory; arms, arm supports, legs, and stretchers, maple; seat, pine. SW 77¼″, SD 20⅜″, SH 17¼″, OH 34″. (Dietrich American Foundation)

Settees such as this are sometimes called "duckbill" Windsors. This is a newer, stylish design not based on the earlier vase-and-ring

style. It is in pieces like this that the bamboo style, with its interesting angles, works best. The center post adds a nice symmetry and strength.

217.   Settee. Lancaster County, Pennsylvania, 1800–1820. Old dark brown paint over yellow paint, over the original salmon-colored paint. Crest rail, back posts, spindles, arm supports, and stretchers, hickory; crest medallions and seat, poplar; arms and legs, maple. SW 78¼″, SD 18⅝″, SH 16¼″, OH 33½″. (Downingtown Antiques)

A variation on the bamboo theme of figure 216, this piece is intended to give the illusion of three chairs side by side. The crest rail steps up distinctively to help create this effect, and the stretcher arrangement echoes that movement. This is a good example of a late settee, and was intended to be a companion piece to the so-called butterfly rod-back Windsor chairs of the period.

216

217

218

218.   Settee. New England, possibly New Hampshire; 1790–1810. Original dark green paint. Made entirely in chestnut, except the pine seat. SW 66¼″, SD 16″, SH 17⅜″, OH 34″. (Privately owned)
Its curved seat, with its back, arms, and medial stretchers curved to conform to it, make this a very rare form. Interestingly, the medial stretchers are square in cross-section and are attached to the underside of the side stretchers with nails. All the spindles penetrate the crest rail and are wedged. The edge of the seat is beautifully carved with a concave chamfer, and the duckbill edges of the arms are nicely perked up.

219.   Settee. New England, possibly New Hampshire; 1790–1810. Mid-nineteenth-century dark green paint over green paint, over the original dark red paint. Crest rail, arms, arm supports, legs, and medial stretchers, chestnut; spindles, hickory; seat, pine; side stretchers, maple. SW 66¼″, SD 16¼″, SH 17½″, OH 35″. (Dietrich Americana Foundation)

This settee was probably made by the same hand as figure 218, but here there is more overhang at the seat edge and an extra spindle in the back.

219

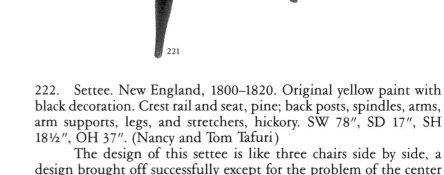

220.   Settee. Pennsylvania, 1800–1820. Original green paint with black decoration. Crest rail, oak; back posts, arms, arm supports, and legs, maple; spindles and stretchers, hickory; seat, poplar. SW 28⅜″, SD 16″, SH 18″, OH 33⅝″. (Privately owned)

     Small loveseats such as this are rare. This one has typical bamboo turning and is well proportioned. The ends of the seat are carved to simulate upholstery. The middle spindle and the third from each end penetrate the crest rail and are wedged.

221.   Settee. Probably Pennsylvania; 1800–1820. Dark green paint over the original green. Crest rail and seat, poplar; back posts, arms, and arm supports, maple; spindles, legs, and stretchers, hickory. SW 31½″, SD 15″, SH 17½″, OH 34⅝″. (Privately owned)

     Although made in the rod-back style, this settee retains the earlier H-stretcher pattern and baluster-turned side stretchers. The legs are double-bobbin turned. The three sets of legs and extra back post, plus the extra blocking on the front edge of the seat to echo the crest rail, make for a pleasing design.

222.   Settee. New England, 1800–1820. Original yellow paint with black decoration. Crest rail and seat, pine; back posts, spindles, arms, arm supports, legs, and stretchers, hickory. SW 78″, SD 17″, SH 18½″, OH 37″. (Nancy and Tom Tafuri)

     The design of this settee is like three chairs side by side, a design brought off successfully except for the problem of the center back post. (Perhaps, instead, the maker should have placed two back posts above the inner legs.) The crest rail is nicely carved and outlined in original paint decoration.

223.   Settee. New England, possibly Maine; 1830–1840. Original yellow paint with green decoration. Made entirely in maple, except the pine seat. SW 78¼″, SD 18½″, SH 18½″, OH 34″. (Steven and Helen Kellogg)

     I think that pieces like this could be called "family settees." This has the look of a Hitchcock chair and the arms of a Boston rocker.

     The paint decoration, added both in freehand and in a plum-and-grape-leaf stencil pattern, creates most of the design interest and is even more important than the architecture of the piece.

222

223

224.   Settee. Philadelphia, 1815–1840. Late nineteenth-century dark brown paint over traces of original stencil decoration. Crest rail, possibly poplar; back posts, spindles, arm supports, legs, and stretchers, maple; arms, oak; seat, poplar. SD 20¾″, SH 16½″, OH 32¼″. (John Bartram Association)

The bamboo spindles of late Philadelphia and other Pennsylvania pieces do not taper. Of course, they are easier to turn that way. This is a feature that is fairly consistent on chairs and settees with three-ring bamboo turnings. On this piece we see a simple board splat with arrow-shaped spindles. The ringing on the back posts gives a slight nod of acknowledgement to the earlier turning patterns. Pieces like this are often called "thumb-backs" because of the flattened terminal of the back posts.

224

CHILDREN'S
and
SCALED-DOWN

Furniture

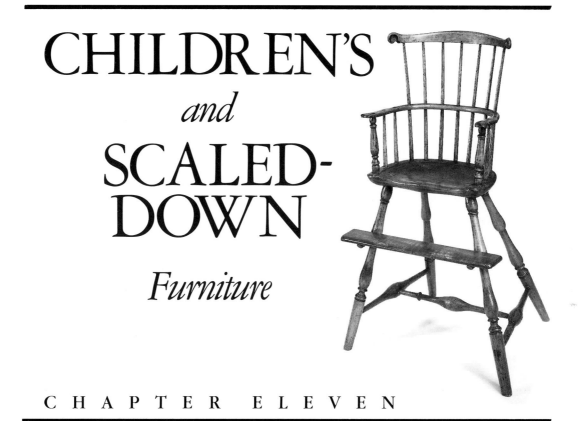

The success of a small chair, high chair, or cradle has much to do with the attention to detail of the maker. When a small chair exhibits the same refinements one hopes to find on a full-size chair—such as knuckle handholds, carved ears, and excellent turnings—it not only says much about the chairmaker but also about the parents!

After all, a child's furniture needs are rather basic, sturdiness being the most important criterion. Parents who were willing and able to pay the extra price for the same refinements they enjoyed in their own Windsor furniture showed not only an appreciation for the Windsor form but an obvious love for their child. I think, too, that one can sense in child-size furniture a delight on the part of the chairmaker.

Fine children's Windsors are rare, not because they did not survive the rigors of childhood but because few were produced in the first place by practical craftsmen on a day-to-day basis. The better pieces were certainly special orders, and it took a truly fine craftsman to understand the problems involved in scaling down a normal chair to child's size. If all the parts are simply made proportionally smaller, the piece will look flimsy (and probably will *be* flimsy). The best Windsor-makers knew that parts such as arm supports and legs often should be made slightly heavier than one might expect to achieve the proper balance and proportion.

---

225. High chair. Philadelphia, 1765–1790. Branded I. [Joseph] HENZEY. Bottoms of knuckles missing; footrest an early replacement. Refinished; traces of original blackish-green paint. Crest rail, arm supports, legs, stretchers, and footrest, maple; spindles and arms, hickory; seat, poplar. SW 14⅞″, SD 10½″, SH 21⅝″, OH 37¾″. (Bernard & S. Dean Levy, Inc.)

Although this is a relatively late chair, it still retains the D-shaped seat of the earlier comb-backs instead of the expected oval or shield-shaped seat. An extra baluster has been added in the leg turnings to accommodate the dowel that holds the footrest; this extra baluster is repeated on the rear legs.

226. High chair. Philadelphia, 1775–1790. Branded I. [John] B. ACKLEY. Footrest an old replacement. Refinished; traces of the original green paint. Crest rail and arms, oak; spindles, hickory; arm supports, legs, and stretchers, maple; seat, poplar. SW 15″, SD 10¼″, SH 21¾″, OH 37¼″. (Mr. and Mrs. R. W. P. Allen)

Like figure 225, this chair has an extra baluster on the front legs, but the design is not repeated on the rear legs. Once again a D-shaped seat has been used. Holes in the arm supports for the missing restraining rod are clearly visible in the photograph.

Since the medial stretcher of this chair is original and in a late style—that is, it does not have turned rings at either end—the chair probably dates from closer to 1790 than to 1775.

225

226

227

227. High chair. Philadelphia, 1780–1800. Footrest an early replacement. Nineteenth-century putty-color paint over the original dark gray paint. Crest rail, oak; spindles, hickory; arms and arm supports, mahogany; seat, poplar; legs and stretchers, maple. SW 14¼″, SD 14″, SH 21¾″, OH 36″. (Privately owned)

Here is a particularly handsome design. The mahogany arms and arm supports are an unusual touch. Note, too, that the arm supports are vase-and-ring turned, while the rest of the chair is bamboo-turned. The legs are turned in the typical Philadelphia style, with rounded shoulders at the tops of the legs. The seat is well saddled. On Philadelphia bow-backs of this type, a bamboo-turned medial stretcher is often found in combination with baluster-turned side stretchers.

228. High chair. Philadelphia, 1780–1800. Remnants of the label of Gilbert and Robert Gaw. Medial stretcher replaced. Original green paint over a salmon-color ground. Crest rail, oak; spindles, hickory; arms, mahogany; arm supports, legs, and stretchers, maple; seat, poplar. SW 14½", SD 11⅝", SH 20¾", OH 36¾". (Mr. and Mrs. Thomas Helm)

The leg turnings of this chair are somewhat better than those of figure 227, and the footrest is original, but from the seat up this chair doesn't quite match the sophistication of figure 227. The seat is not as well saddled, nor is it as deep from front to back. The arms are mahogany, but the arm supports are the more typical bamboo style of the period. There is only one short spindle under each arm of this chair, as opposed to two in figure 227—made possible by that chair's greater seat depth. This chair also has a "stiffer" back, with no pinch to the waist. Finally, the spindles are not as well turned—that is, they are essentially a straight taper with score marks and no articulation of the bamboo turning. The replaced medial stretcher of this chair no doubt originally looked like that of figure 227.

229. High chair. Philadelphia area, 1780–1810. Old dark red paint. Crest rail and arms, oak; spindles, hickory; arm supports, legs, and stretchers, maple; seat, poplar; footrest, pine. SW 14¼", SD 10¾", SH 20⅜", OH 35". (Mr. and Mrs. R. W. P. Allen)

The leg turning pattern of this chair, an interesting variant of the bamboo style, is occasionally found on Philadelphia chairs of this period. Overall, the chair is a fairly simple sack-back design. But it is unusual to find a sack-back, an earlier style, with these later bamboo turnings—the type one would expect to find on a tenon-arm, bow-back Windsor. Thus this chair may be provincial, perhaps from Chester County or Lancaster County. The heavy bamboo score marks and the baluster, rather than bamboo, medial stretcher also suggest a provincial origin.

228

229

230. High chair. New York City, 1770–1800. Refinished; traces of the original green paint. Crest rail, oak; spindles, hickory; arms, arm supports, legs, stretchers, and footrest, maple; seat, pine. SW 13⅜″, SD 13½″, SH 21¼″, OH 35″. (Privately owned)

Here we see one of the truly great examples of a Windsor high chair, with superb proportions and a wonderful splay. Note the innovative footrest: a baluster stretcher turning that is flattened on the top and bottom. New York—and New England—Windsor makers solved the problem of where to place the footrest by using a long leg taper and skortened baluster, so that the footrest could be socketed directly into the baluster. The H-stretchers on these chairs are also generally higher, and thus more graceful, than those on Philadelphia-area high chairs, whose footrests are generally socketed into the narrow part of the upper leg, weakening the leg. Occasionally, Philadelphia Windsor makers solved this problem by adding an extra baluster (as in figures 225 and 226) to receive the footrest instead of a longer bottom taper, but the result is awkward.

230

231. High chair. Salem, Massachusetts, 1800–1810. Branded I.C. TUTTLE. Early nineteenth-century yellow paint with white decoration over original green paint. Crest rail and arms, hickory or oak; spindles, hickory; arm supports, legs, and stretchers, maple; seat, pine. SW 15¾″, SD 10¾″, SH 21″, OH 34″. (Also see color plate VII.) (Doris and Kyle Fuller)

This is a fairly simplified version of a sack-back. On Philadelphia chairs the bamboo ringing is far more rounded, or convex, than it is on this chair, which is typical of the New England style. While most of this chair is bamboo-turned, the stretchers are baluster-turned—a feature not found on Windsors produced in design centers such as Boston.

The bow angles backward nicely, and the simplicity of the chair's design is enhanced greatly by its paint surface.

232

231

232. High chair. Gettysburg, Pennsylvania, or nearby Maryland, 1790–1810. SW 20⅞″, SD 17½″, OH 34⅜″. (The Henry Francis du Pont Winterthur Museum)

This is an interesting variation on the high-chair form, with its great leg splay and graceful but idiosyncratic presence. The point where the arm sockets into the bow is lower than the point where the arm is attached to the arm support—just the opposite of most bow-back Windsor armchairs.

The turning pattern of the arm supports of this chair, especially as they enter the seat, is similar to that of figure 36, an armchair from the same area.[19]

233

234

233. High chair. New England, 1800–1820. Early black paint. Crest rail, two short spindles, arm supports, legs, and stretchers, maple; spindles, hickory; arms, ash; seat and footrest, pine. SW 12½″, SD 9″, SH 20½″, OH 34½″. (Privately owned)

It is not unusual to find a New England comb-back with bamboo turnings, as on this simple, elegant little chair. The bamboo ringing has been placed toward the upper half of the legs, allowing for a long leg taper. Generally, three bamboo rings were used on rod-backs, so even though this chair has a comb-back form, it probably dates from no earlier than 1800.

234. High chair. New England, possibly New Hampshire; 1800–1820. Old dark brown paint. Made entirely in birch, except the pine seat. (Privately owned)

The attractive features of this "duck-bill" Windsor include its high back, the finely mortised corners of the arms and of the crest rail with its little ears, and the D-shaped seat. Perhaps the stretchers could have been placed higher, but the stretchers and legs are well turned, and the chair has good splay.

235

236. Armchair. Massachusetts, 1770–1790. Very old black paint over older black. Crest rail, oak; spindles, hickory; arms, arm supports, legs, and stretchers, maple; seat, pine. SW 14″, SD 13″, SH 10″, OH 32″. (Tom Brown)

This is a wonderful, charming example of a child's comb-back Windsor chair with all the refinements one would hope to find: scrolled ears, a tall back, knuckle handholds, a nicely saddled and chamfered seat, and crisp turnings.

When turning patterns are scaled down, it sometimes becomes difficult to determine where they were made. However, on this chair the arm supports and medial stretcher are just like those found on fan-back armchairs from coastal Massachusetts.

235. High chair. New England, 1800–1820. Nineteenth-century dark red paint over the original yellow. Crest rail, back posts, and legs, maple; spindles and stretchers, hickory; arms and arm supports, oak; seat, pine. SW 12¾″, SD 12″, SH 23½″, OH 36¾″. (Lori and Craig Mayor)

This rod-back high chair has an interesting feature: the back posts are round, with bamboo ringing, but they flatten when they reach the crest rail to conform with its shape. Unlike the arms of figure 234, these arms are totally different from the crest rail. The bamboo legs are nicely proportioned. The box stretcher arrangement is the one usually found on rod-backs.

236

237.   Armchair. New York City, 1775–1800. Old black paint over the original green. Crest rail, probably oak; spindles, hickory; arm supports, legs, and stretchers, maple; seat, poplar. SW 12½″, SD 12½″, tailpiece 2″, SH 12″, OH 25¼″. (Privately owned)

Here we see one of the masterpieces of children's Windsor furniture. It really leaves nothing to be desired and has all the refinements of the great New York City full-scale Windsors: explosive turnings and a strong shield-shaped seat, plus the added attraction of turned "pipe-stem" spindles that are probably a Rhode Island influence. Interestingly, except for a bit of heaviness in the spindles and legs, you would be hard-pressed to tell from this photograph the exact size of this little chair.

237

238. Side chair. Philadelphia, 1765–1780. Some foot loss. Mid-nineteenth-century dark red paint over a salmon ground, over the original green paint. Crest rail, oak; back posts and spindles, hickory; seat, poplar; legs and stretchers, maple. SW 13¼″, SD 13¼″, SH 10¼″, OH 25¼″. (Privately owned)

A fine example of a scaled-down fan-back, this chair is not really as successful as figure 237. The stretchers are a bit clumsy compared with the leg turnings. The seat is well done.

Note how comb-pieces with uncarved ears like these usually turn up at the ends, whereas comb-pieces with scrolled ears turn down, as on figure 236.

238

239. Armchair. Philadelphia, 1765–1790. Refinished; traces of green paint. Crest rail and arms, oak; spindles, hickory; arm supports, legs, and stretchers, maple; seat, poplar. SW 17¾″, SD 11¾″, SH 11″, OH 26¾″. (Mr. and Mrs. R. W. P. Allen)

The leg turnings of this chair are quite simple compared with those of figure 238, but the stretchers are much better and more in proportion to the legs. The arm supports are a bit simplified, the collar over the ring having been omitted. Overall, this is a nicely proportioned chair.

240.   Settee. Philadelphia area, 1790–1810. Refinished. Arm crest, poplar; spindles, hickory; arms, oak; arm supports, legs, and stretchers, maple; seat, poplar. SW 22¼″, SD 11½″, SH 8¾″, OH 17¼″. (Privately owned)

The arm crest on this low-back settee is nailed to the arm rail with original eighteenth-century nails. This settee never had stretchers. The leg turnings are extremely simplified, and it is quite possible that they were made by cutting down the tops of legs turned for a full-scale Windsor.

240

241. Settee. Philadelphia, 1800–1830. Original red paint, with original salmon-color paint on seat. Crest rail, spindles, and stretchers, hickory; back posts, arms, arm supports, and legs, maple; seat, poplar. SW 36¾″, SH 12½″, OH 26¾″. (Sarah Lippincott)

This is a very well-proportioned, scaled-down rod-back settee. The parts are nicely turned in the typical Philadelphia style. Especially attractive is the extra center back post, creating the illusion of a double chair.

241

242. Side chair. Philadelphia, 1785–1800. Branded I. [John] B. ACKLEY. Rockers a later addition. Late nineteenth-century gray paint with green striping. Crest rail, probably oak; spindles, hickory; seat, poplar; legs and stretchers, maple. SW 14⅞″, SD 13¼″, SH 11¾″, OH 26¼″. (Eugene Pettinelli)

A child's version of the very popular Philadelphia bow-back side chair, this has the baluster side stretchers and bamboo medial stretcher characteristic of the form.

243.   Armchair. New England, possibly New Hampshire; 1800–1820. Original black paint. Crest rail, spindles, back posts, arms, and arm supports, hickory; seat, pine; legs and stretchers, maple. SW 16½″, SD 14½″, SH 14″, OH 30″. (Courtesy, James and Nancy Glazer)

Very crisply turned for a bamboo child's chair, especially in the medial stretcher, this piece also has a beautifully chamfered seat that echoes the duckbill design of the arms and crest rail.

244

244.   Armchair. Pennsylvania, 1800–1830. Painted black. Crest rail, back posts, arms, arm supports, and legs, maple; spindles and stretchers, hickory; seat, poplar. SW 11″, SD 10¾″, SH 6¾″, OH 18½″. (Privately owned)

This chair was originally made as a potty chair, and its scale is quite small. Yet even in this size, the legs have the typical Pennsylvania rolled shoulders at their tops where they enter the seat. The turned arms are similar to those found on rush-bottom, slat-back high chairs.

245

245.   Armchair. Pennsylvania, 1800–1820. Original green paint with gilt striping. Crest rail, back posts, arms, arm supports, legs, and stretchers, maple; spindles, hickory; seat, pine. SW 4″, SD 3½″, SH 3½″, OH 7¼″. (See also color plate XV.) (Allan and Joan Lehner)

A true miniature only 7¼″ tall, this little chair could have been a doll's seat, a salesman's sample, or simply a whimsy. It is very well proportioned and an extremely rare piece of Windsor furniture.

OTHER FORMS

of

Windsor
Furniture

CHAPTER TWELVE

Tables, candlestands, and stools made with Windsor construction methods during the third quarter of the eighteenth century are very rare. This may have something do with the psychology of the Windsor-chairmaker of the time.

In the 1750s, it seemed innovative to transpose what were essentially William-and-Mary turning patterns to the new mode of seating furniture—the Windsor chair. However, "joyned" stools, tables, and candlestands had been produced with essentially those same turning patterns all through the late seventeenth and the first half of the eighteenth century. Thus, by the middle of the eighteenth century, while Windsor chairs looked new, tables and stools made with the same turning patterns must have seemed hopelessly old-fashioned.

It was not until the introduction of the bamboo turning pattern in the 1780s that the concept of a product totally Windsor in style but not a chair—the stool—seems to have been realized by Windsor craftsmen from all regions. By the end of the eighteenth century, stools of all shapes and sizes—from desk stools to "cricket" stools to work stools—were produced in large numbers.

In their leg turnings, these stools are usually stylistically similar to the bow-back or rod-back chairs produced in the same region. They also may display decorative beading on the edge of the top of the seat similar to the beading found on a chair's seat edge, and often they are painted in the variety of Windsor colors popular at the time.

Windsor tables and candlestands remained a great rarity, even in the bamboo period.

———————————————————————————————

246. Candlestand. Philadelphia or Chester County, Pennsylvania, 1770–1800. Original black paint. Legs and stretchers, maple. Top 14½″ × 15¼″, OH 26¼″. (Dietrich American Foundation)

Windsor candlestands are rare, and ones that are in all-original condition, like this one, are extremely rare. This dish-top stand has sophisticated turnings in the Philadelphia pattern, but similar pieces have been found in Chester County, Pennsylvania. It is a delicate and graceful piece distinguished by a very long top baluster.

247. Table. Chester County, Pennsylvania, 1770–1800. Attributed to Nathan Jefferis (1773–1823), East Bradford Township. Made entirely in butternut. Top 16⅞″ × 17½″, OH 25″. (Chester County Historical Society)

It is not unusual for Windsor candlestands and tables to be constructed of a single wood, unlike Windsor chairs. The double beading on this table's dish top is an especially nice feature.

246

247

248

249

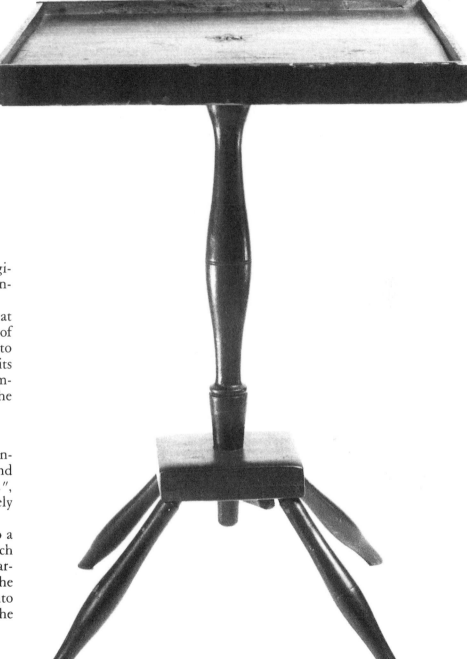

248.   Stool. Pennsylvania, probably Philadelphia; 1780–1800. Original buff-color paint with yellow and green striping. Top, pine; turnings, poplar. Top 11″ × 11¼″, OH 27½″. (Privately owned)

This is a very unusual stool with a wonderfully turned top that shows clear evidence of concentric-circle chisel marks. Like chairs of the period, it has a top with a double banding along its edge made to resemble upholstery. Note the T-stretcher arrangement with its baluster-turned front stretcher and bamboo side stretchers—a combination of turning styles also found on Philadelphia chairs of the period.

249.   Candlestand. Pennsylvania, probably Chester County or Lancaster County; 1750–1780. Original green paint. Top, pedestal, and cross-braces, poplar; plinth, pine; legs, oak. Top 17″ × 17½″, H to top of plinth 8¾″, OH 28″. (Also see color plate V.) (Privately owned)

While the previous forms have three legs that mortise into a circular top, this stand is constructed like a Windsor stool into which is socketed a center post with a top. Similar stands were made with various turning patterns throughout most of the eighteenth century. The top of this piece is held in place by a cross-brace that is mortised into the center post, and the center post is attached to the top of the "stool" with a removable wooden wedge, or key.

250.   Candlestand. New England, 1800–1820. Nineteenth-century brown paint over the original green. Top and edge molding, pine; pedestal, maple; plinth, oak; legs, chestnut. Top 17¼″ × 17⅞″, OH 26″. (Rosemary Beck and Ed Rogers)

This is a more delicate version of figure 249. Each piece has decorative double score marks in the center of its pedestal and a shoulder at the bottom of the turning. The shape of the rectangular top is echoed by the top of the "stool," which in this case has four legs. The rectangular top is attached to the pedestal in typical Windsor fashion, with a wedge joint.

250

251

252

251. Table. New England, possibly Connecticut; 1790–1810. Old black paint over the original buff-color paint. Made in yellow pine, except the maple legs. Top 18½″ × 26″, OH 26¼″. (Privately owned)

Although this table does not have Windsor construction, but, rather, the more traditional frame construction, its leg turning pattern is nonetheless in the late Windsor style. More traditional splay-leg tables without stretchers have legs that are wide at the top and narrow as they approach the floor—no matter what the style of the leg. On this table, the legs are narrowly turned near the top, then swell at midleg, then taper to the floor—like the legs of figure 250. Note, too, the two decorative score marks on the legs, which are like the score marks on the pedestals of the two previous examples. The shape of the legs of this piece is reminiscent of the legs found on late Windsors made by E. B. Tracy, which also have double score marks.

252. Stool. New England, 1780–1800. Nineteenth-century blackish-brown paint over the original green. Top, pine; legs and stretchers, maple. Top 9″ × 9½″, OH 10½″. (Privately owned)

Stools like this are often called crickets, or hearth stools. This one has excellent proportions. Its thick, dished top above well-turned bamboo legs, plus its H-stretcher arrangement and baluster, make it one of the better stools of its type.

254. Stool. New York or eastern Connecticut, 1800–1810. Late nineteenth-century pewter-blue paint with gilt striping over pale gray paint, over white paint. Top, pine; legs and stretchers, maple. Top 9¾″ × 12⅞″, OH 9½″. (Mr. and Mrs. R. W. P. Allen)

Another cricket, this one bears a striking resemblance to a pair of footstools from the same period found on Long Island.[20] The cupid's-bow stretcher seen here is often found on Connecticut Windsor chairs. The box stretcher arrangement indicates a relatively late date.

254

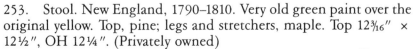

253. Stool. New England, 1790–1810. Very old green paint over the original yellow. Top, pine; legs and stretchers, maple. Top 12³⁄₁₆″ × 12½″, OH 12¼″. (Privately owned)

Here is another well-proportioned stool. Especially effective is the high stretcher arrangement, allowing for a long leg taper—uncommon on a small stool.

256.   Stool. American, 1790–1820. One replaced stretcher: Traces of white paint. Made entirely in oak. Seat 11″ × 11⅜″, OH 20″. (Privately owned)

This exceptionally sturdy stool apparently was made for heavy-duty use. One-quarter-inch-square pegs hold the legs to the seat and the stretchers to the legs. There are three score marks on the stretchers and legs—used not only for decoration but also to mark points of attachment.

255

256

255.   Stool. New England, 1800–1820. Old yellow paint over traces of the original green. Seat, pine; legs and stretchers, maple. Seat 10¾″ × 13½″, OH 19¼″. (Mr. and Mrs. R. W. P. Allen)

Here is a tall stool with typical New England bamboo-turned legs. The high stretchers, long leg taper, and undercut chamfer of the top add a bit of grace to the piece.

257.   Stool. American, 1800–1825. Late nineteenth-century brown paint with green-and-yellow striping over the original red paint. Seat, poplar; legs, maple; stretchers, possibly hickory. SW 12½″, SD 9″, OH 16¼″. (Mr. and Mrs. Victor Johnson)

Unlike most stools, this one has a chairlike seat. Because of its seat shape and leg arrangement, there is just one right way to sit on this stool—otherwise, it would tip over.

258.   Stool. Pennsylvania, 1800–1820. Old gray paint over straw-color paint, over the original dark red. Seat, poplar; legs, maple; stretchers, hickory. Seat 13¾″ × 14″, OH 15½″. (Eugene Pettinelli)

With its staggered stretchers, this three-legged stool looks as though it were built for strength. The bamboo turning pattern is typical of Pennsylvania turnings in the rod-back period.

258

257

259.   Pair of stools. New England, 1800–1820. Original reddish-brown paint with yellow ringing; original upholstery has been replaced. Top, pine; legs and stretchers, maple. Top 9″ × 14″, OH 11½″. (Privately owned)

The feature of these stools that raises them above the norm is their leg turnings with a concave taper. Note how the maker chose to use double score marks to accent the point at which the stretchers enter the legs.

259

261.   Table. Probably Pennsylvania; 1810–1830. Nineteenth-century stain over traces of the original green paint. Top, pine; legs and stretchers, poplar. Seat 11½″ × 20⅝″, OH 24⅜″. (Mr. and Mrs. R. W. P. Allen)

This is a very simple table, with bamboo-turned legs that socket into the top and are wedged.

261

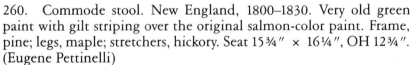

260

260.   Commode stool. New England, 1800–1830. Very old green paint with gilt striping over the original salmon-color paint. Frame, pine; legs, maple; stretchers, hickory. Seat 15¾″ × 16¼″, OH 12¾″. (Eugene Pettinelli)

The hole in the middle of this stool once held a slip seat. The top is framed with mortise-and-tenon joints, just like a slip-seat chair.

262.   Stool. New England, 1800–1820. Original mahoganizing over an ochre ground. Top, pine; legs, maple; stretchers, hickory. Top 10¾″ × 13¾″, OH 11¾″. (Privately owned)

This stool is a rarity because it still has its original—or at least very early—needlepoint upholstery, edge-banded with silk ribbon.

263.   Stool. New England, 1800–1820. Traces of the original reddish-black paint. Seat, pine; legs and stretchers, maple. Seat 11″ × 11″, OH 18⅜″. (Privately owned)

This stool looks rather like a New England Windsor chair, but, of course, there is no evidence that it ever had back spindles. Stools with definite "fronts," such as this one and figure 257, are uncommon.

264.   Stool. New England, 1800–1820. Original dark red stain over salmon-color ground. Seat, pine; legs, maple; stretchers, hickory. Seat 13″ × 13¼″, OH 15½″. (Eugene Pettinelli)

   The seat of this stool is carved to look like a cushion. It seems that stools became quite popular during the 1800–1840 period, judging by the frequency with which they are found in late styles with box stretchers.

265.   Camp stool. Probably Pennsylvania, possibly Bucks County; 1800–1825. Reupholstered. Nineteenth-century dark red paint over black. Made entirely in maple, except for iron leg-joint pins. SW 17½″, SH 15½″, OH 30¾″. (Sam Bruccoleri)

   Here is a novelty: a Windsor "director's chair" with double-bobbin legs and baluster-turned arm supports. Metal pins hold the legs together, and the legs are flattened at the point where they touch. Unlike modern director's chairs, this one cannot be completely folded.

264

265

266. Daybed. New England, 1810–1830. (David Pottinger)
Windsor daybeds are rare. This one is made like a bow-back armchair, with a caned seat for comfort. The arrow-back spindles are nicely carved.

267. Cradle. Vermont, 1810–1830. Branded D. HARVEY. Found in Passumsic, Vermont. Original salmon-color and black paint with black decoration. (Mr. and Mrs. Stephen Score)
Early Windsor cradles are relatively low to the ground, or they sit directly on their rockers, just like early board cradles. Later cradles, like this one, are much more chairlike and taller, perhaps because someone discovered that, since heat rises, an infant would stay warmer in a taller cradle. This particular piece has a plank bottom and a step-down crest rail just like a rod-back Windsor chair. The back posts are bamboo-turned and notched to accept the side rails.

This cradle has an odd feature: it rocks from front to back like a rocking chair, instead of from side to side. In this case, the rockers act as side stretchers.

The only difference between the headboard and footboard of this cradle is that the headboard steps down. The original paint decoration is quite attractive.

266

267

268

268.   Crib. New England, 1810–1830. Original red paint with yellow decoration. Crest rails, headposts and footposts, rails, spindles, legs, and stretchers, maple; bottom, pine. L 22½″, W 12¾″, H 15½″, OH 30″ (head) and 25½″ (foot). (Mr. and Mrs. Victor Johnson)

This "thumb-back" crib has split spindles instead of full-round turnings. It is unusual because it was made to be a crib and never had rockers. The casters seem to be original.

269.   Child-tender. New England, 1800–1830. Crest ring, seat, and drawer, pine; spindles, hickory; legs and stretchers, maple. SW 21¼″, SD 21⅜″, SH 12½″, OH 29¼″. (The Clokeys)

Here is a rarity: a Windsor child-tender. It is basically a large Windsor stool with a circular, cagelike arrangement of spindles. Because it is wide at the bottom and narrow at the top, it is virtually impossible for its small occupant to tip it over.

270.   Baby walker. New England, 1800–1830. Never painted; original casters; legs are probably shortened where casters worked their way loose and had to be refitted. Top, apron, and tray, pine; legs and stretchers, maple; casters, brass. Top 13¾″ square, tray 5″ × 13¾″ × 3″, OH 16″. (Mr. and Mrs. R. W. P. Allen)

This is certainly an unusual example of Windsor furniture. The small knob on the left side of the top of this piece, when turned, allows the top to open so a baby can be placed inside and practice walking while rolling around on the casters. Lest you think this is merely a cut-down Windsor chair fitted with an odd superstructure, look at the legs of this piece: they are turned with blocks at the top, as they would be for a table (or a baby walker!), but not for a chair.

270

269

NEW DISCOVERIES

CHAPTER THIRTEEN

The number of never-before-published Windsor finds of exceptional quality and importance has compelled me to prepare this entire chapter on new discoveries, while previously unrecorded brands have allowed me to add more than a dozen new names to our checklist of chair-makers. I have included details on these new brands, as well as seven photographs of brands and labels not available before, in this updated volume.

271.   Comfort Starr Mygatt and his daughter, Lucy Mygatt (Adams) by John Brewster, Jr. (1776–1854), oil on canvas, 54" x 39 1/4". Signed and dated lower right "March 1st 1799, John Brewster, Pinx." (Sotheby's)

This double portrait by Brewster was an exciting discovery for many reasons, not the least of which is the documentation of the Connecticut green fan-back Windsor with fine turnings and a wonderful red upholstered seat trimmed with green fringe and brass tacks.

272. Braced fan-back armchair. Philadelphia, 1765–1780. Greenish-black paint over the original green. Crest rail and arms, oak; spindles, hickory; seat, poplar; arm supports, legs, and stretchers, maple. SW 19", SD 16", tailpiece 3 7/8", SH 17 1/4", OH 41 1/4". (Privately owned)

Braced Philadelphia fan-back armchairs are very rare, and examples of this quality almost never turn up. In my twenty-five years of collecting, only two have come on the market. One appeared in an antiques magazine ad in April, 1969, and the other was sold at the Mabel Brady Garvan sale at New York's Parke Bernet auction galleries in 1970. Both chairs were the tapered-leg version. (See figures 81 and 82 of *Volume I.*) This brings the total of known examples of both the tapered-leg and blunt-arrow foot type to about a dozen or so, most in collections of prominent museums and historical societies.

This blunt-arrow foot type is, in my opinion, the finest example I have seen. The chairmaker utilized the best features of both Philadelphia brace-back types. The beautifully turned back post is also seen in figure 81 of *Volume I;* the powerful blunt-arrow foot turning pattern is also found in figure 82 of *Volume I.* Further, the feet of this chair are not worn down, so the design statement is complete. The flaring arms have a scrolled termination more complete than other examples I have seen of the blunt-arrow foot type.

272

273

273.   Fan-back armchair. Coastal Connecticut, 1800–1820. Original black paint with gilt decoration over a red primer. Crest rail, white oak; spindles and back posts, hickory; arm supports, arms, legs, and stretchers, maple; seat, pine. SW 20", SD 16 3/4", SH 17 1/2", OH 41". (Dr. George Manger)

This beautifully turned fan-back armchair has many interesting characteristics. The gold decoration, rope carving on the back seat edge, leaf carving on handholds, and floral and rope carving on the crest all suggest a nautical motif. The architecture of the chair relates to a small group of fan-backs with arms that were produced in Connecticut at the beginning of the nineteenth century. These chairs are similar in their shorter backs and mortised cyma-curved arms (see figure 86 of *Volume I*). The unusual urn-shaped neoclassic turning patterns are similar to those of another group of Connecticut decorative Windsors found in the Westbrook area (see figure 77 of *Volume I*). The turned pipestem spindles, arm shaping, and concave vase terminations on the legs are characteristic of many fine Windsors from Newport, Rhode Island, up through coastal Massachusetts.

This chair is a wonderful stylistic hybrid that probably could only have been produced by a coastal chairmaker.

274

274. Continuous-arm chair. New York, 1785–1795. Upholstered. Mid-nineteenth-century black over original green paint. Crest rail, oak; spindles, hickory; arm supports, legs, and stretchers, maple; seat, pine. SW 18", SD 17 1/2", SH 18", OH 38". Upholstered in green moreen and finished with brass nails. (James and Nancy Glazer)

A masterpiece of New York Windsor chairmaking, this chair is a classic example of a Windsor interpretation of the elegant bergère chair popular in Federal America. It is beautifully turned with a high, graceful back terminating in arms that lift slightly as they approach the arm supports—a very fine touch. The finish is a wonderfully textured black paint over the original green paint. The uncarved, unfinished seat retains most of its original padding and stuffing. The green moreen upholstery was made to replicate some original remnants still nailed to the seat bottom. Fringe was occasionally used as a decorative touch on upholstered eighteenth-century Windsors (see figure 271).

275.   Detail showing the seat of an upholstered Windsor stripped of its outer covering and exposing the muslin padding stuffed with horsehair. The stuffed pad is tacked to the front edge of the seat along the sides, and around the back just in front of the spindles. The flat, plank-like shape of the seat gives the front of the seat an apron-like effect. The seat surface is also uncarved (not saddled, like those of Windsors that were not intended to be upholstered).

When the final covering of fabric or leather was applied, two basic methods were most commonly used. The first was to pull the outer covering over the stuffing at the front of the seat to about the midpoint of the front of the seat and finishing with a row of brass tacks around the front edge of the seat. Brass tacks were also used around the back edge of the seat (see figure 274) for a pleasing decorative effect. The second method was to bring the outer covering over the entire front edge of the seat and tack it to the underside of the seat. In this case, plain tacks were usually used. In both methods, a ribbon trim was often used under the row of tacks.

276.   Bow-back side chair, Philadelphia, 1800–1810. Attributed to Thomas Rain. The initials "T.R." are branded twice in a fine script on the back of the seat behind the middle spindle. Original black paint over a salmon-colored base coat with gilt striping over original yellow striping. Crest rail, oak; spindles, hickory; legs and stretchers, maple; seat, poplar. SW 17", SD 16 1/2", SH 17 1/2", OH 38". (Don Walters)

The chairmaker's use of the stylish Sheraton-shaped seat with double-beaded front and side edge, combined with the pinched-waist bow back containing nine spindles, makes an elegant Windsor statement of the Federal period. This chair is one of a set of five truly elegant Federal Windsors. I have seen the branded initials "T.R." on five other bamboo-turned Windsors of the late eighteenth century—one bow-back armchair and a set of four rod-back bird-cage chairs. All were branded on the seat twice, on either side of the middle spindle.

277.   Bow-back side chair. Newport, Rhode Island, circa 1780–1800. Two coats of original black paint. Crest rail, oak; spindles, hickory; legs and stretchers, maple; seat, pine. SW 17 1/4", SD 16 1/2", SH 18 1/2", OH 38 1/2". (Privately owned)

   This Windsor is an exquisite example of its type. It has bold, crisp turnings, a beautifully carved seat, a well-balanced bow with delicate concave beading on the face, and most of all, a wonderful sense of proportion and balance in bringing these parts together. The overall design statement of this fine chair is the quality that separates it from more elaborately turned Rhode Island bow-backs that are not as successful in unifying the variety of parts and patterns that make a Windsor chair.

278.   Bow-back side chair. Connecticut, 1790–1810. Early nineteenth-century black paint with gilt striping and banding over original greenish-black paint. Crest rail; oak; spindles, hickory; legs and stretchers, maple; seat, pine. SW 14 5/8", SD 15 1/2", SH 16 1/2", OH 40 1/2". (Janie and Peter Gross)

   Eccentric and stylized in every way, this chair is an outstanding statement of Windsor chairmaking in Connecticut. Its leg turnings combine both bamboo-and-baluster and Rhode Island patterns, and its elongated bow back has a pinched waist and six tall spindles. It boasts a beautifully carved shield-shaped seat, finely chamfered, and the splay of its legs gives it a wide stance. These features make it a dramatic, charming Windsor chair.

279

279. Rod-back side chair. Maine, 1810–1830. Black paint with red striping added in 1881 (noted in black on seat bottom) over original black. Crest rail, spindles, back post, and stretchers, hickory; legs, maple; seat, pine. SW 16 1/2", SD 15", SH 17 1/4", OH 31 5/8". (Eugene Pettinelli)

This unusual example of a rod-back Windsor is a handsome stylized chair. The fine seat is carved in a modified shield shape with double beading and a strong chamfer on the underside. The placing of the second crest rail creates four unusually spacious compartments in the chair back, resulting in a very effective design.

280. Settee. Philadelphia, 1765–1780. Blackish-green over earlier blue-green, very dry patina. Arm rail and seat, poplar; arm supports, legs, and stretchers, maple; spindles, hickory; arms, oak. SW 84", SD 17 1/2", SH 18", OH 30 5/8". (Privately owned)

This Windsor settee is a superb example of Philadelphia Windsor chairmaking. Ten beautifully turned vase-and-ring baluster legs, joined by baluster-and-ring medial and side stretchers, achieve a level of proportion, placement, and balance I have never seen equaled in a Windsor settee. The chairmaker emphasizes this wonderful undercarriage with his choice of an unusually narrow and gracefully carved seat—an elegant touch, considering that most Windsor settees have broad seats that overshadow the legs and stretchers.

Above the seat, beautifully turned vase-and-ring arm supports frame 44 finely shaped spindles, a carved, molded back crest, and graceful arms that terminate in slightly flaring knuckle handholds. I have never seen a better example of a Philadelphia Windsor settee.

281. Comb-back high chair. Philadelphia, 1750–1770. Footrest missing. Dark brown varnish graining, probably mid-to-late-nineteenth-century, over red paint, over earlier yellow paint, over the original green paint. Crest rail and arms, white oak; spindles, hickory; arm supports, legs, and stretchers, maple; seat, poplar; retaining rod, ash (nineteenth-century replacement). SW 17", SD 12", SH 22 1/2", OH 40 1/2". (Privately owned)

Only a handful of early Philadelphia Windsor high chairs have survived in this condition. One can imagine the heavy and often rough use these high chairs suffered in the service of generations of tots before they reached the status of gently cared-for family heirlooms. This fine high chair has all the important characteristics that place it among the best of its type: a finely carved crest rail, beautifully turned parts, a well-shaped seat, and handsome overall proportions. Its many-layered paint surface lends a mellow patina that enhances the total effect of this classic chair.

280

282. Sack-back high chair. Philadelphia, 1770–1790. Footrest and retaining rod missing. Trace of brownish-red paint over a moss green, over a nineteenth-century green, over the original eighteenth-century dark green paint. Crest rail and arms, white oak; spindles, hickory; arm supports, chestnut; legs, stretchers, maple; seat, poplar. SW 16", SD 12", SH 21", OH 36 3/8". (Privately owned)

This is a beautifully designed and well-built example of an early Philadelphia sack-back high chair. It features fine strong turnings, with particularly well-balanced and turned arm supports. The holes in the arm supports once held the retaining rod. This high chair has survived in great condition partly because of the heaviness of the turned parts and the thick seat. Interestingly, the chairmaker chose to use small nails to secure the bow, arm supports, and first spindle to the arm rail instead of using the more common wooden pegs.

281

282

283.   Fan-back side chair (miniature). Philadelphia, 1790–1810. Early nineteenth-century black paint over original cream or beige-colored paint. Crest rail, white oak; spindles and back posts, hickory; legs and stretchers, maple; seat, poplar. SW 9 1/2", SH 7", SD 9 1/4", OH 15 1/4". (Pook & Pook, Inc.)

Scaled-down Windsors such as children's chairs are rare, especially those that are well-turned, detailed, and well-proportioned. Miniature Windsors (Windsors smaller still) are extremely rare and seldom come to light. This delightful miniature fan-back is a great rarity. Probably made before the close of the eighteenth century, it is not only beautifully turned and well-proportioned, but still retains its original paint surfaces. I have seen only four authentic miniature Windsors in all my years of collecting and studying the form. This chair is in near-perfect condition, showing little evidence of any use.

283

284

284. Stool. Connecticut, 1780–1810. Old green paint over nineteenth-century black paint. Entirely chestnut. Top 13 1/4'', OH 11 1/4''. (Privately owned)

Many small stools survive from the early nineteenth century, but the majority were turned in the bamboo style fashionable in that period. This is a rare example of a stool turned in the early vase-and-ring, baluster-turned style. Judging from the number of stools in this style that survive, very few were turned in this early fashion. This stool is one of three known to have been made by the same anonymous Connecticut maker. One stool is at the Henry Francis du Pont Winterthur Museum in Wilmington, Delaware, the other at the Henry Ford Museum, Greenfield Village in Dearborn, Michigan. I have been looking for baluster-turned stools for a long time, yet in twenty-five years I have seen just four outside museum collections.

APPENDIX I

Brands and Labels: The Maker's Mark

The practice of using printed paper labels to identify the makers of furniture was not common among early American craftsmen, although many case pieces, clock cases, and tables from the 1730s to 1830s retain their original paper labels.

A paper label provided an opportunity for a furniture-maker to create a small advertisement, sometimes listing his products, to accompany each piece produced in his shop. Because of climatic conditions, wood shrinkage, wood smoke, scratching, and peeling, most early paper labels haven't survived, or are in such poor condition as to be illegible, but I suspect that the biggest obstacle to the survival of paper labels is the glue or bonding material used to attach them to the wood. With the passage of time the glue becomes dry and brittle and loses its bonding properties, and the label falls off.

Many of these hazards were overcome on case pieces by the placement of the label: glued to the inside of the pendulum door of a tall case clock, or the outside of a small interior drawer of a slant-lid desk, or under the lid of a blanket box, or cellerette, a paper label is protected from the climate and the general wear and tear of everyday use. Fortunately, this has resulted in the identification of a considerable number of case pieces, clock cases, and other furniture products as the work of individual craftsmen in various regions of early America. Unfortunately, this usually is not the case when it comes to Windsors.

Because Windsors are all exterior, there are no protected places where a label can remain dry or reasonably secure for any length of time. The seat bottom is the only logical place for identification, since it presents the only unused Windsor surface. Nevertheless, that surface is exposed to climatic changes. Although some labeled Windsors have survived, it is difficult to determine to what extent labels were used. If a label was lost or removed in the first few years of a chair's existence, there would be no telltale rectangle of lighter-colored wood to show where the label was once attached.

Most Windsor-makers preferred to use the more permanent and practical method of branding their furniture—an identification not nearly as descriptive or elaborate as a label, but more enduring. Some chairmakers used both label and brand. Gilbert & Robert Gaw of Philadelphia, and Robert Taylor, also of Philadelphia, are examples of Windsor chairmakers whose branded chairs are often found, but whose chairs occasionally turn up with a label instead. I have seen a few chairs by other makers that were both labeled and branded (including one by William Seaver of Boston, illustrated in Appendix II).

By the third quarter of the eighteenth century, the business of exporting Windsors had expanded considerably, as ship captains found a lucrative Windsor market in seaports up and down the eastern seaboard. Often these vessels carried Windsor chairs from several chairmaking shops on the same voyage. On March 10, 1791, four dozen Windsor chairs were shipped to Petersburg, Virginia, on board the Schooner Thomas. The schooner's journal lists a payment of £12.00 to William Cox for two dozen, and a payment of £13.4.0 to Joseph Henzey for two dozen at £11/doz. Identifying the chairs from a particular shop was one very important way of keeping the inventoried cargo in agreement with the ship's manifest. Since loss and damage caused by salt water and dampness were a part of sea shipment at that time, it is not hard to see why Windsor chairmakers preferred branding to paper labels in order to avoid the confusion that could result from peeling labels.

The products of many of the Windsor chairmaking shops were so similar—especially the comb-back, sack-back, and bow-back styles popular during that period—that the method of branding quickly became the most common and practical way to mark a chair for export.

APPENDIX II

A Checklist of Windsor-Makers

This checklist, while admittedly far from complete, should nevertheless be of great help to owners of Windsor furniture in identifying provenance. Many of the makers listed here also are represented in the text of this book (see Index).

Names that appear in brackets denote the full names of makers who used initials to brand their work: for example, A[mos] D[enison] Allen, who branded his work "A. D. ALLEN". Many makers who were named James or John branded their work with the initial I., and in these cases, given names also are listed in brackets: for example, I. [James] Always. Spelling variations of last names are provided in parentheses.

Listings that are only initials, rather than full names, are likely to be owners' marks, as opposed to makers' marks, assuming that makers branded their products with their full names so that shippers and purchasers would know who had made them; nonetheless, initials are included on the off-chance that they may be those of a maker whose name is yet to be discovered.

Dates that appear in parentheses indicate years of birth and/or death. Other dates are known working dates, but are not exclusive; that is, a maker may have been working before or after the date or dates shown. A question mark in a listing indicates information that has been deduced from evidence and that, while probably correct, is nonetheless tentative.

Sources that are cited repeatedly are shown below, and are indicated by numbers in parentheses at the ends of the listings. These sources are not intended to be exhaustive, but only as a reference point if you are interested in learning more about certain makers.

The checklist included as Appendix IV of *The Windsor Style in America*—the predecessor of this book—contained several errors of omission and commission which have been corrected in this new list. The following checklist, which includes nearly 100 new names, supersedes the earlier list.

1. Ethel Hall Bjerkoe, *The Cabinetmakers of America.*
2. Charles Dorman, *Delaware Cabinetmakers and Allied Artisans, 1655–1855.*
3. Dean F. Failey, *Long Island Is My Nation.*
4. Dean A. Fales, Jr., *American Painted Furniture 1660—1880.*
5. William Macpherson Hornor, Jr., *Blue Book of Philadelphia Furniture.*
6. Thomas H. Ormsbee, *The Windsor Chair.*
7. *Plain & Elegant, Rich & Common: Documented New Hampshire Furniture, 1750–1850* (New Hampshire Historical Society, Concord).
8. Alfred Coxe Prime, *The Arts and Crafts in Philadelphia, Maryland, and South Carolina, 1721–1785.*
9. Margaret Berwind Schiffer, *Furniture and Its Makers of Chester County, Pennsylvania.*
10. Esther Singleton, *Furniture of Our Forefathers.*
11. *Winterthur Portfolio Thirteen.*
12. "Early Furniture Made in New Jersey, 1690–1870" (catalog of an exhibit at the Newark Museum, October 1958–January 1959).
13. *Antiques* Magazine.
14. *The Maine Antique Digest.*
15. New York Directories.
16. Philadelphia Directories.
17. Personal correspondence.
18. Personal observation.

ACKLEY, I. [JOHN] B[RIETNALL] (1763–1827). Philadelphia, 1791–1802. Worked at 103 N. Front St., 3 Mulberry St., 13 Elfreth's Alley, and 152 N. Front St. "This same Ackley was later a druggist and apothecary, and sold paints," according to Abraham Ritter, *Philadelphia and Her Merchants,* 1860. (16; 17; 18) *See also* TAYLOR and KING

ACKLEY, M. Pennsylvania?, c. 1790. An Ackley chair is in the collection of the Northampton County (Pennsylvania) Historical Society. (17)

ALDEN, AUSTIN. Gorham, Maine, 1790–1800. (Brand on five signed Federal-style rod-back chairs—four side chairs and one armchair—with serpentine crests, mitered into back posts in the Letchworth and Moon style. Bamboo turnings, H-stretcher arrangement, and cyma-curved arm and arm supports on armchair only; *Art & Antiques)*

ALLEN, A[MOS] D[ENISON] (1744–1855). Lisbon and Norwich, Connecticut (1796–1855). Apprenticed to Ebenezer Tracy; married Tracy's daughter and opened his own shop in 1796. (1; 18) *See also* GREEN, B.

ALLEN, JOB A. White Creek, New York, early nineteenth century. (13: May 1981)

ALLEN, THOMAS. *See* BATES and ALLEN

ALLING, DAVID (1733–1855). Newark, New Jersey, 1800–1850. Also made fancy chairs; the New Jersey Historical Society has a painting titled *David Alling's House and Shop, Newark*. (1; *Sentinel of Freedom* 1808–1809)

ALLVINE (ALLWINE?), JOHN. Baltimore, 1796. (10)

ALLWINE, JOHN. Philadelphia, 1801–1809. Worked at 3 Gray's Alley, 137 S. Front St., 258 N. Second St., and 43 Sassafrass St. (16)

ALLWINE, L[AWRENCE]. Philadelphia, 1786–1799. Worked at 99 S. Front St. and made chairs for Governor John Penn. (5; 16; 18)

ALWAYS, JAMES. New York City, 1786–1815. Worked at 40 James St. (1; 13: May 1981; *New York Weekly Museum*, 28 February 1801)

ALWAYS, I. [JAMES] and HAMTON, I. New York City, 1792 (according to research, in partnership only one year). (13: May 1981; 18)

ALWAYS, JOHN. New York City, 1786–1815. Worked with his brother, James. (1)

ANDREWS, JOEL. Canadaigua, New York, 1804. (17; *Western Repository*, 6 November 1804)

ARMSTRONG, L. Chester County, Pennsylvania, 1790–1800. (Brand on a fan-back side chair, beautifully turned in the vase-and-ring baluster style; Chester County Historical Society)

ASH, J. New York City, 1780–1796. (18; brand on the seat bottom of a very early New York City sack-back with fine turnings)

ASH, THOMAS. New York City, 1774. Worked on Broadway. (1; 10; *Rivington's Gazetteer*, 17 February 1774) *See also* TWEED, RICHARD

ASH, TH[OMA]S and WILLIAM. New York City, 1785–1794. Worked at 17 John St.; claimed to make upholstered Windsors in a "mode peculiar to themselves and never before executed in America." (1; 15; *New York Packet*, 3 March 1785; 18)

ASHTON, THOMAS. Philadelphia, c. 1800. (5; 18)

ATWOOD, T. (1785?–1865). Lived in Worcester, Massachusetts, for several years after 1808; opened a chair factory in New Bedford, New Hampshire, in 1819; opened a furniture warehouse in Nashua, New Hampshire, in 1832, where he sold "flag bottomed, Fancy & Common CHAIRS, of all kinds, by the set or hundreds"; sold his property in 1840; moved to Nunda, New York, and in 1860 to Canaseraga, New York. (7; 18)

AUSTIN, D. Mount Vernon, Maine, c. 1810. Painted signature, plus a drawing of a cat. (17)

AUSTIN, RICHARD (1744–1826). Charlestown and Salem, Massachusetts, 1765?–1826. (1)

B

B., R. Philadelphia?, c. 1765–1780. (Brand on a pair of low-back chairs with cylinder-and-ball feet in the collection of Independence National Historical Park, purchased in New York State; may be an owner's mark)

BAILEY, O., JR. New England, c. 1790. (17)

BALCH, ISRAEL, JR. (d. 1809). Mansfield, Connecticut, c. 1790. (17)

BARNARD, JULIUS. Northampton, Massachusetts, and Windsor, Vermont, 1791–1802. (13: May 1980)

BARNET, S[AMPSON]. Wilmington, Delaware, 1795. Several Barnet chairs are in the collection of the Historical Society of Delaware. (2; 17; 18)

BARNS & HAZLER. Golden Hill, New York, 1785–1815. (17; labeled continuous-arm, bamboo-turned, brace-back chair. Label reads, "Barns & Hazler Windsor Chair Makers from Philadelphia, No. 93 Golden Hill New York")

BATES, WILLIAM and ALLEN, THOMAS. New Bedford, Massachusetts, 1822–1824. Worked on Water St. (13: June 1978)

BEACH, ABRAHAM. Newark, New Jersey, c. 1830. (12)

BEAL, J. New England, c. 1810. (17)

BECK, D. (18; seat of a 1780–1800 Massachusetts sack-back)

BECKWITH, HARRIS. Northampton, Massachusetts, and Marlow, New Hampshire, 1803–1820. (13: May 1980)

BEDORTHA, CALVIN. West Springfield, Massachusetts, 1800–1815. Advertised in the *Federal Spy* in 1800. (Label on a pair of bow-back side chairs; *Art & Antiques*)

BEESLEY, WILLIAM G. (d. 1842). Salem, New Jersey, 1828–1842. Bought Windsor parts from local craftsmen and assembled them in his shop with Elijah Ware. (12)

BELDING & COLLINS. Randolph, Ohio, 1829. (17)

BENDER, L[EWIS]. Philadelphia, 1794. (8; 18)

BERTINE, JAMES. New York City, 1790–1797. Worked on Pearl St. and Queen St. (13: May 1981; 15)

BIGGARD, JOHN. Charleston, South Carolina, 1767. Worked on Queen St.; arrived in Charleston from Philadelphia. (1)

BIRDSEY, JOSEPH, JR. Ridgefield or Huntington, Connecticut, 1790–1805. (17)

BISHOP, G. *See* TOBEY, D., and BISHOP, G.

BISPHAM, J. M. Pennsylvania?, c. 1810. (18)

BLACKFORD, THOMAS, Boston, c. 1795. (14: November 1979; label on the seat bottom of a sack-back with vase-and-ring turnings)

BLOOM, J. Bloom's Corner (near Milford), New York, c. 1800. (13: May 1981; 18)

BLOOM, MATTHIAS. New York City, 1787–1793. (5; 11: May 1981)

BOUND, WILLIAM. Philadelphia, 1785. Worked on Walnut St. and Chestnut St. (16)

BOWEN, O. M. Pennsylvania?, 1790. (18; brand on a Pennsylvania knuckle-arm sack-back chair)

BOWEN, W[ILLIAM]. Philadelphia, 1786–1810. Worked at 83 N. Front St. (16; 17; brand on a bow-back side chair with bamboo turnings)

BOWEN, W. (WILLIAM?). Bowenton or Roadstown, New Jersey, 1823. (10)

BROOKS. *See* HUDSON & BROOKS

BROWN, G. Sterling, Massachusetts, c. 1820. (4)

BROWN, HENRY S. Bangor, Maine, c. 1850. A Brown chair is in the Maine State Museum. (15)

BROWN, JOHN. West Chester, Pennsylvania, 1829. Also made fancy chairs. (9; *Village Record*, 25 March 1829)

BROWN, NATHANIEL. Litchfield, Connecticut, 1797. Made "Windsor, fiddleback, dining room, parlor, kitchen, and children's chairs." (1; *Litchfield Monitor*, 1797)

BROWN, NATHANIEL. Savannah, Georgia, c. 1775–1800. (1)

BUCK, P. New England?, c. 1800. (7)

BULLER, WILLIAM. West Chester, Pennsylvania, 1834. Worked on Gay St.; also made fancy chairs, settees, and rocking chairs. (9; *Village Record*, 18 June 1834)

BURCHALL and WICKERSHAM. West Chester, Pennsylvania, 1822. Also made fancy and rush-bottom chairs. (9; *American Republican*, 14 August 1822)

BURDEN, ALEXANDER. Philadelphia, 1822–1831. (16)

BURDEN, J[OSEPH]. Philadelphia, 1793–1827. Worked at 99 S. Third St. and 90 S. Third St.; in partnership with Francis Trumble in 1796. (16; 17; 18)

BURROWS, SMITH. Cincinnati, Ohio, c. 1810. (17)

C

CAIN, T. New England?, c. 1800–1810. (18; Brand on a vigorously turned rod-back side chair)

CALDWELL, J[OHN]. New York City, 1790s. (15; 18; brand on a New York City continuous-arm chair)

CANNON, FERGUS. Worked at 50 S. Front St., Cincinnati, Ohio, 1819. (17)

CAPEN, WILLIAM, JR. New England?, c. 1810. (17)

CARPENTER, WILLIAM. Philadelphia, 1793. Worked at 296 S. Second St. (8)

CARTER, MINOT (1812–1873). New Ipswich, New Hampshire, c. 1826–1841. Related by marriage to Abijah Wetherbee and Josiah Prescott Wilder; worked at Wilder's chair factory. A set of six Carter chairs is in the collection of The Henry Francis du Pont Winterthur Museum. (7; 18)

CARTERET, D[ANIEL]. Philadelphia, 1793–1820. Worked at 24 Shippen St., 391 S. Front St., and 393 S. Front St. (16; 18)

CASE, A. G. (1769–1828). Norwich, Connecticut, 1790?–1828. (17)

CATE, H. Probably Boston; possibly Rhode Island, c. 1785. (18)

CAULTON, RICHARD. Williamsburg, Virginia, 1745. (Marion Iverson Day, *The American Chair, 1630–1890*)

CHALLEN, WILLIAM. Lexington, Kentucky, 1800; advertised that he had worked in London and New York. (*Kentucky Gazette*, 13 June 1800)

CHAMBERS, DAVID. Philadelphia, 1748. Worked on Walnut St. and Plumb St. (*Pennsylvania Gazette*, 18 August 1748)

CHAMPLIN, H. P. Rhode Island?, c. 1780–1800. (17)

CHAPIN, ELIPHALET. *See* WILLIAMS, EBENEZER

CHAPIN, JUSTIN. West Springfield, Massachusetts, 1803–1810. (Labeled continuous-arm, comb-back chair with bamboo turnings; *Art & Antiques*)

CHAPMAN I. [JOHN]. Philadelphia, 1793–1809. Worked at various addresses on Eighth St. and at 2 Cherry St.; supplied 12 chairs to the Arch Street Meeting House. (16; 17)

CHASE, C. Massachusetts?, c. 1775. (18)

CHESLEY, WILLIAM. Durham, New Hampshire, c. 1800. (7)

CHESNUT. *See* CHESTNUT

CHESTNEY, JAMES. Albany, New York, 1798–1805. Worked at 72 Market St.; also made rush-bottom chairs. (4)

CHESTNUT (CHESNUT), J[ARED]. Wilmington, Delaware, 1804–1814. Was in partnership with James Ross on Hemphill's Wharf in 1804; also worked at 20 Market St. (2)

CHILDRES. *See* POINTER and CHILDRES

CLARK, I. (JOSIAH?). Hartford, Connecticut, c. 1800. (17)

CLARK, OLIVER (b. 1774). Litchfield, Connecticut, 1797. Worked with Ebenezer Plumb, Jr. (1)

CLARK & CROWELL. Cincinnati, Ohio, 1822. Worked on Fourth St. (17)

COFFIN, JOB B. Fishkill, New York, c. 1780. (13: May 1981; 17)

COLE, GEORGE. Baltimore, 1796. (1)

COLE, JACOB. Baltimore, 1796. (10)

COLLINS. *See* BELDING & COLLINS

COMMERFORD, JOHN. Brooklyn, New York, 1829–1832. Worked at 18 Hicks St.; also made fancy chairs. (3)

CONCHITA. Caribbean?, c. 1825. (17; maker's or owner's brand on a simplified rod-back side chair)

CONOVER, MICHAEL F. Philadelphia, 1840. (*Public Ledger*, 14 January 1840)

COUTANT, DAVID. *See* COUTONG

COUTONG (COUTANT), D[AVID]. New York City and New Rochelle, New York, c. 1780–1800. (13: May 1981; 15; brand on the front of the seat pommel of a continuous-arm chair, 1790–1810)

COVERT, ISAAC. Philadelphia, 1772–1786. Apprenticed to Joseph Henzey in 1772. (5)

COWPERTHWAITE, JOHN K. New York City, 1815. Also made fancy chairs. (New York Historical Society)

COX, W[ILLIAM] (d. 1811). Newcastle, Delaware, and Philadelphia, 1767–c. 1804. Worked on Second St.; also made rush-bottom chairs; supplied Stephen Girard with more than 40 dozen Windsors for shipment; used punch marks as shown here as well as his name to brand his chairs. (5; 16; 17)
A. Brand of William Cox.

B. Punch marks of William Cox.

CROWELL. *See* CLARK & CROWELL

CUBBIN. *See* WEAR and CUBBIN

CURTIS and HUBBARD [J. C.?]. Boston, 1828. Also made fancy chairs. (1)

CUSTER, J[ESSE]. Vincent and Coventry Townships, Chester County, Pennsylvania, 1796–1798. (9)

D

DANNLEY, G. D. Pine Grove, Pennsylvania, c. 1825. (18)

DAVID, S. *See* WEST and DAVID

DAVIS, W. *See* RAMSEY and DAVIS

DAVIS WILLIAM. Philadelphia, 1791. Worked at 28 Branch St. (8)

DEGANT, JOSEPH. Halifax, Nova Scotia, c. 1790

DEGROAT, JOHN. New Brunswick, New Jersey, 1791. (12; *Brunswick Gazette*, 9 August 1791)

DE WITT, JOHN. New York City, 1794–1799. Worked at 38 Whitehall St., 225 William St., 47 Water St., and 442 Pearl St.; made Windsors for the Senate and Assembly rooms, Federal Hall, New York City. (4; 15)

DILLER, R. Pennsylvania?, c. 1800. (18)

DIX, E. New Hampshire? or Maine?, c. 1790. (18; brand on a carved-ear fan-back side chair)

DOAK, WILLIAM. Boston, 1789. Worked on Back St., also a cabinetmaker. (1)

DODGE. New England?, c. 1810. (14: October 1976; brand on a pair of braced bow-back side chairs)

DOMINY, NATHANIEL, V. (1770–1852). East Hampton, New York, c. 1780–1840. Made a wide variety of furniture; the Dominy shop and tools are in the collection of The Henry Francis du Pont Winterthur Museum. (3)

DOW, I. (18; brand on a Rhode Island-style bow-back side chair, 1800–1820)

DUNBAR, GEORGE. Canton, Ohio, 1817. Advertised that he made "common Windsor chairs." (17)

DUNHAM, CAMPBELL. New Brunswick, New Jersey, 1793–1805. Worked on Albany St.; also made fancy and rush-bottom chairs. (12)

DUPRAY, F. New England?, c. 1820. (17)

E

EDLING, JOHN. Philadelphia, 1797. Worked on S. Second St. (16)

EDWARDS, BENJAMIN A. (1773–1822). Northampton, Massachusetts, 1790–1822. (13: May 1980)

EUSTACE. Connecticut?, c. 1800. (Brand on a comb-back chair)

EVANS, E[PHRAIM]. Philadelphia, 1785, and Alexandria, Virginia, 1786. In Philadelphia, worked on Front St. (1; 16; 17)

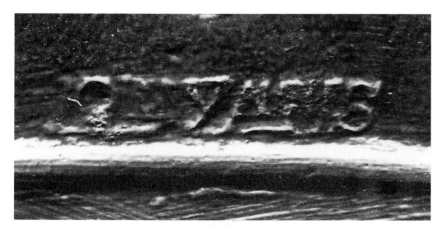

F

F., C., JR. Pennsylvania?, c. 1790. Possibly an owner's mark. (17)

FETTER, I. [JACOB] (1756–1833) and FREDERICK. Lancaster, Pennsylvania, until 1833. (13: May 1979)

FINLAY, JOHN and HUGH. Baltimore, 1803–1833. Made a wide variety of furniture. (4)

FITTS. *See* SPOONER & FITTS

FLINT. *See* WELLS and FLINT

FOLSOM, JOSIAH (1763–1837). Portsmouth, New Hampshire, 1788–1812. Advertised in the *New Hampshire Gazette* (Portsmouth) 19 September 1797 that he "made & kept for sale [Windsor chairs] as cheap as can be purchased at BOSTON or elsewhere"; may have apprenticed in Boston. (7)

FOSTER, J[ESSE]. Boston, 1796. Also a cabinetmaker. (1)

FOX, WILLIAM. Philadelphia, 1796. Worked at 50 N. Front St. (16)

FRANCIS, WILLIAM. Philadelphia, 1791–1800. Worked at 69 Green St., N. Third St., and Race St. (16)

FRAZER. (18; brand on a Pennsylvania "duckbill" child's side chair with bamboo turnings, 1810–1820)

FREEMAN, BENJAMIN, and HOUCK, ANDREW. Philadelphia, 1784. Worked on Front St.; also made rush-bottom chairs. (*Pennsylvania Journal*, 4 September 1784)

FRENCH, JOHN, II. New London, Connecticut, 1807. (1; *Connecticut Gazette*, 18 February 1807)

FROST. *See* SEAVER and FROST

FRY, GEORGE. Philadelphia, 1800?–1820. (4; 16)

G

GALER, ADAM. New York City, 1774. Moved to New York City from Philadelphia. *Rivington's Gazetteer*, 2 September 1774)

GALLUP, WILLIAM. Norwalk, Ohio, 1830. (17)

GAMMON, G. Halifax, Nova Scotia, c. 1800. (14: June 1981)

GAUTIER, ANDREW. New York City, 1746–1766. Worked on Princess St. (15; *New York Journal*, 13 February 1766)

GAW, GILBERT. Philadelphia, 1798–1824. Worked at 90 N. Front St. and 84 N. Front St. (5; 16; 17) *See also* GAW, GILBERT & ROBERT
A. Brand on a bow-back side chair.
B. Gaw used this label while he was working at 90 N. Front St. in Philadelphia.

A

B

GAW, G[ILBERT] & R[OBERT]. Philadelphia, 1793–1798. Worked at 34 Elfreth's Alley. (5; 16; 17)

GAW, R[OBERT]. Philadelphia, 1798–1839. Worked at various addresses on Front St. (5; 16; 17) *See also* GAW, GILBERT & ROBERT

GEYER, JOHN; KERR [?]; and ROSS, WILLIAM H. Cincinnati, Ohio, 1831–1841. Operated the Western Chair Manufactory [sic] at 19 W. Third St. (17)

GIDEON, GEORGE. Philadelphia, 1799–1820. Worked on Slaughter's Court, 33 Vine St., and 202 N. Eighth St. (16)

GILBERT, JABEZ. Windham, Connecticut, 1769. (1)

GILLINGHAM, W. (WILLIAM?) (1783–1850). Morrisville, Pennsylvania, 1800?–1850? (17; 18)

GILPIN, T[HOMAS] (1700–1766). Birmingham and Thornbury Townships, Chester County, Pennsylvania, and Philadelphia, 1735?–1766. Maker of some of the earliest-known branded Windsors. (5; 9; 17)

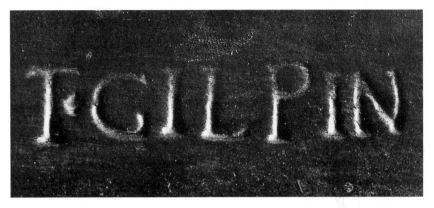

GLADDING, J[ONATHAN]. Newport, R.I., c. 1770. Brand on a braced, bow-back, tenon-arm Rhode Island-style Windsor chair with pipestem spindles. (1; 13: February 1987 advertisement)

GOLDSBURY & MUSSER. Canton, Ohio, 1818. (17)

GOODRICH, ANSEL. Northampton, Massachusetts, 1795–1803. The Northampton (Massachusetts) Historical Society has two Goodrich chairs in its collection. (13: May 1980)

GORDON, JOHN. Baltimore, 1833. Worked at 41 Water St. (1)

GRAGG, SAMUEL. Boston, 1808–1833. Also made a unique form of bent-wood fancy chair. (3)

GRANT & JEMISON. Lexington, Kentucky, 1807. Worked on Main St.; apparently Jemison was a chairmaker and Grant a painter. (*Kentucky Gazette*, 15 December 1807)

GRAY, I. Massachusetts; probably Boston. (Brand on a bow-back, cross-stretcher side chair, probably Boston, 1790–1815; 18)

GREEN, B. South Windham, Connecticut, c. 1810–1820. An apprentice of A. D. Allen. (17)

GREEN, JACOB. Philadelphia, 1823. (16)

H

HAGGET, AMOS. Charlestown, Massachusetts, c. 1815. A Hagget chair is in the collection of The Henry Francis du Pont Winterthur Museum.

HAHN, A. (18; brand on a fan-back side chair, possibly Philadelphia or Bucks County, Pennsylvania, 1760–1780)

HALL, RICHARD. Halifax, North Carolina, 1770. (6)

HALL, WILLIAM. Sag Harbor, New York, 1802–1804. Also a cabinetmaker. (3)

HALLET, JAMES, JR. New York City, 1801. Worked at 8 John St. (*New York Gazette and General Advertiser*, 22 October 1801)

HAMILTON, BENJAMIN. Solebury, Pennsylvania, 1809. Also made "patent churns." (*Pennsylvania Correspondent*, 20 April 1809)

HAMLIN, S. New Hampshire?, c. 1800–1820. Child's bird-cage rod-back side chair. (18)

HAMTON, I. *See* ALWAYS and HAMTON

HAND, RICHARD. Bridgeton, New Jersey, 1826. Also made fancy chairs. (11)

HANNAH, CALEB. Baltimore and Fell's Point, Maryland, 1796. (1)

HARBISON, WILLIAM. Wilmington, Delaware, 1814. Worked at 46 King St. (*Porter's Register*)

HARDWICK, JAMES. Lexington, Kentucky, 1794. (1)

HARRIS, WILLIAM, JR. New London, Connecticut, 1788. (1; 18; *New London Gazette*, 14 November 1788)

HARVEY, D. Passumsic?, Vermont?, c. 1810. (17; brand on the bottom of a Windsor cradle)

HASBROUCK, J. M. Kingston, New York, 1800. (13: May 1981; 15)

HAYS, THOMAS. New York City, 1800. *(Daily Advertiser,* 3 November 1800)

HAYWARD, THOMAS COTTON. Charlestown, Massachusetts, 1770–1800. (Robert Bishop, *The American Chair 1640–1770*)

HEINY, C[HRISTIAN]. Philadelphia, 1791. Worked at 496 N. Second St. (16; brand on a bow-back, Philadelphia-style side chair with bamboo turnings) (Heiny's name was misspelled in the earlier checklist contained in *The Windsor Style in America* due to an apparent typographical error in the original research material.)

HENZEY, I. [JOSEPH] (b. 1743). Philadelphia, 1760?–1806? Worked at 106 S. Eighth St. and 76 Almond St.; made chairs for the Library Company, the State Assembly, and the First Bank of America. Occasionally, the initials I. H. are branded on the later bamboo-turned tenon-arm Henzey chairs. (5; 16; 17)

A   B

HERRCK (HERRICK?), S. N. Rhode Island?, c. 1780. (18)

HEWS, ALPHEUS. New Jersey and New Haven, Connecticut, 1787. In New Haven, worked on Chapel St. (1; 6)

HIGBEE and WALL. Philadelphia, 1800. Worked next to 10 N. Front St. (16)

HILL, B. M. Boston?, c. 1790–1810. Bow-back side chair with Rhode Island turnings, pipestem-turned spindles. (18)

HOLMES, ISAAC. Lexington and Frankfort, Kentucky, 1806–1808. (1)

HOOVER, JACOB. Kendall (Massillon), Ohio, 1817. Operated a Windsor chair factory. (17)

HOPPER, NICHOLAS. Philadelphia, 1795–1796. Worked at 38 High St. (16)

HORN (HORNE), JACOB. Philadelphia, 1797–1800. Worked on Cherry St. and Fifth St. (16)

HORN, SAMUEL. Canton, Ohio, 1835. (17)

HORTON, S. (SAMUEL?). Boston?, c. 1807. (1; 17)

HOUCK, ANDREW. *See* FREEMAN and HOUCK

HOUGH, M. Cleveland, 1848. (17)

HOXIE. Rhode Island?, c. 1790. (17; brand on a brace-back armchair)

HUBBARD, J. C., and WHITE, WILLIAM. Boston, c. 1800. (18) *See also* CURTIS and HUBBARD

HUDSON & BROOKS. Portland, Maine, c. 1815–1823. (*Newtown Bee*, August 26, 1983)

HUEY, JAMES (b. 1805). Zanesville, Ohio, c, 1830–1840. (*Ohio Republican*, 21 May 1829; Columbus Museum of Art, *Made in Ohio; Furniture 1788–1888*)

HUMMESTON, J[AY]. Delaware; Charleston, South Carolina, 1798–1802; and Halifax, Nova Scotia, 1804. (14; 17)

HUMMESTON, JAY, and STAFFORD, THEODORE. Charleston, South Carolina, 1798. (1; *Charlestown City Gazette and Advertiser*, 29 November 1798)

HUMPHREYVILLE, J. D. Morristown, New Jersey, 1828. Also made fancy chairs. (12)

HUNT, J[OSEPH] R[UGGLES] (1781–1871). Eaton (Madison), New Hampshire, c. 1811–1860. Born in Boston, Hunt may have apprenticed there. (7)

HURDLE, LEVI. Alexandria, Virginia, 1835. Worked on King St. in partnership with his brother, Thomas; also made fancy chairs. (1, *Alexandria Gazette*, 1 January 1835)

HUTCHINS, ZADOCK. Pomfret, Connecticut, c. 1820. A Hutchins chair is in the collection of The Henry Francis du Pont Winterthur Museum. (18)

I

ILSLEY, G. L./EXETER. Exeter, New Hampshire, c. 1800. (18; brand on a rod-back side chair)

INMAN. American, nineteenth century. (17)

INTLE. *See* LECOCK and INTLE

J

JACQUES (JAQUES), RICHARD. New Brunswick, New Jersey, c. 1775. Also made spinning wheels. (12)

JACQUES, S. Philadelphia?, 1800–1810. (18; branded Philadelphia-style bow-back with tenoned arms and bamboo turnings)

JEFFERIS, JAMES and EMMOR. West Chester, Pennsylvania, 1830. Worked on Church St. (*Village Record*, 20 January 1830)

JEFFERIS, NATHAN (1773–1823). East Bradford Township, Chester County, Pennsylvania, c. 1800. (Chester County Historical Society)

JEFFERIS, T. Wilmington, Delaware. (Brand on a sack-back chair, c. 1775–1800; Ruth van Tassel)

JEMISON. *See* GRANT & JEMISON

JOHNSON, H. V. Massachusetts, 1780–1800. (Branded seat bottom of a Massachusetts-style sack-back with knuckle arms; *Art & Antiques*)

JOHNSON and TATEM. Bridgeton, New Jersey, 1856. (11)

JUDD, DAVID. Northampton, Massachusetts, 1799–1827. Made a wide variety of furniture. (13: May 1980)

K

KELSO, JOHN. New York City, 1774. Served his apprenticeship in Philadelphia. (1; 6)

KERR. *See* GEYER, KERR, and ROSS

KILBURN (KILBOURNE), S. New London, Ohio, c. 1840. (17; S-KILBOURNE brand appears on a set of thumb-back side chairs)

KING, D. Philadelphia, c. 1800. (14; branded bamboo bow-back armchair)

KING, JESSE. Philadelphia. c. 1770. (5)

KING, PELEG C. Southold, New York, 1804. Also made rush-bottom chairs. (3)

KITCHEL (KITCHELL), ISAAC. New York City, 1789–1812. (3)

KITLER, JOHN L. (16)

L

LAMBERT, JOHN. Philadelphia, c. 1760–1793. His shop had "3 Machines for letting in feet with Propriety & Dispatch." (5)

LAWRENCE, DANIEL. Providence, Rhode Island, 1787. Worked on Westminster St. (1)

LEAGUE, REUBEN. Baltimore, 1796. (10)

LECOCK and INTLE. New York City, 1786. (10)

LEDYARD. Massachusetts?, c. 1790–1810. (18; brand on a sack-back chair)

LEE, JOHN. Newark, New Jersey, 1827–1855? Also made fancy chairs. (12)

LEIGH, JOHN. Trenton, New Jersey, c. 1790. Worked at 107 Factory St.; also a cabinetmaker. (18)

LETCHWORTH, I. [JOHN] (b. 1759). Philadelphia, 1785–1824. Worked on Third St. and at 76 and 78 S. Fourth St.; one of the most prolific of Philadelphia makers; made chairs for the New City Hall. (5; 11)

LEWIS, C. Pennsylvania?, c. 1800. (18; brand on a Pennsylvania-style rod-back chair)

LLOYD, RICHARD. Cincinnati, Ohio, 1830s. Worked on Third St. (17)

LOCKE, HENRY. New York?, c. 1790. (18)

LOVE, B[ENJAMIN]. Philadelphia, 1783–1802. (17)

LOVE, W[ILLIAM]. Philadelphia, 1793–1806. Worked at 150 N. Front St. and 216 N. Second St.; also made spinning wheels; a Love chair is in the collection of Independence National Historical Park. (16)

LOVE and WHITELOCK. Philadelphia, c. 1790. (18)

LOW, HENRY V. New Brunswick, New Jersey, 1804. Worked on Albany St.; also made fancy and rush-bottom chairs. (12)

LUTHER. NATHAN. Salem, Massachusetts, and Providence, Rhode Island, 1810–1837. (1; 14: May 1978)

M

MACBRIDE, W[ALTER]. New York City, 1792–1799. (13: May 1981; brand on a continuous-arm brace-back armchair)

MACY, JOSIAH. Hudson, New York, c. 1810. (13: May 1981; 17)

MCADAN, THOMAS F. Philadelphia, 1820. (16)

MCCORMICK, S. Connecticut?, c. 1790–1810. (18; brand on a fan-back side chair)

MCELROY, W[ILLIAM]. Camden, New Jersey, 1790–1800. (17; 18)

M'KIM, ANDREW and ROBERT. Richmond, Virginia, 1802–1819. (1; Museum of Early Southern Decorative Arts)

274

M'PHERSON, ALEXANDER. Philadelphia, 1793. Worked at 16 George St. (16)

MANNING, CALEB (d. 1810). Salem, Massachusetts, 1803–1810. Worked on Daniel, Federal, Fish, and Derby Sts. (1)

MANSFIELD. Connecticut?, c. 1780. (17)

MARCH, JONES. Lexington, Kentucky, 1833. Also made fancy chairs. (1; *Lexington Observer and Kentucky Reporter*, 21 August 1833)

MARSH, CHARLES. New York City, c. 1800. Worked at 75 John St. (1; 13: May 1930)

MARSH, RICHARD. New York City, 1806. Worked on Greenwich St.; also made fancy chairs. (10)

MARTIN, JACOB. Philadelphia, 1785–1801. Worked on Third St. and at 87 N. Front St.; also a joiner and cabinetmaker. (5; 16)

MASON, JOHN. Philadelphia, 1811. Worked at 49 Pine St. (5; 16)

MASON, T[HOMAS]. Philadelphia, 1793–1817. Worked at 169 N. Third St., various addresses on Vine St., and at 20 Callowhill St. (16; 18)

MASON, WILLIAM. Philadelphia, 1794. Worked at 60 Vine St. (16)

MATTOCKS, JOHN. Litchfield, Connecticut, 1797. Advertised that he would take "bass wood plank" for chair seats in exchange for his work. (1)

METCALF, LUTHER (1765–1838). Medway, Massachusetts, 1770–1838. Apprenticed to Elisha Richardson, 1770–1778. (1)

MILLARD, THOMAS. Philadelphia, 1791–1819. A maker of Windsor chairs and spinning wheels; worked at 128 and 129 S. Water St. in 1791, and at 398 N. Front St. from 1793 to 1800. (16)

MILLER, JOHN. Baltimore, 1796. (10)

MILLS, JOHN. Chillicothe, Ohio, 1842. Also made fancy chairs. (17)

MITCHELL, WILLIAM. Philadelphia, 1799–1817. Worked at various addresses on Lombard St. and at 10 Union St. (16)

MOON, DAVID. *See* MOON, SAMUEL, and MOON, WILLIAM D.

MOON, SAMUEL. Philadelphia, 1800–1802. Worked at 2 Carter's Alley, and, with David Moon, at 66 S. Fourth St. (16)

MOON, WILLIAM D. Philadelphia and Crewcorne (Morrisville, Bucks County), Pennsylvania, 1799–1829. In Philadelphia, worked at 19 Dock St., 299 N. Second St., 32 N. Fourth St., and, with David Moon, at 18 Carter's Alley. (16; 17)

MOON, WILLIAM D., and PRALL, EDWARD. Philadelphia, 1805. Worked at 63 S. Front St. (16; 17)

MOROW, PETER. Philadelphia, 1820. (16)

MORRIS. *See* WORREL and MORRIS

MORSE, R. New England?, c. 1810. (14: November 1984)

MOTZER, A. Connecticut?, c. 1790. (18)

MUCKE, S. Ontario, Canada, and/or northern New England, 1760?–1800? (14)

MURPHY, MICHAEL. Philadelphia, 1793–1800. (16)

MUSSER. *See* GOLDSBURY & MUSSER

N

NELSON, O. Connecticut?, c. 1790. (18; brand on a sack-back chair)

NEWCOMB. *See* WHITAKER and NEWCOMB

NEWMAN, BENJAMIN. Gloucester, Massachusetts, 1815–1825. (4)

NICHOLS, JOSEPH. Savannah, Georgia, 1800. (1)

NICHOLS, SAMUEL. Wilmington, Delaware, 1800. Worked in partnership with George Young at Second and King Sts. (2) *See also* YOUNG, GEORGE.

NORTON, JACOB. Hartford, Connecticut, 1790. (1; *American Mercury*, 8 November 1790)

O

ODELL, REUBEN. New York City, 1815–1836. Worked on Barkley, Duane, Chambers, Rivington, and Bowery Sts. (15; 17)

OGILBY, J. Pennsylvania?, c. 1770–1790. (18; brand on a Philadelphia-style sack-back chair)

OLDHAM, JOHN. Baltimore, 1796. (10)

ORMSBY, ORRIN (b. 1766). Windham, Connecticut, c. 1785. (1)

OSSBACK (OSBECK), JOHN. Philadelphia, 1817–1820. Worked on Adelphia Ave., at 97 N. Front St., and 2 M'Culloch's Court. (16)

P

PACKARD, S. H. Rochester, New York, 1819. (17)

PAINE, S. [STEPHEN?] c. 1760, possibly Charlestown and Medford, Massachusetts, 1743–1752. (18; brand on a comb-back chair)

PAINE, S. [STEPHEN?] O. Philadelphia, c. 1760, or possibly Charlestown and Medford, Massachusetts, 1743–1752. (1; 18; brand on a Philadelphia-style low-back armchair)

PARSONS, JUSTIN. Westhampton, Massachusetts, 1796–1807. (13: May 1980)

PARSONS, THEODOSIUS. Windham, Connecticut, 1792. Also a cabinet-maker. (1; *Connecticut Gazette*, 18 October 1792)

PEARSON, GEORGE (b. 1789). West Chester, Pennsylvania, 1810?–1817. (9)

PEASE, J. M. Connecticut?, c. 1789. (Patricia Kane, *300 Years of American Seating Furniture*)

PENTLAND I. [JAMES]. Philadelphia, 1791–1806. Worked at various addresses from 221 to 227 N. Front St. (16)

PERKINS, D. Pennsylvania?, 1790–1810?. (Brand on a low-back Windsor settee with bamboo turnings; R. Mones)

PHIPPEN, SAMUEL (d. 1798). Salem, Massachusetts, c. 1785. (10)

PINKERTON, JOHN. Philadelphia, 1779. Made two settees for the Courtroom at Independence Hall. (5)

PLUMB, EBENEZER, JR. *See* CLARK, OLIVER

POINTER and CHILDRES. Richmond, Virginia, c. 1782. (1)

POMEROY, OLIVER. Northampton, Massachusetts, and Buffalo, New York, 1795–1818. (13: May 1980)

PRALL, EDWARD. Philadelphia, 1805–1820. Worked at 56 and 64 N. Sixth St. and at 72 N. Fifth St. (16) *See also* MOON, WILLIAM D., and PRALL, EDWARD

PRALL, HENRY. Philadelphia, 1798–1802. Worked at 8, 15, and 17 Dock St. (16)

PRATT, JOEL, JR. Sterling, Massachusetts, c. 1835. A Pratt chair is in the collection of the Henry Ford Museum. (1)

PRESCOTT, LEVI (1777–1823). Boylston, Massachusetts, 1799. A Prescott chair is in the collection of Old Sturbridge Village. (13: October 1979)

PRESTON, J.S. New York, 1775–1800. (14; branded brace-back continuous armchair with bulbous New York City turnings.

PRUYN, JOHN V. L. New York?, c. 1800. (18; maker's or owner's brand on a child's bow-back side chair with bamboo turnings)

PUGH, S. Pennsylvania, c. 1810. (14: September 1979; 18)

R

R., J. N. Philadelphia?, c. 1765–1780. (18; brand on a Philadelphia-style low-back armchair with blunt-arrow feet)

RAIN THOMAS, Philadelphia, 1790–1815. Worked at various addresses on Front St. and at 135 N. Water St. and 15 Coombs Alley. I have seen Thomas Rain's unusual brand "T.R." branded twice in script on seat surfaces—once on either side of the center spindle: on a set of six Philadelphia bamboo-turned, bow-back side chairs; on one Philadelphia bow-back tenoned armchair; and on a set of four bird-cage side chairs with bamboo turnings. (16, 18)

RAMSEY, T., and DAVIS, W./PITTSBURGH, c. 1790. (17; brand on a pair of bow-back side chairs)

RAYBOLD, THOMAS. Philadelphia, 1823. (16)

REDMOND, ANDREW (d. 1791). Charleston, South Carolina, 1784–1791. Worked at 27 Meeting St. (1; *South Carolina Gazette*, 13 January 1784)

REED, E. New England?, c. 1825. (14: September 1984)

RICHARDSON, ELISHA. Franklin, Massachusetts, 1743–1798. (1)

RICHMONDE. Philadelphia, 1763. (5)

RILEY [?], & ROBINSON, JOHN. Wilmington, Delaware, 1811. (2)

ROBERTS, S. New Mills, New Jersey, c. 1810. (12)

ROBERTS, W. W. Philadelphia?, (18; brand on a pair of Philadelphia-style, bow-back tenoned mahogany armchairs with bamboo turnings, c. 1790–1800)

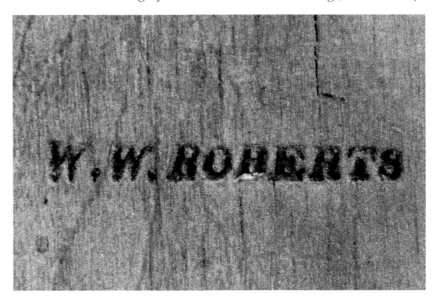

ROBINSON (ROBISON), JOHN. Wilmington, Delaware, 1811. Worked on Front St., two doors from Market St. (2) *See also* RILEY & ROBINSON

ROGERS, M. New York or Connecticut, c. 1780–1800. (18; brand on a sack-back Windsor)

ROSE, E. P. New England?, c. 1810. (13: November 1979)

ROSS, JAMES. *See* CHESTNUT, JARED

ROSS, WILLIAM H. *See* GEYER, KERR, and ROSS

RUSSEL, WILLIAM, JR. New Bedford, Massachusetts, c. 1800. Worked on Union St. (6; *American Collector*, 6 September 1934)

S

SAGE, LEWIS. Middletown, Connecticut, and Northampton, Massachusetts, 1790?–1822. (13: May 1980)

SAMLER, I. New York, c. 1780. (17)

SANBORN [REUBEN], BOSTON. Boston, 1799. (1; 14: October 1979; brand on a pair of rod-back side chairs with bamboo turnings)
A. Brand of Reuben Sanborn.
B. Chalk signature of Reuben Sanborn

SCHUMM, J. [JACOB?]. Pennsylvania?, c. 1810. (14: February 1981; 17; brand on a set of rod-back chairs with bamboo turnings)

SCOTT, EDWARD. Boston, 1801. (1)

SEAVER, WILLIAM. Boston, 1789–1896. (1; 10; at left of brand is a large "O"[?])
A. Brand of William Seaver.

B. Label and brand of William Seaver on seat bottom.

B

SEAVER, WILLIAM, and FROST, JAMES. Boston, 1798. (1; 10; 13: January 1957)

SHARPLESS, BENJAMIN (1748–1833). Bridgeton, New Jersey, and Chester County, Pennsylvania, c. 1810. (12; Schiffer, *Miniature Furniture*)

SHAW, AARON. Plumstead (Plumsteadville), Pennsylvania, 1806. Also made spinning wheels. (*Pennsylvania Correspondent*, 31 March 1806)

SHEPPARD, C. Philadelphia?, c. 1810. (18; brand on a Philadelphia-style rod-back armchair)

SHERALD, JOSIAH. Philadelphia, 1765. Worked on Second St.; also made rush-bottom chairs. (*Pennsylvania Gazette*, 5 September 1765)

SHIPMAN, WILLIAM. Middletown, Connecticut, 1785. (1)

SHOUSE, I. Pennsylvania?, c. 1820. (17)

SHOVE, BENJAMIN, Berkley, Rhode Island, 1815–1835. (17; branded on bamboo rod-back and bow-back side chairs; brand reads, "Shove Berkley")

SHREADER, I. Pennsylvania?, c. 1790. (18)

SHUREMAN, WILLIAM. New York City, 1817. Worked at 17 Bowery St.; also made fancy chairs. (10)

SIMMS, ISAAC. P. Massachusetts, c. 1780. (1)

SKELLORN, GEORGE W., FANCY WINDSOR CHAIRMAKER. New York City, 1800–1827. Worked at 356 Pearl St. (18; label on a bamboo rod-back armchair, one of a set of two armchairs and four side chairs)

SMALL, ISAAC. Newport, Rhode Island, 1803. Worked on Marlborough St. (1)

SMITH, CARMAN. Huntington, New York, 1826. Also made fancy chairs. (3)

SMITH, THOMAS. West Chester, Pennsylvania, 1842. Worked on Church St. (9)

SMITH, WILLIAM V. Brooklyn, New York, 1826. Also made fancy chairs. (3)

SNOWDEN, JEDEDIAH. Philadelphia, 1748. Was also a cabinetmaker. (5)

SNYDER, ADAM. Philadelphia, 1798–1820. Worked on Brown, Green, and Third Sts.; also made fancy chairs. (16)

SNYDER, WILLIAM. Philadelphia, 1793–1801. Worked on Brown St. and Third St. (16)

SPOONER & FITTS. Athol, Massachusetts, c. 1800. (18; brand on a rod-back side chair)

SPRINER. Probably Pennsylvania, c. 1810–20. (18; brand on a bow-back side chair with bamboo turnings)

SPROSON (SPROSEN, SPROWSON), I. [JOHN]. Philadelphia, 1783–1788, and New York City, 1789–1798. (5; 8; 15; 16; brand on a braced bow-back side chair)

STACKHOUSE, DAVID. Philadelphia, 1772. Was apprenticed to Joseph Henzey in 1772. (5)

STACKHOUSE, STACY. Hartford, Connecticut, 1786–1792. Moved to Hartford from New York City. (1; *Connecticut Courant*, 30 January 1786) *See also* WADSWORTH, JOHN

STAFFORD, THEODORE. Charleston, South Carolina, 1801. Worked at 98 Tradd St. (1) *See also* HUMMESTON and STAFFORD

STALCUP, ISRAEL. Wilmington, Delaware, 1798. (*Delaware Gazette*, 24 March 1798)

STANYAN, J. (18; brand on a Pennsylvania Windsor stool, 1790–1820)

STEEL, A[NTHONY]. Philadelphia, 1791–1817. Worked at various addresses on S. Wharves, Spruce St., Little Dock St., and S. Second St. (16)

STEWART, DANIEL. Farmington, Maine, 1812–1827. (17)

STEWART, DAVID. Philadelphia, 1797. Worked on Eighth St. (16)

STIBBS, SAMUEL. Cincinnati, Ohio, 1819. Worked at 107 Main St. (17)

STONE, EBENEZER (b. 1793). Boston, 1787. (1)

STONER, MICHAEL. Lancaster or Berks County, Pennsylvania, c. 1770. (18)

STOUT,^{S} C. Pennsylvania?, c. 1790. Stout chairs have been found in the Reading, Pennsylvania, area. (18; brand on a bow-back side chair with bamboo turnings)

STOW, J[OHN] PHIL^A *fecit*. Philadelphia, c. 1780. (18; brand on a fan-back side chair)

SWAN, OLIVER. Otsego County (Cooperstown area), New York.

SWANN, E. New England?, c. 1790. (18)

SWIFT, R[EUBEN] W[ILLIAM] (or REUBEN and WILLIAM). New Bedford, Massachusetts, 1800–1825. (13: May 1978)

T

TATEM. *See* JOHNSON and TATEM

TAYLOR, N. New England?, c. 1810. (17)

TAYLOR, ROBERT. Philadelphia, 1799?–1817. (16; 17)

TAYLOR and KING, Philadelphia, c. 1800. Successors to John B. Ackley. (5)

TEBBETTS. New England, 1800–1830. (17; branded set of six bow-back bamboo side chairs with H-stretcher arrangements)

TENNY, S. Rhode Island?, c. 1790. (17)

TERRY, L. E. Boston?, c. 1780. (Marsh, *The Easy Expert in American Antiques*)

THAYER, A. New Jersey?, c. 1800. (18; brand on a low-back writing-arm chair)

THORNTON, J. Pennsylvania?, c. 1765. (18)

TMPSON (TIMPSON), THOMAS. New York City, 1801. (13: May 1981)

TOBEY, D. [DANIEL?], and BISHOP, G. [GEORGE?]. Maine, c. 1810. (17)

TOMKINS, SQUIER. Morristown, New Jersey, 1808–1812. Worked on Bridge St.; also made fancy chairs. (12; *Genius of Liberty*, 24 November 1808)

TOOKER, BENJAMIN. Elizabethtown, New Jersey, 1820–1830. Worked with A. Tooker, Jr.; also made fancy chairs. (12; *New Jersey Journal*, 2 February 1830)

TOV, P. S. Philadelphia?, 1800–1820. (18; brand on the back of the crest medallion of a Philadelphia rod-back armchair)

TRACY, E[BENEZER] B. (1744–1803). Lisbon, Connecticut, 1764?–1803. One of the most prolific makers of Windsors, Tracy seems to have specialized in writing-arm chairs. (13: December 1936; 18)

TRACY, E[LIJAH] (1766–1807). Lisbon, Connecticut, 1790s. Was a tenant on land owned by his father, Ebenezer Tracy. (17)

A

B

TRACY, S. Connecticut, c. 1790. (18)

TROVILLO, P. New England?, c. 1800. (18)

TRUMBLE, F[RANCIS] (1716?–1798). Philadelphia, 1740?–1798. Worked at various addresses on Front St. and Second St.; made a wide variety of furniture and other items; made 78 Windsors for the State House and 12 chairs for the House of Representatives. The brand on his earlier furniture (figure A) differs from one he used later (figure B). (5; 18; *Winterthur Portfolio One*)
A. Brand on a fan-back side chair with vase-and-ring turnings, c. 1765.
B. Brand on a bow-back side chair with bamboo turnings, c. 1780.

A

B

TUCKE (TUCK), S[AMUEL] J. Boston, 1790–1796. Worked on Battery March St.; a Tucke chair is in the collection of Colonial Williamsburg. (1; 17; *Massachusetts Sentinel*, March 1790)

TUFTS, U[RIAH]. Rhode Island, c. 1785. (17; 18)

TUTTLE, J[AMES] C[HAPMAN] (1772?–1849). Salem, Massachusetts, 1796. Worked on Federal St.; was also a cabinetmaker. (1; *Salem Gazette*, 19 August 1796)

TWEED, RICHARD (b. 1790). New York City, c. 1815. Worked at 24 Cherry St.; served his apprenticeship with Thomas Ash. (1; 6)

TYSON, JONATHAN. Philadelphia, 1808–1812. (Branded bird-cage settee in the bamboo style; *Art & Antiques*)

V

VANHORN, NATHANIEL. Philadelphia, 1820–1823. (16)

VOSBURGH, HERMAN. New York City, 1785?–1800. (16; *New York Weekly Museum*, 29 March 1800)

W

W., P. N. Rhode Island?, c. 1790. (18; the owner's or maker's brand on a Rhode Island-style continuous-arm chair)

WADSWORTH, JOHN. Hartford, Connecticut, 1793–1796. Took over the shop of Stacy Stackhouse; made furniture for the Old State House. (1; *American Mercury*, 10 June 1793)

WALKER, S. Possibly Rhode Island. (17; branded set of five bow-back side chairs)

WALL. *See* HIGBEE and WALL

WALL, JOHN (JONATHAN). Philadelphia, 1805–1820. Worked at various addresses on N. Front St.; also made fancy chairs. (16)

WARD, JOSEPH. New Brunswick, New Jersey, 1796–1798. Worked on Church St. and Albany St. (12; *The Guardian*, 28 June 1796)

WARE, ELIJAH. *See* BEESLEY, WILLIAM G.

WARNER, EVERADUS. Brooklyn, New York, 1801. *(3; Long Island Courier,* 18 November 1801)

WATERHOUSE, TIMOTHY. Newport, Rhode Island, c. 1764. A set of 12 low-back chairs in the collection of the Redwood Library and Atheneum is attributed to Waterhouse. (Redwood Library and Atheneum)

WATERMAN. New England. c. 1800. (Branded set of four bow-backs with bamboo turnings and 11-stretcher arrangement. *Art & Antiques)*

WEAR and CUBBIN. Philadelphia, 1785. Worked on Water St. (16)

WEATHERSFIELD WINDSOR MANUFACTORY. Weathersfield, Vermont, c. 1825. (6)

WEBSTER, B. F. New England, 1810–1830. (18; brand on the seat bottom of a triple-back chair with bamboo turnings)

WELLS, JOHN I. Hartford, Connecticut, 1798–1807. (1; *Connecticut Courant*, 19 February 1798)

WELLS, JOHN I., and FLINT, ERASTUS. Hartford, Connecticut, 1807–1812. (1)

WEST, THOMAS. New London, Connecticut, 1815–1828. (1; *New London Gazette*, 26 April 1815)

WEST, THOMAS, and DAVID, S. New London, Connecticut, 1807. (18)

WETHERBEE, A[BIJAH] (1781–1835). New Ipswich, New Hampshire, 1813–1835. Was in partnership with Peter Wilder, Josiah Prescott Wilder, and John B. Wilder. (7)

WEYMOUTH, E. Maine, c. 1825–1840. (*Newtown Bee*, 26 August 1983)

WHITAKER, JAMES. Philadelphia, 1800–1820. Worked at 19 and 33 Dock St., 70 Spruce St., and 26 Lombard St.; also made fancy chairs. (16)

WHITAKER and NEWCOMB. Bridgeton, New Jersey, 1856. (11)

WHITE, SAMUEL K. Exeter, Maine, nineteenth century. (17)

WHITE, WILLIAM. *See* HUBBARD and WHITE

WHITELOCK. *See* LOVE and WHITELOCK

WICKERSHAM. *See* BURCHALL and WICKERSHAM

WIDDIFIELD (WIDDEFIELD, WIDOWFIELD), WILLIAM (d. 1822). Philadelphia, 1768–1779. A branded Widdifield chair is in the collection of Independence National Historical Park. (5; 8; 17)
A. Label of William Widdifield.
B. Brand of William Widdifield.

A

B

WILDER, JOHN B. *See* WETHERBEE, A.

WILDER, J[OSIAH] [PRESCOTT] (1787–1825). New Ipswich, New Hampshire, c. 1807. (7; 13: May 1979) *See also* WETHERBEE, A.

WILDER, PETER. *See* WETHERBEE, A.

WILES, WILLIAM W. Lebanon, Ohio, 1831. (17)

WILLIAMS, EBENEZER. East Windsor, Connecticut, 1790. Worked in the shop of Eliphalet Chapin. (17; *Connecticut Courant*, 3 May 1790; "A Selection of Nineteenth-Century American Chairs," Stowe-Day Foundation, 1973)

WILLIS, JOHN. Philadelphia, 1792–1811. (16)

WILSON, E. H. Wooster, Ohio, 1820–1850. (17)

WILSON, H. A. Wooster, Ohio, 1820–1850. (17)

WING, SAMUEL (1774–1854). Sandwich, Massachusetts, 1800?–1854. Made a wide variety of furniture; Wing chairs are in the collection of Old Sturbridge Village. (13: May 1968)

WIRE, I. [JOHN]. Philadelphia, 1791–1813. Worked at 207 and 109 S. Front St. and 208 S. Water St.; made chairs for Governor John Penn. (5; 16; 17)

WOOD, N. F. Philadelphia, 1852. (11)

WORREL and MORRIS. Pennsylvania?, c. 1800–1810. (18)

Y

YATES, J. New York City?, c. 1790. (6)

YOUNG, GEORGE. Wilmington, Delaware, 1800. Worked in partnership with Samuel Nichols. (2)

Z

ZUTPHEN, W. Pennsylvania?, c. 1800. A Zutphen chair is in the collection of Colonial Williamsburg. (18)

Notes

1. A very rare example of a stylish low-back made during this period is shown as figure 64 in *The Windsor Style in America* by Charles Santore (Philadelphia: Running Press, 1981), p. 80.

2. For an example of a typical English armchair in the High Wickham style, see *The Windsor Style,* p. 39, figure 11.

3. An example of the English design is pictured as figure 80 of *The Windsor Style,* p. 89.

4. For a chair of related design, see *The Windsor Style,* p. 109, figure 118.

5. An armchair version of this side chair, one produced in the same region during the same period, is pictured as figure 151 of *The Windsor Style,* p. 129.

6. Patricia E. Kane, "Samuel Gragg: His Bentwood Fancy Chairs," *Yale University Art Gallery Bulletin,* V. 33, No. 2, Autumn, 1971, p. 28.

7. Ibid.

8. Ibid., *29.*

9. Ibid.

10. Three other examples from the New York area are shown in *The Windsor Style* as figures 134 and 135, p. 120, and figure 235, p. 177.

11. Ethel Hall Bjerkoe, *The Cabinetmakers of America* (New York: Doubleday & Company, 1957), p. 31.

12. See *The Windsor Style in America,* p. 115, figure 128.

13. Robert Bishop, *The American Chair, 1640–1970* (New York: E. P. Dutton, Inc., 1972), p. 267.

14. Nancy Goyne Evans, "Fancy Windsor Chairs of the 1790s," *The Newtown* (Pa.) *Bee,* November 6, 1981, p. 66.

15. For a similar chair with Tracy's brand, see *The Windsor Style,* p. 112, figure 121.

16. Ibid., 51. This attribution is based upon the chair shown in color plate V.

17. Ibid., p. 140, figure 170.

18. Ibid., p. 153, figure 190. The design of this settee is virtually identical to one that bears Tracy's brand, with the exception of the crest rail.

19. Ibid., p. 129, figure 151. The shape of the arms, seat, medial stretcher, and the swellings at the ends of the side stretchers of figure 232 are similar to those of the Maryland armchair pictured.

20. Ibid., 182, figure 244.

Index

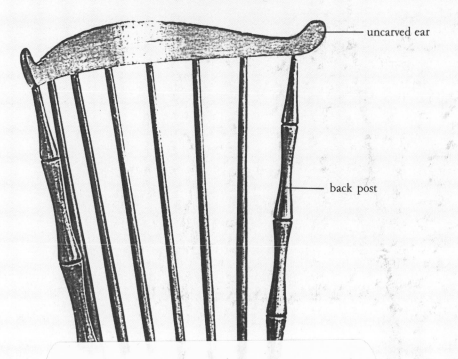

uncarved ear

back post

bamboo-turned leg

bamboo ringing

bul